# Simply
# Lutheran

## A PRACTICAL GUIDE
## TO LUTHERAN TEACHINGS

Arthur A. Eggert

NORTHWESTERN PUBLISHING HOUSE
Milwaukee, Wisconsin

Cover Illustration: Shutterstock
Design Team: Lynda Williams, Pam Clemons, Diane Cook

Northwestern Publishing House
N16W23379 Stone Ridge Dr., Waukesha, WI 53188-1108
www.nph.net
© 2020 by Northwestern Publishing House
Published 2020
Printed in the United States of America
ISBN 978-0-8100-3008-4
ISBN 978-0-8100-3009-1 (e-book)

22  23  24  25  26  27  28  29      10  9  8  7  6  5  4

# Contents

Preface . . . . . . . . . . . . . . . . . . . . . . . . . . . . . . . . . . . . . . . . . . . vii

SECTION I  The Bible . . . . . . . . . . . . . . . . . . . . . . . . . . . . . . . . .  1

Chapter 1        Choosing a Standard. . . . . . . . . . . . . . . . . . . .  3

Chapter 2        Structure of the Bible . . . . . . . . . . . . . . . . . .  11

Chapter 3        Understanding the Bible . . . . . . . . . . . . . . . .  21

SECTION II  God . . . . . . . . . . . . . . . . . . . . . . . . . . . . . . . . . . . . . 39

Chapter 4        The Lord God Almighty . . . . . . . . . . . . . . . . . 43

Chapter 5        The Trinity . . . . . . . . . . . . . . . . . . . . . . . . . . . . . 57

Chapter 6        God and the Universe. . . . . . . . . . . . . . . . . . . . 67

SECTION III  Plan of Salvation—Historical View . . . . . . . . 81

Chapter 7        God's Beginnings With Humans . . . . . . . . . 83

Chapter 8        The Role of Israel . . . . . . . . . . . . . . . . . . . . . . . 93

Chapter 9        The Savior. . . . . . . . . . . . . . . . . . . . . . . . . . . . . . 117

Chapter 10       The First-Century Church . . . . . . . . . . . . . . . 143

Chapter 11       End Times . . . . . . . . . . . . . . . . . . . . . . . . . . . . . 155

**SECTION IV**   Plan of Salvation—Theological View . . . . . . .**169**

Chapter 12        Kingdom of God . . . . . . . . . . . . . . . . . . . . . . . .**171**

Chapter 13        Predestination. . . . . . . . . . . . . . . . . . . . . . . . . .**185**

Chapter 14        Law. . . . . . . . . . . . . . . . . . . . . . . . . . . . . . . . . .**195**

Chapter 15        Gospel . . . . . . . . . . . . . . . . . . . . . . . . . . . . . . .**205**

Chapter 16        Work of the Holy Spirit . . . . . . . . . . . . . . . . .**215**

**SECTION V**   Life in the Church . . . . . . . . . . . . . . . . . . . . . . . .**229**

Chapter 17        Mission of the Church . . . . . . . . . . . . . . . . . .**231**

Chapter 18        Civil Estates. . . . . . . . . . . . . . . . . . . . . . . . . . .**257**

Chapter 19        Saints, Angels, and Demons. . . . . . . . . . . . . .**277**

Epilogue. . . . . . . . . . . . . . . . . . . . . . . . . . . . . . . . . . . . . . . . . . . . . .**289**

For Further Reading . . . . . . . . . . . . . . . . . . . . . . . . . . . . . . . . . . .**291**

Scripture Index . . . . . . . . . . . . . . . . . . . . . . . . . . . . . . . . . . . . . . . .**293**

Subject Index . . . . . . . . . . . . . . . . . . . . . . . . . . . . . . . . . . . . . . . . .**307**

# Reviewers and Commenters

The author wishes to thank the following people who read all or part of this manuscript and made useful comments on its content and format.

John Brenner, MDiv, PhD—
: WELS, seminary professor of church history and dogmatics

Joan E. Eggert, BS—
: WELS, medical technologist (retired)

Sharon Grinyer, BA—
: WELS, insurance claims adjuster (retired)

Michael N. Hart, MD—
: RCC, professor emeritus of pathology and lab medicine & department chair

Anne Heller, BS—
: WELS, elementary school teacher and deaconess

Patricia A. Horstmeier, BS—
: ELS, medical technologist & lab administrator (retired)

Geoffrey Kieta, MDiv—
: WELS, circuit pastor

Marsha J. Konz, PhD—
: LCMS, professor emerita of education & college administrator

Bonnie Schmidt, BS—
: LCMS, archiving assistant and high school teacher (retired)

Luke Werre, MDiv—
: WELS, circuit pastor

# Preface

To write about Lutheran theology, one must first define what it is to be Lutheran. Anyone can claim to be a "Lutheran," just as anyone can claim to be a "Christian." There is no legal standard, enforceable by some court of law, that people must meet to use these titles. To define "Lutheran," one must start by looking at where the name "Lutheran" came from.

Martin Luther (1483–1546) was the firstborn son of Hans Ludder, a miner and small businessman in Saxony, Germany. Many scholars of his time translated their names into Latin or Latinized the spellings of their names, and Martin Luther did the same.[1] His father wanted him to be a lawyer and sent him to the University of Erfurt. Responding to the guilt that the Roman Catholic Church used to motivate both good works and contributions to the church, Martin Luther was deeply troubled that he had not done enough to be saved. When he feared for his life during a thunderstorm, he promised St. Anne[2] he would enter a monastery if she saved his life. He subsequently entered the local Augustinian monastery to fulfill that vow.

Even the rugged life of the monastery could not calm Luther's troubled soul. He therefore became a priest, and he earned the degree of doctor of theology in biblical studies. He hoped to improve his standing before God through these efforts. Assigned by his abbot to teach at the University of Wittenberg, he continued to study the Bible and the writings of the early church fathers. As he did so, he became increasingly convinced that the Roman Catholic Church had lost its way and was no longer teaching biblical theology. While many others objected to the moral corruption in the church, to Luther the central issue was always how a person could be saved from eternal damnation. When a Dominican monk named Johann Tetzel traveled near Wittenberg to hawk papal indulgences, which were intended to raise money to build St. Peter's Basilica in Rome, Luther

---

[1] Philipp Melanchthon, for example, was born Philipp Schwartzerdt, which means "black earth" in German.

[2] The Roman Catholic Church claims that Jesus' maternal grandmother was named Anne, and it has made her a saint under this name. There is no historically valid record of the name of this woman.

became concerned for the souls of the members of his congregation. On
October 31, 1517, the eve of All Saints Day, he posted for debate 95 Latin
theses (i.e., statements) on the door of the Castle Church in Wittenberg,
which also served as a community bulletin board. More details of Luther's
life can be found in biographies.[3]

The issues raised by Luther struck a chord with both scholars and lay-
men. Translated into German, his theses spread throughout northern
Europe. Over the next several decades, Luther and his colleagues at the University of Wittenberg began to study the Bible from a doctrinal perspective,
using its original Greek and Hebrew manuscripts. This had not been done
in the Roman Catholic Church for 1,100 years, since the time of St. Jerome.[4]
Luther's team translated the Bible into German and reconstructed biblical
Christianity. The Roman Catholic Church, which bases its teachings on
both the Bible and church tradition,[5] excommunicated Luther, and the Holy
Roman Emperor Charles V declared Luther to be an outlaw.

Faced with growing religious divisions within his empire and with a
Turkish military threat, Charles V called upon all parties to state their religious beliefs at a meeting (called a "diet") of the imperial estates in Augsburg in 1530. Luther could not attend because he was an outlaw, so Philipp
Melanchthon, one of Luther's associates, drafted a statement of Lutheran
beliefs. Some of the princes and some of the councils of the free cities in the
empire accepted this document as a statement of their faith. On June 25,
1530, this Augsburg Confession was presented to the emperor in both Latin
and German. It was read aloud in German by Dr. Christian Beyer, a layman
and chancellor of Electoral Saxony. Thus, the Lutheran church was born.

After Luther's death in 1546, there was considerable political, military,
and doctrinal turmoil in Germany over Luther's teachings. This turmoil
threatened to tear the Lutheran movement apart. The situation was bleak.
Therefore, Dr. Martin Chemnitz and Dr. Jacob Andreae began working with
the various Lutheran factions to define the internal issues dividing Lutheranism. Through a series of intermediate steps, they drafted a document called
the Formula of Concord of 1577. This document was signed by more than
eight thousand pastors. It, together with key documents prepared by Martin

[3]Roland Bainton, *Here I Stand* (New York: Abingdon Press, 1950).

[4]St. Jerome (A.D. 347–420) was a priest and theologian who translated the Bible into Latin from Greek
and Hebrew. His translation was called the Vulgate and has been used in the Roman Catholic Church
ever since.

[5]*Catechism of the Catholic Church* (Washington D.C.: United States Catholic Conference, Inc., Vatican
City: Libreria Editrice Vaticana, 1994, 1997), no. 82.

Luther and Philipp Melanchthon and with the historical creeds of the church (see Table 1), was published in 1580 under the title of *The Book of Concord*.[6] Today those who accept the teachings of *The Book of Concord* as being fully in agreement with the Bible are called confessional Lutherans. When the word *Lutheran* is used in this book, it will mean "confessional Lutheran" for reasons that will become apparent when standards of belief are discussed.

| TABLE 1—Contents of the *Book of Concord* | |
|---|---|
| **Ecumenical Creeds** | **Confessions** |
| Apostles' Creed | Augsburg Confession |
| Nicene Creed | Apology to the Augsburg Confession |
| Athanasian Creed | Smalcald Articles |
| **Catechisms** | Formula of Concord |
| Luther's Small Catechism | **Discourse** |
| Luther's Large Catechism | Treatise on the Power and Primacy of the Pope |

Confessional Lutheranism has maintained the practice of training its pastors to work in the original Greek and Hebrew languages in which the Bible was written. Lutheran church bodies in the United States, such as the Evangelical Lutheran Synod (ELS), the Lutheran Church—Missouri Synod (LCMS), and the Wisconsin Evangelical Lutheran Synod (WELS), have school systems in which future pastors are trained to understand the Bible in terms of its Greek and Hebrew grammar and its original cultural setting. In the WELS, for example, the training program is integrated through the high school, college, and seminary levels so that pastors emerge with a good understanding of the interrelationships within the complex mosaic of biblical teachings. The LCMS has a much larger number of colleges and two seminaries in its training system.

In comparison to the training of their pastors, the spiritual training of average Lutheran laypersons is considerably more haphazard. While some laypeople have had the opportunity to attend a Lutheran elementary school

---

[6]Paul T. McCain, ed., *Concordia: The Lutheran Confessions,* 2nd ed. (St. Louis: Concordia Publishing House, 2006).

and a Lutheran high school—or even a Lutheran college—many have had no formal training beyond Sunday school and confirmation instruction as children or beyond Bible information classes as adults. Sermons and Bible classes, of course, also add to their knowledge of the Christian faith, but these things do not provide the comprehensive training available for the ordained ministers. Stated another way, most laypeople know various pieces of biblical teachings that they have acquired throughout the years, but the pieces may not be well understood, and the knowledge of the inter-relationships among them may be weak or lacking. This can produce frustration in the face of temptation and can even result in failure to grasp the gospel message correctly.

I find it easy to relate to the plight of the common layperson because that is where I started. I had a good Lutheran elementary school education and excellent instruction before confirmation. However, that is where my formal religious education ended. There were many things that I did not understand well or know about at all. Fortunately, being a science professor and a businessman by profession, I realized the need for continuing education. I have therefore read several hundred books on theology and church history. I have learned biblical Hebrew and Greek, to go with my school languages of Latin and German, so I can comprehend the points the theologians are making. This has helped me build the mental framework needed to understand Christian doctrines and put them into the proper relationship to one another. For more than 30 years, I have taught religion classes in Lutheran congregations, ranging in topics from biblical books to church history to dogmatics.

Martin Luther recognized the plight of the laypeople already in the 1520s. This led him to write the Small Catechism in 1529, so pastors and parents could train children systematically in at least the basic doctrines of Christianity. In the same year, he also wrote the Large Catechism, which explained key doctrines in much more depth so that lay adults could understand and apply the Christian faith. These books became part of *The Book of Concord* and are still used in the Lutheran church today. *Note well that these books do not establish any new doctrines, but they merely present biblical doctrines in a way that pastors and laypeople can readily understand them.*

Luther realized that as cultural norms would change, it would be necessary to update and amplify how things are presented. While the underlying teachings of Christianity are constant, how they are explained so they can be understood by laypeople requires new writings as we move from generation to generation. In this book, I will attempt to do what Luther would do if he were living today; I will try to explain Christian teachings and their relationships both to one another and to the challenges and issues of this era so that laypeople can better understand them.

For the convenience of the reader, short biblical quotations that are necessary to the flow of the writing are inserted in the text. Short passages that serve as good references to the points being made in the text are included as footnotes. Longer biblical passages are merely referenced in the text in keeping with the fair use practice of the Bible publisher. The English Standard Version (ESV) of the Bible is the source of the quotations unless otherwise indicated. Occasionally, I have retranslated a word or phrase if I feel the ESV has inadequately represented the biblical text. Generally, I have identified the people speaking or being spoken to, unless they are the author of the biblical book quoted or are already indicated in the quotation.

# The Bible

From its very beginning, the Christian church has had a close relationship to the Bible. This relationship has been expressed in many ways by various theologians and church bodies throughout the years. When one reads what these people and these church bodies have written, however, it becomes clear that while almost all Christians claim that the Bible is critical to their theology, they differ widely in how they use the Bible.

In this section of the book, we look at why a standard for religious teaching is needed and why the Bible is that standard for confessional Lutherans. This section describes the structure of the Bible and discusses how the Bible is used and, sadly, often misused. It explains the classical Lutheran approach to biblical interpretation and why this is the only approach that can really enable someone to understand the Scriptures independent of passing fads and quirks in the current culture.

# CHAPTER I

# Choosing a Standard

Some years ago, the manager of a British factory needed an unusual chemical for a manufacturing process that his company asked him to implement. He specified the composition of the chemical and contracted with a specialty chemical firm to manufacture it. When the chemical arrived, he sent a sample of it to an independent testing laboratory to determine whether it met his specifications. The analysis report showed that the water content was higher than specified. He called the manufacturer of the chemical to say that he would not pay for the inaccurate formulation. Assured by his own laboratory staff that the formulation was correct and desiring to get paid for his product, the manager of the specialty firm also sent a sample of it to an outside testing laboratory. It reported that the chemical did indeed meet the specifications. After several sharp exchanges between the two managers over the correctness of the formulation, they agreed to meet face-to-face, each bringing his independent assayer along to defend his results. Imagine the surprise on the faces of the two managers when they discovered that they had sent their samples to the same reference laboratory! Unfortunately, one had asked that the analysis for water be done by weight and the other by volume.[1] This is an example of what happens when two people try to resolve an issue without having a common standard of truth.

The lack of a standard is an extremely common problem. Sometimes it is a case of intentional dishonesty, such as when a double standard is used.

---

[1] A measurement of composition is made by separating one or more components from a mixture or a solution. Measurement by weight compares the weight of a component substance to the weight of the initial mixture, while measurement by volume compares the volume of a component substance to the volume of the mixture.

Already when God gave his law in the Old Testament, he warned merchants against carrying two stones of supposedly the same weight for weighing merchandise, a heavier one for when they bought it and a lighter one for when they sold it (Deuteronomy 25:13-16).[2] At other times, the lack of agreement is caused by different ways of looking at things. All of us have had the experience of entering a clothing store knowing our correct size, then picking a garment from the rack of that size and finding it didn't fit. It was either too big or too small, because the various manufacturers size their garments somewhat differently from one another. It was annoying, and we returned to the rack to try to find a larger or smaller garment of the same style and color.

Under other conditions, the lack of standards could be much worse. Imagine everyone driving on whichever side of the road they pleased. Imagine going to the lumber yard and discovering that the length of an 8-foot board varied between 6½ and 9½ feet, depending on who had cut it. Imagine a football league where every game was played under whatever rules were devised by the two teams at the beginning of the game. In fact, a major function of governments and of professional associations is to establish standards for weights, measures, and rules of conduct. Without standards, there is continual conflict and suspicion, because no one can trust what someone else does.

The role of standards, therefore, is to enforce conformity. Standards are assumed to be without error by those who use them, because if they had internal inconsistencies, conformity would not be assured. If we buy a package in a grocery store that claims to contain 4 pounds of sugar, we expect that, within some small tolerance of measurement error,[3] there will be exactly 4 pounds of sugar in the package. We expect everyone to stop at a red traffic light. If a business meeting starts at 11:00 A.M., we expect people to be there at 11:00 A.M. The industrial age and electronic technology are possible only because standards require products to be made to meet specifications so that they are compatible and/or interchangeable. When products do not meet their advertised claims, that is, do not meet the standards that have been set for them, we bitterly complain and often return them for a refund. Standards are essential to our way of life.

---

[2][Moses said,] "You shall not have in your bag two kinds of weights, a large and a small. You shall not have in your house two kinds of measures, a large and a small. A full and fair weight you shall have, a full and fair measure you shall have, that your days may be long in the land that the LORD your God is giving you. For all who do such things, all who act dishonestly, are an abomination to the LORD your God." (Deuteronomy 25:13-16)

[3]The law might require precision of ±0.05 percent, or 5 parts per 10,000, for example.

Looking at standards more closely, we see that they are composed of two parts. The first part is the rule that sets boundaries in which actions must occur or for the variances of behavior that will be tolerated. For example, when driving on a highway, motorists must keep their autos completely between the lines on either side of their lane, except when changing lanes is necessary. The second part of the standard is the enforcement mechanism for the rule. If drivers fail to stay within their lanes, they may be ticketed for erratic driving, they may go into a ditch, or they may collide with other vehicles. To avoid these negative consequences, the great majority of drivers strive to adhere to the standard. In the same way, devices that weigh or measure must present the result to within a small percentage of the measured quantity. Governments regularly check grocers' scales, gasoline pumps, and numerous other commercial measuring devices for accuracy to guarantee that the customers are getting the amount indicated.

Now consider an even more chaotic situation, one in which there is a complete absence of standards. Suppose a woman walks into a clothing store simply to pick out a pair of jeans. She discovers, however, that the task will be anything but simple. No sorting has been done of the merchandise by clothing type, style, color, or size. Pairs of jeans are scattered among the shoes, formal dresses, ties, underwear, blouses, and top coats. Moreover, the sizes have not even been marked on the clothing. If she finds something she likes that is too big or too small or is not the desired color, there is no easy way for her to find if there is a version of the apparel in the appropriate size and color. Because standards have been completely ignored, shopping in such a store would try anyone's patience.

This clothing store is a good representation of the religious scene in the 21st century. Society is overrun by religious teachers, but finding one who actually teaches the Word of God rather than his or her own ideas of God's will is difficult. So many churches tolerate such diversity of teaching that the person seeking religious truth cannot even be sure that the same message is being proclaimed in churches claiming to be part of the same religious denomination or association. Where can one find a reliable standard to measure the teachings of these preachers and parishes?

Christianity recognized the need to standardize its doctrine from its very beginning. Jesus said, "False christs and false prophets will arise and perform great signs and wonders, so as to lead astray, if possible, even the elect" (Matthew 24:24). The apostles, whom Jesus had commissioned (Luke 24:44-48), quickly saw that others were beginning to introduce their own ideas and to claim divine authority for them. St. Paul wrote,

"Even if we or an angel from heaven should preach to you a gospel contrary to the one we preached to you, let him be accursed" (Galatians 1:8). To combat the threats of fragmentation and false doctrine, the apostles and their successors called the recognized church leaders to gatherings known as councils, or synods, to make certain that everyone was teaching the correct message. The first recorded council occurred in Jerusalem and is described in Acts 15. Such councils were held locally and regionally during the first several hundred years after Christ. Beginning in the fourth century, churchwide councils were held, and church leaders (bishops) from the whole Christian area of the world were invited.[4]

A major concern of the early Christian church councils was to prevent the written Word of God from becoming diluted by the writings of others. They recognized the 39 books of the Hebrew Bible (i.e., the Jewish Old Testament) as the Word of God. This was natural, because Christians believed that the life and work of Jesus Christ was the fulfilment of the promises of the Old Testament. All but three of the Old Testament books (Esther, Ecclesiastes, and Song of Songs) are quoted in the New Testament to explain events in Jesus' life or to justify actions taken by the church. The books that became part of the New Testament were the recognized writings of those commissioned by Jesus to spread the gospel message or of their close associates (Matthew 28:19,20).[5] More than 70 percent of the New Testament was written by just three men: Paul, Luke, and John. Most of the books of the New Testament were already recognized and accepted during the first century A.D., while many were still alive who had known the writers. Spurious writings were easy to detect and reject. The rest of the books were included as the church councils had the opportunity to verify their authors and their content. Many copies of the texts of the various New Testament books exist today because early church leaders, dating back to the beginning of the second century A.D., included lengthy quotations from them in their own writings. Jesus predicted the role his apostles would play in defining the content of the New Testament when he promised that the Holy Spirit would be with them and teach them (John 14:16,17; John 14:26;[6] John 16:12-15) (also see chapter 2).

---

[4]Philip Schaff and Henry Wace, ed., *The Seven Ecumenical Councils* (Peabody: Hendrickson Publishers, 1900).

[5][Jesus said,] "Go therefore and make disciples of all nations, baptizing them in the name of the Father and of the Son and of the Holy Spirit, teaching them to observe all that I have commanded you." (Matthew 28:19,20)

[6][Jesus said,] "But the Helper, the Holy Spirit, whom the Father will send in my name, he will teach you all things and bring to your remembrance all that I have said to you." (John 14:26)

The Bible is called the standard of the Christian faith because the Bible can be used to reliably establish what people need to believe if they desire to be followers of Jesus Christ. Just as anyone who wants to play football in the National Football League (NFL) needs to know those things that are contained in the official league rulebook, so Christians need to know what is in the Bible. Players who continually ignore the rules are first penalized, then fined, then suspended, and eventually expelled from the NFL. In the same way, those who ignore the teachings of the Bible are first instructed, then disciplined, then excommunicated, and finally eternally punished for their unbelief or impenitence. Unlike the NFL rulebook, however, the Bible never changes because the God who gave the Bible never changes. This will be discussed more in chapters 3 and 4.

It is reasonable to ask why the Bible should be the standard of true religion rather than some other book written by some other person or group of people. What is the proof that this is the case? In fact, there can be no such proof because the Bible is the primary standard for knowing the will of God. If this could be proven from some external set of arguments, then that set of arguments would be the primary standard of truth. The next natural question would be, "Why are these arguments themselves, which are used to prove the validity of the Bible, valid?" This would produce a never-ending chase of some absolute that is always one step out of our reach. In all systems of information, primary assumptions must be made, which are taken as true without proof. This is even the case in science and mathematics, as will be discussed later.

But why should the Bible, and not some other book, be the source and final arbitrator of all doctrine? Why can we make that assumption? To answer those questions, one must read the Bible. Certainly, the Bible claims to be the infallible Word of God. St. Paul wrote, "All Scripture [i.e., the Bible] is breathed out by God and is profitable for teaching, for reproof, for correction, and for training in righteousness, that the man of God may be thoroughly equipped for every good work" (2 Timothy 3:16,17). St. Peter wrote, "No prophecy was ever produced by the will of man, but men spoke from God as they were carried along by the Holy Spirit" (2 Peter 1:21). Moses quoted the Lord God himself as saying,

> Hear, O Israel: The LORD our God, the LORD is one. You shall love the LORD your God with all your heart and with all your soul and with all your might. And these words that I command you today shall be on your heart. You shall teach them diligently to your children, and shall talk of them when you sit in your house, and when you walk by the way, and

when you lie down, and when you rise. You shall bind them as a sign on your hand, and they shall be as frontlets between your eyes. You shall write them on the doorposts of your house and on your gates. (Deuteronomy 6:4-9)

Indeed, the same claim of the superiority of the contents of the Bible is made in numerous other biblical verses.

Can this biblical claim be taken seriously? Using the Bible to prove that it is the true and inerrant[7] Word of God has been labeled "circular reasoning." The Bible is indeed being used to authenticate itself. In a logical sense, the charge of circular reasoning is therefore true. But that is not the relevant issue here. Either the Bible is what it claims to be, or it is not! *There is no middle ground.* The only way to resolve the issue is to read the Bible with an open mind. It is a most unusual book, having been written by more than 40 authors over 1,600 years, and yet on careful reading, one finds it has but a single major theme, which is laid out in its first three chapters and reaches its climax in its last three chapters. The writers differ greatly in style; some require a lot of thought to understand. The Bible offers a way of eternal salvation that is counterintuitive and at variance with every other way of salvation ever proposed (1 Corinthians 2:9).[8] Its "heroes of faith" often did horrible things, unlike the legendary heroes of other cultures. The Lord God Almighty, the God whom the Bible proclaims, is very different from humans, hardly the type of God the human mind would create (see chapter 4). People have become convinced from the content of the Bible, and the Lord working on their hearts and minds through that content, that the Bible is completely reliable. Because of this, Christians have historically made the primary assumption that the Bible is indeed the Word of God. It is upon this assumption of divine inspiration and inerrancy that confessional Lutherans build all their doctrines and practices. The Bible is their sole source and standard of doctrine.

What about other "holy books" and the teachings of "gurus" (sometimes called charismatics) who supposedly have received revelations from God? Are they all worthless for developing a relationship with the true God? Put bluntly, they are! If one reads *The Book of Mormon*,[9] for example, one finds a boring, muddled story with lots of wars and very little theology, except that

[7]In order for something to be a standard, it must be inerrant; otherwise, when you used the standard, you could never know whether the answer was correct or not. This is labeled the "mathematical" or "formal logical" requirement of standards.

[8]As it is written, "What no eye has seen, nor ear heard, nor the heart of man imagined, what God has prepared for those who love him." (1 Corinthians 2:9; quote of Isaiah 64:4)

[9]Joseph Smith, *The Book of Mormon* (originally published by Smith in 1830, The Church of Jesus Christ of Latter-day Saints, Salt Lake City, 1980).

which was copied from the King James Version of the Bible. The book is supposedly a translation by Joseph Smith of writings by refugees who escaped Judah before the Babylonian captivity, but it contains numerous errors concerning Jewish practices that are inconsistent with that claim. The original was supposedly written in an Egyptian dialect that could only be translated with the Urim and Thummim (which Mr. Smith supposedly received with the book),[10] rather than in Hebrew, which scholars could have read and evaluated. The supposed translation appeared soon after the extensive publicity that followed the discovery of the Rosetta Stone.[11]

The Qur'an was an effort to create a monotheistic Arab religion based on what Muhammad had learned from the local Jewish rabbis, because there are references in the Qur'an to things both in the Old Testament and in the Talmud.[12] Muhammad, however, credited these sayings to the angel Gabriel. Stories of Abraham and others were recast with an Arab slant. The Jews rejected Muhammad, and he turned bitterly against them. His statements about the teachings of Christianity show that he was ill-informed. Editors compiled the Qur'an from what people had remembered of Muhammad's unwritten suras (i.e., sayings) and did not arrange them in historical order. If the suras are read in historical order, one sees the transformation of Muhammad from someone claiming to be a humble messenger to someone seeking recognition next to Allah himself. The Qur'an is law without gospel.[13]

Other holy books are not any better. They all give sets of rules by which the reader can supposedly gain the favor of one or more gods. These rules are almost always updated by subsequent revelations to leaders and teachers of the religion because they become culturally irrelevant. All these "holy books" expound variations of what is labeled "natural religion," the inherent human belief that one can earn temporal[14] blessings and/or eternal salvation by following the right set of rules. The Bible is not this kind of book. Rather, it declares that there is no way to earn the Lord's favor through human effort.

---

[10]The Urim and Thummim were tools given to the high priest of Israel for determining God's judgments. Of what they consisted or how they were used is not known.

[11]The Rosetta Stone was created in the second century B.C. and has a message written in two Egyptian writing styles and Greek. It has aided linguists in understanding these Egyptian ways of writing. It was discovered in Egypt by a French soldier just before the end of the 18th century.

[12]The Talmud is a collection of Jewish scholarly and pharisaical writings. There are several versions, but the Babylonian Talmud with its 22 volumes is the most common.

[13]Mohammad, *The Koran*, ed. Zaid Ibn Thâbit, tr. J. M. Rodwell (Mineola, NY: Dover Publishers, Inc., 2005).

[14]The word *temporal* is used in religious writings to designate things that happen during humankind's existence on earth. Man is dwelling "in time," in contrast to God, who is dwelling "in eternity."

But couldn't some of these gurus have it right? Couldn't God be talking directly to people and telling them what his will is? This would make sense only if God had a very specific program of tasks that people had to follow for salvation. But which of the gurus has that program right? By what standard can one judge their sayings? How can anyone know whether they are speaking under the influence of God or of evil forces or of their own delusions? If God has truly enlightened them, why don't they agree with one another? What about people who died before a particular guru spoke? Is there any hope for them? If so, are that guru's words really very significant if they are not essential for salvation? If God has not given a standard for identifying truth, what hope does humankind have of finding it? And if God doesn't care how he is worshiped, why should anyone bother with him? The search for the truly wise guru is therefore a wild goose chase.

The Bible has none of the guru problems. It begins at the beginning of the human race, so everyone is included. The key issues are revealed immediately. When the Lord gave the law through Moses, it was complete; no additions were needed. When Jesus the Messiah came to fulfill the law, his apostles (those men whom he commissioned) wrote a message not to be changed. Their message was complete. When Martin Luther led the Reformation of the church, he did not invent anything new. He taught only what he found in the Bible, and he discarded what Roman Catholic gurus had added to the teachings of the Bible over the years.[15] Confessional Lutherans believe that they dare say no more and no less than what is in the Bible (see chapter 3 for how to understand the Bible). While some confessional Lutheran teachers are better than others at teaching in particular situations, their message is the same. The Bible is the standard for all their teaching because everyone can read the Bible and determine whether the teacher is teaching according to it. The knowledge needed for salvation is available to all. The Lord does not hide it in secret communications to only a few. The Bible is indeed a reliable standard of truth.

---

[15]The Roman Catholic Church by Luther's time had created many rules and requirements that were not in the Bible that people had to follow to have a chance to gain salvation (e.g., the celibacy of the priesthood and the veneration of saints). The biggest issue, however, was that the church had placed itself between God and the people as the only means of grace. People had to do the works and participate in the ceremonies prescribed by the church so that the church would advocate their cause before the Lord, in hopes of gaining for them entrance into heaven and of minimizing their time in purgatory (if they were saved). Faith in Christ's promise of free salvation without human contributions was ignored and even actively condemned, as at the three sessions of the Council of Trent (1545–1563).

# CHAPTER 2

# Structure of the Bible

The Bible, which is also called the Scriptures, has two main divisions, as becomes evident when the book is opened (see Table 2-1 at the end of this chapter). One is called the Old Testament, and it covers the time before the birth of Jesus Christ. The other is the New Testament, which covers the life of Jesus, as well as the work and writings of his apostles. These names do not completely explain what is in these two sections of the Bible, but they are historical and therefore continue to be used. The Old Testament consists of 39 books, and the New Testament consists of 27 books.

The word *covenants* might be a better choice than the word *testaments* to describe the major biblical divisions. The Old and New Testaments discuss the two major covenants[1] that the Lord made as part of his plan for humankind. Both of the Lord's covenants are based on promises he made. In fact, he made the promise on which the new covenant is based before he made the promise on which the old covenant was based. The new covenant is the covenant of justification through the atonement of the Messiah,[2] which leads to eternal salvation. The promise for this covenant was first given to Adam and Eve (Genesis 3:15),[3] and it was renewed many times,

---

[1] A covenant is an agreement between two parties that obligates one or both parties to act in a specific manner.

[2] *Messiah* means "anointed one" in Hebrew. The Greek word is *Christ,* which is more commonly used.

[3] [The Lord said,] "I will put enmity between you [the serpent Satan] and the woman [Eve], and between your offspring and her offspring; he shall bruise your head, and you shall bruise his heel." (Genesis 3:15)

particularly to Abraham (Genesis 12:3)[4] and David (2 Samuel 7). It was a one-sided covenant, because in it the Lord promised to act for the benefit of humankind and required nothing from humankind in return. The old covenant was based on a separate promise to Abraham that the Lord would give a subset of Abraham's descendants the land of Canaan as a homeland. The Lord made the covenant two-sided by requiring obedience to a large set of rules on the part of the descendants of Jacob, Abraham's grandson,[5] in exchange for the land of Canaan and prosperity (see the whole book of Leviticus and Deuteronomy 6:1-12). It also contained terrible punishments if these descendants, the Israelites, failed to keep the terms of the covenant (Deuteronomy 28:15-68).

## The Old Testament

The Old Testament, which was written almost entirely in Hebrew, is the Word of God that was given to the descendants of Abraham. Before it was written, the Lord used the lengthy life spans that he had granted the people, sometimes over 950 years (Genesis 5), to allow them to proclaim the message of his covenant promise (Genesis 4:26),[6] which he had first given to Adam. When humankind's abysmal depravity had troubled the Lord long enough (Genesis 6:5-7),[7] he eradicated most of humankind and started again with Noah and his family (Genesis 6:9–8:19). After this, the Lord gradually shortened the life spans of people. The need for a written record became more and more important so that his message would not be lost or become garbled. Moses, a man trained in all the learning of the Egyptians (Acts 7:22)[8], was the first biblical writer.

Moses, obviously with divine guidance, wrote the history of humankind from creation until the end of his own life. The pre-Moses account, contained in the book of Genesis, has only enough detail to carry the theme of the Bible, which is that the Lord was trying to deal graciously with a totally

---

[4][The LORD said,] "I will bless those who bless you, and him who dishonors you I will curse, and through you all the families of the earth shall be blessed." (Genesis 12:3)

[5]The Lord later gave the name "Israel" to Jacob; therefore his descendants are called Israelites.

[6]At that time people began to [proclaim] the name of the LORD. (Genesis 4:26)

[7]The LORD saw that the wickedness of man was great in the earth, and that every intention of the thoughts of his heart was only evil continually. And the LORD regretted that he had made man on the earth, and it grieved him to his heart. So the LORD said, "I will blot out man whom I have created from the face of the land, man and animals and creeping things and birds of the heavens, for I am sorry that I have made them." (Genesis 6:5-7)

[8][Stephen, speaking under the influence of the Holy Spirit, said,] "Moses was instructed in all the wisdom of the Egyptians, and he was mighty in his words and deeds." (Acts 7:22)

depraved humankind.[9] To a large extent, it follows the family through which he had chosen to carry out his plan of salvation. At the beginning of the book of Exodus, Moses' first 80 years are briefly covered. Then begins the description of Moses' epic task of leading the people of Israel out of Egypt and to the doorstep of Canaan, where Moses died. During this time the Lord revealed the details of his old covenant, often called the Mount Sinai covenant or Mosaic covenant. The covenant was given to establish the Israelites as a "chosen people" and was a consequence of the Lord's promise to give the land of Canaan to Abraham's descendants. Moses struggled for 40 years with the "stiff-necked" Israelites (Exodus 32:9)[10] who rebelled continually. This account is given in Exodus, Leviticus, Numbers, and Deuteronomy. Some people doubt that Moses wrote these books, but Jesus himself often stated Moses' authorship of them, such as in Luke 16:31,[11] and Moses certainly had the training to write them.

Moses and his brother Aaron were descendants of Levi,[12] who was the third son of Israel. The Lord gave the priesthood for the Israelites to Aaron and his descendants (Exodus 28:1).[13] The rest of the Levites served in various capacities related to religious worship, the material support of the place of worship, and the teaching of God's Word. Some of the Levites were scribes who faithfully made copies of the words of the Lord for future generations. They were probably also the chroniclers of the events in the history of Israel. These events are in the biblical books of Joshua, Judges, Ruth, 1 & 2 Samuel, and 1 & 2 Kings, which give the history of the Israelites until the Babylonian captivity.

The Lord also gave the Israelites teachings that have come to be labeled "wisdom literature." King David wrote many psalms (2 Samuel 23:1,2),[14] as did other poetically gifted men. These became a hymnal for Israel, called the book of Psalms. Solomon wrote many proverbs (1 Kings 4:32).[15] Some of

---

[9]The phrase "total depravity" appears here and elsewhere in the text, and it may be a little unsettling. It will be discussed more fully in sections 3 and 4 of this book.

[10]And the LORD said to Moses, "I have seen this people, and behold, it is a stiff-necked people." (Exodus 32:9)

[11]He [Father Abraham] said to him [the rich man in hell], "If they do not hear Moses and the Prophets, neither will they be convinced if someone should rise from the dead." (Luke 16:31)

[12]Collectively, the descendants of a person in the Bible are often called a tribe.

[13][The LORD said,] "Then bring near to you Aaron your brother, and his sons with him, from among the people of Israel, to serve me as priests—Aaron and Aaron's sons, Nadab and Abihu, Eleazar and Ithamar." (Exodus 28:1)

[14]Now these are the last words of David: The oracle of David, the son of Jesse, the oracle of the man who was raised on high, the anointed of the God of Jacob, the sweet psalmist of Israel: "The Spirit of the Lord speaks by me; his word is on my tongue." (2 Samuel 23:1,2)

[15]He [Solomon] also spoke 3,000 proverbs, and his songs were 1,005. (1 Kings 4:32)

these were collected with those of other wise men in the book of Proverbs. In addition, Solomon wrote a book about romantic love (Song of Songs) and another about the futility of the human situation without the Lord (Ecclesiastes). The other book in this biblical section is Job, which describes the struggles of faith of a pious man after the Lord let Satan test him severely. Together these books helped the Israelites deal with the joys and the sorrows, the trials and the successes of life on earth or, as Solomon put it, "life under the sun."

The Lord used messengers (prophets) to remind the Israelites that faithful obedience to the covenant made at Mount Sinai could only come from a loving heart and a trust in the Lord. Many of the Israelites had set their minds on their own affairs and were only going through the motions of religious ceremonies without having their hearts in them (Isaiah 1:11-17). Some of these prophets put their messages from the Lord into written form. The longer books are referred to as the books of the major prophets (Isaiah, Jeremiah, Lamentations of Jeremiah, and Ezekiel). The shorter books are referred to as the writings of the minor prophets (Hosea, Joel, Amos, Obadiah, Jonah, Micah, Nahum, Habakkuk, Zephaniah, Haggai, Zechariah, and Malachi.) Some of these writings were directed against specific problems, and some were against general apostasy.[16]

The Babylonian captivity, inflicted upon the Israelites by the Lord because of their unfaithfulness to the old covenant (2 Chronicles 36:11-21), dramatically changed their lives and their ability to practice their religion. Another set of books describes the changed situation that resulted from God's punishment. The books of Daniel and Esther were written about the Israelites while they lived under foreign captivity in present-day Iraq. Most of the Israelites had disappeared, having been killed or absorbed into foreign cultures. Those who remained were called Jews because they came primarily from the tribe of Judah. The descendants of Benjamin and Levi also had a significant representation among the Jews, but there were relatively few people from the other tribes. The books of Nehemiah and Ezra describe the political and religious problems that the Jews faced after they were allowed to return to Canaan. Finally, 1 & 2 Chronicles were prepared to document the important genealogies in Israel, particularly those of the priests and Levites, and to summarize the activities involving the men in David's line, the royal family of Judah. This family was important because the Lord had promised that the

---

[16]For example, Hosea prophesied against the lifestyles of excess and idolatry that existed among Israel's leaders late in its history, while Obadiah declared the Lord's judgment against the Edomites for their treatment of the Jews as they went into captivity in Babylon.

Messiah would be a descendent of David (2 Samuel 7:16).[17] Although some of the minor prophets did write during the period after the Jewish return, their work has traditionally been grouped with those who wrote before the Babylonian captivity. Because the second half of Daniel contains visions, it has been placed with the major prophets in many Bibles, even though Daniel wrote somewhat later.

The arrangement of the books in the Hebrew Bible is significantly different from that of the Bibles in general use in the rest of the world. The Hebrew Bible does not separate Samuel, Kings, and Chronicles into two books each. The prophets immediately follow Kings. The wisdom literature comes next. Ruth is placed within the wisdom literature and Lamentations after it. The historical books written after the fall of Babylon are placed at the end. It is generally thought that Ezra was involved in writing and gathering these books, perhaps including the writing of Chronicles, during the century after the Jews returned from Babylon.

### The Jewish Apocrypha

The last book of the Old Testament is by the prophet Malachi, who wrote about 430 years before the birth of Christ. After this time, the Lord sent no more men who wrote additional revelation. The Levitical scribes who maintained the Scriptures added no more materials. The contents, sometimes called the canon, of the Hebrew Bible (i.e., the Old Testament) were complete. Because the dominant language in the eastern Mediterranean area had become Greek more than two centuries before the birth of Jesus, the Jews in Alexandria, Egypt, began to translate the Hebrew Bible into Greek. This translation became known as the Septuagint because of the legend that it had been translated by 70 Jewish scholars who, working independently, had quickly produced identical Greek translations of the Hebrew text. The translation actually took many years and likely involved much discussion. The translators added some additional writings to the final product that were not part of the Hebrew Bible and were of dubious quality. These are called the Old Testament (or Jewish) Apocrypha. Luther translated the Old Testament Apocrypha into German, but he noted that while it might be profitably read by Christians, it should not be considered part of the inspired Scriptures. The Septuagint was the version of the Bible used by the Greek-speaking members of the early Christian church. Its phrasing is frequently quoted in the New Testament when reference to the Old Testament is made.

---

[17][The Lord spoke to David through Nathan,] "Your house and your kingdom shall be made sure forever before me. Your throne shall be established forever." (2 Samuel 7:16)

## The New Testament

The New Testament, written in Greek, is organized into three sections: history, letters, and prophecy. The first four books are accounts written about the life of Jesus Christ. They were written from different perspectives. Matthew, one of Jesus' disciples and a former tax collector, emphasizes that Jesus had fulfilled the Old Testament prophesies of the coming Messiah, which was important to Jewish readers (e.g., Matthew 1:22,23).[18] Mark, a close associate of the apostles, shows in his writings that Jesus was a bold religious teacher and leader, which appealed to Roman readers (e.g., Mark 1:22).[19] Luke, a physician and historian, researched and wrote based on the input of numerous witnesses who had known Jesus (Luke 1:3,4).[20] These three authors wrote probably within 35 years of Jesus' resurrection. John, also a disciple, may have written closer to the end of the first century and emphasizes Jesus' key teachings and his conflict with the religious leaders over his deity (e.g., John 7:14-52). The last historical book of the New Testament is the Acts of the Apostles, which was also researched and written by Luke (Acts 1:1-3). Luke did much of his early study with the Jewish disciples in Palestine and later traveled with Paul as he did missionary work among the Gentiles. It is interesting to note that Luke's two books were written to Theophilus. This could be a personal name, but the Greek word means "lover of God," so it could be addressed to any Christian.

The second section of the New Testament contains letters, most of them written by Paul, an anti-Christian zealot who became a great gospel missionary and writer (1 Corinthians 15:9,10).[21] Paul's 13 letters are Romans, 1 & 2 Corinthians, Galatians, Ephesians, Philippians, Colossians, 1 & 2 Thessalonians, 1 & 2 Timothy, Titus, and Philemon. These letters explain Christian theology so that it can be understood by those who were not first-century Jews. While the Jewish missionary team, composed initially of the apostles trained by Jesus during his earthly ministry, worked in the areas with significant Jewish settlements from Alexandria in Egypt to Babylon (southern

---

[18]All this took place to fulfill what the Lord had spoken by the prophet [Isaiah]: "Behold, the virgin shall conceive and bear a son, and they shall call his name Immanuel" (which means, God with us). (Matthew 1:22,23)

[19]They [the people] were astonished at his [Jesus'] teaching, for he taught them as one who had authority, and not as the scribes. (Mark 1:22)

[20]It seemed good to me also, having followed all things closely for some time past, to write an orderly account for you, most excellent Theophilus, that you may have certainty concerning the things you have been taught. (Luke 1:3,4)

[21]I am the least of the apostles, unworthy to be called an apostle, because I persecuted the church of God. But by the grace of God I am what I am. (1 Corinthians 15:9,10)

Iraq), Paul teamed with other Greek-speaking Christians and worked in the Greek-speaking world from Asia Minor (present-day Turkey) to Spain. The contact points for the two teams were Antioch in Syria and Jerusalem, before the latter was largely destroyed in A.D. 70. The letters of Paul, after being received by congregations, were copied and circulated to neighboring congregations. Most of the letters were sent to or from Greece and Asia Minor. It was in these areas where collections of Paul's letters were made and verified by traveling missionaries of Paul's team. Later John moved to Ephesus, from which most of his writings originated. Because John lived nearly to the end of the first century, he probably knew every New Testament writer personally and could validate their work.

Paul's letters were written to both congregations and individuals. They contain both theology and practical advice. Other letters were written by John (1, 2, & 3 John), Peter (1 & 2 Peter), James, and Jude. The author of one letter, the epistle to the Hebrews, is unknown. It is generally thought that a member of Paul's missionary team wrote it because of the depth of its theology, the thorough knowledge of Jewish religious law the writer had, and the reference to Timothy.

The final section of the New Testament has but one book, the book of Revelation by John. Its first several chapters contain seven letters that Jesus directed John to send to seven churches in Asia Minor. The rest of the book consists of seven visions John was given of spiritual events that use intense symbolism. The visions conclude the biblical theme begun at the start of Genesis.

The centers where the books of the New Testament were collected were in Asia Minor, particularly Ephesus, and in Antioch in Syria. The four gospels, Acts, the writings of Paul, as well as 1 Peter and 1 John were quickly and universally accepted as God's inspired Word. The authors were well-known and their writings verifiable. Greek Christians at first questioned the books of James and Jude because they did not know these men personally and were concerned over their more legalistic approach. They wondered whether Peter was still alive to write 2 Peter. The Christians in Jewish areas wondered whether John had really written 2 John, 3 John, and Revelation. That Hebrews did not have the author's name on it raised questions for some. As these books—and numerous others that were purported to be works of the apostles—were circulated among the churches, reliable witnesses (perhaps even the authors) were found who were present when the books were written or received. The final canon for the New Testament was set at 27 books. The other books are sometimes called the New Testament

Apocrypha (or pseudepigrapha) and contain some truly strange, inconsistent, and even blasphemous material.

Since the canon of the Bible was established, various people have proposed adding other books to it. These are usually books that were supposedly recently discovered works of Jesus' close associates, such as Peter or Judas. These supposedly "lost books" were usually lost for good reasons. Most of them were known about and were dismissed by the early church leaders as forgeries, when these leaders mentioned them in their own writings. These "new" books or letters either add nothing to what is already in the New Testament or they contradict what is there. While stories about them are frequently spread by the sensationalist press, they have no theological significance. Although it is true that some early writings by church leaders were lost, those of significance were copied and quoted so often that anything important to the salvation of souls did not disappear from the church. Of particular concern to some people are the so-called Gnostic Gospels. In the second century, Bishop Irenaeus, who received training from Polycarp, a disciple of the apostle John, wrote extensively against the heresies of the Gnostics, who reject Christ as he was presented in the Bible.[22] There is no new fount of wisdom in them.

As one examines the Bible, one notes that almost all of the biblical books are divided into chapters and that the chapters are divided into verses. This was not done by the original authors and is therefore not part of the inspired text. Scholars recognized that to easily identify what passages in the Bible they were referencing, some sort of bookmarking system was needed. The division into chapters was developed in the 13th century, based on the work of Archbishop Stephen Langton. The division into verses occurred during the 16th century when the Bible was translated into languages that the common people spoke. The systems of division used by different translators were not identical, so there is some variation between languages even today. This can be seen in Bibles that are multilingual. More information about the Bible can be found in one of the books in the People's Bible Teachings series.[23]

---

[22]Gnostics claimed to have "secret" knowledge that was essential to salvation. They believed the physical world had been made by a lesser, ill-willed god and that one had to reach the ultimate good god to be saved. Gnosticism was disorganized but growing in the first century and became a real problem for the Christian church in the second century, particularly among the Greeks who loved anything new, as Luke notes (Acts 17:21).

[23]Brian R. Keller, *Bible,* People's Bible Teachings series (Milwaukee: Northwestern Publishing House, 2002).

| TABLE 2-1—The Sections of the Bible | | |
|---|---|---|
| **Old Testament** | | |
| **History** | **Wisdom** | **Prophecy** |
| Genesis | Job | Isaiah |
| Exodus | Psalms | Jeremiah |
| Leviticus | Proverbs | Lamentations |
| Numbers | Ecclesiastes | Ezekiel |
| Deuteronomy | Song of Songs | Daniel |
| Joshua | | Hosea |
| Judges | | Joel |
| Ruth | | Amos |
| 1 Samuel | | Obadiah |
| 2 Samuel | | Jonah |
| 1 Kings | | Micah |
| 2 Kings | | Nahum |
| 1 Chronicles | | Habakkuk |
| 2 Chronicles | | Zephaniah |
| Ezra | | Haggai |
| Nehemiah | | Zechariah |
| Esther | | Malachi |
| **New Testament** | | |
| **History** | **Paul's Epistles** | **Other Epistles** |
| Matthew | Romans | Hebrews |
| Mark | 1 Corinthians | James |
| Luke | 2 Corinthians | 1 Peter |
| John | Galatians | 2 Peter |
| Acts | Ephesians | 1 John |
| | Philippians | 2 John |
| | Colossians | 3 John |
| | 1 Thessalonians | Jude |
| | 2 Thessalonians | |
| | 1 Timothy | |
| | 2 Timothy | |
| | Titus | **Prophecy** |
| | Philemon | Revelation |

CHAPTER 3

# Understanding the Bible

Many people repeat the old cliché, "You can prove anything by quoting the Bible." In fact, when one looks at the different things that people claim the Bible says, one is tempted to agree. Yet the statement is totally false. It would be correct to say, "You can prove anything by quoting the Bible out of context," or perhaps, "You can read anything into the Bible if you are determined enough."

The difficulty many people have trying to interpret the Bible is that they start with the assumption that the Bible is a collection of writings of varying quality by writers representing the religious thoughts of their time periods. They fail to recognize that the Bible is a highly integrated book, despite the fact that it was written by numerous writers over many centuries. The Bible begins by talking about an incredibly powerful God, the Lord God Almighty, and it ends by talking about the same incredibly powerful God. It begins with a perfect world, and it ends with a perfect paradise. It begins with humankind's disastrous fall into sin, and it ends with the Lord having completed his rescue of humankind from its sin. Between the beginning and the end is the account of the numerous efforts that the Lord made to bring humankind to its senses and of humanity's total self-centeredness and rebellion against him. The Lord even pictures himself in a parable as a loving, generous, and patient husband trying to deal with an adulterous wife (Ezekiel chapter 16). If the Bible is studied from this perspective, then everything fits together. Because the biblical theme never changes, any proper approach to understanding the Bible must produce the same result, regardless of the generation in which it is studied.

The Bible is both a very simple book and a very complex book. It is simple in that humankind's problem (total depravity) and the Lord's solution (free grace) can be understood even by the young. Bible stories commonly read to children illustrate these themes, and children understand them. The Bible is complex because the Lord is a God beyond our understanding who works in ways that do not make sense to us. Isaiah quoted the Lord as saying, "As the heavens are higher than the earth, so are my ways higher than your ways and my thoughts than your thoughts" (Isaiah 55:9). The adult mind must struggle hard to keep from rationalizing the Lord and his actions or from reengineering them into something that is more intellectually or emotionally satisfying. A proper approach to understanding the Bible must use reason to sort the information given but must not use it to limit or define the Lord where he has not limited or defined himself. Believing is a matter for the heart, but understanding is a matter for the mind.

It is also essential to recognize the language and cultural barriers that exist in trying to understand the Bible. The Old Testament was written almost entirely in Hebrew, and the New Testament was written in a dialect of Greek. Neither of these languages allows for a word-for-word translation into English, and both languages require understanding word usage and phrase structures within them. Writers in Hebrew developed means of expression and emphasis that are sometimes a challenge to represent in English, and the Jewish writers of the New Testament carried this writing style into portions of their Greek writing as well. It therefore takes cultural and historical study, as well as linguistic study, to get a comprehensive understanding of any portion of the Bible. People who try to establish their theology using an English Bible translation will sometimes base their doctrines on translation artifacts rather than the real meaning of the biblical text. Bible commentaries by people who cannot read biblical Hebrew and Greek are therefore not trustworthy, no matter how sincere the writers.

Any approach to an in-depth understanding of the Bible must start with a working knowledge of biblical Hebrew and Greek. If one does not have such knowledge, then one must use reference materials written by people who do. This, however, will be somewhat limiting because one will not see the play on words, the use of acrostics, or the phrase structure that can be important to meaning. One must learn the ways in which Hebrew writers expressed ideas and not read their words in the context of contemporary culture. For example, Hebrew writers often use chiasmus[1] (an inverted style) instead of

---

[1] A modern example of chiasmus: Drivers must be aware that children might be playing in the road. The children could become injured. The drivers must be careful not to hit them.

logical progression (Matthew 7:6).[2] Jewish customs at the time of Christ were dominated by laws of ceremonial cleanliness, which are necessary to know to properly understand biblical stories like the good Samaritan (Luke 10:25-37).[3] While casual reading of the Bible has merit, the systematic study of whole books is much more useful in increasing one's understanding and faith. Understanding takes effort.

The starting point of any honest effort to understand the Bible is to accept the Bible for what it claims to be, namely, the inerrant, verbally inspired Word of the Lord (2 Timothy 3:16,17).[4] Even if one doubts the assumption is true, that is no reason not to use the assumption as a working hypothesis. When people try to understand any book, they will make little progress if they start with the assumption that the author's writing is haphazard and illogical. First, one has to give the author a fair chance to impress the reader.[5] Second, one has to assume that the Bible can be understood with effort that is both sufficient and appropriate. If this is not the case, then its meaning will be forever hidden.

## False approaches that prevent understanding the Bible

It is best to first consider what happens if either of the two assumptions in the previous paragraph is false. Suppose the assumption that the Bible can be understood with sufficient study is false, and it requires a specially gifted guru to understand the Bible. If this were the case, then the source of teaching in the church would be the words of the guru, *not* the words of the Bible, because one would never know if the guru was telling the truth or not. In fact, this is the approach to the Bible of the Roman Catholic Church. In the *Catechism of the Catholic Church,* the source of doctrine is declared to be the Bible and the tradition of the fathers, with the final authority on the meaning of either being the Magisterium of the church,[6] in particular, the Bishop of Rome, i.e., the pope.[7] The meaning of the Bible must therefore

---

[2] [Jesus said,] "Do not give dogs what is holy, and do not throw your pearls before pigs, lest they trample them underfoot and turn to attack you." (Matthew 7:6)

[3] A lawyer, who was the one who came to Jesus and led to him telling this parable, would have recognized that the priest and Levite avoided contact with the wounded man because it would have made them unclean for service before the Lord. The gentile Samaritan's compassion, even for someone from a hostile nation, wasn't hampered by ceremonial considerations.

[4] All Scripture is breathed out by God and profitable for teaching, for reproof, for correction, and for training in righteousness, that the man of God may be complete, equipped for every good work. (2 Timothy 3:16,17)

[5] In literature, Samuel Coleridge labeled this the "willing suspension of disbelief."

[6] The Magisterium is the teaching office of the Roman Catholic Church that defines its theology.

[7] *Catechism of the Catholic Church,* no. 100.

be understood in terms of papal pronouncements, regardless of how poorly they may fit the biblical text. In effect, the Roman Church is saying that the Bible is a dark book (i.e., beyond our understanding) until whoever is the current pope enlightens it.

Suppose the assumption that the Bible *is* the inerrant Word of God is false and that the Bible merely *contains* the Word of the Lord. The rest of the material put into the Bible by its writers would then be results of their own cultures and of their own limited knowledge of the world. If that were true, then what would be the standard for determining which parts of the Bible are the Word of the Lord and which parts are not? As new information becomes available, interpreters would have to change their opinion of whether a particular passage is from the Lord or from a mere human. This would produce the same type of situation one sees in medical research, where researchers frequently change their recommendations about what is good and bad for one's health. For example, the cholesterol level, the blood pressure, and the blood glucose level that are believed to make medical intervention necessary have been changed nearly every decade. In theology, at one point in the 20th century, many liberal scholars convinced themselves, without any real evidence, that the book of Mark had been written by someone other than Mark in the middle of the second century. They were forced to abandon their fantasy when subsequent discoveries showed that it was already in use long before the end of the first century. If one's understanding of the Bible is based on a standard outside of the Bible, then it must change with each new discovery. This approach can hardly produce the solid ground for faith that one would desire. God's will would be forever clouded with uncertainty, awaiting the next discovery or theory.

Finally, suppose both the above assumptions about the Bible are false. Evidence both internal and external to the Bible would then be untrustworthy, and one would have to understand the Bible based on the promptings of one's own heart. The heart, it has been argued, is able to judge even if the mind is troubled by uncertainty. Yet the vast differences in beliefs among those who adopt this approach show the heart is not a reliable guide to anything, because emotionalism rules. Jesus states that what comes out of the heart is not wisdom but evil (Mark 7:21-23).[8] Moses documents that the Lord saw this in humankind from the beginning (Genesis 6:5).[9]

---

[8] [Jesus said,] "From within, out of the heart of man, come evil thoughts, sexual immorality, theft, murder, adultery, coveting, wickedness, deceit, sensuality, envy, slander, pride, foolishness. All these evil things come from within, and they defile a person." (Mark 7:21-23)

[9] The LORD saw that the wickedness of man was great in the earth, and that every intention of the thoughts of his heart was only evil continually. (Genesis 6:5)

The heart is always looking for ways to justify itself (Jeremiah 17:9),[10] and it seeks to find its own ideas in the Bible to validate them. This approach results in reading a meaning *into* the Bible rather than reading its meaning *from* the Bible. Our desires, instead of God's will, then become the guiding hand in our theology.

Without the assumptions that the Bible is the inerrant Word of the Lord and that it can be understood through faithful study, there is no firm standard that endures from generation to generation. Instead, the Bible becomes a book with no real meaning at all. It becomes merely a crutch to support what people want to believe, a means to convince themselves that they really are good and God-pleasing people. Many who scoff at religion use the continually changing standards of interpretation used by some church bodies to make the charge that all religion is really man-made and not God-given. And if it is man-made, then it is subject to change for the benefit of humankind. The changes that many churches have made in their teachings in recent years, such as in their views on sexual behavior and abortion, are a direct result of trying to interpret the Bible by external standards of their own creation. In other words, many people's god is a creature of their own imagination, whom they lead around like a bull with a ring in his nose. This does not impress the Lord God Almighty (Psalm 2:4).[11]

## The Lutheran approach

The Lutheran approach to understanding the Scriptures (see Table 3-1) is called the historical-grammatical method and goes back to Martin Luther himself. Luther abandoned the convoluted approach of the Scholastic theologians with its multiple meanings of every verse of the Bible. Instead, he argued each Bible passage had one basic meaning that was firmly rooted in the historical truth of the situation in which it was written or spoken and that could accurately be understood using the common principles of human language. This tethered the truth of the Scriptures to real, historical events and gave a way to study the Scriptures according to the well-established principles of human language.

The tools of grammatical analysis are well-understood and independent of the text being studied. One starts by identifying the general context in which the passage (i.e., verse or verses) of interest is located. This gives clues as to how the passage can be understood. One next determines the literary

---

[10]The heart is deceitful above all things, and is [incurable]; who can understand it? (Jeremiah 17:9)

[11]He who sits in the heavens laughs; the Lord scoffs at them. (Psalm 2:4)

style of the passage and uses the characteristics of that style to develop possible meanings. Sometimes the clarity of the passage points to only one possible meaning. Other times several meanings might be possible, or no obvious meaning can be deduced. One next validates the information against the rest of Scripture by using the rules of formal, nonnumerical mathematical logic. While these logical methods cannot be used to understand the hidden things of God, they allow Scriptural constraints to be rigorously applied to possible meanings to determine which meanings agree with other parallel passages (i.e., those discussing the same topics). This process yields consistent results, because scholars working independently, even centuries apart, will assign the same meaning to biblical passages.

Although Luther did not realize it, he had selected an approach to biblical understanding that took it out of the realm of philosophical reasoning and into the realm of mathematical logic. The strength of this is that when mathematical reasoning is appropriately applied, it always gives the same correct answer, unlike philosophy or science. It forces clear definitions and relationships to be used and allows one to determine necessary and sufficient conditions for the truth of assertions. While Lutheran dogmaticians (i.e., systematic theological scholars) do not write their arguments in the symbolism of the predicate calculus,[12] their verbal arguments adhere to the same rules.

Some examples will show how the process works.

### Understanding Joshua 24:15

Suppose we desired to understand Joshua 24:15: "As for me and my house, we will serve the LORD." The biblical table of contents places the book of Joshua in the Old Testament. If we consult a study Bible, such as *The Lutheran Study Bible*,[13] we learn that the book of Joshua is a historical narrative of the Israelites as they entered Canaan (present-day Palestine). It was prepared by Joshua and/or his scribes and discusses how the Lord fulfilled his promise to Abraham by bringing the Israelites into the land he had promised them. The audience for the book was subsequent generations who

---

[12]Mathematical systems are ideal because they can be defined independently of the physical and literary worlds. Therefore, any operation (i.e., action) performed in a mathematical system will always yield the same result. The predicate calculus is a mathematically rigorous, therefore always truthful, approach to applying the rules of mathematics to situations that contain verbal statements rather than numbers. It has a complex set of symbols that can be used to represent statements, variables, etc. When this type of logic is applied to the statements of the Bible, it must never be used to try to reconcile the things of God to human reason, but must only be used to consider and compare statements that are in the realm of human understanding.

[13]E. A. Engelbrecht, ed., *The Lutheran Study Bible* (St. Louis: Concordia Publishing House, 2009).

needed to know that the Lord was a faithful God. The passage appears near the end of the book, and its surrounding verses show that Joshua is making a farewell speech to the Israelites, whom he had led since the death of Moses. In the verses immediately before this verse, Joshua had issued a challenge to the Israelites to choose which god they would serve now that they were in the land that the Lord had promised to them. Joshua was still speaking in the passage of interest.

---

### TABLE 3-1—The Rules for Understanding Scripture (Hermeneutics)

I. Determine the general context (i.e., the setting) of the passage verse of interest.

  A. Which testament is it in?

  B. What type of book of the Bible is it in (e.g., narrative, poetical, letter)?

  C. What is the purpose of the book and its historical setting?

  D. Who is the writer? Is he quoting someone else in the words of interest?

  E. Who is the audience?

  F. What verses on the same topic bracket the passage?

II. Identify the literary context.

  A. Narrative and letter

    1. Use the literal sense of the words unless the text itself indicates to do otherwise.

    2. Construe the meaning using the established rules of grammar in the original language.

    3. Consider the popular use (i.e., the spoken use) before any derived use.

    4. Compare uncommon words with their usage elsewhere in Scripture and in secular writings.

    5. Be aware that special usages might occur (e.g., idioms, figures of speech).

    6. Consider general usage before a specialized use.

  B. Poetical (e.g., Psalms, Proverbs, much of Isaiah)

    1. Become familiar with the patterns and forms in Hebrew poetry.

    2. Evaluate the picture language carefully; don't over-read what is written.

    3. Be sensitive to the Lord's attitude toward his people in the poetry.

## TABLE 3-1 — The Rules for Understanding Scripture (Hermeneutics) *continued*

    C. Comparison (e.g., parables, similes, metaphors)
       1. Identify what is being compared.
       2. Do not go beyond the point of comparison in figurative language.
    D. Picture language in prophetic revelation (e.g., Revelation, Daniel)
       1. Interpret the picture language in the context of other scriptural uses of it picture language.
       2. Never use it to establish doctrine because it is only a dim reflection of future reality.

III. Apply the scriptural constraints.

    A. Every acceptable meaning of a passage must be consistent with the Scriptures' own stated purpose for its existence, namely, to teach the wisdom necessary for salvation.

    B. Scripture is the only reliable interpreter of Scripture—the plain passages help to make the difficult clear. Any interpretation that does not agree with all of a passage's parallels is unacceptable (analogy of Scripture).

    C. Every doctrine necessary to our spiritual welfare is taught in one or more clear passages (seat of doctrine).
       1. One may not add to or subtract from teachings of the Scriptures.
       2. One may not assert what the Bible does not mention (argument from silence).
       3. One may assert doctrine only when the necessary and sufficient conditions are met.
       4. One may not use descriptive passages as prescriptive for Christian living.
       5. One may not establish doctrine when the Bible does not speak definitively (adiaphoron).

    D. *Sola Scriptura* (i.e., Scripture Alone), not reason, experience, tradition, or church practices, governs how Scripture is to be understood.

Because this section of the Bible is a narrative, one must first try to understand everything literally as it is written. In the introductory phrase, Joshua identifies a group: "me and my house." In the main clause, he states what that group would do. The main clause is clear English, indicating that the group of which the speaker is a part would serve the Lord God, the God who brought them out of Egypt. Because there was no restriction placed on that service, it could be given in various ways. The introductory phrase contains the word *house*, which most commonly means a building. Certainly, a building is not going to serve the Lord, who hardly needs it as a shelter. Instead, we must consider that the word *house* can also refer to those who dwell in it or who are associated with the family who lives in it. For example, people say that the United Kingdom is ruled by the "House of Windsor." Furthermore, the Hebrew word used by Joshua can also mean "household." A clear meaning can therefore be assigned: Joshua and his family and his servants will worship and work for the Lord.

One must always ask a final question, namely, whether such a proposed meaning is consistent with the rest of the teachings of the Bible. Because this is both a historical statement and a personal statement of intent, it is merely descriptive of what happened, and it places no requirement on the reader. Nothing is commanded for the reader to do, so most potential conflicts with other things written in the Bible are eliminated. Certainly, his action was an example that Joshua wanted all the Israelites to follow, and in the next verse, they did indeed commit themselves to do as Joshua was doing. Moreover, this was what the Lord clearly commanded the Israelites to do in many places within the first five books of the Bible (e.g., Exodus 20:2-5;[14] Deuteronomy 6:1,2[15]). Therefore, one can be certain that this is the meaning of the passage.

## Understanding Psalm 1:1,2

Let us consider Psalm 1:1,2: "Blessed is the man who walks not in the counsel of the wicked, nor stands in the ways of sinners, nor sits in the seat of scoffers; but his delight is in the law of the LORD, and on his law he meditates day and night." We find that the biblical table of contents places the book of Psalms in the Old Testament. If we consult a study Bible or a Bible commentary on the psalms,[16] we learn that the book of Psalms is poetical; in

---

[14]"I am the LORD your God, who brought you out of the land of Egypt, out of the house of slavery. You shall have no other gods before me. You shall not make for yourself a carved image, or any likeness of anything that is in heaven above, or that is in the earth beneath, or that is in the water under the earth. You shall not bow down to them or serve them." (Exodus 20:2-5)

[15][Moses said,] "Now this is the commandment—the statutes and the rules—that the LORD your God commanded me to teach you, that you may do them in the land to which you are going over, to possess it, that you may fear the LORD your God, you and your son and your son's son, by keeping all his statutes and his commandments, which I command you, all the days of your life, and that your days may be long." (Deuteronomy 6:1,2)

[16]John F. Brug, *Psalms*, Vol. 1, The People's Bible series (Milwaukee: Northwestern Publishing House, 1989).

fact, it was the hymnal of the Israelites. No one person wrote all the psalms, although King David wrote more psalms in the book of Psalms than any other poet. The author of Psalm 1 is unknown. Because each psalm is a separate work, the context of the passage of interest is limited to Psalm 1 itself.[17] The psalm mentions no historical events to which it might be related, but it is rather a poem for general use.

To understand poetry, it is essential to determine the style of the poet. In Hebrew poetry, repetition with variations is the standard tool to advance a theme or to intensify it. In the first verse, we find the progression "walks," "stands," and "sits." This is a progression of commitment. At a Renaissance Faire, for example, one might walk past a stage area to see if an act looks interesting. One might then stand in the back to see whether one can pick up some of what is going on. Finally, one might find a seat and enjoy the performance. In this psalm the poet uses a similar progression. The reader is first warned against walking to where people are talking about wicked things. The next warning is against standing around to soak up the conversations. The final warning is against sitting in on the scheming for evil and on the ridiculing of the "simple fools" who will suffer from the schemes. The psalm says the man who does not get involved in such activities is "blessed." Perhaps a better translation would be "happy" or even "content," because in the end, doing evil is not the way of happiness.

The psalmist then contrasts such playing with sin to what should truly delight a person. In so doing, he uses three references that require further study. What is "the law of the LORD" (Issue 1)? The initial reaction is to think of the Ten Commandments and perhaps other regulations that the Lord has given. That is a possible interpretation, but another meaning for the Hebrew word *Torah* is "instruction." So the phrase might mean "but his delight is in the instruction of the LORD." This must be left an open question at this point. The second unclear phrase is "on his law he meditates day and night" (Issue 2). Does this imply that unless someone is constantly mediating on "his law," he is not living as the Lord wishes? For centuries the Roman Catholic Church argued that true sanctification required doing precisely this. Therefore, the monastic lifestyle was the only one that was truly pleasing to God, because only monks and nuns separated themselves to serve God "day and night." A related issue that might be considered is whether these statements apply only to males, because a Hebrew word for "man" is used (Issue 3).

---

[17] Later in the book of Psalms, there are cases where consecutive psalms are linked by a common theme, but Psalm 1 is not in such a section.

To resolve the issues left unanswered by looking at the literary evidence, one must search the rest of the Bible to see what it says on these matters. Issue 3 is resolved by Galatians 3:25-28,[18] which explains that in spiritual matters, there is no differentiation between classes of people, such as male and female. Because Psalm 1 is discussing a spiritual matter, what is true for men is also true for women and is also true for children. Issue 2, the "meditates day and night" phrase, can be understood with the aid of Deuteronomy 6:4-9,[19] which discusses the same subject. In these verses, the Lord instructed the Israelites to always have the words of the Lord about them. They were to talk about his teachings whenever the opportunity arose. They were to put up signs of their faith around them so that they would see them and remember them. They were to teach the words of the Lord to their children. The knowledge of the Lord's will needed be an active part of their lives. His commands were not an obligation they could periodically fulfill and then forget about. This explains what the psalmist was encouraging by using the phrase "meditates day and night." Issue 1 is addressed in John 5:39.[20] When Jesus was confronting the teachers of the law, he said they should examine the Scriptures (at the time, only the Old Testament existed) because they testified of him. Jesus, however, personifies the gospel, not the law. He was telling them that the Bible was more than rules; it pointed to him and his coming to save humankind. To be consistent with Jesus' teaching, therefore, "instruction" is a better translation than "law" for the word *Torah* in Psalm 1. The Christian's delight should be in the instruction that is received by studying the Bible.

## Understanding John 15:5

Another interesting verse is John 15:5: "I am the vine; you are the branches. Whoever abides in me and I in him, he it is that bears much fruit, for apart from me you can do nothing." The book of John is in the New

---

[18]Now that faith has come, we are no longer under a guardian, for in Christ Jesus you are all sons of God, through faith. For as many of you as were baptized into Christ have put on Christ. There is neither Jew nor Greek, there is neither slave nor free, there is no male and female, for you are all one in Christ Jesus. (Galatians 3:25-28)

[19][Moses said,] "Hear, O Israel: The LORD our God, the LORD is one. You shall love the LORD your God with all your heart and with all your soul and with all your might. And these words that I command you today shall be on your heart. You shall teach them diligently to your children, and shall talk of them when you sit in your house, and when you walk by the way, and when you lie down, and when you rise. You shall bind them as a sign on your hand, and they shall be as frontlets between your eyes. You shall write them on the doorposts of your house and on your gates." (Deuteronomy 6:4-9)

[20][Jesus said,] "You search the Scriptures because you think that in them you have eternal life; and it is they that bear witness about me." (John 5:39)

Testament. It is one of the gospels, so the verse can be expected to be closely tied to the life of Jesus Christ. In fact, the words can be seen to be a quotation of Jesus, which was recorded by John, who particularly emphasized Jesus' doctrinal statements in his writings. To find when these words were spoken and to whom, we need to go back to the beginning of John 13. Here we find that they were spoken by Jesus to his disciples on the night before his crucifixion. Since these are some of his last words to those who would carry his message to the world, the words can be expected to have great significance. Lastly, we need to identify all the surrounding verses that are directly related, in this case, John 15:1-8.[21]

The words in John 15:5 are part of a narrative, but it is pretty obvious that they cannot be taken literally.[22] Jesus certainly was not indicating by his words that he was a woody piece of plant, but he was using the word *vine* to indicate some characteristic that he shared with a vine. This is a very important principle in understanding Jesus' words. Whenever he used a form of the verb "to be" to relate himself to a physical object, it was because he wanted to illustrate some property he shared with the object.[23] In the next part of the verse, his followers were described as being "branches" on the vine. What passes between a vine and its branches is the sap that the branches need to live and bear fruit. Could it be that Jesus was saying he supplied what his followers needed to physically survive? That interpretation would not be consistent with the New Testament's picturing Jesus as a poor man (Matthew 8:20).[24] As a result, it cannot mean that his disciples were depending on him for support for their physical lives. That forces one to conclude that he was talking about spiritual nourishment rather than physical nourishment. The rest of the verse confirms this meaning. His followers were not about to begin sprouting grapes on their bodies, but they were going to produce

---

[21] [Jesus said,] "I am the true vine, and my Father is the vinedresser. Every branch in me that does not bear fruit he takes away, and every branch that does bear fruit he prunes, that it may bear more fruit. Already you are clean because of the word that I have spoken to you. Abide in me, and I in you. As the branch cannot bear fruit by itself, unless it abides in the vine, neither can you, unless you abide in me. I am the vine; you are the branches. Whoever abides in me and I in him, he it is that bears much fruit, for apart from me you can do nothing. If anyone does not abide in me he is thrown away like a branch and withers; and the branches are gathered, thrown into the fire, and burned. If you abide in me, and my words abide in you, ask whatever you wish, and it will be done for you. By this my Father is glorified, that you bear much fruit and so prove to be my disciples." (John 15:1-8)

[22] John 15:5 is, in reality, a string of metaphors.

[23] See the "Scriptural Doctrine of the Lord's Supper" in Francis Pieper, *Christian Dogmatics*, Vol. 3 (St. Louis: Concordia Publishing House, 1953).

[24] And Jesus said to him [a teacher of the Law], "Foxes have holes, and birds of the air have nests, but the Son of Man has nowhere to lay his head." (Matthew 8:20)

something that had a property similar to fruit. But is this understanding of John 15:5 consistent with other parts of the Bible? Indeed, it is. St. Paul wrote to the Romans (Romans 11:13-24) that the believing Gentiles are like wild olive branches that are grafted into Christ. The picture of Christ as a "vine" or a "root" supplying spiritual nourishment is therefore consistent with biblical teaching.

In the second part of the verse, Jesus made clear that the purpose of being the vine was so that the branches would bear much fruit. Paul confirmed this relationship to Christ was for the purpose of bearing fruit (Romans 7:4).[25] As long as branches are attached to the vine, they are, at least theoretically, able to bear fruit. If they are cut off, they will soon die and no longer have the ability to bear fruit. This point is stated emphatically in the final part of the verse. Those who are not attached to Christ cannot bear any fruit whatsoever. Can it really be the meaning of this verse that those who are not attached to Christ, that is, do not believe in him, can produce no God-pleasing fruit in their lives? To see whether this meaning is consistent with the rest of biblical teaching, one must find other passages on the subject. The writer to the Hebrews (Hebrews 11:6)[26] wrote that without faith it is "impossible to please" God. In chapter 3, John quotes both Jesus (John 3:17,18)[27] and John the Baptizer (John 3:36)[28] as saying that anyone who does not believe in Christ is under the wrath of God. Other sections of the Bible present this teaching as well.

John 15:5 is one of the "seats of doctrine" in the Bible. The teaching that there is no ability to "bear fruit" (i.e., do God-pleasing works) without being a Christian is clearly stated here, as it is in the other three verses referred to in the previous paragraph. The context of each verse prevents any other meaning from being assigned to it. This meaning, however, seems to contradict common sense. Numerous unbelievers in this world do great things for their neighbors and/or for humanity in general. Two principles essential

[25]Likewise, my brothers, you also have died to the law through the body of Christ, so that you may belong to another, to him who has been raised from the dead, in order that we may bear fruit for God. (Romans 7:4)

[26]Without faith it is impossible to please him, for whoever would draw near to God must believe that he exists and that he rewards those who seek him. (Hebrews 11:6)

[27][Jesus said,] "God did not send his Son into the world to condemn the world, but in order that the world might be saved through him. Whoever believes in him is not condemned, but whoever does not believe is condemned already, because he has not believed in the name of the only Son of God." (John 3:17,18)

[28][John the Baptizer said,] "Whoever believes in the Son has eternal life; whoever does not obey the Son shall not see life, but the wrath of God remains on him." (John 3:36)

to biblical understanding, however, must be observed here. When considering a comparison as we have in this verse, only one point of comparison exists between the figure of speech and reality. In this case, it is that nourishment is necessary to produce fruit. Because it is spiritual nourishment that is being provided, what is expected is spiritual fruit. Such fruit might not have a physical component that can be seen by human observation (e.g., praying for others in one's home), and what can be observed may not be true spiritual fruit (e.g., deeds of civic righteousness done for political advantage). Second, human reason cannot set criteria that the Lord has to follow. There is no way for frail humans, even en masse, to compel the Lord God Almighty to have the same view of human works and human morality as they do. In examining the nature of the God of the Bible in the next chapters, this will become even more apparent.

### Understanding Revelation 20:1-3

A final passage we will consider is Revelation 20:1-3: "Then I saw an angel coming down from heaven, holding in his hand the key to the bottomless pit and a great chain. And he seized the dragon, that ancient serpent, who is the devil and Satan, and bound him for a thousand years, and threw him into the pit, and shut it and sealed it over him, so that he might not deceive the nations any longer, until the thousand years were ended. After that he must be released for a little while." The book of Revelation is the last book in the New Testament. It was written by the apostle John, but it bears little resemblance to the gospel he wrote. Revelation is a book of prophetic revelation, which means that it cannot be used to establish doctrine. It does not show us clear pictures but rather images of the spiritual world in visions that stagger the mind. There are seven visions in Revelation. The passage being considered is at the beginning of the last of these visions. This vision presents Christ's final victory. In these visions, John saw only what the Lord wanted him to see, and he put what he saw into the best words he could to describe things that must have been truly inexpressible.

It is immediately clear that this passage is presenting spiritual things, as do all the visions in Revelation. Satan is not a physical dragon or serpent but rather a powerful angel. He masqueraded as a serpent to deceive Eve, so that action is alluded to here by calling him a serpent. One cannot bind a spirit with a physical chain or lock him in a physical bottomless pit with a physical key. Given this situation, one is forced to consider everything in this passage symbolically. The only being powerful enough to constrain Satan is the Son of God himself, who came down to earth and assumed a human nature (Genesis 3:15).[29] He is the only option for being the "angel" of this vision (Jude 9). The Son of God did appear in the role of an angel several times in the Old Testament (e.g., Genesis 22:11-18; Exodus 3:2-6;[30] Judges 2:1-4), so understanding him to be the angel in this vision is consistent with other parts of the Bible. What binds Satan must be something that hampers his operations. The only thing that will prevent Satan from working freely to corrupt souls is the gospel, which is being proclaimed throughout the world, because it gives people a way to escape Satan's kingdom. Any effort to assign the means of his confinement (i.e., key, chain, pit, seal) to specific things in the operation of the Lord's dispensing of his grace would be speculative. The information in the vision is too limited.

But what about the "thousand years"? Because everything else in this vision is spiritual and symbolic, it would be inconsistent reasoning to conclude that the thousand years is a period measured by some human calendar. The number 1,000 is used in various places in the Bible, including Revelation, to indicate an indefinitely large but finite number (Joshua 23:10;[31] Job 9:3;[32] Psalm 50:10;[33] Psalm 90:4;[34] Revelation 5:11; Revelation 9:16). The thousand years mentioned here must therefore be regarded as a long but finite period of time. The purpose of confining Satan is so that the gospel can be preached to the "nations." Yet the Greek word translated here as "nations" can also be translated as "Gentiles." This makes more sense. The completion of Christ's work on earth has led to missionaries spreading the gospel throughout the Gentile world, which, before Christ, was almost exclusively Satan's domain. Being constrained, Satan is losing Gentiles to Christ's kingdom. Sadly, the last sentence indicates that a time is coming when the forces opposing the spread of the gospel will gain such power that Satan will again

---

[29] [The Lord said,] "I will put enmity between you and the woman, and between your offspring and her offspring; he shall bruise your head, and you shall bruise his heel." (Genesis 3:15)

[30] The Angel of the Lord appeared to him in a flame of fire out of the midst of a bush. He looked, and behold, the bush was burning, yet it was not consumed. And Moses said, "I will turn aside to see this great sight, why the bush is not burned." When the Lord saw that he turned aside to see, God called to him out of the bush, "Moses, Moses!" And he said, "Here I am." Then he said, "Do not come near; take your sandals off your feet, for the place on which you are standing is holy ground." And he said, "I am the God of your father, the God of Abraham, the God of Isaac, and the God of Jacob." And Moses hid his face, for he was afraid to look at God. (Exodus 3:2-6)

[31] [Joshua said,] "One man of you puts to flight a thousand, since it is the Lord your God who fights for you, just as he promised you." (Joshua 23:10)

[32] [Job said,] "If one wished to contend with him [the Lord], one could not answer him once in a thousand times." (Job 9:3)

[33] [The Lord said,] "Every beast of the forest is mine, the cattle on a thousand hills." (Psalm 50:10)

[34] [Moses said,] "A thousand years in your sight are but as yesterday when it is past, or as a watch in the night." (Psalm 90:4)

be effectively free to suppress the saving message. This understanding of this section of Revelation is consistent with the rest of the Bible, which elsewhere (Matthew 24) speaks of days of tribulation just before Christ returns.

Some church bodies argue, based on this section of Scripture, that there will be a thousand-year period, called the millennium, in which Christians will dominate the world and in which there will be great prosperity (see chapter 11). Whether Christ comes before or after the Millennium is a matter of hot debate among people who hold such a belief. Such an interpretation of this section of Scripture is incompatible with clear descriptions of the return of Christ on judgment day and of his heavenly kingdom (Matthew 24). Christ sought no earthly kingdom (John 6:15;[35] John 18:36[36]). Why would he? He is the Lord God Almighty. There is no "seat of doctrine" for a physical millennium in the narrative parts of the Bible; rather, people try to read it into verses where the context will not support it.

### Mistakes that prevent understanding the Scripture correctly

The millennium is a good introduction to one of the main ways that people get lost in their efforts to understand the Bible. Rather than reading *from* the Bible, they read *into* the Bible. For example, someone may think that the consumption of alcohol is a bad idea. With great zeal they then search for supporting passages that mention the ills of drunkenness or warn against it (e.g., Proverbs 23:31,32[37] and Luke 1:15[38]). They next string these together and add encouraging passages for leading an exemplary Christian life (e.g., 1 Peter 5:8).[39] They ignore passages such as when Jesus turned water into wine for a wedding party where significant alcohol had already been consumed (John 2:1-11) and those that speak against judging people based on what they eat or drink (Colossians 2:20-23).[40] The result of their efforts

---

[35]Perceiving then that they [the crowd of listeners] were about to come and take him by force to make him king, Jesus withdrew again to the mountain by himself. (John 6:15)

[36]Jesus answered, "My kingdom is not of this world. If my kingdom were of this world, my servants would have been fighting, that I might not be delivered over to the Jews. But my kingdom is not from the world." (John 18:36)

[37][Solomon said,] "Do not look at wine when it is red, when it sparkles in the cup and goes down smoothly. In the end it bites like a serpent and stings like an adder." (Proverbs 23:31,32)

[38][Gabriel, an angel, said,] "He must not drink wine or strong drink, and he will be filled with the Holy Spirit, even from his mother's womb." (Luke 1:15)

[39]Be sober-minded; be watchful. Your adversary the devil prowls around like a roaring lion, seeking someone to devour. (1 Peter 5:8)

[40]If with Christ you died to the [basic principles] of the world, why, as if you were still alive in the world, do you submit to regulations—"Do not handle, Do not taste, Do not touch" (referring to things that all perish as they are used)—according to human precepts and teachings? These have indeed an appear-

appears to be a good case for prohibition, which the Bible never makes if one uses a proper method of interpretation.

Another approach that will lead to trouble is using a principle to guide one's translation that is not found in the Bible. For example, John Calvin[41] used the principle that "the finite cannot contain the infinite" to develop his theology of the relationship between the divine and human natures of Christ. But the relationship between the two natures of Christ is in the divine realm and transcends human understanding. There is far too little information to apply analysis tools to it. By trying to impose a non-biblical condition, a condition that makes perfect sense to the rational human mind, Calvin got himself in a bind. He was forced to draw conclusions about some clear passages of Scripture, such as those that describe the nature of Christ's presence in Holy Communion, which made them cloudy and untenable. Those seeking to understand the Scriptures have to allow themselves to be limited by the principle of reading no more and no less from the Bible than the Bible says (2 Corinthians 4:2).[42]

Perhaps one of the most deceptive approaches to understanding the Bible is called the analogy of faith.[43] This approach assumes that the human mind is smart enough to reconcile all the different doctrines the Bible teaches into a clear picture. The first difficulty with this approach is that the Bible never says that this is possible (2 Peter 3:15,16).[44] The second difficulty is that the Lord has only revealed to us what he decided we needed to know. When the six blind men in the fairy tale went to "see" the elephant, each came back with a different impression of the nature of an elephant because each had felt a different part of the animal, from its rope-like tail to its tree-like legs. If

---

ance of wisdom in promoting self-made religion and asceticism and severity to the body, but they are of no value in stopping the indulgence of the flesh. (Colossians 2:20-23)

[41] John Calvin was a Frenchman and was 25 years younger than Luther. He fled for safety to Geneva and did extensive theological writing. He was unduly influenced by Humanism, and sometimes he felt he needed to give rational explanations for spiritual concepts that seemed to be at variance to human logic.

[42] We have renounced disgraceful, underhanded ways. We refuse to practice cunning or to tamper with God's Word, but by the open statement of the truth we would commend ourselves to everyone's conscience in the sight of God. (2 Corinthians 4:2)

[43] The concept of "analogy of faith" is not the same as the concept of "analogy of Scripture." Applying the analogy of Scripture means using everything that Scripture teaches about a specific doctrine to understand it. Using the analogy of faith means trying to reconcile the different doctrines taught in Scripture by editing them so that they fit together in one humanly comprehensible picture. The latter approach uses human reason to judge Scripture and invariably forces additions to and/or subtractions from the teachings of Bible.

[44] Our beloved brother Paul also wrote to you according to the wisdom given him, as he does in all his letters when he speaks in them of these matters. There are some things in them that are hard to understand, which the ignorant and unstable twist to their own destruction, as they do the other Scriptures. (2 Peter 3:15,16)

these men had tried to pool their knowledge into a unified picture of an elephant, they almost certainly would still not have had something that looked anything like an elephant. Too much information would have been missing to form a correct picture. The same is true if we try to put together a complete picture of the Lord and his ways from the limited information he has given us in the Bible. We must restrict ourselves to believing what the Lord has made known and to trusting that he will take care of the rest (Acts 1:7).[45]

The ultimate meddling with the meaning of Scripture, however, involves allegory. Rather than assuming the Bible means what it says, allegorists assume that there is a hidden meaning in every passage, which can be deduced by the skilled practitioner of hidden meanings. As it is with astrologers interpreting the Zodiac signs, where different people reach different conclusions, so it is with allegorists interpreting the Bible. Such interpretations might best be described as whimsy. During the Middle Ages, theologians greatly confused biblical understanding by insisting that every verse of the Bible had not only a literal meaning but also three spiritual meanings: the allegorical (figurative) sense, the moral sense, and the anagogical (allusions to the afterlife) sense. Whole books of these interpretations were assembled and taught in the universities. Luther struggled to escape the allegory trap, which had plagued Christianity since the theologian Origen in the second century. These struggles led him to methods employed by the Antiochene School (Antioch, Syria) in the third century, and from these Luther developed the historical-grammatical approach to the Scriptures, which Lutherans continue to use. Sadly, even today, people are tempted to see allusions and coded information in the Scriptures that have nothing to do with the real message of the Bible.

To prevent misunderstanding the Bible, we must accept the Bible for what it claims to be, namely, the inerrant Word of the Lord. It was written around his plan of salvation and centers on Jesus the Christ, the Messiah. We must read what is there in the context in which it was given. We must let the clear passages illuminate the cloudy. If passages refer to the nature and/or work of the Lord, they may be beyond our ability to completely understand and reconcile. If they discuss earthly things, then they should be comprehensible by the human mind with sufficient study. If we cannot find a clear seat of doctrine on some matter, then it is unimportant for salvation. The Lord is a hidden God, but he loves people enough to give them what they need to know for their eternal salvation.

---

[45] He [Jesus] said to them [his disciples], "It is not for you to know times or seasons that the Father has fixed by his own authority." (Acts 1:7)

# God

"Then men said, 'Let us make gods in our own image so that we can have dominance over them and so they will bless us, so they will overlook our faults, and so they will curse our enemies.' So men made gods in their own images out of wood and stone and the desires of their hearts. And men served them so long as it suited their fancy. And then they made other gods to serve which had even more potential to please them." (Folly 1:17-19)

The above quotation is from a fictitious source and parallels Genesis 1:26,27. However, to a large extent, the quotation reflects the way most people subconsciously behave. People seek gods to which they can relate, and the best place for them to find such gods is in the feelings of their own hearts. People give moral values to their god or gods, that is, things their gods will or will not tolerate. They define what their gods will or will not do in particular situations, when they can be of assistance, and in what matters they will be of no use. They size their gods to what they need and bargain with their gods for things they hope their gods can help them obtain. They promise their gods that they will behave uprightly in exchange for blessings either in this life or in the afterlife. They permit themselves to turn off their gods when they want to do something of which they don't think their gods would approve. In effect, they figuratively keep their gods in a breadbox or a closet, except when they need them to grant some request or when they want to feel comfort or piety.

The reason that people behave this way is twofold. They look around themselves and see a universe that is both huge and scary. They feel insignificant and helpless in the face of nature, which can unleash immense power in storms, earthquakes, landslides, floods, and forest fires. They want some validation of their personal worth and some sense that help is available in dealing with the things of nature. This has led people in virtually every culture in the world to create gods, i.e., supernatural beings, to help them in their perceived needs. The interaction of gods with the physical world is therefore the first theme of religions.

But people are also troubled by their consciences. They have an innate sense that there are things that are right and that there are things that are wrong for humans to do. They feel responsible to something greater than themselves. They therefore assign moral judgment to their gods and create ways to regain their gods' favor if they feel they have offended them. They often codify rules to guide their actions, and they force others to conform to those rules to prevent their gods from becoming angry. Obeying the rules helps to soothe their consciences; enforcing the rules gives them a feeling of moral superiority. Obedience and reconciliation with the gods is the second major theme in religions.

When these two themes are put together, one gets what is called natural religion. All natural religions function the same way. People believe that they need to placate some god(s) so that they can gain an improved standing before them. These gods then manipulate the physical world to the extent necessary to grant people's desires. Therefore, one is tempted to say, all religions are really pretty much alike and should be able to get together and coexist.

The God whom the Bible proclaims is not like one of the gods of natural religion. He can in no way be defined by the mind of man, and he cannot be limited by the desires of individuals or nations. He must be dealt with on his terms, not on our terms, because no one can impose anything upon him. In this section of the book, the nature of the God of the Bible and his interaction with the universe will be described, including what can and cannot be known about him.

CHAPTER 4

# The Lord God Almighty

We become familiar with the nature of the God of the Bible by learning his characteristics. In making a formal description of some thing or being, these characteristics are called attributes. For example, to describe a dog, one might say that it is a mammal and that it has four feet. Both of these are attributes of the common dog, so they help someone to reliably identify a dog vis-à-vis an earthworm, for example. If we wanted to differentiate between a dog and a cat, however, many more attributes of "dogliness" would be necessary. Yet the two attributes just mentioned are of different types. To be a dog, an animal must be a mammal. It is an "essential attribute." An animal could, however, have only three feet and still be a dog, because it might have lost a foot as the result of a misadventure. Such an attribute is a "nonessential attribute." Nonessential attributes are sometimes called accidents by technical writers because they are the results of events rather than integral parts of the entity being described.

As will become evident, the God of the Bible has no nonessential attributes. Every attribute the Bible uses to describe him is essential to his being. When John wrote, "Anyone who does not love does not know God, because God is love" (1 John 4:8), he was saying that the essence of God is love. It cannot be separated from God as wool can be shaved off a sheep and it is still a sheep. Moreover, the attributes that are ascribed to God cannot be separated from one another, but they blend together. God has no internal boundary within himself among his love, his justice, and his omnipotence. These attributes as they are expressed in human terms are but clouded views into the nature of the incomprehensible essence of God. The Bible uses such attributes as separate entities so the human mind can gain some appreciation of the nature of God's being. We will follow the same convention in this chapter.

The first of God's attributes to examine is his name. For a person, his or her name is not an essential attribute. People can change their names or go by aliases without changing their natures in the least degree. That is not true for the God of the Bible. Like all of his other attributes, his name *is* his essence. When Moses asked God what his name was so that he could tell the Israelites which god had sent him, God replied, "I AM WHO I AM" (Exodus 3:14).[1] God's formal Hebrew name, in fact, is derived from the Hebrew word for "to be" (Isaiah 42:8)[2] and was written in the original text by the Hebrew letters YHWH.[3] Present-day Jews regard this name as so holy that they never pronounce it when they read the Bible but substitute another word meaning "Lord," namely *Adonai*. Initially, vowels were added in English to the Hebrew letters to make it pronounceable as "Jehovah" (jeh-HOE-vah), but in recent years it has become common to add only two vowels to yield "Yahweh" (YAH-vay). Following the Greek practice, "LORD" has been used in most English Bible translations for God's name. "Lord" is not really a good translation, however. An accurate translation of his name would be "he who is" (always in the present tense). Yahweh is translated spelled "LORD" (with small capital letters) in most English Bibles to distinguish it from *Adonai*, translated as "Lord," with lowercase letters. That one of the Ten Commandments, which God himself gave from Mount Sinai, specifically prohibits the misuse of his name shows its importance.

His name means still more. His existence means that no other god can exist. Isaiah quotes the Lord concerning this: "'You are my witnesses,' declares the LORD, 'and my servant whom I have chosen, that you may know and believe me and understand that I am he. Before me no god was formed, nor shall there be any after me. I, I am the LORD, and besides me there is no savior. I declared and saved and proclaimed, when there was no strange god among you; and you are my witnesses,' declares the LORD, 'and I am God. Also henceforth I am he; there is none who can deliver from my hand; I work, and who can turn it back?'" (Isaiah 43:10-13). His uniqueness is the basis of the first commandment, which the Lord thundered from

---

[1] God said to Moses, "I AM WHO I AM." And he said, "Say this to the people of Israel, 'I AM has sent me to you.'" (Exodus 3:14)

[2] "I am the LORD; that is my name; my glory I give to no other, nor my praise to carved idols." (Isaiah 42:8)

[3] Biblical Hebrew did not originally have written vowels. The Masoretes (groups of Jewish scribes) added "vowel points" between the fifth and tenth centuries A.D.

Mount Sinai (Exodus 20:3).[4] It is the "greatest commandment of the Law" according to Jesus (Matthew 22:35-38), who references Moses' charge to the Israelites (Deuteronomy 6:4,5).[5] It is further amplified through the Lord's declaration to Isaiah (Isaiah 45:21).[6] Because the name of the Lord means his very essence, all should be careful how they use it.

To assist us in studying the rest of the Lord's attributes, we can group them into three categories: size and power, holiness, and love. The size and power attributes describe the Lord in terms of the physical universe. They present the incredibleness of a being who is off the scale of all our methods we have to measure. The holiness attributes describe the Lord independent of any human comparison as he exists within himself. To be holy is to be completely separated from any falseness of purpose. The love attributes describe the Lord in his interactions with his creatures, particularly mankind. They tell of a God who acts in the best interests of others.

## Attributes that define the size and power of the Lord

The Bible reveals the Lord God through attributes that people can use to compare him to the things of this world with which they are familiar. People think in terms of how much time it takes for a concert to be performed or how much parking space a bus occupies. They think in terms of how much power an aircraft engine produces or how long a furnace filter will last. They think in terms of the amount of knowledge it takes to play chess at the level of a grandmaster. They want to know when a rainstorm began and when it will end. These "sizing attributes" are a good place to start when considering the Lord.

Underlying all of these attributes that help to picture his immenseness is that the Lord has no physical dimensions. He is a spirit, as Jesus pointed out in John 4:24.[7] St. Paul also wrote of the Lord as a spirit in 2 Corinthians 3. The Lord told Moses that no one could see his face and live (Exodus 33:20). Physical eyes cannot see a spirit, and the Lord implied that if he revealed his glory through a means that a person could experience, that person's mental capacity would be overwhelmed and be destroyed. Yet to accomplish his purposes, the

---

[4] [The LORD said,] "You shall have no other gods [besides] me." (Exodus 20:3)

[5] [Moses said,] "Hear, O Israel: The LORD our God, the LORD is one. You shall love the LORD your God with all your heart and with all your soul and with all your might." (Deuteronomy 6:4,5)

[6] "Declare and present your case; let them take counsel together! Who told this long ago? Who declared it of old? Was it not I, the LORD? And there is no other god besides me, a righteous God and a Savior; there is none besides me." (Isaiah 45:21)

[7] [Jesus said,] "God is spirit, and those who worship him must worship in spirit and truth." (John 4:24)

Lord did sometimes limit (i.e., attenuate) his glory so that people could get a sense of its magnitude (Exodus 24:10,11), but this was a rare occurrence. In addition, sometimes the Lord took on human form to appear to chosen people (e.g., Genesis 18; Joshua 5:13-15; Judges 6). To help people understand how the Lord was caring for them, he sometimes personified his attributes by talking about his eyes (2 Samuel 15:25), his ears (1 Samuel 8:21), and his arms (Deuteronomy 26:8), for example, or by saying he was building (Psalm 127:1) or sitting (Psalm 2:4). A spirit certainly has none of these physical characteristics and does none of these actions. They are picture language in the same way in which people might say that a woman has a "heart of gold" to indicate she is generous or that a family is "putting down roots" in a new community to indicate that they are becoming settled in a new place.

If the Lord is a spirit, where can he be found? The inspired psalmist posed this question in another way and realized the answer is that the Lord is everywhere. He wrote, "Where shall I go from your Spirit? Or where shall I flee from your presence? If I ascend to heaven, you are there! If I make my bed in Sheol [an abyss,] you are there! If I take the wings of the morning and dwell in the uttermost parts of the sea, even there your hand shall lead me, and your right hand shall hold me" (Psalm 139:7-10). The Lord made similar statements to Jeremiah (Jeremiah 23:23,24)[8] and to Amos (Amos 9:1-6). This attribute of the Lord is called omnipresence (i.e., being present everywhere). Yet the Lord is not spread thinly across the universe; his essence is completely present everywhere. The psalmist noted that the Lord can hear prayer everywhere (Psalm 145:18),[9] and King Solomon wrote that the Lord has the ability to see everywhere (Proverbs 15:3).[10] He is not a God who is far off in any sense.

That something could be completely present everywhere has always been beyond human comprehension. Within the last century, however, two technical concepts have been developed that can perhaps give a better understanding to this biblical revelation. When one works with a database, one can link the attributes in two tables together so that each record in one table links to all the records in the other. This one-to-many (or one-to-infinity) relationship is used frequently. The power of one record is indeed

---

[8]"Am I a God at hand, declares the LORD, and not a God far away? Can a man hide himself in secret places so that I cannot see him? declares the LORD. Do I not fill heaven and earth? declares the LORD." (Jeremiah 23:23,24)

[9][David said,] "The LORD is near to all who call on him, to all who call on him in truth." (Psalm 145:18)

[10][Solomon said,] "The eyes of the LORD are everywhere, keeping watch on the evil and the good." (Proverbs 15:3)

effectively present in many places at once. The mathematical term for creating such a relationship is "mapping"; one point is mapped to many. Another useful concept is that of parallel universes, which is often mentioned in science fiction books and movies. Such universes appear to occupy the same position in time and space, but no relationship exists between their time-space coordinates. There is, in effect, no mapping between the points within them. Dr. Siegbert Becker, a 20th-century Lutheran theologian, suggested that if the Lord is pictured as being in a universe called eternity, then one might consider that he has mapped his location in that universe to every point in the physical universe. That would make him completely present everywhere. Neither of these explanations is given in the Bible, so they are not a matter of doctrine. Some people might find them helpful to better understand an otherwise unfathomable attribute of the Lord. What is clear from numerous biblical references is that one can never be in a place where the Lord is not present.

Our sense of time is an artifact of the earth's rotation and orbit around the sun, by which we establish hours, days, and years. Yet the nature of time is that it is a continuum in which events occur. The Bible also tells us that the Lord is not a creature of time, as everything else is that exists in the universe (Psalm 102:25-27).[11] What happened yesterday is out of every person's reach. Nor can one do anything tomorrow until tomorrow becomes the present. Time carries humankind as a stream carries a leaf. The leaf has no way to return and no control over its forward motion. All the events of history can therefore be considered to be laid out on a time line. The Lord sees this time line of the universe end-on, that is, as a single point. All history is effectively simultaneous to the Lord. Using the previous example of a parallel universe, the Lord has mapped himself not only to every spatial point in the present universe but to every time-space coordinate that has ever existed. He is not only everywhere but also "everywhen." He exists in an "eternal now" (i.e., *eternally present*) relative to the human view of time. As a consequence, the Lord cannot change (i.e., he is *changeless* or *immutable*) because he has no time component (Malachi 3:6).[12] To him a day is as long as a year or as a millennium (2 Peter 3:8);[13] they are all dimensionless to him. When he is making a promise at one

---

[11]Of old you laid the foundation of the earth, and the heavens are the work of your hands. They will perish, but you will remain; they will all wear out like a garment. You will change them like a robe, and they will pass away, but you are the same, and your years have no end. (Psalm 102:25-27)

[12]"I the LORD do not change." (Malachi 3:6)

[13]Do not overlook this one fact, beloved, that with the Lord one day is as a thousand years, and a thousand years as one day. (2 Peter 3:8, paraphrase of Psalm 90:4—the song of Moses)

point in human history, he is fulfilling it at some later point (Numbers 23:19).[14] It is the same action to him because, from his viewpoint, he is simultaneously at both places and times and must be consistent with himself (2 Timothy 2:13).[15] He is not "slow" to fulfill his promises as people reckon slowness (2 Peter 3:9), but he has placed their fulfilments at the times in human history to make his plan to save humankind work as he intends (Galatians 4:4,5).[16] This attribute will be mentioned again when his plan of salvation is discussed.

If an observant individual is present at some place at a particular time, one would expect that person to know what is happening at that location. The same is true of the Lord. Because the Lord is present at every place at every time, he must know everything (Hebrews 4:13).[17] The Bible therefore teaches that the Lord is *omniscient* (i.e., all-knowing). In Psalm 139, David wrote about how completely the Lord knows everything about him. The Lord spoke to Job (Job 38–41) and claimed a thorough knowledge of the forces of nature. Jesus pointed out to his disciples that not a sparrow dies without the Lord knowing about it and that the very hairs on people's heads are numbered by the Lord (Matthew 10:29,30). Furthermore, the Lord is not limited by what human eyes can see (1 Samuel 16:7),[18] but he also looks at the thoughts and attitudes of a person. John noted that Jesus also did the same thing (John 2:24,25).

The implications of the Lord's total knowledge of the universe are overwhelming. It is so beyond human comprehension that the mind staggers at trying to imagine how it could be. Because the Lord is everywhere at all times, it is impossible for him to be caught by surprise. He knows where every particle of the universe has been during every moment of its existence and where those particles have been going at every instance of time. It is impossible for anyone or anything to hide from him. There is nothing for him to learn, for he already knows it all. Moreover, because he knows the attitudes of each human heart, he knows exactly what people will do

---

[14]"God is not man, that he should lie, or a son of man, that he should change his mind. Has he said, and will he not do it? Or has he spoken, and will he not fulfill it?" (Numbers 23:19—The Lord put these words into the mouth of the rebellious prophet Balaam.)

[15]If we are faithless, he remains faithful—for he cannot deny himself. (2 Timothy 2:13)

[16]But when the fullness of time had come, God sent forth his Son, born of a woman, born under the law, to redeem those who were under the law, so that we might receive adoption as sons. (Galatians 4:4,5)

[17]No creature is hidden from his sight, but all are naked and exposed to the eyes of him to whom we must give account. (Hebrews 4:13)

[18][The LORD said,] "For the LORD sees not as man sees: man looks on the outward appearance, but the LORD looks on the heart." (1 Samuel 16:7)

if given a chance to do it, even if they never get that chance. The Lord's words to Isaiah summed up the situation when he said, "My thoughts are not your thoughts, neither are your ways my ways, declares the LORD. For as the heavens are higher than the earth, so are my ways higher than your ways and my thoughts than your thoughts" (Isaiah 55:8,9). His knowledge will be reviewed again when his relationship to the physical universe is examined.

The omniscience of the Lord bothers many people. They would like to believe that they can bring the Lord around to their way of thinking by educating him. They would like to fool him by cutting deals with him that they never expect to keep. That his knowledge of the future is exact because he is already there leaves them helpless to finesse the Lord. They therefore refuse to accept what the Bible says about him, and they recreate him as a god who has much less ability to thwart their plans. That they will accomplish this is less likely than making the weather warm and sunny by sitting outside on a chaise lounge in a bathing suit in a blizzard at -10° F. Threatening the Lord with unbelief if he fails to accept our way of thinking is indeed folly.

Finally, one must consider the power of the Lord, that is, his ability to control the physical universe. The Bible contains numerous examples of the extent of the Lord's control of nature. Together they show a God whose power is absolutely limitless (Isaiah 43:13).[19] He can do anything he pleases (Psalm 115:3;[20] Psalm 135:5,6[21]). But he is not just more powerful than any other being or thing; everything else is totally powerless unless he delegates power to them (Psalm 127:1,2;[22] Nahum 1:6[23]). They are like electrical appliances that are wholly dependent on the power being turned on to operate. That which is inanimate does nothing without his command (Matthew 5:45),[24] and that which is animate does nothing without his permission

[19][The LORD said,] "Also henceforth I am he; there is none who can deliver from my hand; I work, and who can turn it back?" (Isaiah 43:13)

[20]Our God is in the heavens; he does all that he pleases. (Psalm 115:3)

[21]I know that the LORD is great, and that our Lord is above all gods. Whatever the Lord pleases, he does, in heaven and on earth, in the seas and all deeps. (Psalm 135:5,6)

[22][Solomon said,] "Unless the LORD builds the house, those who build it labor in vain. Unless the Lord watches over the city, the watchman stays awake in vain. It is in vain that you rise up early and go late to rest, eating the bread of anxious toil; for he gives to his beloved sleep." (Psalm 127:1,2)

[23]Who can stand before his indignation? Who can endure the heat of his anger? His wrath is poured out like fire, and the rocks are broken into pieces by him. (Nahum 1:6)

[24][Jesus said,] "He makes his sun rise on the evil and on the good, and sends rain on the just and on the unjust." (Matthew 5:45)

(Isaiah 14:27;[25] Psalm 104:27-29[26]). He is truly *omnipotent*, that is, all-powerful, with his power being limited only by his own will.

The Lord's control over the universe is usually carried out through his decreeing a set of interactions among pieces of matter and their energy, which scientists call natural laws. Seedtime and harvest continue year after year (Genesis 8:22),[27] the earth turns, and stars give off radiation. The Lord is a being of order (Jeremiah 33:20,25), and this order makes life possible. If everything were to behave randomly, no structure in any sense of the word *structure* could survive. Yet the Lord is not so bound to such perfect order that he cannot use the natural laws for his own purpose. For example, there can be floods (Joshua 3:15),[28] earthquakes (Luke 21:11),[29] bad harvests (Deuteronomy 28:38-40),[30] disease (Deuteronomy 28:22),[31] and numerous other events that affect people and the things in the universe. But how does the Lord do this? If one rolled a perfect cubic die infinitely often, each side would appear on top the same number of times, because each side has an equal probability of being in that position. If one rolled it only a few times, however, one could not be sure that each side would come to the top with equal frequency. Moreover, there is no scientific way to determine which side will appear on top on the next roll of the die, even if one knows the results of all the previous rolls. Because of this, if the Lord makes the die to have four dots on the top side on a particular roll, there is no way to determine that this was just a random event rather than a specific action of the Lord. By acting within the laws of probability, he can create changes of events that carry out his purpose without arousing the slightest suspicion.

---

[25]For the LORD of hosts has purposed, and who will annul it? His hand is stretched out, and who will turn it back? (Isaiah 14:27)

[26]These all look to you, to give them their food in due season. When you give it to them, they gather it up; when you open your hand, they are filled with good things. When you hide your face, they are dismayed; when you take away their breath, they die and return to their dust. (Psalm 104:27-29)

[27][The LORD said,] "While the earth remains, seedtime and harvest, cold and heat, summer and winter, day and night, shall not cease." (Genesis 8:22)

[28]Now the Jordan overflows all its banks throughout the time of harvest. (Joshua 3:15)

[29][Jesus said,] "There will be great earthquakes, and in various places famines and pestilences. And there will be terrors and great signs from heaven." (Luke 2:11)

[30][Moses said,] "You shall carry much seed into the field and shall gather in little, for the locust shall consume it. You shall plant vineyards and dress them, but you shall neither drink of the wine nor gather the grapes, for the worm shall eat them. You shall have olive trees throughout all your territory, but you shall not anoint yourself with the oil, for your olives shall drop off." (Deuteronomy 28:38-40)

[31][Moses said,] "The LORD will strike you with wasting disease and with fever, inflammation and fiery heat, and with drought and with blight and with mildew. They shall pursue you until you perish." (Deuteronomy 28:22)

We might call this "flying-below-the-radar" mode of action the Lord's "natural hand." He uses his almighty power and his complete knowledge of the universe to work through means of what appears to the observer as completely natural events. But the Lord can also work in total disregard of the laws by which he runs the universe. When he does, the observed events are called miracles, or actions by the Lord's "nonnatural hand." For example, he confused the languages at the tower at Babel (Genesis 11:1-9). To bring the Israelites out of Egypt, he carried out plagues on the Egyptians (Exodus 7:19–12:32) and parted the Red Sea—called the Sea of Reeds in Hebrew (Exodus 14:21-28). He parted the Jordan at flood stage (Joshua 3), made the earth to appear to stop rotating (Joshua 10:12-15), made an iron axe head float (2 Kings 6:5-7), struck an entire army with blindness (2 Kings 6:18), and slaughtered the Assyrian army as it besieged Jerusalem (2 Kings 19:35). The Lord used miracles at critical times for his people in the Old Testament, and he continued to use them in the New Testament. These miracles included the virgin birth (Luke 1:26-38), curing diseases and handicaps (dozens of examples in the four gospels), calming the lake (Matthew 8:23-27; Matthew 14:25-32), feeding large crowds (Matthew 14:19-21; Matthew 15:35-38), and raising the dead (Luke 7:11-15; Mark 5:35-43; John 11:1-44). The number of miracles was so large that it was clear even to Jesus' opponents that he was not a normal man limited by the processes of nature (John 3:1,2; John 11:47,48) (see Table 9-1 on p. 128).

The Lord's almighty power is not limited to physical events. Knowing everything people will do if given an opportunity, he can arrange events so that people will follow their own purposes and accomplish his in the process. For example, the Lord drew the king of Assyria from Judah with a rumor (Isaiah 37:7).[32] He saved Jacob's family by arranging for one of his sons to be sold into slavery (Genesis 50:20).[33] He even led a high priest to prophesy against his own scheme (John 11:50).[34]

## Attributes that define the Lord's holiness

To understand the Lord's "holiness," we must have the proper definition of *holy*. When applied to the Lord, holiness is perhaps best stated as "being

---

[32] [The LORD said,] "Behold, I will put a spirit in him, so that he shall hear a rumor and return to his own land, and I will make him fall by the sword in his own land." (Isaiah 37:7)

[33] [Joseph said,] As for you [his brothers], you meant evil against me, but God meant it for good, to bring it about that many people should be kept alive, as they are today." (Genesis 50:20)

[34] [Caiaphas the high priest said,] "Nor do you understand that it is better for you that one man should die for the people, not that the whole nation should perish." (John 11:50)

set aside and dedicated to a purpose." The Lord's attributes define his being, and there is nothing within them that is false to that being. He is complete within himself, and he is separate and distinct from everything else that does or can exist. His being cannot be contaminated or turned aside from its intent and purpose.

The Lord is what he wills to be. His *will* drives what he does. Being omnipotent, when he acts directly, his will always prevails. If he wills to dispose of the unrepentant, it happens (1 Samuel 2:25).[35] When he wills to save humankind, the steps in the preordained plan are carried out (Isaiah 53:10).[36] Lutherans accept the will of the Lord even when it does not agree with their will, and in the Lord's Prayer they even pray for it to be carried out: "Your will be done, on earth as it is in heaven" (Matthew 6:10). They know that the Lord's will must happen, so they are eager to learn about it from the Bible and desire to follow it (Ephesians 5:15-17).[37] More will be said about the Lord's will and the Christian's response in subsequent chapters.

The will of the Lord is consistent with his plan for the universe. Therefore, it is *perfect,* because only by following his plan can his will be accomplished. The perfection of the Lord's will is mentioned by Paul in his letter to the Romans (12:2).[38] It is declared in the psalms (18:30)[39] and by Moses (Deuteronomy 32:3,4).[40] Jesus urges his followers to seek to conform to the perfection of their God (Matthew 5:48).[41]

Some of the Lord's other attributes follow naturally from those already discussed. Because the Lord is both willful and unchanging, he is *faithful* (2 Timothy 2:13).[42] He cannot deviate from his will, so he can be trusted

---

[35] They would not listen to the voice of their father, for it was the will of the LORD to put them to death. (1 Samuel 2:25)

[36] Yet it was the will of the LORD to crush him; he has put him to grief; when his soul makes an offering for guilt, he shall see his offspring; he shall prolong his days; the will of the LORD shall prosper in his hand. (Isaiah 53:10)

[37] Look carefully then how you walk, not as unwise but as wise, making the best use of the time, because the days are evil. Therefore do not be foolish, but understand what the will of the Lord is. (Ephesians 5:15-17)

[38] Do not be conformed to this world, but be transformed by the renewal of your mind, that by testing you may discern what is the will of God, what is good and acceptable and perfect. (Romans 12:2)

[39] [David said,] "This God—his way is perfect; the word of the LORD proves true; he is a shield for all those who take refuge in him." (Psalm 18:30)

[40] [Moses said,] "I will proclaim the name of the Lord; ascribe greatness to our God! The Rock, his work is perfect, for all his ways are justice. A God of faithfulness and without iniquity, just and upright is he." (Deuteronomy 32:3,4)

[41] [Jesus said,] "You therefore must be perfect, as your heavenly Father is perfect." (Matthew 5:48)

[42] If we are faithless, he remains faithful—for he cannot deny himself. (2 Timothy 2:13)

to do what he has committed himself to do (Deuteronomy 7:9).[43] Being perfect and faithful, the Lord can also be said to be "true" (Romans 3:3,4). True means that he is honorable in his actions, not needing to be deceitful to accomplish his purposes.

Being both willful and faithful, the Lord is determined that his actions be carried out and that he be credited for them (Isaiah 42:8).[44] People are to credit neither themselves nor luck nor randomness nor some other supernatural being for what happens, lest they deceive themselves as to who controls the universe. The Lord himself describes this as being "jealous" (Exodus 20:5,6).[45] He is intolerant of disloyalty and infidelity because such things contradict his very essence (Deuteronomy 4:24).[46] They are incompatible with his existence. Because he has all the power, his jealousy is not based on the fear that others will take what is his. It is rather that he knows doing other than his will is folly (Isaiah 32:6).[47] He judges everything by his will, without partiality, and therefore he is "just" (Revelation 15:3).[48] Because he needs nothing, he cannot be bribed or influenced by his creatures (Ezekiel 33:12-20). If he could, he would no longer be perfect. Man needs to fear the Lord's justice if he acts against the Lord's will (2 Chronicles 36:16).[49]

If the Lord seems to be self-centered, he might very well appear to be from a human viewpoint. After all, everything comes from him and depends on him. The world was created because he desired it, and he made it for the glory of his name. As frail humans we cannot fully grasp the actions of the Lord, but the Bible assures us that the Lord is wise (Isaiah 46:9,10).[50] His

---

[43]Know therefore that the LORD your God is God, the faithful God who keeps covenant and steadfast love with those who love him and keep his commandments, to a thousand generations. (Deuteronomy 7:9)

[44]"I am the LORD; that is my name; my glory I give to no other, nor my praise to carved idols." (Isaiah 42:8)

[45]"You shall not bow down to them or serve them, for I the LORD your God am a jealous God, visiting the iniquity of the fathers on the children to the third and the fourth generation of those who hate me, but showing steadfast love to thousands of those who love me and keep my commandments." (Exodus 20:5,6)

[46]The LORD your God is a consuming fire, a jealous God. (Deuteronomy 4:24)

[47]The fool speaks folly, and his heart is busy with iniquity, to practice ungodliness, to utter error concerning the Lord. (Isaiah 32:6)

[48][Angels in heaven:] "Great and amazing are your deeds, O Lord God the Almighty! Just and true are your ways, O King of the nations!" (Revelation 15:3)

[49]They kept mocking the messengers of God, despising his words and scoffing at his prophets, until the wrath of the LORD rose against his people, until there was no remedy. (2 Chronicles 36:16)

[50]"For I am God, and there is no other; I am God, and there is none like me, declaring the end from the beginning and from ancient times things not yet done, saying, 'My counsel shall stand, and I will accomplish all my purpose.'" (Isaiah 46:9,10)

*wisdom* is just as great and incomprehensible as the rest of his attributes (Psalm 104:24).[51] His wisdom extends beyond his will and omniscience to his interaction with all that he created, and therefore his wisdom bridges his holiness attributes and his loving attributes. While he always acts in the best interests of his glory, he also acts in the best interests of his servants. In his wisdom he acts in ways beyond human understanding to give people more than they could ever deserve or arrange to get for themselves (Isaiah 55:8,9).

## Attributes that define the Lord's love

To say that "God is *love*" is to quote the Bible (1 John 4:8). But what is love? There is romantic love, puppy love, sexual love, tough love, parental love, platonic love, and love of blueberry ripple ice cream. To describe the love that is the essence of the Lord, the Bible uses the Greek word *agape*. As used in the Scriptures, this love is a selfless love that has only the welfare of the recipient of the love as its purpose (John 3:16;[52] Romans 5:8[53]). The rest of the Lord's love attributes can be thought of as being attached to this root.

*Mercy* is the attribute of the Lord that shows his willingness to reach out to those who have no reason to expect anything from him because they have violated his will and rebelled against his rule (Psalm 145:9).[54] It is because he is merciful that the Lord devised a plan of salvation for vile sinners whom, according to his justice, he should have immediately annihilated or consigned to eternal punishment (Luke 1:54).[55] When sinners seek forgiveness, they flee to the Lord as a God who is merciful (Ephesians 2:4,5).[56]

The *grace* of God is the favorable attitude of the Lord toward humankind. The Lord does not merely look in pity at the miserable state humankind is in and extend his mercy, but he looks at humankind as it could be if freed

---

[51] O LORD, how manifold are your works! In wisdom have you made them all; the earth is full of your creatures. (Psalm 104:24)

[52] [Jesus said,] "God so loved the world, that he gave his only Son, that whoever believes in him should not perish but have eternal life." (John 3:16)

[53] God shows his love for us in that while we were still sinners, Christ died for us. (Romans 5:8)

[54] [David said,] "The Lord is good to all, and his mercy is over all that he has made." (Psalm 145:9)

[55] [Jesus' mother Mary said,] "He has helped his servant Israel, in remembrance of his mercy." (Luke 1:54)

[56] God, being rich in mercy, because of the great love with which he loved us, even when we were dead in our trespasses, made us alive together with Christ—by grace you have been saved. (Ephesians 2:4,5)

from sin. Although people do not deserve more chances than they have already had, the Lord has gone beyond all human reason to create a way to allow people to again become his loving children rather than his vile enemies (Romans 3:23,24).[57] It is only through God's grace that anyone can reach heaven (Ephesians 2:8,9).[58] Moreover, the Lord does not treat humans like the rest of his creation, but from the very beginning he linked humankind to what he saw in himself (Genesis 1:26).[59] Humankind received God's "image," an imprint of his will. Humankind's link to the Lord is God's attribute of *favor*. It is a non-understandable orientation of the Lord to humans (Psalm 8:4).[60]

Because of the light of God's favor, humankind sees the result of the *goodness* of the Lord. The Lord would have been good even if he had immediately punished humankind for its evil, but people would never have known it. Wrapped up in themselves, all people would have regarded the Lord as cruel and hateful. Certainly, that is how the people condemned to hell will view him. Nevertheless, he has continued to give humankind countless blessings through his goodness (Psalm 68:10).[61] Only those who come to faith in Christ can truly appreciate this attribute of the Lord (Psalm 31:19).[62]

Finally, there is the Lord's *patience*. In a world driven by the tyranny of the immediate, the Lord takes his time. He seldom strikes down his enemies immediately, but he gives them time to repent (Exodus 34:6,7).[63] He does not fulfill his promises immediately, but he tests those to whom he gives these promises to see if they really will believe him and will wait patiently (2 Peter 3:9).[64] Because he is omniscient and not a creature of time, he knows

---

[57] All have sinned and fall short of the glory of God, and are justified by his grace as a gift, through the redemption that is in Christ Jesus. (Romans 3:23,24)

[58] By grace you have been saved through faith. And this is not your own doing; it is the gift of God, not a result of works, so that no one may boast. (Ephesians 2:8,9)

[59] Then God said, "Let us make man in our image, after our likeness. And let them have dominion over the fish of the sea and over the birds of the heavens and over the livestock and over all the earth and over every creeping thing that creeps on the earth." (Genesis 1:26)

[60] [David said,] "What is man that you are mindful of him, and the son of man that you care for him?" (Psalm 8:4)

[61] [David said,] "In your goodness, O God, you provided for the needy." (Psalm 68:10)

[62] [David said,] "Oh, how abundant is your goodness, which you have stored up for those who fear you." (Psalm 31:19)

[63] The LORD passed before him and proclaimed, "The LORD, the LORD, a God merciful and gracious, slow to anger, and abounding in steadfast love and faithfulness, keeping steadfast love for thousands, forgiving iniquity and transgression and sin." (Exodus 34:6,7)

[64] The Lord is not slow to fulfill his promise as some count slowness, but is patient toward you, not wishing that any should perish, but that all should reach repentance. (2 Peter 3:9)

precisely when he must act to accomplish his plan, even when his followers wait and wonder—and sometimes wander (Galatians 4:4,5).[65]

The attributes of the Lord are truly amazing. Looking at them one at a time, like looking through the windows of a cathedral from the outside, one can gain an appreciation of the greatness of what is present, but one cannot grasp its full magnitude. As one studies the Bible and sees the Lord in action, one comes more and more to stand in awe of this God, who has chosen to reveal himself to humankind as their Creator, Preserver, and Savior. For those who believe in such a God, there is never a reason to fear the future since the Lord has all things under his control.

---

[65]When the fullness of time had come, God sent forth his Son, born of woman, born under the law, to redeem those who were under the law, so that we might receive adoption as sons. (Galatians 4:4,5)

CHAPTER 5

# The Trinity

As discussed in the previous chapter, the Lord, the God of the Bible, over-whelms our imagination. In addition to his name "LORD," he also refers to himself as the "LORD of Hosts" (armies) (1 Samuel 15:2),[1] "*El Shaddai*" (usu-ally translated as "God Almighty") (Genesis 17:1),[2] the "Holy One of Israel" (Isaiah 12:6),[3] and the "King of kings and Lord of lords" (Revelation 19:16).[4] Even some of the heathen during Old Testament times referred to him as the "God of heaven" (Ezra 6:10).[5] Yet the most perplexing of the titles that are applied to the Lord in the Bible is "gods." It appears already as the third word of the Hebrew Bible (*Elohim*) and is the subject of the Bible's first sentence. The word is always translated as "God" when it refers to the Lord because the verb is singular, but the plurality of the noun certainly cannot be without meaning in a book the Lord himself has given us. In Genesis 1:26, "God" uses the pronoun "us" in reference to himself. In fact, throughout the Old Testa-ment there is a trail of divine references that imply that the Lord is a more

---

[1] Thus says the LORD of Hosts, "I have noted what Amalek did to Israel in opposing them on the way when they came up out of Egypt." (1 Samuel 15:2)

[2] When Abram was ninety-nine years old, the LORD appeared to Abram and said to him, "I am God Almighty; walk before me, and be blameless." (Genesis 17:1)

[3] "Shout, and sing for joy, O inhabitant of Zion, for great in your midst is the Holy One of Israel." (Isaiah 12:6)

[4] On his robe and on his thigh he has a name written, King of kings and Lord of lords. (Revelation 19:16)

[5] [Darius the king wrote,] "That they may offer pleasing sacrifices to the God of heaven and pray for the life of the king and his sons." (Ezra 6:10)

complex being than those with whom we are used to dealing (e.g., Genesis 3:22;[6] Isaiah 48:16;[7] Jeremiah 23:5,6[8]).

When we study the whole biblical text, the complex structure of the Lord becomes apparent, and like everything about the Lord, it exceeds the ability of our human mind to grasp. The Lord is clearly pictured as a single God. "Hear, O Israel: The LORD our God, the LORD is one" (Deuteronomy 6:4) is the beginning of the *Shema*,[9] the prayer many Jews say every morning. Again and again the Lord emphasizes that he is the only God (Deuteronomy 32:39). Yet he also reveals a threefold nature about himself in such verses as the Aaronic Blessing, which he commanded to be placed upon his people: "The LORD bless you and keep you; the LORD make his face to shine upon you and be gracious to you; the LORD lift up his countenance upon you and give you peace" (Numbers 6:24-26). He alludes to his complex nature in the writings of the prophets (e.g., Isaiah 42:1)[10] and in the Psalms (e.g., Psalm 2:7).[11]

What, then, is the internal structure of God? How are we to visualize him? In fact, there is no word in the Bible that describes his internal nature. The Latin scholar Tertullian coined the Latin word *Trinitas*, that is, "Trinity," to describe this God who is three-in-one. To know what the word stands for, and the profession of faith based on it, we must look at the various pictures that the Scriptures give us of the Lord. We must, however, be aware that the Bible gives only those limited views into the divine nature that the Lord thinks we need to see. We should not try to go further and attempt to reconcile or enhance these views to obtain some kind of complete picture recognizable by the human mind.

### Nature of God

The Bible regularly proclaims that there is only one God (Psalm 83:18; Isaiah 43:10; 1 Corinthians 8:4). Theologians have used the word *essence* to

---

[6] Then the LORD God said, "Behold, the man has become like one of us in knowing good and evil." (Genesis 3:22)

[7] Now the LORD God has sent me, and his Spirit. (Isaiah 48:16)

[8] "Behold, the days are coming, declares the LORD, when I will raise up for David a righteous Branch, and he shall reign as king and deal wisely, and shall execute justice and righteousness in the land. In his days Judah will be saved, and Israel will dwell securely. And this is the name by which he will be called: 'The LORD is our righteousness.'" (Jeremiah 23:5,6)

[9] *Shema* is the first word in the Hebrew of this sentence.

[10] [The LORD said,] "Behold my servant, whom I uphold, my chosen, in whom my soul delights; I have put my Spirit upon him; he will bring forth justice to the nations." (Isaiah 42:1)

[11] I will tell of the decree: The LORD said to me, "You are my Son; today I have begotten you." (Psalm 2:7)

describe the basic existence of a being. Every person is a separate essence, and God is but one essence. God is not a committee, and there are no disagreements within God. He is perfect in his being (Deuteronomy 32:3,4), and what is perfect cannot be in conflict with itself.

The Bible also frequently mentions what theologians label "persons" of the Lord: God the Father (John 3:35; 1 Peter 1:3[12]), God the Son (Matthew 17:5; John 1:18[13]), and God the Holy Spirit (John 15:26; Acts 5:3,4[14]). It never mentions any others. We further learn from studying the Scriptures that these persons are not separate parts of God. They are also not different aspects of the one God, as if he were different when looked at from different vantage points. Neither are they masks, as Greek actors would use so the same person could appear in different roles. Each person is completely God, and each person is equal to the others. Having made these summary statements, it is necessary to validate them from the only reliable source of information about God: his Word, i.e., the Bible.

The oneness of the Lord was seen from his claims about himself in chapter 4. He claims to be one being (Deuteronomy 6:4). He also claims to be the only God (Isaiah 44:6-8).[15] While the Bible acknowledges the existence of created spiritual forces hostile to the Lord, it always places them in inferior roles and asserts the Lord's control over them (Job 1:6-12; Romans 16:20[16]). Hostile spiritual beings will be placed into eternal punishment when the time comes (Matthew 25:41)[17] (see chapter 19).

Although the multiplicity of the Godhead is alluded to in the Old Testament, its nature is clearly established in the New Testament. The three persons of the Trinity are named in Matthew 28:19 in connection with the command to baptize. All appeared together at the time of the baptism

---

[12]Blessed be the God and Father of our Lord Jesus Christ! (1 Peter 1:3)

[13]No one has ever seen God; the only Son, who is at the Father's side, he has made him known. (John 1:18)

[14]But Peter said, "Ananias, why has Satan filled your heart to lie to the Holy Spirit and to keep back for yourself part of the proceeds of the land? While it remained unsold, did it not remain your own? And after it was sold, was it not at your disposal? Why is it that you have contrived this deed in your heart? You have not lied to a man but to God." (Acts 5:3,4)

[15]Thus says the LORD, the King of Israel and his Redeemer, the LORD of hosts: "I am the first and I am the last; besides me there is no god. Who is like me? Let him proclaim it. Let him declare and set it before me, since I appointed an ancient people. Let them declare what is to come, and what will happen. Fear not, nor be afraid; have I not told you from of old and declared it? And you are my witnesses! Is there a god besides me? There is no Rock; I know not any." (Isaiah 44:6-8)

[16]The God of peace will soon crush Satan under your feet. (Romans 16:20)

[17][Jesus said,] "Then he will say to those on his left, 'Depart from me, you cursed, into the eternal fire prepared for the devil and his angels.'" (Matthew 25:41)

of Jesus (Matthew 3:16,17)[18] and are mentioned in the apostolic blessing (2 Corinthians 13:14).[19] Multiple persons of the Godhead are often mentioned, in various orders, in the same Bible passage (e.g., John 17:1;[20] John 15:26;[21] Galatians 4:6[22]). They are all given divine attributes, and the deeds of each of them are referred to as the actions of God (e.g., John 8:41,42;[23] Titus 3:4-6;[24] 2 Peter 1:20,21).

When the persons of the Trinity interact with the physical universe, they always act together. For example, the Bible refers to God the Father as the creator of the universe (Exodus 20:11),[25] but it also mentions the Son (John 1:3)[26] and the Holy Spirit (Genesis 1:2)[27] being present. Jesus' resurrection from the dead is credited to the Son (1 Thessalonians 4:14),[28] the Father (Galatians 1:1),[29] and the Holy Spirit (Romans 1:4).[30] Bringing people to faith involves

---

[18]When Jesus was baptized, immediately he went up from the water, and behold, the heavens were opened to him, and he [John the Baptizer] saw the Spirit of God descending like a dove and coming to rest on him; and behold, a voice from heaven said, "This is my beloved Son, with whom I am well pleased." (Matthew 3:16,17)

[19]The grace of the Lord Jesus Christ and the love of God and the fellowship of the Holy Spirit be with you all. (2 Corinthians 13:14)

[20]When Jesus had spoken these words, he lifted up his eyes to heaven, and said, "Father, the hour has come; glorify your Son that the Son may glorify you." (John 17:1)

[21][Jesus said,] "When the [Counselor] comes, whom I will send to you from the Father, the Spirit of truth, who proceeds from the Father, he will bear witness about me." (John 15:26)

[22]God has sent the Spirit of his Son into our hearts, crying, "Abba! Father!" (Galatians 4:6)

[23][Jesus said,] "You are doing the works your father did." They [the Jews] said to him, "We were not born of sexual immorality. We have one Father—even God." Jesus said to them, "If God were your Father, you would love me, for I came from God and I am here. I came not of my own accord, but he sent me." (John 8:41,42)

[24]When the goodness and loving kindness of God our Savior appeared, he saved us, not because of works done by us in righteousness, but according to his own mercy, by the washing of regeneration and renewal of the Holy Spirit, whom he poured out on us richly through Jesus Christ our Savior. (Titus 3:4-6)

[25][The LORD said,] "In six days the LORD made heaven and earth, the sea, and all that is in them, and rested on the seventh day. Therefore the LORD blessed the Sabbath day and made it holy." (Exodus 20:11)

[26]All things were made through him, and without him was not anything made that was made. (John 1:3)

[27]The earth was without form and void, and darkness was over the face of the deep. And the Spirit of God was hovering over the face of the waters. (Genesis 1:2)

[28]Since we believe that Jesus died and rose again, even so, through Jesus, God will bring with him those who have fallen asleep. (1 Thessalonians 4:14)

[29]Paul, an apostle—not from men nor through man, but through Jesus Christ and God the Father, who raised him from the dead. (Galatians 1:1)

[30][He] was declared to be the Son of God in power according to the Spirit of Holiness by his resurrection from the dead, Jesus Christ our Lord. (Romans 1:4)

the Father (John 6:44),[31] the Son (Matthew 28:18-20),[32] and the Holy Spirit (1 Peter 1:12).[33] We know of the relationships and interactions among the persons of the Trinity within the Godhead to the very limited extent that they are mentioned within the Scriptures. We can only acknowledge and believe what the Bible says, without trying to embroider upon it.

## The persons of the Trinity

Although all three persons of the Trinity are involved in all interactions outside the Godhead, God the Father is often referred to as the creator (Exodus 20:11), preserver (Joshua 24:17),[34] and lawgiver (2 Kings 10:31).[35] He acted as a father to his people Israel during the Old Testament times (Malachi 2:10). The Jews at Jesus' time continued to regard him as their father (John 8:41). Jesus called him my Father (John 17:1), and the New Testament writers also referred to him as God the Father (Romans 15:6).

God the Son is already referred to as being the equal of God the Father in the Old Testament (Psalm 110:1),[36] and this verse is also quoted several times in the New Testament (Matthew 22:44; Acts 2:34; Hebrews 1:13). He is called God in John 1:1,[37] where John uses the name "Word" to describe him because he is the expression of God to humankind. God the Son, eternally God like God the Father, is best known through his incarnation as Jesus Christ and is therefore often called the Redeemer of humankind (Titus 2:13,14). This will be discussed more in chapter 15. It is important to realize at this point that he existed before he became incarnate (John 1:1). But how is he related to the Father if both are eternal? The term that the Bible uses to describe the relationship is "begotten" (Psalm 2:7). Because the Son

---

[31] [Jesus said,] "No one can come to me unless the Father who sent me draws him." (John 6:44)

[32] [Jesus said,] "All authority in heaven and on earth has been given to me. Go therefore and make disciples of all nations, baptizing them in the name of the Father and of the Son and of the Holy Spirit, teaching them to observe all that I have commanded you. And behold, I am with you always, to the end of the age." (Matthew 28:18-20)

[33] It was revealed to them that they were serving not themselves but you, in the things that have now been announced to you through those who preached the good news to you by the Holy Spirit sent from heaven, things into which angels long to look. (1 Peter 1:12)

[34] [Joshua said,] "It is the LORD our God who brought us and our fathers up from the land of Egypt, out of the house of slavery, and who did those great signs in our sight and preserved us in all the way that we went, and among all the peoples through whom we passed." (Joshua 24:17)

[35] But Jehu was not careful to walk in the law of the LORD, the God of Israel, with all his heart. (2 Kings 10:31)

[36] The LORD says to my Lord: "Sit at my right hand, until I make your enemies your footstool." (Psalm 110:1)

[37] In the beginning was the Word, and the Word was with God, and the Word was God. (John 1:1)

existed from the beginning, he was involved with the creation of all things (John 1:3). There never was a time when he did not exist. Lutheran theologians therefore say that he is "eternally begotten" of the Father. How God the Father could beget a Son who is of the same essence that he is cannot be grasped by human reason. We are not able to peek behind the curtain of the Lord's majesty and understand how he functions internally, except to the extent that he has revealed that information to us. Moreover, because the Father and the Son are of the same essence (John 10:29,30),[38] they have all the same attributes and are therefore equal in all respects.

The third person in the Trinity is God the Holy Spirit. His role is often pictured as the giver of the Holy Scriptures (2 Peter 1:20,21) and the sanctifier of believers (1 Corinthians 12:1-11). The term *Holy Spirit* is found in the Old Testament (Psalm 51:11),[39] as well as the New Testament. The Bible describes him as "proceeding" from God the Father (John 15:26) and also as being the Spirit of God the Son (Galatians 4:6). Because the Holy Spirit is God, and therefore not a creature of time, his proceeding is an "eternal proceeding." Like the relationship between the Father and Son, it is beyond our comprehension. While at times the Holy Spirit appears to be merely an agent of the Father and the Son, sins against him are labelled as the most severe that anyone can commit (Matthew 12:32). This will be discussed in chapter 16.

The human mind often understands something better if a picture can be created to show the relationships that exist between the parts of the item of interest. Various figures have been created to try to help the mind grasp the Trinity, such as an equilateral triangle, three interwoven circles, a triangle interwoven with three circles, two overlapping equilateral triangles pointed in opposite directions, various triquetrae,[40] and various shields with arcs and bars, among others (Figure 5-1). There is nothing wrong in using such figures, as long as one recognizes that none of them show a true representation of the Trinity but only hint at the complexity of the Lord who is three in one.

### False teaching about the Trinity

Because the existence of the Trinity and the internal relationship among its persons defy human understanding, it was only natural that false teach-

---

[38] [Jesus said,] "My Father, who has given them to me, is greater than all, and no one is able to snatch them out of the Father's hand. I and the Father are one." (John 10:29,30)

[39] [David said,] "Cast me not away from your presence, and take not your Holy Spirit from me." (Psalm 51:11)

[40] A triquetra is a symmetrical, triangular design of three interlaced arcs used on metalwork and stone crosses.

## Figure 5-1 Symbols Used to Represent the Trinity

ings would arise in the church about the Trinity. This happened almost from the beginning. For example, some have claimed that the Son and the Holy Spirit are creations of the Father and are therefore lower-level gods. Some have claimed that the persons of God are merely masks that the one essence wears, depending on what role he is playing. Some have dismissed the Holy

Spirit from the Godhead and have claimed that "the spirit of God" is the force that God exerts when he acts.

To evaluate such challenges to the nature of the Trinity, we must consult the Scriptures. If the Son and the Holy Spirit were lesser gods, then what are their powers? The Bible quotes the Lord himself claiming that he is the only God, and there is no other (Isaiah 44:6-9). It also states that the Son and the Holy Spirit have divine attributes, which are inherent in the Lord's essence and nowhere else, and that their actions are divine actions. While one can question how such an internal structure of the Trinity is possible, one cannot question the clear grammatical construction of the Bible or the cultural implications of its statements. In Old Testament Jewish culture, the oldest son was regarded as the equivalent of his father because he would replace his father in the family structure when the father died. When Jesus stated that he was the Son of God, the Jewish leaders knew that he was claiming to be God and they were ready to stone him because they regarded what he said as blasphemy (John 10:22-39). In the same way, things done by God are credited to the Holy Spirit (compare 2 Timothy 3:16,17[41] with 2 Peter 1:20,21[42]). If the Holy Spirit isn't God, then the primary assumption of the Bible being the inerrant Word of God has been violated.

The other false teachings are also contradicted by the clear words of the Bible. When an actor wears a mask, he can only play one character at a time. Yet different persons of the Trinity appear together (John 15:26; Galatians 4:6). The Son prays to the Father (John 17:1). God addresses himself in the plural (Genesis 11:7).[43] Similarly, if the Holy Spirit were not a person, how could he be lied to (Acts 5:3,4)? How could he be grieved (Ephesians 4:30)?[44] These false teachings are a result of trying to apply human logic to the things of God, reconstructing God to fit into an image with which one's reason is comfortable and then editing the Bible to support those ideas. In other words, people are still making idols to worship,

---

[41]All Scripture is breathed out by God and profitable for teaching, for reproof, for correction, and for training in righteousness, that the man of God may be complete, equipped for every good work. (2 Timothy 3:16,17)

[42]No prophecy of Scripture comes from someone's own interpretation. For no prophecy was ever produced by the will of man, but men spoke from God as they were carried along by the Holy Spirit. (2 Peter 1:20,21)

[43][The LORD said,] "Come, let us go down and there confuse their language, so that they may not understand one another's speech." (Genesis 11:7)

[44]Do not grieve the Holy Spirit of God, by whom you were sealed for the day of redemption. (Ephesians 4:30)

except now they are making them out of their thoughts instead of wood, metal, and stone.

## Nicene Creed

The false teaching that the Son of God was a creation of God the Father became popular in the fourth century due to the work of Arius, a renegade churchman from Egypt. His teachings so disturbed the church that Emperor Constantine called all the bishops together in Nicea to discuss the nature of God. During this meeting (called the Council of Nicea) Arius was condemned, and a confession was drafted stating the nature of the Godhead and the person of Jesus Christ. This statement was later refined at the first Council of Constantinople into the statement of faith that is called the Nicene Creed (Figure 5-2). This creed has remained unchanged for more than 1,600 years, except that the churches in the west added the phrase "and the Son" to indicate more exactly from whom the Holy Spirit proceeds. This is a biblically correct addition because the Bible calls the Holy Spirit the "Spirit of his Son" (Galatians 4:6), as well as the Father. Because the Nicene Creed clearly states the teachings of the Bible, to disagree with what is confessed in it is to put oneself outside of the Christian church. The doctrines of this creed will be discussed throughout the rest of this book.

### Figure 5-2 Nicene Creed

We believe in one God, the Father, the Almighty,
    maker of heaven and earth, of all that is, seen and unseen

We believe in one Lord, Jesus Christ, the only Son of God,
    eternally begotten of the Father,
    God from God, Light from Light, true God from true God,
    begotten, not made, of one being with the Father.
Through him all things were made.
For us and for our salvation, he came down from heaven,
    was incarnate of the Holy Spirit and the virgin Mary, and became
    fully human.
For our sake he was crucified under Pontius Pilate.
He suffered death and was buried.
On the third day he rose again in accordance with the Scriptures.
He ascended into heaven and is seated at the right hand of the Father.
He will come again in glory to judge the living and the dead,
    and his kingdom will have no end.

We believe in the Holy Spirit, the Lord, the giver of life,
> who proceeds from the Father and the Son,
> who in unity with the Father and the Son is worshiped
> and glorified,
> who has spoken through the prophets.

We believe in one holy Christian and apostolic Church.
We acknowledge one baptism for the forgiveness of sins.
We look for the resurrection of the dead and the life of the world to come.

CHAPTER 6

# God and the Universe

There is an active and very bitter argument going on continually between those who believe the universe was created by a supernatural being (or beings) and those who believe that it evolved through natural processes. The conflict often becomes emotional because both sides are prone to overstating their positions and failing to reveal their underlying assumptions. In this chapter we will look at the underlying assumptions of both sides, clarify the nature of the conflict, and determine what is at stake in the argument.

## God the Creator

In chapter 1 we noted that the primary assumption of confessional Lutheran teachings is that the Bible is the inerrant, verbally inspired Word of God. If that is the standard by which all teachings are to be judged, it is incumbent upon the Lutheran church that it abides by that standard. It must neither add to nor subtract from what the Scriptures say. Subtractions occur when those parts of the Bible about which people feel uncomfortable are ignored or denied. Additions usually occur when the zeal to guard biblical truths causes defenders to draw unsupported conclusions or to add human filler to deal with what appear to be unintended omissions in the written Word that was given by the Holy Spirit. Care must be taken in studying the Bible that we do not fall into either trap.

It is important to understand the nature of the Lord's interaction with the physical world in terms of the theme of the Bible. That theme is the Lord's love for his central creature (i.e., man), who has rebelled against him. The Bible describes the whole story from the beginning to the end, emphasizing man's total depravity and the incredible acts of love with which the Lord has tried to bring people back to a holy relationship with him. Everything described in the Bible serves this theme (Romans 15:4).[1] For this reason, it is only natural for the Lord to start his account of his relationship with man at the very first meeting.

The Bible begins by setting the stage on which the story will occur. The first chapter of Genesis describes how the Lord created an entire, perfect universe in which humankind would live. It then explains in the second chapter of Genesis how he created man and woman to be his special creatures and to live in this perfect world. Genesis chapter 3 tells how humankind rebelled against the perfect relationship that the Lord had created and thereby instigated a chain of unintended consequences that spread evil throughout the entire world. It also tells of the promise of a Savior who would restore the perfect relationship between the Lord and humankind. After that, the account of the Lord and humankind goes through many twists and turns until its final conclusion with the blessing of eternal life in heaven for those who believe in the promised Savior. The premise of the biblical account is completely dependent, however, on humankind initially receiving both life and a perfect world from the Lord. It was these things that gave the Lord the right to set the terms and conditions by which humankind was to live and interact with him. If the Lord did not create humans, what right would he have to place demands upon them?

In Genesis chapter 1 the Lord created the whole universe out of nothing by merely commanding that it exist. The timeless God then took six days on the human timeline to refine the stage he had created so it would be ready for his special creatures, humankind. He did not do this in what would be considered a logical fashion by human standards, but he did it in a sequence that showed his absolute control over everything physical, as was discussed previously in chapter 4. The days were defined by a Hebrew idiom for a calendar date, "evening and morning," rather than by just the generic word *day*, which could mean an extended period of time in other contexts. He reinforced this definition of *day* when he introduced the Sabbath concept as part of his giving the law from Mount Sinai (Exodus 20:11).[2] At the end of each day, he

---

[1] Whatever was written in former days was written for our instruction, that through endurance and through the encouragement of the Scriptures we might have hope. (Romans 15:4)

[2] [The LORD said,] "In six days the LORD made heaven and earth, the sea, and all that is in them, and rested on the seventh day. Therefore the LORD blessed the Sabbath day and made it holy." (Exodus 20:11)

proclaimed his work "good" by his standards (Genesis 1:31),[3] which are far better than any human standard. On the last of these days of creation, he created his special creatures with a special relationship to him ("in his own image," Genesis 1:27) and a special position to rule over his other creatures.

A curious humankind wants to know more about how the Lord carried out his creation. People ask questions. How could plants live without the heat and light from the sun? How could barren soil sustain plants? How many species did the Lord really create? To these and many more questions, the Lord gives no answer. He doesn't think people need to know. Moreover, because God was using his nonnatural hand in creation (Genesis 1:24),[4] it is unlikely that we could understand the "how" anyway. God's ways are beyond us when he resorts to acting outside the laws of nature (Job 38:32).[5] If he had so chosen, he could have created the entire universe in a nanosecond, and he could destroy it equally as quickly.

More questions arise from what is said in Genesis chapter 2. Did Adam really name every animal in existence, or just the common animals? How could he do this in a short time? How could he remember the names? Why did the Lord create woman in such a strange way? How could people live forever by eating the fruit of a tree? Once again, the Lord chose not to tell us his thinking in detail. Although later we do learn a little more about the Lord's thinking in how he created woman (Acts 17:26),[6] much information that human minds might desire is never revealed. Some people have argued that Genesis chapter 2 is a different account of creation from Genesis chapter 1, but this argument contradicts the whole fabric of the Bible. Genesis chapter 2 merely looks in more detail at the part of the creation process the Lord deemed critical, his creation of his special creatures, humans. Genesis chapter 2 begins using the name "LORD" (i.e., YHWH) as well as the word *God* (*Elohim*), which was used in Genesis chapter 1 to designate the Creator. The name "LORD" shows that he has a special relationship to humans, in contrast to his generic relationship to the rest of his creation.

Genesis chapter 3 is tightly bound to the first two chapters because it completes the background needed for what happens in the rest of the Bible.

---

[3] God saw everything that he had made, and behold, it was very good. And there was evening and there was morning, the sixth day. (Genesis 1:31)

[4] God said, "Let the earth bring forth living creatures according to their kinds—livestock and creeping things and beasts of the earth according to their kinds." And it was so. (Genesis 1:24)

[5] [The LORD said,] "Can you lead forth the Mazzaroth [constellations] in their season, or can you guide the Bear with its children?" (Job 38:32)

[6] He made from one man every nation of mankind to live on all the face of the earth. (Acts 17:26)

It tells how the Lord's beloved creature was led into rebellion against him by the fallen angel Satan. This rebellion instantly changed humankind. It caused people to try to hide from the Lord. That physical act by Adam and Eve of trying to hide was the beginning of a continual human effort to hide from God, which has characterized the spiritual relationship between humankind and the Lord ever since. It has been a separation that the Lord calls death, that is, spiritual death (Ephesians 2:1).[7] It points forward to another separation people will experience, "temporal death," where the spiritual element of a person (his or her soul) leaves the physical element (his or her body) (Ecclesiastes 12:7).[8] Of even more concern, the Lord tells us that it portends eternal separation from the Lord—"eternal death," which is the punishment of hell (2 Thessalonians 1:9).[9]

The story would have been a tragedy, and the Bible could have ended with Genesis chapter 3, if the Lord had not given a promise that the original relationship between himself and humankind would be restored. It was the promise of a Savior who would crush the one that tempts humankind that makes this chapter the beginning of the story of the Lord's incredible love.[10] Man had lost his close relationship to the Lord with all its benefits and could do nothing to restore it. If the Lord had not acted, man would have been forever separated from him. But the Lord did act, though in his own way and at his own time, as the rest of the Bible documents.

If the Lord created a perfect world, one that was "very good" even in his perfect sight, how did the world reach its current state of existence where there are numerous natural disasters, as well as those caused by people? The Bible states that this happened because of sin (Genesis 3:17,18; Romans 8:20,21[11]), but unfortunately (or so people think), it does not tell us the details. Instead, it leaves us with a dilemma. Because the Lord can act by both his natural hand, working through the laws of nature, and his nonnatural hand, performing miracles by direct commands, we do not know in what way he has changed which things unless he tells us. During such events as the fall into sin, the great flood (Genesis 6–8), and the lengthening of the day for Joshua (Joshua 10:12-14), the Lord might have made many other mirac-

---

[7]You were dead in the trespasses and sins. (Ephesians 2:1)

[8]The dust returns to the earth as it was, and the spirit returns to God who gave it. (Ecclesiastes 12:7)

[9]They will suffer the punishment of eternal destruction, away from the presence of the Lord and from the glory of his might. (2 Thessalonians 1:9)

[10]The Savior is also called Messiah (the anointed one) and Christ in the Bible.

[11]The creation was subjected to futility, not willingly, but because of him who subjected it, in hope that the creation itself will be set free from its bondage to corruption and obtain the freedom of the glory of the children of God. (Romans 8:20,21)

ulous changes, or maybe he didn't make them at those times. He might have switched back and forth between his natural and miraculous ways of working over the years. We do not know, and there is no way to find out. As we shall soon see, when the Lord acts in a miraculous way, it cannot be studied and explained by scientific investigation. The Lord did not think it was necessary for us to know any more about his creating acts than he has told us. We can fantasize, but we must not pretend to know. This is an example of where we must not add anything to the Bible that is not there.

## The nature of science

Because of its characteristics as a means of investigation, the approach of science to the origins of the universe is radically different than that of biblical Christianity. To understand the nature of science, one must distinguish it from mathematics. Mathematics is of human origin, and it is abstract. It is not inherently related to the real world. Mathematics is the study of sets of domains devised and defined by human minds in fields such as geometry, calculus, topology, and symbolic logic. In every field of mathematics, an investigator can create his or her own domain by definition, and the validity of any thesis within that domain can be established as true, false, or indeterminate based solely on how the domain is defined. In effect, the person defining a domain is the "god" who rules over it. The standard of truth used to establish the validity of a thesis in a mathematical domain is that every possible case to which a thesis applies must be tested and found to meet the statement of that thesis. Mathematics has powerful tools to allow cases to be examined systematically so as to accomplish this seemingly onerous task (see endnote i at the end of the chapter). In mathematics, absolute truth can therefore be determined within each system.

The basic sciences (as opposed to the applied sciences like medicine, engineering, or business) are the study of the universe, which the Bible teaches is the Lord's creation. Scientists, however, are not the masters of events, because scientists can only observe the events of nature that occur. They cannot alter the underlying natural forces or the properties of matter and energy that they assume cause them. It is true that in some fields experiments can be performed in which as many variables as possible are controlled, but even in these cases, what is observed is the result of forces involving matter and energy that are beyond the control of the scientists. Scientists attempt to explain their observations of nature in terms of the most elementary principles possible. Their efforts are labeled "modeling." The goal of science is to build models that explain observed phenomena in terms of the fundamental properties of matter and energy. (Note that scientists often use the words *law, model,* and *theory* interchangeably, but *model* is the best term for what they develop because it is not emotionally charged.)

Often scientists use mathematics to support their work by attempting to match an abstract mathematical domain with known properties to the domain they are studying in the "real world." If they can find a good match, the properties of the mathematical domain, which are known with certainty, can be used to predict what is happening in the scientific domain of study, where things can be observed only within the reliability of the measuring devices available. This is an extremely useful practice, but there is a danger. People, even scientists, sometimes confuse the validity of the mathematical model with the validity of the scientific model it is being used to approximate. This causes them to imagine the scientific model is equally as good as the mathematical. Because scientific models usually cover an incredibly large number of cases and because scientists do not have the ability to study cases by abstraction as do mathematicians, scientists cannot use the same standard of truth as mathematicians use. Scientists instead employ what is called the scientific method to approximate truth, because, as we shall see, scientific truth can never be completely established. The steps of the scientific method are (1) scientists observe phenomena, (2) they develop a model to explain them, (3) they evaluate their model by its ability to predict further phenomena, and (4) they continuously refine the model until it proves satisfactory or until it is supplanted by a better model.

## The assumptions of science

For confessional Lutherans, the primary assumption on which their theology is built is that the Bible is the inerrant, verbally inspired Word of God. This statement is accepted without external proof. In the same way, the basic sciences, i.e., the physical and biological sciences, also have assumptions on which they are built and that are accepted without external proof.

Let us contrast mathematics and science at their most basic levels. In mathematics, everything is known about the fundamental properties of the domain being studied from the beginning due to the way the mathematicians defined it. Scientists, on the other hand, have not been handed a list of the properties of matter and energy, but they must deduce them from their observations. Therefore, *the primary assumption of science is that all observations can be explained in terms of the inherent properties of matter and energy.* As more observations are made, more useful information is discovered. Each discovery adds to the amount of knowledge that exists in a specific field of science, but each observation also places all the related scientific models in jeopardy. One new piece of evidence may overturn a generally accepted model, causing a major revision in scientific thought. For example, for many years the interactions among physical objects were calculated based on "laws" of physics developed from the work of Isaac Newton. In the 19th century, however, scientists discovered that as objects traveled closer to the speed of light, the Newtonian model no longer explained what was seen. A new model had to be developed to explain the behavior of high-speed objects but also to approximate the Newtonian model for low-speed interactions. *The first major limitation of science is that its models are fragile—they can be overturned or require significant alteration because of a single new observation.* They are not a manifestation of truth, but a manifestation of the best explanations based on current data known from observations.

Moreover, the primary assumption of science eliminates the possibility of the existence of any supernatural being that can interact with the physical universe. Why is this true? If any god, angel, demon, or other being not governed by natural laws (hence, a "supernatural being") existed who could affect the physical world, then scientists would not know whether what they observed was a result of the natural properties of matter and energy or the action of the supernatural being(s). The scientists would be like blind people trying to walk through a room where someone periodically rearranges the furniture. The primary assumption of science forces scientists in their work to act as if there were no god. If there is anything a scientist does not want, it is a "miracle" being performed by some supernatural being during an experiment, thereby making his or her work non-reproducible and unpublishable. *A second major limitation of science is that if a supernatural being exists, such as the Lord God Almighty of the Bible, then all scientific observations are of uncertain validity, and the reliability of scientific models ranges somewhere between questionable and complete junk.* Even the best scientific model would be only as reliable as the supernatural being wanted it to be. In such a situation, the primary assumption of science is reduced from being a reliable pillar for building models of nature to being, at best, a useful guideline for investigation. (Concerning Lutherans being scientists, see endnote ii.)

In addition, if the primary assumption of science is true, then the universe had to develop through evolution at all levels. The primary assumption says that the only processes available are natural processes. Therefore, that the universe evolved is a logical (i.e., a mathematically true) corollary of the primary assumption of science, not something scientists have proven or can prove. The role of scientists is to take the available evidence and develop models that explain the evidence in terms of the inherent properties of matter and energy. They must exclude any consideration of divine intervention in the evolutionary processes of the universe or of humankind because divine intervention would violate their primary assumption. When scientists make statements about their models, those statements must always be regarded in light of the assumptions of science, not regarded as absolute truth, which cannot be found by the scientific method due to the first limitation.

This is easier to understand if we look at another limitation of science. If two scientists develop different models to explain a set of data, the scientific community will attempt to find new tests for evaluating the models to determine which better predicts the existence of new data points. If one model does so more accurately, then the acceptance of that model by the scientific community increases and the other model falls into disfavor. If, however, no test can be found that is able to differentiate between the models, then either or neither might be true, but both cannot be true because they conflict with each other. Therefore, *a third limitation of science is that if no cases can be found that differentiate between two models attempting to explain the same phenomenon, then either or neither might be the correct explanation.* Why is this important? The Bible claims that the universe as it now exists was created and readjusted by the Lord God Almighty, a supernatural being, and science claims that it evolved from natural processes based on the inherent properties of matter and energy.[12] *Key point: There is no test that can differentiate between these two models!* On one hand, an almighty God can, by definition, make anything happen that he chooses to happen and can operate in manners that scientists cannot measure. On the other hand, the scientific method permits data to be gathered continuously to enhance evolutionary models[13] so that they are never completely finished and therefore cannot be proven inadequate. Because the two approaches are based on different primary assumptions, there is no common standard by which they can be compared. *Key point: This situation can actually be reduced to a formal mathematical proof that it is impossible for either creation or evolution to be established logically in preference to the other.*

Even though it can be shown through mathematical methods that the controversy between creationists and evolutionists is irresolvable, the dispute is encouraged by those having other agendas. Secular Humanists[14]

---

[12]Certainly, an almighty God could have brought the world into existence through evolutionary processes, but the Bible says that was not the way he chose to do it.

[13]Evolution simply means "change." In reality, everyone believes in evolution at some level, because everyone sees changes occurring in the world. The point of contention between Christianity and science is "macroscopic evolution," that is, changes on a massive scale that form planets, radically alter geography, and create life.

[14]While there is a Secular Humanist Manifesto of its beliefs as a formal group, the label is appropriately applied to all those who believe that humankind can better society through human ingenuity rather than

want to build a better, and eventually a utopian, world based on moral principles that they themselves develop. Secular Humanists know that if the universe has been created by the Lord, then they are rebels against him and cannot escape his wrath and eternal punishment. They believe that if they can eliminate the acceptance of the historical biblical interpretation, then the Lord cannot possibly exist to challenge them. In effect, they desire to overwhelm and outvote him. Even though the argument is logically false that something cannot be true unless someone believes it, Secular Humanists are passionately devoted to it. They are convinced that if they can use science to undermine the credibility of the teachings of the Bible, Christianity will quickly decline or be redirected to social purposes, as it has already been in many nominally Christian church bodies. Secular Humanists have much more at stake in the validity of evolutionary models than scientists, although some people are, of course, both.

The other group stoking the creation versus evolution debate is composed of those who believe it is possible to reconcile all the teachings of the Bible through human reasoning. They think that they can establish the truthfulness of the Bible by using the methods of science and that scientists are intentionally misusing their data to promote evolution out of personal motives. Certainly, not all scientists have the purest motives for the way they carry out their research any more than all Christians have the purest motives for everything they do. This, however, is a minor issue, and the tolerance of misbehavior is often less in the scientific communities than in the Christian communities. The real issue is that those arguing for "creation science" are practicing both bad theology and bad science. Their theology is bad because they develop models of how the Lord acted to alter the world after creation that are not mentioned in the Bible. They ignore that the Lord can intersperse actions of his miraculous hand with those of his natural hand and thereby try to dictate to him how he had to manage his creation. Their science is bad because they reject the primary assumption of science and the scientific method. They therefore cannot submit their claims to a process of independent testing as legitimate science requires. (See endnote iii for examples of such bad practices of creation science.)

While the battles over creation and evolution are often heated, they are generally irrelevant. On a daily basis, models of macroscopic evolution play little or no role in most scientific investigation. Trying to model what is

acknowledging that humans' inherent sinfulness prevents permanent peace and prosperity and that even physical improvements in living conditions are transitory and given based on divine good will.

happening in their fields of study is at the center of most scientists' attention, rather than how things on a macroscopic level got to be the way they are. Moreover, there is no way to reconcile the two views of the world's origin. Those who try to do so by arguing for theistic evolution or intelligent design are forced to abandon the biblical timeline of creation and therefore have conceded defeat at the start. Those pushing creation science quickly abandon the rigorous methods of science for pseudoscience. Because the primary assumptions of confessional Lutheranism and of science are incompatible, either one or both of them must be false. Neither primary assumption is provable, so it is a matter of faith which assumption a person accepts.

There are two other limitations of science that show its nature is not infallible. The study of the universe is based on what the human brain can comprehend and what the human senses can detect. The human brain understands spatial relationships in three dimensions and a one-dimensional time vector. Scientific models are therefore built according to this understanding of space and time. What if there were more than three spatial dimensions to the universe? Models might have to be dramatically changed to accommodate additional dimensions of matter. Humans observe phenomena based on their five senses, which they amplify through measuring technology. Suppose there are key properties of matter and energy that cannot be measured by our senses? Once again, current models might be silly in regard to the true structure of the universe. *A fourth limitation of science is that models are limited by what the human mind and senses, extended by instrumentation, can observe and comprehend.*

Finally, scientists must do their measurements with instruments that are themselves part of the environment being measured or that are isolated from it by other environments that can affect the values recorded by the measuring devices. For example, the energy of the radiation needed to determine the location of an object will cause the object to move. This is a significant issue with atomic-sized or smaller particles. For example, the temperature of a substance will be affected by energy transfer between it and the instrument measuring its temperature. For example, metal rulers will change length based on their temperature, thereby altering the standard of measure. For example, light can be bent and can change wavelength depending on the relative motion of the source and of the detector, as well as by what the light passes through or near while traveling between the two. *A fifth limitation of science is that the quality of observations is limited by the quality of the instruments and how well they can be employed to isolate the target object from other factors.* The changing recommendations concerning good dietary practice by the medical community shows how hard it can be to isolate and measure all important factors involved in a complex process.

## The Lord as preserver

The Bible teaches not only that the Lord created the universe but also that he preserves it. He has not abandoned it to run itself under a set of inviolate laws of nature. He provides different levels of preservation for creatures, for humankind in general and especially for the believers in his Messiah. He is concerned with the details in each case.

After the great flood (Genesis 6:9–8:19), the Lord declared that seasonal cycles would be preserved (Genesis 8:22).[15] He actively sets limits on physical processes (Job 38:8-11).[16] Jesus noted that even the lives of small birds are of concern to the Lord (Matthew 10:29).[17] The Lord feeds all the animals (Psalm 104:27).[18] He even makes the flowers beautiful (Matthew 6:28,29).[19] Without him, all things die and decay (Psalm 104:29).[20]

The Lord has committed himself to preserving humankind until the final judgment (Matthew 24:36-39). He gives rain and good weather (Matthew 5:45).[21] Without his help, not even the mundane things like building a house can occur (Psalm 127:1).[22] Man can plan, but it is the Lord who decides whether those plans are realized (Luke 12:16-21; James 4:13,14[23]).

---

[15] [The LORD said,] "While the earth remains, seedtime and harvest, cold and heat, summer and winter, day and night, shall not cease." (Genesis 8:22)

[16] [The LORD said,] "Who shut in the sea with doors when it burst out from the womb, when I made clouds its garment and thick darkness its swaddling band, and prescribed limits for it and set bars and doors, and said, 'Thus far shall you come, and no farther, and here shall your proud waves be stayed'?" (Job 38:8-11)

[17] [Jesus said,] "Are not two sparrows sold for a penny? And not one of them will fall to the ground apart from your Father." (Matthew 10:29)

[18] These all look to you, to give them their food in due season. (Psalm 104:27)

[19] [Jesus said,] "Why are you anxious about clothing? Consider the lilies of the field, how they grow: they neither toil nor spin, yet I tell you, even Solomon in all his glory was not arrayed like one of these." (Matthew 6:28,29)

[20] When you hide your face, they are dismayed; when you take away their breath, they die and return to their dust. (Psalm 104:29)

[21] [Jesus said,] "He makes his sun rise on the evil and on the good, and sends rain on the just and on the unjust." (Matthew 5:45)

[22] [Solomon said,] "Unless the LORD builds the house, those who build it labor in vain. Unless the LORD watches over the city, the watchman stays awake in vain." (Psalm 127:1)

[23] Come now, you who say, "Today or tomorrow we will go into such and such a town and spend a year there and trade and make a profit"—yet you do not know what tomorrow will bring. What is your life? For you are a mist that appears for a little time and then vanishes. (James 4:13,14)

The Lord's highest level of concern, however, is for those who believe in him and seek to do his will. He promised tremendous blessing to the Israelites if they would remain faithful to his covenant given at Mount Sinai (Deuteronomy 28:1-13). He promised guidance (Isaiah 58:11).[24] He promised deliverance (Romans 11:26).[25] Jesus grieved over those who fell away (Matthew 23:37,38)[26] and pointed out how even the angels rejoice over one sinner who repents (Luke 15:7).[27] The Lord assured his New Testament followers that all things would work together for their good (Romans 8:28).[28]

## Summary

The Lord's relationship to humankind is closely bound to his creation and his control of the physical universe. The latter is necessary because of his love for the former. That love is so strong that the Lord devised a plan of salvation for humankind, who had become totally repulsive to his very essence, so that he might bring humans back to the perfect relationship that they had destroyed in Eden. Compared to the salvation of the souls of people, the creation and management of the complexity of the physical world is child's play for the Lord God Almighty.

The discoveries of science should not trouble the Christian nor should Christians feel the necessity to argue with those who accept the conclusions of science. No scientific model, no matter how well accepted, can invalidate the teachings of the Bible. The existence of the Lord means that the most fundamental assumption of science is false and that all of the conclusions of scientists must therefore be uncertain or limited in scope.

## Endnotes

[1]*Examples of mathematical principles in determining truth*
**Positive integers**—A mathematical domain can be defined as the set of positive integers (1, 2, 3, 4 . . .). For that domain, the thesis that addition is a valid operation is true (e.g., 3 + 2 = 5, and 5 is a positive inte-

---

[24]The LORD will guide you continually and satisfy your desire in scorched places and make your bones strong; and you shall be like a watered garden, like a spring of water, whose waters do not fail. (Isaiah 58:11)

[25]And in this way all Israel will be saved, as it is written, "The Deliverer will come from Zion, he will banish ungodliness from Jacob." (Romans 11:26)

[26][Jesus said,] "O Jerusalem, Jerusalem, the city that kills the prophets and stones those who are sent to it! How often would I have gathered your children together as a hen gathers her brood under her wings, and you were not willing! See, your house is left to you desolate." (Matthew 23:37,38)

[27][Jesus said,] "Just so, I tell you, there will be more joy in heaven over one sinner who repents than over ninety-nine righteous persons who need no repentance." (Luke 15:7)

[28]We know that for those who love God all things work together for good, for those who are called according to his purpose. (Romans 8:28)

ger) and so is the thesis that multiplication is a valid operation (e.g., 3 x 2 = 6, and 6 is a positive integer). These statements are true because both operations always yield results within the domain. The domain is said to be "closed" under these operators. This can be shown to be the case for all integers through a technique called "recursion." The theses that subtraction and division are valid operations are not true, however, because these operations can produce values outside the domain (e.g., 2 - 3 = -1, or 3 / 2 = 1.5, neither result being a positive integer). The theses that the set of positive integers is closed under subtraction and division are shown to be false by a technique called "counterexample."

*Triangles*—An isosceles triangle is a figure on a plane (i.e., a flat surface) in which three non-linear points are connected by line segments and in which two of the line segments are of equal length. It constitutes a domain in which theses can be proven or disproven. Because proofs are general, e.g., they are not based on specified lengths for any of the sides of the triangle, the proofs cover all possible isosceles triangles. It can be proven that the base angles of an isosceles triangle are equal; therefore, anything that fits the definition of the domain we call an isosceles triangle will have equal base angles.

## II *Can a confessional Lutheran be a scientist?*

Because the primary assumption of science leads to conflicts with the primary assumption on which confessional Lutherans build their faith, it would seem that they could not be scientists. If this were the case, however, then Lutherans also could not play games. For example, when one plays a computer game that requires one to kill an evil troll or steal a villain's treasure, one does not have to commit oneself to killing and thieving in the real world. While one accepts the rules of the game as "working assumptions" for playing the game, one does not have to morally bind oneself to those actions, even if they are necessary in the game. If one did, then even such games as chess and checkers would be unscriptural. In the same way, a scientist can accept as a working hypothesis that all observations are a result of natural forces without personally believing this must always be the case. If this seems hypocritical, consider what people who believe in the inerrancy of the Bible do every day. Do they leave their homes in the morning with a tether tied to their front porches and wearing parachutes so that they can get back to the ground safely in case gravity would fail for a few minutes? No, they assume that gravity will always work, even though they believe that it is possible for the Lord to suspend it. In fact, they assume a large number of the "laws of nature" will always work, never planning for an instance when they might not. In the same way, a Lutheran can do his or her scientific work without having to abandon faith in the omnipotence of God. He or she trusts the Lord to govern his created universe in an orderly fashion unless the Lord has a reason to do otherwise. In many fields of science, a Lutheran can use the primary assumption of science as a working hypothesis without abandoning his belief that it is the Lord who actually controls everything in the universe.

## III *Examples of problems with the approaches of creation science*

*Laws of thermodynamics*—Some have argued that life could not have evolved because that would involve greater complexity in nature, violating the laws of thermodynamics, which require all systems to run downhill to the state of lowest potential energy. The general laws of thermodynamics, however, apply only to closed systems, and virtually everything in the physical world is an open system. (A closed system is one that does not exchange energy or matter with the outside world.) Consider this example: Ocean water at sea level is at a much lower potential energy than the relatively pure water in a snowpack on the top of a mountain. Once the snow melts in summer, by the laws of thermodynamics, it would seem that it would never again appear on the mountaintop, as it would not be able to gain the potential energy to do so. Because the earth's environment is an open system, however, the sun supplies the energy to evaporate the water and move the clouds over the mountain to reestablish the snowpack the next winter. In an open system, things can indeed become more complex.

*Probability*—Some have often argued that the probability of life evolving is so low that it could not happen. Sometimes this is done by comparing evolution with some other highly improbable event. Developing an accurate probability expression for a complex phenomenon requires that the probability be known for each path the phenomenon could follow. In reality, virtually none of this information is available for complex systems, and the time to gather it would take at least many centuries. Without a doubt, the evolution of life is improbable, but so are the chances of any specific person winning a big lottery jackpot, yet it happens.

Improbable does not mean impossible, particularly when long periods of time or many actors are involved.

*Scientific "laws"*—In its simplest form, the "law of biogenesis" states that living things can come only from living things. Some have argued that this proves life cannot originate from nonliving materials. Louis Pasteur developed this assertion several centuries ago to demonstrate that milk could be prevented from bacterial decay by killing the bacteria in the milk through heating it (Pasteurization) and by then keeping it in a sealed container. It cannot, however, be considered an established universal law. It was tested in only a small domain for a short time interval. Since Pasteur's time, even the scientific definition of what life is has changed. Calling something a law does not make it any more valid than calling it a theory. Laws do not trump theories. They are the same thing, that is, models developed to explain observations.

*Counterexamples*—Some have often attacked evolutionary models with counterexamples. While these are a deadly effective technique in mathematics, they are much less so in science and are often easily overcome by tweaking the model being attacked or by improving the method of measurement employed to build the model. In fact, scientists are continuously challenging one another's models—this tactic is the heart of classical science. If creation scientists actually did find anything significant, scientists working on evolutionary models would rapidly use the information to strengthen the models.

*Dated arguments*—Scientists are continually learning from flaws in their past models. Newer and more accurate means of measuring routinely replace older methods. Arguments against a particular scientific approach are only valid while it is being used as the primary means of observation or modeling. For example, one approach that geologists have historically used to determine the age of landscapes is based on the rate at which sediment builds up. They would measure the current rate of sedimentation and extrapolate how long it would have taken for the various layers of sediment they observed to develop. Because there are cases where such an approach has been shown to be grossly inaccurate, geologists long ago concluded they needed more supporting data. They now gather additional evidence by doing core sampling to determine what fossils and other time markers, such as rocks with radioactive materials, are present in the various layers. Skeptics often concentrate on attacking older methods that are easily understood by nonscientists rather than newer methods currently in use that are not so easily understood by the laity. Before accepting an argument, one must ask an expert in the field whether it represents current scientific thinking.

# Plan of Salvation—Historical View

The Bible is the account of the Lord's interactions with humankind. Any interaction between two parties will naturally have two perspectives. In the current section of this book, we will look at this interaction from the viewpoint of what humankind has seen and what the Lord intended humankind to see. In section four, we will look at the interaction from the Lord's vantage point—to the extent that he has given us the information to do so.

As we saw in chapter 4, the Lord is omniscient. Before the Lord created humankind, he knew precisely what humankind in general and every person in particular would do. He foresaw the fall into sin and how people would fail to accept all his efforts to turn them from their sinful course. Yet just because the Lord foresaw what would happen does not mean that he either caused it or desired it. Moreover, throughout all his interactions with humankind, the Lord learned nothing because he already knew everything. His actions, therefore, were not trial-and-error efforts on his part to deal with a developing situation, but they were carried out in order to teach people of his greatness and of natural humans' total helplessness to accept the Lord's guidance. Throughout this section we will look at the

Lord's efforts to teach us, heeding the words of St. Paul: "Whatever was written in former days was written for our instruction, that through endurance and through the encouragement of the Scriptures we might have hope" (Romans 15:4).

A second factor that will strongly color our study of the Lord's education of humans is humanity's total depravity. The Lord said, "I will never again curse the ground because of man, [even though] the intention of man's heart is evil from his youth" (Genesis 8:21). Jeremiah added, "The human heart is deceitful above all things, and is [incurable]; who can understand it?" (Jeremiah 17:9). When it comes to the things of God, every person is very dense. St. Paul wrote, "The natural person does not accept the things of the Spirit of God, for they are folly to him, and he is not able to understand them because they are spiritually discerned" (1 Corinthians 2:14). Because people are always looking for their own advantage, they seldom stop to determine the meaning of what has happened to them in the past and continue to plow forward to gain whatever they can before they lose their opportunities to others. As we review the history of humankind under the Lord's efforts to train its members, we will rely heavily on the writings of the later prophets and the New Testament apostles, following the principle that Scripture must interpret Scripture. This is necessary because the Lord's purpose in the various accounts may not be obvious if they are read as simple historical narratives rather than as part of an overall plan.

# CHAPTER 7

# God's Beginnings With Humans

As discussed in chapter 4, the Lord God is perfect, and he is perfect in all his actions (Psalm 145:17).[1] Therefore, when he decided to make a universe, he made it to be perfect. It had no blemish or deficiency. In the creation account, the reader is reminded at the end of each day that even the Lord thought his creation was very "good."[2] Being almighty, he certainly could have made it run unerringly forever, just like an ideal clock. Yet in creating the world, the Lord did something truly amazing, and it is because he did this that history happened the way it is described in the Bible.

The Lord resolved to make two types of creatures into whom he placed his divine will and to whom he gave the ability to obey it. However, he also gave them the freedom to choose to follow his will or to act contrary to it (Deuteronomy 30:19,20).[3] Unlike a clock that can only do what it is built to do, these creatures could choose to "violate their programming" and follow their own course of action, at least to the extent to which the Lord would allow them to do so. However, only the Lord's way is the right way, the way that will not cause conflict and grief. Giving creatures the ability to make choices, therefore, created the risk that those who had the

---

[1] [David said,] "The LORD is righteous in all his ways and kind in all his works." (Psalm 145:17)

[2] Genesis 1:10,12,18,21,25,31

[3] [The LORD said,] "I call heaven and earth to witness against you today, that I have set before you life and death, blessing and curse. Therefore choose life, that you and your offspring may live, loving the LORD your God, obeying his voice and holding fast to him." (Deuteronomy 30:19,20)

ability would go astray and make bad moral choices. Why the Lord chose to give any creatures the ability to make choices has not been specifically revealed to us, but we can draw some conclusions from what is revealed in the Bible.

One set of creatures who received the freedom of choice was the angels. Angels are creatures who, like the Lord, are spirits with no permanent physical form (Hebrews 1:14),[4] although they can assume a physical form under certain conditions (Genesis 19:1).[5] Angels will be discussed in more detail in chapter 19. It is only important at this point to note that they were created to be very powerful, to be rational, and to have freedom of choice. The Lord created a very large number of them, many tens of thousands (Daniel 7:10). They were to be the Lord's perfect servants, carrying out his will throughout the realm of created things (Psalm 91:11,12). Unfortunately, one of the leading angels, Satan, led a rebellion of some of the angels against the Lord (Jude 6).[6] Certainly, the omniscient Lord knew that this would happen and how he would deal with the situation. Why Satan did not realize that the Lord was not bound by time, as were Satan and everything else, is puzzling. Because the Lord is already in the future, there was no way that Satan could gain an advantage against the Lord by subterfuge, nor could he overpower the Almighty in strength. The Lord dealt swiftly with the rebellion, expelling Satan and his angels (now called demons or devils) from heaven and consigning them to eternal punishment in hell (Matthew 25:41).[7] The essence of the Lord cannot tolerate rebellion, and the fate of the devils was a necessary result of their opposing the Lord. Perhaps the devils did not realize this beforehand, but it was clear to both the faithful angels and the fallen angels afterward what the result of disobedience and rebellion would be. The Lord apparently decided that the angels needed no further lessons. For the angels that had remained faithful, he confirmed them in their state of holiness, that is, he removed their freedom of choice so that they could no longer fail to obey him. The demons had lost their freedom to choose by their act of rebelling. Their spiritual nature had become evil, and therefore they could no longer choose to do God-pleasing deeds (Matthew

---

[4] Are they not all ministering spirits sent out to serve for the sake of those who are to inherit salvation? (Hebrews 1:14)

[5] The two angels came to Sodom in the evening, and Lot was sitting in the gate of Sodom. When Lot saw them, he rose to meet them and bowed himself with his face to the earth. (Genesis 19:1)

[6] The angels who did not stay within their own position of authority, but left their proper dwelling, he has kept in eternal chains under gloomy darkness until the judgment of the great day. (Jude 6)

[7] [Jesus said,] "Then he will say to those on his left, 'Depart from me, you cursed, into the eternal fire prepared for the devil and his angels.'" (Matthew 25:41)

7:18,19).[8] They were literally "hell-bent" to oppose the Lord at every turn for the suffering that he inflicted on them.

The other creature who received the freedom of choice was humankind. The Lord, however, did not handle humankind as he did the angels. There were several clear differences. First, the Bible tells us that he took counsel with himself before the creation of humans (Genesis 1:26).[9] It does not record that he did this with any other species. He furthermore created humankind "in his own image." This does not mean that humans looked like the Lord, because the Lord is a formless spirit. Instead, the will of the Lord was written into him so that he reflected God's desires for him and wanted to serve the Lord wholeheartedly. Moreover, unlike the angels, the Lord gave men and women physical bodies to go with their spiritual component, namely, the soul, which remains attached to the body as long as the body lives (Genesis 2:7). He made a special place on earth for his first man, a garden that was a pleasant dwelling place (Genesis 2:8,9). He gave the man work to do tending the garden (Genesis 2:15) and authority over the animals the Lord had created (Genesis 1:28). He made humans weaker than the angels (Isaiah 37:36).[10]

A major difference between humans and the angels is how the Lord chose to populate the species. On one hand, he created a large number of angels, which is fixed because they do not reproduce (Matthew 22:30).[11] On the other hand, he started the human race with but one person, Adam, whose Hebrew name is derived from the word for earth. The Lord created a wife for Adam by extracting a rib from him and then brought her to him as his companion (Genesis 2:21-23). In so doing, the Lord caused all humans to truly come from only one person. He commanded his first couple to bring forth more people by procreation, rather than to expect him to directly create more people himself (Genesis 1:28). The manner in which the Lord created the human race caused him to deal with it much differently than how he dealt with the angels.

As with the angels, the Lord started off humankind with a perfect internal understanding of his will by making humans in his own image. In addition,

---

[8] [Jesus said,] "A healthy tree cannot bear bad fruit, nor can a diseased tree bear good fruit. Every tree that does not bear good fruit is cut down and thrown into the fire." (Matthew 7:18,19)

[9] Then God said, "Let us make man in our image, after our likeness. And let them have dominion over the fish of the sea and over the birds of the heavens and over the livestock and over all the earth and over every creeping thing that creeps on the earth." (Genesis 1:26)

[10] The angel of the LORD went out and struck down 185,000 in the camp of the Assyrians. (Isaiah 37:36)

[11] [Jesus said,] "In the resurrection they neither marry nor are given in marriage, but are like angels in heaven." (Matthew 22:30)

the Lord gave Adam and Eve an external commandment,[12] forbidding them to eat the fruit of one of the trees in the garden paradise (Genesis 2:17).[13] The tree offered Adam and Eve a clear choice: They could obey the Lord and live in harmony with him by ignoring the tree, or they could experience death by rebelling against his will and eating the fruit of the tree.

Satan, having rebelled against and having been easily defeated by the Lord, began a campaign to undermine the Lord's physical creation and corrupt his favored species, the human race (John 8:44).[14] Satan surmised that if he could get humans to follow him into sin, then they would certainly get the same sentence that he got, namely, eternal punishment (Matthew 25:41). He also may have surmised that contact with a sinful humankind would contaminate the physical world and thereby cause the Lord to destroy it (Romans 8:20,21). Satan therefore launched his attack on Eve by suggesting that the Lord was perhaps holding back what he could have given her, namely, the ability to know good and evil (Genesis 3:4,5).[15] Moreover, Satan assured her that she could gain this knowledge independently, apart from the Lord, thereby establishing herself as a force to be reckoned with. Eve bought into the deception, ate the fruit, and quickly brought Adam into the rebellion as her ally. It seemed like Satan had obtained his goal.

The Lord indeed had righteous anger against Adam and Eve, and even more so when they began to place the blame for their sins on others, including him (Genesis 3:9-13). But Satan had once more underestimated the Lord. Although their sin had made Adam and Eve liable to immediate physical death, spiritual death (i.e., spiritual separation from the Lord), and eternal punishment, the Lord had foreseen humankind's sin and had prepared a plan to deal with it, a plan that did not set aside his abhorrence of sin. First, he put on hold the immediate sentence of temporal death (i.e., physical death), commuting it to a long lifetime in a hostile world where toil and trouble would abound (Genesis 3:16-19).[16] Inevitable physical death, however, continued to hang over their heads (verse 19). Second, he prom-

---

[12] August Pieper, "The Law Is Not Made for a Righteous Man," in *The Wauwatosa Theology*, Curtis A. Jahn, ed., Vol. II (Milwaukee: Northwestern Publishing House, 1997), pp. 73-100.

[13] [The LORD said,] "Of the tree of the knowledge of good and evil you shall not eat, for in the day that you eat of it you shall surely die." (Genesis 2:17)

[14] [Jesus said,] "You are of your father the devil, and your will is to do your father's desires. He was a murderer from the beginning, and does not stand in the truth, because there is no truth in him. When he lies, he speaks out of his own character, for he is a liar and the father of lies." (John 8:44)

[15] The serpent said to the woman, "You will not surely die. For God knows that when you eat of it your eyes will be opened, and you will be like God, knowing good and evil." (Genesis 3:4,5)

[16] To the woman he [the LORD] said, "I will surely multiply your pain in childbearing; in pain you shall

ised a way for humankind to escape the punishment of eternal death because he would give to humankind a human descendent who would destroy Satan and repair humankind's relationship with the Lord (Genesis 3:15).[17] Few details about the plan were given to them at this point, but by believing the offer (Genesis 4:1), Adam and Eve were restored to a positive relationship with God. They again had spiritual life and could be sure that they would be freed from the punishment of eternal death, that is, endless suffering for their sins in complete separation from the Lord (see chapter 11).

The difference in how the Lord responded to the rebellion of the angels and to the rebellion of man is striking. A fixed number of angels had been created, and they had learned there were consequences to sin (that is, rebellion) against God. There was no more for any of the angels to learn about this matter, and there would be no more angels to teach. Without God's grace, the good could not remain faithful to him and the evil could never be restored to goodness. The Lord therefore made a judgment concerning all the angels. Those who had remained faithful would no longer be able to choose to sin, while those who had rebelled would no longer be able not to sin and would be condemned to eternal punishment. Humankind, on the other hand, had begun with but one pair of people. The whole of humankind had been corrupted in Adam and Eve's rebellion. Because they were corrupt, they could never know if they might have been able to remain in a favorable relationship to God if they had acted differently. They did not know whether they could check the degree of corruption they had incurred. Therefore, the Lord decided that, as rational creatures, they needed to learn more before a final judgment would be placed on them.

It is easy for the human mind to ask why the Lord did things the way he did. Why did he permit the possibility of evil? Why didn't he destroy evil into nothingness when it first appeared? Why didn't he start with more people or different people? Who gave the Lord the right to behave in such a manner, anyway? The same answer to each of these questions is that the Lord is the Lord. As should be obvious from chapter 4, he does what he pleases and is not answerable to human thoughts or agencies. It is his universe. The Lord

---

bring forth children. Your desire shall be [for] your husband, and he shall rule over you." And to Adam he said, "Because you have listened to the voice of your wife and have eaten of the tree of which I commanded you, 'You shall not eat of it,' cursed is the ground because of you; in pain you shall eat of it all the days of your life; thorns and thistles it shall bring forth for you; and you shall eat the plants of the field. By the sweat of your face you shall eat bread, till you return to the ground, for out of it you were taken; for you are dust, and to dust you shall return." (Genesis 3:16-19)

[17][The LORD said,] "I will put enmity between you and the woman, and between your offspring [followers] and her offspring; he shall bruise your head, and you shall bruise his heel." (Genesis 3:15)

made it, he owns it, and he can do what he pleases with it. To challenge his fairness is to recommit the sin of Eve. Giving us the answers in this life to questions such as those above is not something the Lord chooses to do (Acts 1:7).[18] The Lord asks for our trust, not our questions (Job 38–41).

If the first humans had believed that sin could be contained to small acts of rebellion and disobedience against the Lord, they were soon proven wrong. They had lost the image of God through their first sin, and therefore they no longer had that unerring sense of what the Lord wanted, nor did they have a written code to guide them (Romans 2:14,15).[19] Satan continued to distort their knowledge of the Lord's will, which he had corrupted with his first temptation. The full ugliness of their sinful condition became visible in the actions of Cain. When his sacrifice did not please the Lord as much as his brother's, he ignored the Lord's warnings and killed his brother (Genesis 4:1-16). He was then far less than repentant, and the Lord banished him from his family. In his sin, Cain's heart showed the same arrogance that Adam and Eve showed when they first rebelled (Matthew 15:19,20).[20]

The Lord has given us very little information about the early history of humankind. In this period, which might be called the Pre-Flood Age, the few people who are mentioned are usually only mentioned by name and perhaps by lifespan. Lines of descendants are given, but they may not be complete because the Hebrew word for "father" can also mean "ancestor." The lives of the people were very long, hundreds of years, causing some people to suggest that perhaps conditions on earth were somewhat different than they are now. The Bible mentions no written records from this time, nor any landmarks that can be used to identify the events of this period. How the Lord communicated with people is also not explained. Whether he appeared to people directly or spoke through chosen representatives is unknown. The long lifespans allowed for good oral history and transmission of the creation account and of the Lord's interactions with people. If the genealogies are anywhere near complete, Noah could have learned of the creation and fall from someone who had heard it from Adam himself. Even if some generations are missing, the information chain would have needed very few links to cover the time

---

[18]He [Jesus] said to them [the apostles], "It is not for you to know times or seasons that the Father has fixed by his own authority." (Acts 1:7)

[19]When Gentiles, who do not have the law, by nature do what the law requires, they are a law to themselves, even though they do not have the law. They show that the work of the law is written on their hearts, while their conscience also bears witness, and their conflicting thoughts accuse or even excuse them. (Romans 2:14,15)

[20][Jesus said,] "Out of the heart come evil thoughts, murder, adultery, sexual immorality, theft, false witness, slander. These are what defile a person." (Matthew 15:19,20)

period. Imagine being able to hear about Martin Luther and Elizabeth I of England from someone who had known both of them personally!

One person who is given special attention is Lamech, a descendant of Cain (Genesis 4:19-24). In our trying to gain information about this Pre-Flood Age, we must be careful not to read more into the account of Lamech than the Bible actually records.[21] Lamech would appear to have been a man who was fairly well-off financially. He could afford two wives. One of his sons had time to become an expert metal smith, a craft that would have been profitable only after some investment of money and time. Another of his sons was a skilled musician, an even less profitable career that would have likely required familial support. The Lord therefore continued to bless all humankind materially, even the descendants of unrepentant Cain (Matthew 5:45).[22] Lamech, however, was arrogant, even more than his ancestor. He rejoiced in revenge killing, claiming a legacy even more notorious than Cain's.

Lamech serves as an example of the general apostasy that was in progress. Even those who had accepted the direction of the Lord during the early centuries of the Pre-Flood Age began to weaken in their resolve. Perhaps they envied the wealth of the unbelievers, perhaps they concluded that the Lord really didn't care, or perhaps they merely took what appeared to be the expedient course. The Bible mentions marriages between believers and unbelievers as a major reason for the growing apostasy (Genesis 6:1-3).[23] Men used selfish rather than Godly motives in choosing spouses, and in the process they lost their faith in the Lord. Finally, the Lord lost patience with the gross immorality of his favored creatures and decided to show humankind the depth of the evil into which it had fallen (Genesis 6:5,6).[24]

There were, however, some people who followed the Lord. Enoch was

---

[21] Reading more into these early accounts is a constant temptation because so little is given. One can help to limit this temptation by considering the question, "How many wives did Adam have?" The obvious answer of "one" may not be correct. For example, Adam might have married a great-granddaughter, either before or after Eve died, for the purpose of having more children. We do not know because the Bible tells us nothing about Adam after the birth of Seth except for his lifespan. The correct answer to the question is therefore "at least one," because that is all we can say with certainty from the Scriptures.

[22] [Jesus said,] "He [the heavenly Father] makes his sun rise on the evil and on the good, and sends rain on the just and on the unjust." (Matthew 5:45)

[23] When man began to multiply on the face of the land and daughters were born to them, the sons of God saw that the daughters of man were attractive. And they took as their wives any they chose. Then the LORD said, "My Spirit shall not abide in man forever, for he is flesh: his days shall be 120 years." (Genesis 6:1-3)

[24] The LORD saw that the wickedness of man was great in the earth, and that every intention of the thoughts of his heart was only evil continually. And the LORD regretted that he had made man on the

a faithful follower of the Lord, and the Lord decided to take him from the world by some unusual means (Genesis 5:21-24). Noah was another man who followed the Lord (Genesis 6:8), and he was chosen by God for a huge task that would take years to complete. Note well that neither of these men was commended for his good deeds. The source of their "righteousness" (Genesis 6:9) is not attributed to any deeds mentioned in Genesis, but what is mentioned is that they believed in ("walked with") the Lord. They believed his promise rather than scoffing and turning aside to their own pursuits. Other men and women may also have been faithful, but the Lord did not feel we needed to know about them. None of us is so important that we deserve a permanent footnote in human history merely for believing the Lord's promises.

Noah was commissioned to build an ark (Genesis 6:11-22). The Bible does not say how long it took to build the ark, but due to its size and the relatively primitive tools that were available, it may have taken several years. One can only imagine what others thought of this project. When Noah had finished the ark, the Lord arranged for it to be filled with animals appropriate for his plan (Genesis 7:1-9). The ensuing flood destroyed land-based life on the earth's surface. Noah then had to wait for the floodwaters to recede to see what the revamped world looked like. The nature and the extent of the changes to the earth are not detailed in the Bible. They may have been extensive, or maybe they weren't. The sign of the rainbow (Genesis 9:13-16) is mentioned, as is the permission to eat clean animals (Genesis 9:3). Whatever the changes were, Noah and his family proceeded with their task of making a living in a lonely world.

Care must be used so as not to allegorize the details of the flood account, as if they individually have some deeper theological meaning. The Lord gave these details because this was an important event, and he wanted to show the care he had put into his planning. The flood was not a haphazard deluge during which the Lord rushed in like Superman to rescue his chosen. It was an event under his control that was intended to advance his plan for humankind. He destroyed whom he wished and saved whom he wished (Exodus 33:19).[25]

Using the flood as a punishment on humankind was intended as a lesson for Noah, his family, and subsequent generations. The Lord is able to destroy all of humankind, and he will do so when he deems it the appropriate response. Evil is an affront to the Lord's very essence, which is perfect, and

---

earth, and it grieved him to his heart. (Genesis 6:5,6)

[25] [The LORD said,] "I will be gracious to whom I will be gracious, and will show mercy on whom I will show mercy." (Exodus 33:19)

he will not tolerate rebellion any longer than it serves his greater purpose. The Lord takes no vote as to the reasonableness of his actions, nor does he fill out an environmental impact statement. He does not allow himself to be judged by human standards. Those who doubt the Lord's resolve are given no excuse for such thoughts as a result of the account of the flood. The evil of man, however, could not derail the Lord's plan of salvation. The Lord merely started over with a subgroup of the human race. From the Pre-Flood Age, we should take the lesson that without God's grace, even those who should have known better because they had firsthand witnesses who told them of the wonders of creation could not keep every inclination of their hearts from turning to evil.

After the flood, the Lord started over with eight people (Genesis 7:13), who literally should have had "the terror of God" put into them. He made a covenant with them to reassure them. Again, it was a one-sided covenant in which he promised not to eradicate the human race by another universal flood and to preserve them (Genesis 9:8-17). Neither was the covenant of final salvation rescinded. Alas, the lesson of the Lord's wrath still had not caused men to abandon their evil ways. Soon Noah was getting drunk, and one of his sons was laughing at him lying naked in his tent (Genesis 9:20-27).

After the flood, people began to multiply and to grow in confidence in their own abilities (Genesis 10). Many perhaps took the Lord's promise that he would not destroy all human life again as permission to live as they pleased. Rather than spreading out as the Lord had commanded Noah and his sons (Genesis 9:1), people wanted to show they were strong and began building a monument to themselves at a place that would come to be called Babel (Genesis 11:4). The Lord found it necessary to befuddle their speech so that they could not cooperate in their projects and would flee from one another to be with those whose language they could understand (Genesis 11:5-9). The commands of the Lord, even when backed by incredible acts of punishment, were not enough to convince the restarted human race to take the Lord seriously and to diligently obey him. But in spite of sinful humans rebelling against the Lord, his plan of salvation for sinners would continue to unfold.

CHAPTER 8

# The Role of Israel

In chapter 7 we saw that without the Lord's active intervention, humankind quickly strayed off into grosser and grosser sins. Even after experiencing severe punishments—expulsion from Eden, destruction by the flood, and the dispersal after the building of the tower at Babel—the people still insisted on following their own ways and ignoring the Lord's commands. Human will had been totally corrupted by the fall (Genesis 8:21).[1] While people could strive to improve their lot for their own selfish ends, they could not regain that relationship in which they willingly served the Lord, the relationship that humankind had lost through its own folly. The Lord had shown humankind that punishment alone would not correct its ways, so he needed to teach the next lesson.

The Lord had promised Adam and Eve a deliverer for humankind (Genesis 3:15), but he had given no more details to be transmitted from generation to generation. After the people had begun to scatter over the earth, he deemed the time was right to specify from which family the promised deliverer would come. Perhaps such a designation would keep that family, at least, faithful to him over the subsequent generations. To help that family deal with the long wait, he added an intermediate temporal promise to show them that he would eventually fulfill the spiritual promise as well.

---

[1] [The LORD said,] "The intention of man's heart is evil from his youth." (Genesis 8:21)

## The patriarchs

The man whom the Lord chose to be the father of the people who would bear the Savior was Abram (Genesis 12:1–25:10). He came from a family from present-day Iraq (Genesis 11:31), a family that seemed to have had some knowledge of the Lord but that also practiced idolatry (Joshua 24:2; Genesis 31:19[2]). Abram was called from his family to go to the land of Canaan, a land he was promised his descendants would receive as an inheritance from the Lord when the time was right (Genesis 12:1-3).[3] While Abram was a nomadic herdsman of some wealth, he was not one of the merchant class, nor was he a ruler of one of the city-states. He might not have seemed like the best choice from a human standpoint, but he believed the Lord, accepted his call, left his family, and moved several hundred miles to the west.

Abram's situation was not an easy one. He was in a pagan land in which he had no real estate (Acts 7:5). He had no children, but he had a beautiful wife, Sarai. Several times he tried to pass her off as his sister to keep from being killed on account of her, but each time the Lord rescued her for him (Genesis 12:10-20; Genesis 20). Abram's nephew Lot caused him troubles as well. His herdsmen struggled with Abram's herdsmen over pastureland (Genesis 13). When Lot moved near Sodom, he was captured by enemy kings, and Abram needed to launch a military campaign to gain his release (Genesis 14). Finally, Abram needed to plead with the Lord for Sodom, so as to spare Lot from being destroyed with the evil men of that city (Genesis 18:16-33).

But it was his childlessness that most troubled Abram. The Lord appeared to him several times (Genesis 15:1-6; Genesis 17:1-22; Genesis 18:1-15) to reaffirm both the promise of the Savior and the promise of the land of Canaan. The Lord pointed to the stars as an example of how numerous Abram's descendants would be (Genesis 15:5). The Lord validated his covenant by using the local custom of passing between the halves of slain animals (Genesis 15:7-21). He gave Abram the sign of circumcision for all the males in his household (Genesis 17:9-14). He changed Abram's name to Abraham (Genesis 17:5) and his wife's name to Sarah (Genesis 17:15). Despite his childlessness, Abraham believed the Lord, and he therefore received the righteousness that counts before him (Genesis 15:6).[4]

---

[2] Rachel stole her father's household gods. (Genesis 31:19)

[3] Now the LORD said to Abram, "Go from your country and your kindred and your father's house to the land that I will show you. And I will make of you a great nation, and I will bless you and make your name great, so that you will be a blessing. I will bless those who bless you, and him who dishonors you I will curse, and in you all the families of the earth shall be blessed." (Genesis 12:1-3)

[4] He [Abraham] believed the LORD, and he counted it to him as righteousness. (Genesis 15:6)

However, Abraham's desperation for a son led him and his wife to plan to get a son through Abraham's having a sexual liaison with Sarah's slave Hagar and through Sarah then adopting the child as her own (Genesis 16). This was how surrogate motherhood was practiced at that time. While the Lord blessed this son, Ishmael, he was not the heir that the Lord had intended for Abraham (Genesis 17:20). When the time was right, the "impossible child" was born to Sarah, who was beyond the age of conceiving. Yet the Lord still tested Abraham by telling him to sacrifice this son of promise, Isaac, as a whole burnt offering (Genesis 22:2). When Abraham tried to comply, the Lord gave him a substitute in the form of a ram (Genesis 22:13,14).[5] The lesson that the Lord would provide a sacrifice to save his people was dramatically demonstrated in this account.

Abraham obtained a wife for Isaac from his own family, who stilled lived to the east (Genesis 24). Isaac had twin sons by his wife, Rebekah (Genesis 25:23).[6] The Lord chose the younger son, Jacob, to be the heir to the promise,[7] and he too would find a wife—two, in fact—from Abraham's relatives (Genesis 29:16-30). The account of Jacob and his family dominates the second half of the book of Genesis. Jacob, like his father and grandfather, was not a sinless role model for his descendants. He engaged in deceptions of his relatives and was, in turn, deceived by them. His first four sons (Reuben, Simeon, Levi, and Judah) by the older of his wives (Leah) were all involved in murder or sexual misconduct. Most of his sons sold their brother Joseph into slavery (Genesis 37:28), only to have him emerge as second to Pharaoh among the rulers of Egypt (Genesis 45:26). Despite all the wickedness, the Lord protected Jacob, brought him along in his faith, and renamed him Israel (Genesis 32:28). Genesis closes with the descendants of Israel in Egypt, awaiting their return to Canaan. This fulfilled the promise that the Lord had given to Abraham that his descendants would be "afflicted" in a foreign land for four hundred years (Genesis 15:13).

Abraham, Isaac, and Jacob are called the patriarchs of the people of Israel. The promises of the Lord for the land and for the Savior, given to each in turn,

---

[5] Abraham lifted up his eyes and looked, and behold, behind him was a ram, caught in a thicket by his horns. And Abraham went and took the ram and offered it up as a burnt offering instead of his son. So Abraham called the name of that place, "The LORD will provide." (Genesis 22:13,14)

[6] The LORD said to her [Rebekah, Isaac's wife], "Two nations are in your womb, and two peoples from within you shall be divided; the one shall be stronger than the other, the older shall serve the younger." (Genesis 25:23)

[7] The phrase "heir to the promise" was used to describe Old Testament people who were descended from Abraham and who held to the promise of the Savior (i.e., the Messiah) given to him. Eventually, the gentile believers in Christ in the New Testament were added to this group.

helped to keep the family worshiping him, even though they often strayed. Without the constant renewal of the promise to the Israelites in Egypt, however, the collective memory of the people weakened. The Lord had to teach another lesson through his deliverance of them from their oppression under the hand of Pharaoh.

## The rescue from Egypt

As the years turned to decades and the decades to centuries, the descendants of Jacob made a home in the new land, and many probably grew content. The Lord disturbed this contentment by allowing the Egyptian ruler, Pharaoh, first to begin distrusting the growing Israelite population and then to enslave it (Exodus 1). Finally, Pharaoh decided to exercise population control by killing the male babies of the Israelites. It was in this situation that the Lord intervened by bringing about the birth of Moses. Through a series of events, Moses was saved from dying in the Nile River and then trained in the royal palace like one of the princes of Egypt (Exodus 2). Moses later got into trouble by taking the law into his own hands in defense of an Israelite and was forced to flee into the Sinai Peninsula, where he learned humility as a shepherd.

The Lord called Moses, much against his will, to return to Egypt and lead the Israelites out of Egypt (Exodus 3–14). Moses and his brother Aaron faced Pharaoh in a number of meetings and, at the direction of the Lord, called down ten plagues upon the Egyptians. Finally, Pharaoh allowed the Israelites to leave Egypt and travel to the east. When Pharaoh changed his mind and tried to make the Israelites return by force, the Lord opened a path through the Red Sea (called the Sea of Reeds in Hebrew) for his people but drowned the pursuing Egyptians by returning the water to its place. The amazing rescue from Egypt became the centerpiece of the Israelite consciousness, celebrated in the Passover even today, as the Jews recall how the angel of the Lord "passed over" their houses when he slew the firstborn in Egypt (Exodus 12:14).[8]

With such demonstrations of the Lord's power, one might think that the Israelites would have been eager to move forward under the Lord's leadership, fearing nothing. Quite the contrary, the people grumbled over every new difficulty, big or small (Exodus 15:22–17:7). They always imagined the

---

[8][The Lord said to the Israelites,] "This day shall be for you a memorial day, and you shall keep it as a feast to the Lord; throughout your generations, as a statute forever, you shall keep it as a feast." (Exodus 12:14)

worst scenario of events possible, and on many occasions they longed to go back to slavery in Egypt. Time after time, the Lord responded to complaints of his people (for example, supplying manna and quail as food [Exodus 16] and producing water from a rock to quench their thirst [Exodus 17:1-6], but nothing satisfied them for long. It was against this background that the Lord brought forth the greatest of his teaching tools in the Old Testament—the covenant of Sinai (Mosaic covenant).

To the Israelites who had lived in the lower Nile delta, the wilderness of Sinai with its desert landscape and mountains was a dramatic change. The Lord heightened the drama with thunder, lightning, and earthquakes on Mount Sinai (Exodus 19:16–20:17). The Israelites had never seen anything like this, and they were terrified. The Lord spoke to them in a loud voice, and they wanted to hear no more (Exodus 20:18,19).[9] The Lord then gave his covenant to Moses. The Israelites would receive the land of Canaan, as the Lord had promised the patriarchs, and they would receive prosperity from his hand. However, keeping the land and the prosperity depended on their agreeing to and keeping a covenant based on a large set of laws that were designed to make them a people set apart, a people awaiting the coming of their final redemption. This is often referred to as the "Old Covenant." With the "terror of God" literally having been put into them, they agreed to the covenant (Exodus 24:3)[10] and built the tabernacle (tent enclosure), for which the Lord gave them a pattern (Exodus 35–40). It might seem that they were ready to be the Lord's faithful people, but the Lord was under no illusions that they would be.

## The law as schoolmaster

The Old Covenant, also called the Mosaic covenant, had three types of commandments and regulations within it. They were interwoven because the Lord wanted the people to be obedient in things both large and small. Moreover, in Israelite society the various regulations supported one another, forming one structure or tapestry of law. The three components of the Mosaic Law were the moral law, summarized in the Ten Commandments and applicable to every individual Israelite; the civil law, a legal code for Israel as a nation; and the ceremonial law, which governed the commu-

---

[9] Now when all the people [the Israelites] saw the thunder and the flashes of lightning and the sound of the trumpet and the mountain smoking, the people were afraid and trembled, and they stood far off and said to Moses, "You speak to us, and we will listen; but do not let God speak to us, lest we die." (Exodus 20:18,19)

[10] Moses came and told the people all the words of the LORD and all the rules. And all the people answered with one voice and said, "All the words that the LORD has spoken we will do." (Exodus 24:3)

nity's worship life. Obedience was required, and major violations would lead to execution or exile.

The moral law in the form of the Ten Commandments (Exodus 20:2-17) is shown in Table 8-1. In Hebrew these are called ten words or statements of God, and different groups number them differently. The numbering is unimportant because it is not prescribed by the Scriptures. What is prescribed in the commandments are the two great principles of the moral law: "You shall love the Lord your God with all your heart and with all your soul and with all your mind" (Matthew 22:37) and "You shall love your neighbor as yourself" (Matthew 22:39). These commandments are reflected in the civil laws in almost all communities throughout the world. This is because these commandments are present in the remnants of God's law that were given to humans at the creation and are therefore universal (Romans 2:14,15).[11] Because the image of God was lost in the fall, people now have only a corrupted sense of what is God-pleasing, and they do not willingly obey the moral law in the way the Lord wants. By giving the moral law as an external standard for humankind, the Lord was telling people that their internal sense of right and wrong was inadequate to produce God-pleasing works.[12]

While the Ten Commandments stated principles, those principles had to be applied to individual cases in daily living. That was one of the functions of the civil law code, to detail to the people how to live in conformity with the principles and to tell the authorities how to deal with people who violated the principles. The civil law of Israel, therefore, was an example of how the moral law can be put into practical application. The civil law also covered such things as inheritance, provision for the poor, family relations, and legal processes. It is presented primarily in the last half of Exodus, in Leviticus, and in Deuteronomy. The Israelites had lived for four centuries in the pagan land of Egypt, so they needed to know how the Lord wanted them to live under his direction. By establishing the civil law for the nation himself, the Lord wanted to prevent the people from perverting the intent of his moral law by gradually changing the civil law code so that it would be in conflict with his moral law (Deuteronomy 4:2).[13]

---

[11] When Gentiles, who do not have the law, by nature do what the law requires, they are a law to themselves, even though they do not have the law. They show that the work of the law is written on their hearts, while their conscience also bears witness, and their conflicting thoughts accuse or even excuse them. (Romans 2:14,15)

[12] August Pieper, "The Law Is Not Made for a Righteous Man," in *The Wauwatosa Theology*, Curtis A. Jahn, ed., Vol. II (Milwaukee: Northwestern Publishing House, 1997), pp. 73-100.

[13] [The LORD said,] "You shall not add to the word that I command you, nor take from it, that you may keep the commandments of the LORD your God that I command you." (Deuteronomy 4:2)

The ceremonial law told the Israelites how they were to worship the Lord. Its regulations appear in various places from Exodus through Deuteronomy, but most heavily in Leviticus. Part of this law contained the rites of worship and the celebration of festivals. These created a worship practice that would be carried out from generation to generation. Its intent was to prevent the false teaching of the neighboring religions from being added to the

| Jewish | Catholic/ Lutheran | Reformed | Statement |
|---|---|---|---|
| **TABLE 8-1—The Ten Commandments (Exodus 20)** The numbers in the table represent the order in which the religions list the Ten Commandments | | | |
| **First Table – Love of the Lord** | | | |
| 1 | – | – | I am the LORD your God, who brought you out of the land of Egypt, out of the house of slavery. |
| 2 | 1 | 1 | You shall have no other gods before me. |
| 2 | 1 | 2 | You shall not make for yourself a carved image, or any likeness of anything that is in heaven above, or that is in the earth beneath, or that is in the water under the earth. |
| 3 | 2 | 3 | You shall not take the name of the LORD your God in vain. |
| 4 | 3 | 4 | Remember the Sabbath day, to keep it holy. |
| **Second Table – Love of one's neighbor** | | | |
| 5 | 4 | 5 | Honor your father and your mother, that your days may be long in the land that the Lord your God is giving you. |
| 6 | 5 | 6 | You shall not murder. |
| 7 | 6 | 7 | You shall not commit adultery. |
| 8 | 7 | 8 | You shall not steal. |
| 9 | 8 | 9 | You shall not bear false witness against your neighbor. |
| 10 | 9 | 10 | You shall not covet your neighbor's house. |
| 10 | 10 | 10 | You shall not covet your neighbor's wife, or his male servant, or his female servant, or his ox, or his donkey, or anything that is your neighbor's. |

worship of the Lord, gradually turning it into idolatry. The second part of the ceremonial law involved cleanliness, which represented holiness before the Lord. The Lord wanted the Israelites to be a people set apart from their sinful neighbors (Leviticus 20:26).[14] The regulations concerning cleanliness showed how difficult it was to maintain purity in their service of the Lord. It was something that had to be on their minds continually, lest they made themselves unclean through careless living. It also inconvenienced them to become clean again if they had become unclean (e.g., Numbers 19:11,12).[15] Finally, the ceremonial law prescribed the contributions they were to make to the Lord on various occasions, such as firstfruits (Exodus 23:19),[16] tithes of their produce (Leviticus 27:30),[17] the firstborn of their cattle (Exodus 13:12),[18] and purification after the birth of a child (Leviticus 12:7,8).[19] The Lord included offerings they were to make on various occasions so they would realize that all they had had come from the Lord. Even more offerings were required if they violated the covenant and needed to repent (Leviticus 4:3).[20]

The regulations of the Mosaic covenant were a heavy burden that the Lord placed upon the people of Israel in exchange for their getting the land of Canaan as their homeland. He made it clear that they were mere tenants in the land he allowed them to use while they served him and his plan of salvation (Leviticus 25:23).[21] What was true for the Israelites is also a lesson that must be preached to the New Testament church. Everything on earth is the Lord's, and he loans it to people while they serve his purpose in this world (1 Timothy 6:7).[22] When they die or it pleases the Lord, he will take it from them.

---

[14]"You [the Israelites] shall be holy to me, for I the LORD am holy and have separated you from the peoples, that you should be mine." (Leviticus 20:26)

[15][The LORD said,] "Whoever touches the dead body of any person shall be unclean seven days. He shall cleanse himself with the water on the third day and on the seventh day, and so be clean. But if he does not cleanse himself on the third day and on the seventh day, he will not become clean." (Numbers 19:11,12)

[16][The LORD said,] "The best of the firstfruits of your ground you shall bring into the house of the Lord your God." (Exodus 23:19)

[17][The LORD said,] "Every tithe of the land, whether of the seed of the land or of the fruit of the trees, is the Lord's; it is holy to the LORD." (Leviticus 27:30)

[18][The LORD said,] "All the firstborn of your animals that are males shall be the LORD's." (Exodus 13:12)

[19][The LORD said,] "This is the law for her who bears a child, either male or female. And if she cannot afford a lamb, then she shall take two turtledoves or two pigeons, one for a burnt offering and the other for a sin offering." (Leviticus 12:7,8)

[20][The LORD said,] "If it is the anointed priest who sins, thus bringing guilt on the people, then he shall offer for the sin that he has committed a bull from the herd without blemish to the Lord for a sin offering." (Leviticus 4:3)

[21][The LORD said,] "The land shall not be sold in perpetuity, for the land is mine. For you are strangers and sojourners with me." (Leviticus 25:23)

[22]We brought nothing into the world, and we cannot take anything out of the world. (1 Timothy 6:7)

The severity of the Mosaic covenant was intended to remind the people that their God was perfect and expected them to be perfect. From the covenant they needed to learn that they were incapable of living such perfect lives. In fact, the Lord left little doubt about the lesson that he was trying to impart by blatantly labeling them "stiff-necked" a number of times throughout the period they spent in the desert (Exodus 32:9; 33:3; 34:9). He warned them not to develop pride when they prospered (Deuteronomy 8:17).[23] Only in this way would they realize that all they received was a gift of which they could never be worthy. It was a lesson that applied to the Promised Land of Canaan, but it was also a lesson that they needed to apply to the salvation from sins that the Lord had promised. They were weak and sinful and could contribute nothing to the rescue that the Lord would carry out to save them from the consequences of Adam's fall.

## The Israelites and the priests

The Mosaic covenant was built around sacrifices and the office of the priest. The sacrifices showed that uncleanliness could only be removed by the shedding of blood (Hebrews 9:22).[24] Blood theology is the heart of the Lord's plan of salvation, as will be discussed in section IV. The Lord directed Moses to anoint his brother Aaron to be high priest and Aaron's sons to be priests (Exodus 30:30).[25] This priesthood would be hereditary, restricted to the male members of Aaron's descendants (Exodus 29:9).[26] To assist the priests, to carry out the other functions needed for the place of worship, and to teach the people, Moses was instructed to ordain the remainder of the descendants of Israel's son Levi (the "Levites") (Numbers 1:50).[27] Priests offered animal sacrifices, offered prayers for the people, served as judges in matters related to the covenant, and acted as public health officers. Through them the Lord ran the nation of Israel as a theocracy.[28]

---

[23] [The Lord said,] "Beware lest you say in your heart, 'My power and the might of my hand have gotten me this wealth.'" (Deuteronomy 8:17)

[24] Indeed, under the law almost everything is purified with blood, and without the shedding of blood there is no forgiveness of sins. (Hebrews 9:22)

[25] [The Lord said,] "You shall anoint Aaron and his sons, and consecrate them, that they may serve me as priests." (Exodus 30:30)

[26] [The Lord said,] "The priesthood shall be theirs by a statute forever. Thus you shall ordain Aaron and his sons." (Exodus 29:9)

[27] [The Lord said,] "Appoint the Levites over the tabernacle of the testimony, and over all its furnishings, and over all that belongs to it. They are to carry the tabernacle and all its furnishings, and they shall take care of it and shall camp around the tabernacle." (Numbers 1:50)

[28] A theocracy is a government in which God rules directly through directives to chosen individuals.

The place of worship was an elaborate tent, called the tabernacle or the tent of meeting, which was specified by the Lord in great detail (Exodus 25:9).[29] It was divided into two sections—a Holy Place and a Most Holy Place—and it was surrounded by a courtyard (Exodus 35:4–38:31). In the courtyard was the large altar on which the priests continually made offerings for the people and to meet the Lord's requirements at festivals. In the Holy Place was the altar of incense, a lampstand, and a table with twelve loaves of bread, representing the twelve sons of Israel (Leviticus 24:5,6). In the Most Holy Place was a chest called the ark of the covenant, which held the two tablets containing the covenant. On top of the chest was the "atonement cover" or "mercy seat" of God, the place where the Lord dwelt in an earthly sense among his people. Symbolically, the Lord's mercy covered the law. Above the atonement cover were two cherubim representing the angel hosts that serve the Lord. Everything in the Most Holy Place was made of or plated with gold. The tabernacle could be disassembled by the priests and moved by the Levites, which was necessary while the people wandered in the wilderness before they reached Canaan. To facilitate this, the furniture was even equipped with brackets for poles. Eventually a jar of manna and Aaron's staff were also placed before the atonement cover (Numbers 17:10).

All the priests and Levites could help with the work involved with the sacrifices at the altar in the courtyard of the tabernacle. Only the priests, however, could enter the Holy Place to burn incense and say prayers for the people. Only the high priest was allowed to enter the Most Holy Place, and that was only once a year. It would only happen on the great Day of Atonement (Leviticus 16:2-34). The process would start with a bull and two goats being selected. By lot, one goat would be chosen as the scapegoat. The sins of the people would be confessed over its head by the high priest, and then the goat would be led into the wilderness, symbolically bearing the people's sins away from them. The high priest would kill the bull. Because sinful men cannot come into the Lord's presence, the high priest would fill the temple with the smoke of the incense he burned in the Holy Place. He would then step into the Most Holy Place and sprinkle the blood of the bull he sacrificed onto the atonement cover for his own sins and the sins of his family (the priests). Next, he would leave and return with the blood of the second goat, sacrificed for the people's sins, and he would also sprinkle that blood onto the atonement cover. The Lord accepted this ritual as both purifying the priests so that they could serve for the people for the next year and purifying the

---

[29] [The LORD said,] "Exactly as I show you concerning the pattern of the tabernacle, and of all its furniture, so you shall make it." (Exodus 25:9)

people so that they would have a fresh start before the Lord for the next year. These sacrifices were the absolute center of Israelite worship because they reconciled the people to their God. Without these sacrifices and the scapegoat, the Lord would not have accepted the Israelites because of their many sins. This taught the people that only through the shedding of blood could their sins be removed (Hebrews 9:22),[30] and it prepared them for the Lord's perfect sacrifice, which would remove their sins permanently (1 John 1:7).[31]

The Israelites were terrified at Mount Sinai and readily agreed to accept the terms of the covenant. Moses came and told the people all the words of the Lord and all the rules. "All the people answered with one voice and said, 'All the words that the Lord has spoken we will do'" (Exodus 24:3). The fear soon disappeared, however, and so did their obedience. When Moses went up the mountain to get all the details of the covenant, the people decided they needed a visible god to lead them and made a golden calf like those they had seen the Egyptians worship (Exodus 32). Chastised for that sin, they still refused to advance into Canaan because most of the spies they had sent into the land told them they would not be able to conquer it (Numbers 14:1-10). At that point, the Lord decided he had given the Israelites enough chances to follow his leadership and decreed that all the rebellious men of military age would die in the wilderness and never see the land of promise. Only the two faithful spies survived to cross the Jordan into Canaan (Numbers 26:65).[32] Not even Moses and Aaron were allowed to cross because their rash actions at the waters of Meribah stole glory from the Lord (Numbers 20:10-12).

The dreadful punishment of the destruction of the whole adult male population of Israel changed the people's mind-set for a generation. When the Lord directed the Israelites to move toward Canaan a second time, the rebellious attitude was much less severe (Numbers 32:1-27). While some incidents still occurred, the people generally followed Moses and, afterward, his lieutenant and successor Joshua. With the Lord's aid, they first captured the land to the east of the Jordan (Numbers 21:21-24:25; 31:1-18). After Moses' death, Joshua led them across the Jordan at flood stage by means of another miracle, and a further miracle caused the walls of Jericho to fall flat so that the Israelites could take the city (Joshua 3-6). After several more campaigns, a

---

[30] Indeed, under the law almost everything is purified with blood, and without the shedding of blood there is no forgiveness of sins. (Hebrew 9:22)

[31] The blood of Jesus his Son cleanses us from all sin. (1 John 1:7)

[32] The LORD had said of them, "They [Israelites of military age] shall die in the wilderness." Not one of them was left, except Caleb the son of Jephunneh and Joshua the son of Nun. (Numbers 26:65)

large portion of the land of Canaan was conquered and ready to be divided among the families (tribes) of Israel. During Joshua's life and the lives of the leaders who had been with him, the Israelites followed the Lord's covenant (Joshua 24:31). A generation later, however, many of the people were again in rebellion, this time worshiping the gods of the people who had foolishly been allowed to remain in the land.

To cleanse the land of Canaan of the indigenous peoples, the Lord commissioned the Israelites to practice genocide. They were to kill all the males and frequently also all the females. Sometimes they were even commanded to destroy all the physical property and to kill all the animals of the native peoples (Joshua 6:21).[33] The Lord had judged these people (Deuteronomy 18:12),[34] and Israel was specially told to carry out that judgment. This troubles many people today, but the Lord is not bound by human standards of right and wrong (Deuteronomy 32:39).[35] He continued to use war throughout the Old Testament to carry out his judgments, as the Bible notes in various places, and he still controls the fates of nations today. However, the Lord has not established theocracies since the birth of Christ, nor has he commissioned any modern nation to carry out genocide. Certainly, he has not commissioned his church to kill, torture, or coerce unbelievers.

After the death of Joshua, the Lord did not appoint another political leader for the Israelites. His people were to live under the rule of the priests and the patriarchal system in existence within the tribes of Israel, with the Lord himself serving as ruler through his law and his communications with the high priest. This era in Israelite history is known as the period of the judges and is presented in the book of Judges and the early chapters of 1 Samuel. During this period, the same cycle repeated itself numerous times. The Israelites would begin to worship false gods, and the Lord would send a neighboring people against them to punish them. After several years of occupation, the Israelites would repent and call on the Lord for aid. The Lord would send a deliverer who would defeat the enemy and guide Israel as a judge until his death. The people would worship the Lord more faithfully until the judge died, and then they would go back to their idolatry.

---

[33] Then they devoted all in the city [Jericho] to destruction, both men and women, young and old, oxen, sheep, and donkeys, with the edge of the sword. (Joshua 6:21)

[34] [The LORD said,] "Because of these abominations the LORD your God is driving them [residents of Canaan] out before you." (Deuteronomy 18:12)

[35] [The LORD said,] "See now that I, even I, am he, and there is no god beside me; I kill and I make alive; I wound and I heal; and there is none that can deliver out of my hand." (Deuteronomy 32:39)

A list of the judges is given in Table 8-2. The details given about the individual judges in the Bible vary greatly, so it is not possible to give a generalized description of what they did. Most of the judges seem to have been

| TABLE 8-2—The Judges | | |
|---|---|---|
| **Judge** | **Reference** | **Summary** |
| Othniel | Judges 3:7-11 | Defeated the Syrian king Cushan-Rishathaim after he had occupied Israel for 8 years. |
| Ehud | Judges 3:12-30 | Killed the Moabite king Eglon after he had occupied Israel for 18 years. |
| Shamgar | Judges 3:31 | Killed 600 Philistines but no additional information is given. |
| Deborah | Judges 4:1–5:31 | Was a judge who summoned Barak to attack the Canaanite king Jabin, who had ruled parts of Israel for 20 years because he had 900 chariots. Together they defeated Sisera, Jabin's commander, who was killed by Jael, wife of Heber. |
| Gideon | Judges 6:1–8:35 | Defeated the Midianites and their allies with 300 men after sending home most of his troops at the direction of the Lord. |
| Tola | Judges 10:1,2 | Led Israel for 23 years, but nothing else is known about him. |
| Jair | Judges 10:3-5 | Led Israel for 22 years, but little else is known about him. |
| Jephthah | Judges 10:6–12:7 | Was of illegitimate birth but was called upon to drive out the Ammonites after they had overrun Israel for 18 years. This led to a civil war between the Gileadites and the Ephraimites. |
| Ibzan | Judges 12:8-10 | Led Israel for 7 years, but little else is known about him. |
| Elon | Judges 12:11,12 | Led Israel for 10 years, but nothing else is known about him. |
| Abdon | Judges 12:13-15 | Led Israel for 8 years, but little else is known about him. |

| Judge | Reference | Summary |
|-------|-----------|---------|
| | **TABLE 8-2—The Judges** *continued* | |
| Samson | Judges 13:1–16:31 | Was a child promised to Manoah and his wife. He was raised as a Nazirite, a person dedicated to the Lord living by special rules (see Numbers 6:1-21), but he was unruly. He was attracted to Philistine women and killed many Philistines for various reasons. The Lord gave him strength because of his long hair, but he foolishly lost his hair and his strength. |
| Eli | 1 Samuel 1:9–4:18 | Was a priest who judged Israel for 40 years but had corrupt sons who lost the ark of the Lord in battle. |
| Samuel | 1 Samuel 1:1–25:1 | Was a sought-for child who was dedicated to the Lord upon weaning. He led Israel for many years, but his sons were a problem and caused Israel to abandon the judge system. |

natural leaders, but they were not always eager leaders. Some, like Samson, had their own personality problems, which detracted from their work as judges. Accounts not involving judges—but included in the book of Judges—show how bad the behavior of the people became, including gang rape, fratricide, gross idolatry, and civil war. The spiritual leadership of the priests was largely a failure. Even though the people had detailed rules for serving the Lord, they did not follow them. Even though the Lord spread the priests and the Levites throughout Israel so that they could minister to the people, either they failed to minister or the people failed to listen or both. It broke Samuel's heart when he realized that he would be the last judge (1 Samuel 8:6,7) because the people no longer had confidence in the system. The Lord gave him the task of moving Israel from a theocracy to a monarchy. The Lord had known that this would happen, and he had included provisions in the Mosaic covenant to handle it (Deuteronomy 17:14,15).[36] Samuel accepted what he could not change.

---

[36] [The LORD said,] "When you come to the land that the Lord your God is giving you, and you possess it and dwell in it and then say, 'I will set a king over me, like all the nations that are around me,' you may indeed set a king over you whom the LORD your God will choose. One from among your brothers you shall set as king over you. You may not put a foreigner over you, who is not your brother." (Deuteronomy 17:14,15)

## The Israelites and the kings

In the Mosaic covenant, the Lord had insisted that he needed to be the one who chose the kings to rule Israel. His first choice was a man from the tribe of Benjamin. From a human point of view, Saul appeared to be an excellent choice. He was tall but humble. He came from the smallest tribe of Israel, so he would not be able to strong-arm the other tribes but would need to gain their support through wise and decisive actions (1 Samuel 9:1,2).[37] As might be expected, some grumbled about the choice, but Saul convinced the doubters by rescuing a city that was about to be overrun (1 Samuel 11:1-11). He forgave those who had doubted him. The Lord was with him, and he was successful in establishing more security to overcome the attacks from the neighboring nations (1 Samuel 14:47).

As so often happens with those given power, however, Saul gradually began to think too highly of himself and stopped carrying out the Lord's commands given to him through Samuel. The Lord became angry with Saul and regretted making him king (1 Samuel 15:10,11).[38] Of course, the Lord knew that Saul would fail to be a faithful king, but he wanted to teach his people the lesson that a king would not automatically be the solution to all of their problems. The final failure of Saul that caused the Lord to abandon him came when he failed to completely destroy the Amalekites, the nation that had attacked the Israelites when they came out of Egypt (Exodus 17:8-16). The Spirit of the Lord left Saul, and an evil spirit troubled him (1 Samuel 16:14).

Meanwhile, the Lord sent a frightened Samuel to anoint a new king to replace Saul (1 Samuel 16:1-13), even though Saul insisted on keeping his throne. The Lord chose David, the youngest son of Jesse, from the tribe of Judah. Although not yet mature, he was fearless, having killed a bear and a lion that had tried to attack the flock of sheep that he tended. When the Israelites faced the Philistines and were taunted by a giant soldier named Goliath, David volunteered to engage him in one-on-one combat and killed the giant with a slingshot and stone (1 Samuel 17). David was quickly promoted and became a favorite of the soldiers. Although Saul did not immediately realize that David had been anointed to replace him, he soon became jealous of David's military successes and tried to find ways first to control and then to kill David. David

---

[37]There was a man of Benjamin whose name was Kish, the son of Abiel, son of Zeror, son of Becorath, son of Aphiah, a Benjaminite, a man of wealth. And he had a son whose name was Saul, a handsome young man. There was not a man among the people of Israel more handsome than he. From his shoulders upward he was taller than any of the people. (1 Samuel 9:1,2)

[38]The word of the LORD came to Samuel: "I regret that I have made Saul king, for he has turned back from following me and has not performed my commandments." (1 Samuel 15:10,11)

took to flight and built his own strong company of soldiers. Saul chased him for a while but eventually was killed, along with most of his sons, in a battle with the Philistines. The account of Saul and David is in 1 Samuel chapters 18–31.

After Saul's death, David became king over the tribe of Judah (2 Samuel 2:4), but Ish-bosheth, a son of Saul, ruled the rest of Israel (2 Samuel 2:8). After seven years, during which Israel and Judah raided each other's land continually, the Israelites lost faith in Ish-bosheth and his own servants killed him. David then became king over both Israel and Judah (2 Samuel 3–5). David's total reign was 40 years. It was filled with frequent wars against the neighboring countries as he established Israel as the dominant power in the region. He had several rebellions within his own family and several times fell into gross sins. Unlike Saul, however, he repented and kept the Lord first in his life. He wrote a number of psalms that are in the Bible. He was called "the sweet psalmist of Israel" (2 Samuel 23:1)[39] and "a man after [the Lord's own] heart" (Acts 13:22).[40] The Lord promised to establish David's kingdom eternally through the promised Savior, as well as to give David's descendants an earthly kingdom as long as they remained faithful to him (Psalm 132:11,12).[41]

The Lord chose Solomon to succeed David as king (1 Kings 1:13). Solomon inherited a large kingdom that controlled the neighboring peoples. He therefore became rich and built Jerusalem lavishly. He asked the Lord for wisdom and received it in great measure. His father, David, had longed to build a great temple for the Lord, but the Lord had refused to allow him to do so because he had been involved in so much bloodshed. Nevertheless, David accumulated many of the materials needed to build the temple, and Solomon constructed it (1 Chronicles 28–29; 2 Chronicles 1–4). This was the high point of Solomon's reign. Solomon became involved in idolatry because he married many pagan wives. His high taxes caused unrest among many of the people. Although Solomon wrote all or most of three books of the Bible (Proverbs, Ecclesiastes, and Song of Songs), the Lord did not overlook his idolatry. Instead, the Lord removed a substantial portion of the kingdom from Solomon's son. Israel as a united kingdom lasted for less than 120 years, through only three kings.

---

[39] Now these are the last words of David: "The oracle of David, the son of Jesse, the oracle of the man who was raised on high, the anointed of the God of Jacob, the sweet psalmist of Israel." (2 Samuel 23:1)

[40] [Paul said,] "He raised up David to be their king, of whom he testified and said, 'I have found in David the son of Jesse a man after my heart, who will do all my will.'" (Acts 13:22)

[41] The LORD swore to David a sure oath from which he will not turn back: "One of the sons of your body I will set on your throne. If your sons keep my covenant and my testimonies that I shall teach them, their sons also forever shall sit on your throne." (Psalm 132:11,12)

Rehoboam, Solomon's son and successor, rapidly alienated the northern tribes by threatening even more taxation. This caused Jeroboam to lead a revolt, which nominally included 10 of the 12 tribes (1 Kings 12). Only the tribes of Judah and Benjamin remained loyal to Rehoboam. These numbers are somewhat deceiving, however, because much of the tribe of Simeon lived within the territory of Judah and remained with Rehoboam, and many of the priests and Levites moved to Judah after the revolt. The split in the kingdom, the northern part being called Israel and the southern part being called Judah, had a dramatic effect on the balance of power in the region. Not only did the two kingdoms often carry on warfare with each other at some level, but they were less effective at holding the gains that David had made. Subjugated people revolted, and powerful neighbors took their opportunities to grab territory. Israel survived only 200 years after the split, while Judah lasted almost 350 years. Table 8-3 shows the kings of Israel and Judah, as well as important prophets who served during the various kings' reigns. Accounts of the two kingdoms are given in 1 Kings 12–22 and in 2 Kings 1–25. Judah is covered in more detail in 2 Chronicles 10–36.

The new nation of Israel was in religious trouble from its beginning. Jeroboam I decided that he could not risk having his people go to worship the Lord at Jerusalem, lest they gradually be won back to supporting Rehoboam and to dumping him. He was well aware of the fate of Ish-bosheth. He therefore set up two images of calves for his people to worship as their gods, one at Bethel on the way to Jerusalem and one in Dan in the far north. Priests and Levites abandoned the Northern Kingdom rather than serve these idols, so Jeroboam I established a new religious order of priests. The number of people worshiping the Lord steadily dwindled.

The idolatry that Jeroboam I introduced did not lead to the stability in Israel for which he had hoped. His son was overthrown, and eight dynasties ruled Israel during its history as an independent country. Many kings died at the hands of their successors. The fourth dynasty, which came to power after only 45 years of independence, further corrupted Israel by the introduction of Baal worship from Lebanon. In his effort to strengthen his position in a civil war, Omri allied his family to the king of Sidon by marriage (1 Kings 16:31). Soon Omri's daughter-in-law, Jezebel, was queen in Israel, and Baal worship, a fertility cult, became the state religion. The cult spread into Judah through intermarriage with Judah's royal family. Jezebel and her husband, King Ahab, were so wicked that the Lord introduced his final positive tool for managing his people—his prophets. Against Ahab the Lord sent the prophet Elijah.

## TABLE 8-3—The Kings and Prophets

| Years (B.C.) | Israel | Judah | Prophets |
|---|---|---|---|
| 1052 | Saul▲ | Saul | Samuel |
| 1010 | | David▲ | |
| 1003 | David<sup>☞</sup> | " | Nathan |
| 970 | Solomon<sup>☞</sup> | Solomon | |
| 930 | Jeroboam I▲ | Rehoboam | Ahijah, Shemiah |
| 913 | " | Abijah | |
| 910 | " | Asa | |
| 909 | Nadab | " | |
| 908 | Baasha▲ | " | Jehu (son of Hanani) |
| 886 | Elah | " | |
| 885 | Zimri▲ | " | |
| 885-880 | Tibni* | " | |
| 885 | Omri▲ | " | |
| 874 | Ahab | " | Elijah |
| 872 | " | Jehoshaphat | Elijah, Micaiah |
| 853 | Ahaziah | " | Elijah |
| 852 | Joram | " | Elisha |
| 848 | " | Jehoram | Elisha, Obadiah<sup>☞</sup> |
| 841 | " | Ahaziah | " |
| 841 | Jehu▲ | Athaliah● | Elisha, Joel<sup>☞</sup> |
| 835 | " | Joash | Elisha, Zechariah<sup>☞</sup> |
| 812 | Jehoahaz | " | " |
| 797 | Jehoash | Amaziah | " |
| 795 | Jeroboam II | " | Hosea<sup>☞</sup>, Amos<sup>☞</sup>, Zechariah |
| 791 | " | Uzziah | Hosea, Jonah<sup>☞</sup>, Zechariah |
| 753 | Zachariah | " | " |
| 752 | Shallum▲ | " | " |
| 752 | Menahem▲ | " | " |
| 741 | Pekahiah | " | " |
| 740 | Pekah▲ | " | Hosea, Oded |
| 739 | " | Jotham | Hosea, Isaiah<sup>☞</sup> |
| 732 | Hoshea | Ahaz | Hosea, Isaiah, Micah<sup>☞</sup> |
| 728 | " | Hezekiah | Isaiah, Micah |
| 723 | Assyria exile | " | " |

**Key:**   ▲ 1st of a dynasty    <sup>☞</sup> Biblical author    * Rival king    ● Usurper

**Note:** Sometimes sons became kings while their fathers still reigned,
making some dates approximate.

| TABLE 8-3—The Kings and Prophets *continued* | | | |
|---|---|---|---|
| **Years (b.c.)** | **Israel** | **Judah** | **Prophets** |
| 723 | Assyria exile | Hezekiah | Isaiah, Micah |
| 699 | | Manasseh | Nahum<sup>∞</sup> |
| 643 | | Amon | " |
| 640 | | Josiah | Jeremiah<sup>∞</sup>, Zephaniah<sup>∞</sup>, Habakkuk<sup>∞</sup>, Huldah |
| 609 | | Jehoahaz | " |
| | | Jehoiakim | Jeremiah, Daniel<sup>∞</sup>, Ezekiel<sup>∞</sup>, Uriah, Hanania |
| 598 | | Jehoiachin | Jeremiah, Daniel, Ezekiel |
| | | Zedekiah | " |
| 586 | | Babylon exile | " |
| After return from exile | | | Malachi<sup>∞</sup> |

**Key:**  ▲ 1st of a dynasty   ∞ Biblical author   * Rival king   ● Usurper

**Note:** Sometimes sons became kings while their fathers still reigned, making some dates approximate.

In Judah the political situation was more stable. Except for a six-year interlude when Omri's granddaughter Athaliah seized the throne (2 Kings 11:1-3), Judah was ruled by descendants of David, as the Lord had promised David. The religious situation in the Southern Kingdom, however, was not nearly so positive. Some kings followed the Lord strongly, some partially, and a few not at all. Many of the people practiced idolatry at some level or switched back and forth to worship whatever god was popular at the moment. Even when the kings of Judah followed the Lord, they often did not attempt to suppress idol worship (2 Kings 15:34,35),[42] fearing the resistance of the people who could desert across the northern border into Israel (Jeremiah 44:15-19). As first Assyria and then Babylon grew in power, the pressure to conform to the practices in use in the neighboring countries also grew, and eventually meaningful worship of the Lord became rare even in Judah (Isaiah 29:13).[43]

---

[42] [Jotham] did what was right in the eyes of the LORD, according to all that his father Uzziah had done. Nevertheless, the high places were not removed. The people still sacrificed and made offerings on the high places. (2 Kings 15:34,35)

[43] The Lord said: "Because this people draw near with their mouth and honor me with their lips, while their hearts are far from me, and their fear [worship] of me is a commandment taught by men." (Isaiah 29:13)

The kings who ruled in Israel and Judah, beginning with Solomon, failed to keep their countries free from entanglements with the pagan nations that surrounded them. In the Northern Kingdom, marriage was used to form alliances with surrounding nations. With the worship of the Lord already diminished greatly by the calf idols of Jeroboam I, pagan customs overran the country at all levels. The struggles for power were frequently as bloody as those in the adjacent pagan nations. Judah fought the influence of its pagan neighbors more effectively, but the desire of the people for the "good life" led to increased trade, including the purchase and manufacture of idols. Pagan gods were less demanding than the Lord and offered solutions to problems, such as unwanted children, that the Lord would not tolerate (Leviticus 18:21).[44] The rule of the kings did not keep the people faithful to the Mosaic covenant and often merely encouraged them to transgress it. The lesson of "trust [not] in princes" (Psalm 118:9) can well be drawn from the sorry history of Israel and Judah.

## The Israelites and the prophets

The Lord's next effort to repair the covenant relationship between himself and his chosen people was his sending of prophets to call the people of Israel and Judah to repentance. Prophets were people, generally men, who were sent with specific messages from the Lord, even though they might not have been part of the priestly clan. While prophets had played a minor role in Israel and Judah throughout its history, their role increased dramatically with the appearance of Elijah the Tishbite. With paganism running rampant and Baal worship promoted by the royal family in the Northern Kingdom, Elijah got their attention by calling down the power of the Lord upon them (1 Kings 17:1).[45] His ominous prefix of "by my word" signaled the intervention of the Lord in ways that Israel had not seen since the time of Joshua. Three and a half years of drought, fire falling from heaven upon a sacrifice, and fire falling to consume soldiers who came to seize Elijah all showed that he was a man on a mission from the Lord and was not to be contradicted. He and his successor Elisha got attention in Israel, but they did not change many hearts for very long.

Some prophets were sent by the Lord to the Northern Kingdom, but many more were sent to Judah as time passed. The early prophets directed

---

[44]"You shall not give any of your children to offer them to Molech, and so profane the name of your God: I am the LORD." (Leviticus 18:21) (Molech worship involved child sacrifice.)

[45]Now Elijah the Tishbite, of Tishbe in Gilead, said to Ahab, "As the LORD, the God of Israel, lives, before whom I stand, there shall be neither dew nor rain these years, except by my word." (1 Kings 17:1)

their messages primarily orally to the rulers. Later the prophets began writing their words onto scrolls so that the people as well as the rulers would be aware of the words of the Lord (Jeremiah 36:2). Unlike the Mosaic covenant, the prophets did not introduce new rules for the people to obey or new sacrifices for the people to offer. Quite the contrary, the prophets declared the Lord's wrath on those people who did not keep the Lord's covenant and even on those who did the outward actions but without a sincere love for the Lord in their hearts (Isaiah 1:11-17).[46] They also taught the people about the Lord's love for them and his willingness to forgive the sins of the penitent (Isaiah 1:18).[47] They gave additional details concerning the Savior of humankind whom the Lord had promised Adam and Eve that he would send (Micah 5:2).[48]

The prophets were the point men for the Lord, and they were generally not well liked, even if some people and rulers did fear them because of their message. In fact, "good times" prophets were frequently there to contradict them and say, "All will be well" (Jeremiah 6:14).[49] The genuine prophets were hated because they called for repentance and because they promised the Lord's wrath on the nations if the people did not repent. They spoke of captivity and of only a remnant being saved (Isaiah 10:22).[50] They promised a Savior who didn't sound like he would have what it would take to remake the world as they wanted it remade (Isaiah 52:13–53:12). The Lord was not surprised. In fact, he told the prophets to expect to be rejected because people did not want to hear the truth (Ezekiel 2:5).[51] They did not want to repent of their sins and repudiate their self-centeredness. Because they didn't listen to the prophets, the Lord fulfilled the prophecies by first destroying Israel at the hands of the Assyrians and then Judah at the hands of the Babylonians. The Lord would not let himself be mocked by his chosen people of the Old Testament, and he will not let himself be mocked by Christians today

---

[46] The Latin phrase *ex opere operato* is used by theologians to describe trying to gain merit by performing rites even without faith. It is a theological error practiced by both the Roman Catholic and Eastern Orthodox churches.

[47] "Come now, let us reason together," says the LORD, "though your sins are like scarlet, they shall be as white as snow; though they are red like crimson, they shall become like wool." (Isaiah 1:18)

[48] But you, O Bethlehem Ephrathah, who are the least among the clans of Judah, from you shall come forth for me one who is to be ruler in Israel, whose coming forth is from of old, from ancient days. (Micah 5:2)

[49] [The LORD said,] "They [prophets and priests] have [bound the fracture] of my people lightly, saying, 'Peace, peace,' when there is no peace." (Jeremiah 6:14)

[50] Though your people Israel be as the sand of the sea, only a remnant of them will return. (Isaiah 10:22)

[51] [The LORD said,] "Whether they [the Jews] hear or refuse to hear (for they are a rebellious house) they will know that a prophet has been among them." (Ezekiel 2:5)

(Galatians 6:7,8).[52] That is a lesson he teaches for our learning as well as it was a lesson for the learning of his people in Canaan. To address their continued unfaithfulness, the Lord still had one more lesson to teach his Old Testament flock.

### Israel during the silent period

In 586 B.C., what was left of the kingdom of Judah was taken into captivity in Babylon. It had been weakened over the years by incursions of its neighbors and had been reduced in geographical size and population. Three times the Babylonians deported some of the people eastward, and the third time they left almost no one behind. Those who remained mostly fled to Egypt, and Judah was no more. For 70 years the people remained in the homeland of the Babylonians until Babylon was defeated by the Medes and the Persians. Eventually, the Persian king Cyrus allowed the Israelites to return to Canaan and rebuild Jerusalem, but only a fraction of the people decided it was worth their effort. Most disappeared through assimilation into other cultures, although some Jewish communities continued to exist in Iraq for many centuries.

Those who returned found a changed landscape. It was no longer "a land flowing with milk and honey" as it had been when the Israelites first saw it (Exodus 3:8). Decades of neglect and the rubble of destroyed buildings were not a welcoming sight (Jeremiah 9:10,11). Other peoples who had infiltrated into the area were not eager to see the Jews, as they were then called, returning and rebuilding anything. Several leaders such as Zerubbabel, Nehemiah, and Ezra pushed the rebuilding forward, but it was slow and often disputed. More disturbing to faithful followers of the Lord was that some of the returning people intermarried with the local peoples and made no effort to keep themselves separate and ceremonially clean. The struggle of the returning remnant to faithfully serve the Lord had begun.

In biblical terms, the struggle was fought in silence, with no additional words from the Lord to proclaim his faithfulness to his people. After Malachi, there were no more prophets to call the people back to the Lord for four hundred years. The people were without king or prophet. Again, it fell to the priesthood to keep the people faithful. During this period, political efforts were made to free the Jews from the Greeks who ruled in both Egypt and Syria. There was a spiritual revival by groups, such as the Pharisees and the

---

[52]Do not be deceived: God is not mocked, for whatever one sows, that will he also reap. For the one who sows to his own flesh will from the flesh reap corruption, but the one who sows to the Spirit will from the Spirit reap eternal life. (Galatians 6:7,8)

Essenes, who wanted to increase religious piety, mostly through expanding the demands of the law or through Spartan living. The priests themselves became more political and began to be more open to the ways of the Greeks and the Romans. Finally, the Romans occupied Canaan, then called Palestine, and installed the worst thing the Jews could imagine, an Edomite king named Herod to rule them (Matthew 2:1).[53]

The Lord's lessons for his Old Testament people were complete. He had shown them that no matter what he did for them and no matter how he treated them, they would fail to live up to the Mosaic covenant he had graciously given to them. They would break it, they would ignore it, and they would pervert it. Priests, kings, and prophets had all failed to keep the people faithful. Despite this, the Lord had remained faithful to his people and his covenants. The people could not produce the obedience that was needed to please the Lord because it was something beyond what sinful humans could do. They needed a Priest, a Prophet, and a King only the Lord could supply. In the process of teaching his lessons, the Lord had set the stage (which is the world) in the play (which is human history) for his central act. The "fullness of time had come" for the promised Savior to enter the scene (Galatians 4:4,5).[54]

---

[53]Edomites were the descendants of Esau, Jacob's brother, over whom the Israelites had ruled for many years. There had long been animosity between the two peoples. In blessing his son Judah, Jacob said that the office of ruler would not depart from his descendants until the real Ruler came. With the throne no longer in the hands of the descendants of Judah, it was time for the "bringer of peace" [Hebrew] to come and claim his position. (Genesis 49:10)

[54]When the fullness of time had come, God sent forth his Son, born of a woman, born under the law, to redeem those who were under the law, so that we might receive adoption as sons. (Galatians 4:4,5)

CHAPTER 9

# The Savior

How would the Lord accomplish his rescue of the world? What would he do? Throughout the Old Testament accounts, humankind's situation did not improve. At the national level, empire replaced empire in the world, and little changed. Nations that started out with high purposes soon fell into moral bankruptcy. Hittites, Egyptians, Assyrians, Babylonians, Persians, Greeks, and Romans all rose to power and, after a few centuries, proved inadequate to establish lasting dominance and moral governments. Cruelty and corruption were rampant in even the best of times, and wars were frequent and bloody. These things were true through the time of Caesar Augustus. They have continued to be true down to our time, and there is no sign it will ever be different. The Lord did not choose to bring salvation using a new earthly kingdom (Psalm 118:8,9).[1]

At the personal level, profound evil was also evident. The Lord's chosen people, the Israelites, who should have become the cream of the moral crop, failed to live up to God's covenant, even with the help of the priests, kings, and prophets sent by the Lord to guide them (2 Chronicles 36:14-16).[2] The

---

[1] It is better to take refuge in the Lord than to trust in man. It is better to take refuge in the Lord than to trust in princes. (Psalm 118:8,9)

[2] All the officers of the priests and the people likewise were exceedingly unfaithful, following all the abominations of the nations. And they polluted the house of the Lord that he had made holy in Jerusalem. The Lord, the God of their fathers, sent [word] to them persistently by his messengers, because he had compassion on his people and on his dwelling place. But they kept mocking the messengers of God, despising his words and scoffing at his prophets, until the wrath of the Lord rose against his people, until there was no remedy. (2 Chronicles 36:14-16)

pillars of the Lord's Old Testament people—men like Noah, Abraham, Jacob, Moses, David, Solomon, and Hezekiah—fell short of the obedience that the Lord demanded. They could not save themselves from God's judgment, much less anyone else. The total depravity that spread through the human race because of the first sin of Adam and Eve meant that no one could stand before the Lord without incurring his wrath (Genesis 6:12).[3] Relying on sinful people was not the Lord's answer to this situation. Unless he himself provided a way to address humankind's sin-caused problems, the evils of history would merely repeat themselves under the names of different people, different nations, and different eras. The Lord had allowed his people to think about this situation during the four hundred years of silence when he sent no prophets. He had promised Adam and Eve a deliverer (Genesis 3:15), but where was this deliverer? Had the Lord lost interest? Had he forgotten? Had he disappeared?

## The coming of the Savior

The Lord had done none of the above. He was waiting until his time was right (Galatians 4:4,5).[4] Then the Lord swung into action in a way that surprised those who waited faithfully for his deliverance and befuddled those who wanted a Savior only under their own terms. He did it according to the prophecies that he had given his people (Matthew 1:22),[5] but he did not do it in the way that his people had expected. He did not create a grand sequel to the life of Moses or David or Elijah, with divine justice for the unbelievers and great signs in the heavens. He instead worked through the humble stations of common people so that all people would see that he cared for everyone, not just for those with special gifts or great accomplishments. He started with an aged childless couple, a virgin, and a cattle stall to change the destiny of humankind. Then he sent his own divine Son to become a humble man.

The Lord had told the Israelites what was to come so that they could recognize the unfolding of the plan, if only they had bothered to look. First there was to be the "messenger in the power of Elijah" (Malachi 4:5,6)[6] who would alert the world to the arrival of the Savior. To fulfill that prophecy, the Lord

---

[3] God saw the earth, and behold, it was corrupt, for all flesh had corrupted their way on the earth. (Genesis 6:12)

[4] When the fullness of time had come, God sent forth his Son, born of a woman, born under the law, to redeem those who were under the law, so that we might receive adoption as sons. (Galatians 4:4,5)

[5] All this took place to fulfill what the Lord had spoken by the prophet. (Matthew 1:22)

[6] [The LORD said,] "Behold, I will send you Elijah the prophet before the great and awesome day of the LORD comes. And he will turn the hearts of fathers to their children and the hearts of children to their fathers, lest I come and strike the land with a decree of utter destruction." (Malachi 4:5,6)

chose an old priest named Zechariah and his childless wife, Elizabeth, who was past the time of producing offspring, and he promised them a son who would call the world to repentance (Luke 1:5-25). And so it was—a miracle. After initial skepticism, there was great joy. Their son became John the Baptizer,[7] who dressed in the wilderness prophet garb of Elijah and preached a message of repentance and preparation for the promised Savior (Luke 3:1-20). He caused quite a stir in a world dominated by the Roman and Greek cultures, and for his efforts he was killed like so many of the Old Testament prophets (Mark 6:21-29).

The Lord selected as mother for the Savior an engaged virgin named Miriam (called Mary in English) and made her pregnant by direct divine action—another miracle (Luke 1:26-38). This did not cause nearly the same level of joy experienced by Elizabeth. While Mary accepted the role the Lord had planned for her, it was not an easy assignment. She was probably still a teenager. How would she explain the pregnancy to her intended husband, Joseph, and the people who knew her in Nazareth? Would they believe that an angel had appeared to her and that God had made her pregnant? How many people today would believe their daughter if she said something like that? The prescribed punishment for an engaged woman becoming pregnant by someone other than her betrothed was to be stoned to death (Deuteronomy 22:23,24).[8] Divine intervention was needed to explain the situation to her fiancé (Matthew 1:20-23). We can easily imagine the gossip. It is small wonder that Mary headed off to spend some time away from Nazareth with her cousin Elizabeth (Luke 1:39-45). A virgin birth was an announced part of the Lord's plan, however, and so it had to be (Isaiah 7:14).[9]

The place of the birth had also been specified by the prophets. The Savior was to be born in Bethlehem of Judea[10] (Micah 5:2).[11] In addition

---

[7]This man named John is generally referred to as "John the Baptist" in English books, but that title misrepresents him. He was a "baptizer," not someone just in favor of Baptism or someone who believed the doctrines of the Baptist Church. He will therefore be called John the Baptizer in this book to accurately reflect the Greek text.

[8][The Lord said,] "If there is a betrothed virgin, and a man meets her in the city and lies with her, then you shall bring them both out to the gate of that city, and you shall stone them to death with stones, the young woman because she did not cry for help though she was in the city, and the man because he violated his neighbor's wife. So you shall purge the evil from your midst." (Deuteronomy 22:23,24)

[9]Therefore the Lord himself will give you a sign. Behold, the virgin shall conceive and bear a son, and shall call his name Immanuel. (Isaiah 7:14)

[10]Judea was similar in size and location to the nation of Judah discussed in chapter 8.

[11]You, O Bethlehem Ephrathah, who are [least] among the thousands of Judah, from you shall come forth for me One who is to be ruler in Israel, whose coming forth is from of old, from ancient days. (Micah 5:2)

to being born of a virgin, the promised Savior was to be of the lineage of King David (Matthew 22:41,42),[12] and Bethlehem was David's hometown (1 Samuel 16:1).[13] The Lord used a Roman census to cause Joseph and Mary, who were both descendants of David, to travel from Nazareth to Bethlehem (Luke 2:1-5). Perhaps he also used the leverage of one of the three Jewish pilgrimage holidays (Exodus 23:17)[14] in nearby Jerusalem to fix the time when the journey was made. In Bethlehem, filled with pilgrims for the census and/or for activities in Jerusalem, Joseph and Mary were forced to find shelter in animal quarters (Luke 2:7).[15] It was not uncommon for poorer people in Palestine to do this while traveling in the summer months when the animals were pastured away from the village, but it shows the lack of fanfare the birth of the Savior would have received had the Lord not intervened.

The promised Savior was given the personal name "Jesus" at the direction of the Lord (Matthew 1:21).[16] Jesus, which is the same as the Hebrew name Joshua, means "the LORD saves." Isaiah had prophesied that the Savior would be "Immanuel," meaning "God with us" (Isaiah 7:14), because he truly is God. Jesus is also called the Christ, which is the Greek word for the Hebrew "Messiah," meaning "the anointed one" (John 1:41).[17] Together these names and titles help us understand who the Savior is.

Outside of Bethlehem, shepherds were tending sheep during the night. It was a job that David himself had done in those hills. The Lord sent a host of angels to tell the shepherds of his fulfillment of his prophecy (Luke 2:8-20). Once again, an air of disbelief surrounded the story that the shepherds told to the people whom they met to explain why they had left their sheep to come into town. Jesus was circumcised on the eighth day (Luke 2:21), as were all Jewish boys, thereby being formally placed under the Law. He was stepping into the place of humankind as a member of humankind.

---

[12] Now while the Pharisees were gathered together, Jesus asked them a question, saying, "What do you think about the Christ? Whose son is he?" They said to him, "The son of David." (Matthew 22:41,42)

[13] [The LORD said,] "Fill your horn with oil, and go. I will send you to Jesse the Bethlehemite, for I have provided for myself a king among his sons." (1 Samuel 16:1)

[14] [The LORD said,] "Three times in the year shall all your males appear before the Lord God." (Exodus 23:17)

[15] She [Mary] gave birth to her firstborn son and wrapped him in swaddling cloths and laid him in a manger, because there was no place for them in the inn. (Luke 2:7)

[16] [An angel of the Lord said,] "She [Mary] will bear a son, and you [Joseph] shall call his name Jesus, for he will save his people from their sins." (Matthew 1:21)

[17] He [Andrew, Simon Peter's brother] first found his own brother Simon and said to him, "We have found the Messiah" (which means Christ). (John 1:41)

When Mary and her family went to the temple in Jerusalem for her purification, several old seers recognized the child through special revelation from the Lord, but otherwise the Savior's presence caused little stir (Luke 2:22-38). When magi (stargazers) from farther east came in response to a celestial observation that they had made and that they related to the house of Judah, they were surprised to find that no one in Jerusalem knew of or seemed to care about the important birth of a new king (Matthew 2:1-12). While the religious leaders knew the appropriate scriptural reference, they did not take it seriously enough to check it out. Only Herod, the Edomite king who was paranoid about losing his throne, was interested in the tale of the stargazers and followed up with subterfuge and murder to guard his interests (Matthew 2:16-18). After presenting their gifts to the new king, the stargazers left, and Joseph fled with his family to Egypt (Matthew 2:13-15).

Jesus' early life is not discussed in detail in the Bible. The only incident mentioned after his return from Egypt to Nazareth is his remaining in the temple at age 12 after his parents departed for home (Luke 2:41-51). Stories about Jesus' youth written later contain many strange tales and are part of what is called the New Testament Apocrypha.[18] They were not recognized as being historical by the early church fathers. The Lord wants his church to focus on his ministry, not his childhood.

Jesus began his ministry soon after John the Baptizer had begun his, because Jesus was about six months younger than John. As was typical in Jewish society, they started their ministries on reaching age 30, the age at which temple service began for the priests (Numbers 4:1-3). John preached repentance and baptized people in the Jordan (Matthew 3:1-12). He soon was attracting people from Judea and even from Jerusalem, but the religious leaders were not pleased with what they heard. They were interested in externals, and John preached about changes in their hearts and actions. Jesus came to John to be baptized, marking the official start of his ministry (Matthew 3:13-17). Jesus then went into the wilderness in order to fast for 40 days and nights and to be tempted by Satan (Matthew 4:1-11). Although Jesus was tempted throughout all his ministry, he allowed himself to be tempted early under adverse conditions to draw a line against Satan, thereby showing that he would be a faithful servant of the Lord and replacing the unfaithful service of Adam and Eve, who early fell for Satan's lies. In dealing with Satan, Jesus always returned for authoritative support to the Old Testament Scriptures, the very words that the Lord had given to humanity through his chosen writers.

---

[18] *The Lost Books of the Bible* (New York: Bell Publishing Company, 1979).

## Jesus' ministry—message of repentance

If there is anything about Jesus that is commonly misunderstood, it is his ministry, and it is misunderstood in numerous ways. People love to reshape his ministry to read into it their own agendas rather than try to understand what he did in terms of who he was. Jesus was God (John 10:30,33).[19] He was man (Galatians 4:4).[20] He came at a specific point in history (Luke 2:1,2).[21] He was a first-century rabbi (Mark 11:21).[22] He had a mission to accomplish (Luke 19:10).[23] He needed to reveal himself appropriately and to complete his mission. The four gospels of the New Testament—Matthew, Mark, Luke, and John—must be viewed from this perspective to gain an understanding of Jesus' ministry that is consistent with the rest of the Bible.

The center of Jesus' ministry was his message. The first part of that message was this: "I have not come to call the righteous but sinners to repentance" (Luke 5:32). Because everyone was a sinner, Jesus wanted to reach everyone with the message of repentance. Yet not everyone realized they were sinners. The Jewish religious leaders—scribes, lawyers, Pharisees, and Sadducees—had worked to undermine the people's understanding of the message of the Old Testament Scriptures. The Pharisees taught that one could become righteous by keeping not only the rules of the Old Testament but also the rules that they had devised for a more devout life. Such people did not want to hear that they were sinners. The Sadducees had gone the other way and reduced the Bible to the ceremonies of the Mosaic Law. They taught that if one offered the sacrifices and performed the rites, then one was under no further obligation. The scribes taught rules, and the lawyers speculated on obscure cases. All these leaders saw Jesus' message, as they had seen the message of repentance preached by John the Baptizer, as an attack on their teachings and way of life. They believed they were righteous in their lives and therefore did not need to repent.

It was not only the religious leaders who had trouble with the message of repentance. The common people of Galilee often came out to hear Jesus

---

[19][Jesus said,] "I and the Father are one." . . . The Jews answered him, "It is not for a good work that we are going to stone you but for blasphemy, because you, being a man, make yourself God." (John 10:30,33)

[20]When the fullness of time had come, God sent forth his Son, born of a woman, born under the law. (Galatians 4:4)

[21]In those days a decree went out from Caesar Augustus that all the world should be registered. This was the first registration when Quirinius was governor of Syria. (Luke 2:1,2)

[22]And Peter remembered and said to him [Jesus], "Rabbi, look! The fig tree that you cursed has withered." (Mark 11:21)

[23][Jesus said,] "The Son of Man came to seek and to save the lost." (Luke 19:10)

speak, but most did not want to repent either. Jesus declared that the Lord's wrath would fall upon them for their unbelief (Matthew 11:20-24). When he got specific about his teachings and the life of repentance, many did not want to continue to learn (John 6:60).[24] He noted that while he would reach out to many with his message, few would believe it (Matthew 22:14).[25] He particularly grieved over Jerusalem, the city where the Lord had chosen to put his name, that its people refused his message (Matthew 23:37).[26] It is because of the determined refusal of the people to repent that Jesus spoke more than any other biblical figure about people being condemned to eternal punishment in hell.

Jesus emphasized the issue of the life of repentance in his Sermon on the Mount. He told his hearers that "unless your righteousness exceeds that of the scribes and Pharisees, you cannot be saved" (Matthew 5:20). But how was that possible? The Pharisees were the best of the best; the type of people one might love to have as a neighbor. Did Jesus have yet more onerous regulations they would have to follow to gain God's favor? No, quite the contrary. He was telling them that there was no way they could gain the righteousness they needed for their salvation by their own efforts. If the Pharisees with all their rules and strivings couldn't, how could they? The righteousness that would allow them to obtain heaven and please God would have to come from another source. That was the second part of his message.

Jesus showed the difference in the two forms of righteousness in the parable of the Pharisee and the tax collector (Luke 18:9-14). The Pharisees were viewed as the most righteous people in Jewish society. When the Pharisee entered the temple, he naturally thought he had something to show the Lord. He could call God's attention to how he had kept God's law and gone beyond. How could such righteousness not be recognized by the Lord? But it wasn't recognized, because the Pharisee had a proud heart that relied on himself. The tax collectors were the scum of Jewish society because they worked for the hated Romans and were frequently dishonest in the amount of taxes they collected. The tax collector in the temple had nothing to offer the Lord, so all he could do was plead for mercy. And the Lord showed him mercy, declaring him justified, that is, righteous in God's sight. Was the

---

[24]When many of his [Jesus'] disciples heard it, they said, "This is a hard saying; who can listen to it?" (John 6:60)

[25][Jesus said,] "Many are called, but few are chosen." (Matthew 22:14)

[26][Jesus said,] "O Jerusalem, Jerusalem, the city that kills the prophets and stones those who are sent to it! How often would I have gathered your children together as a hen gathers her brood under her wings, and you were not willing!" (Matthew 23:37)

point of the parable that being humble before the Lord was all that is necessary to please him and gain his favor? No, humility can also be a human work
and therefore is no better than a Pharisee's intense efforts.

The gospel of John states the second part of Jesus' message very clearly.
"Whoever believes in the Son has eternal life; whoever does not believe the
Son shall not see life, but the wrath of God remains on him" (John 3:36). Salvation does not depend on the righteousness of deeds but on what the Son of
God, that is, Jesus Christ, gives to those who believe in him. What the Son of
God gives is the forgiveness of sins and reconciliation with God (2 Corinthians 5:18,19).[27] Martin Luther labeled this a "foreign righteousness" because
it does not come through anything we do or are but is purely a gift from
the Lord (Ephesians 2:8,9).[28] When a paralyzed man was brought to Jesus,
he forgave him his sins before he healed him of his physical ailment (Matthew 9:1-7). The sins the man had committed were much more important
in the sight of the Lord, so Jesus addressed that issue first. This irritated the
Pharisees because they thought that only God could forgive sins, and then
only after sufficient works of obedience and after the appropriate sacrifices
to show God that the person had really repented. Jesus could see repentance
in the heart and did not require a quid pro quo payment (i.e., a payment for
goods received) to forgive sins.

As Jesus neared the end of his ministry, he emphasized that while the
righteousness that gives salvation is free, it is not cheap. He told his followers, "If anyone would come after me, let him deny himself and take up his
cross and follow me. For whoever would save his life will lose it, but whoever
loses his life for my sake will find it. For what will it profit a man if he gains
the whole world and forfeits his soul? Or what shall a man give in return for
his soul?" (Matthew 16:24-26). The righteousness that brings salvation will
also cause changes in the heart and in the actions of the believer in this life.
Once one has received the righteousness granted through Christ, one cannot continue to love the ways of the world and still continue to retain that
righteousness. The love for the Lord and the service of one's fellow people
must replace self-centeredness in the life of the believer.

This message of sin, repentance, free salvation, and the Christian life will
be discussed in detail in section IV of this book. It is a message that is at

---

[27] All this is from God, who through Christ reconciled us to himself and gave us the ministry of reconciliation; that is, in Christ God was reconciling the world to himself, not counting their trespasses
against them, and entrusting to us the message of reconciliation. (2 Corinthians 5:18,19)

[28] By grace you [the readers] have been saved through faith. And this is not your own doing; it is the gift
of God, not a result of works, so that no one may boast. (Ephesians 2:8,9)

variance to the natural way in which people think, so it is not surprising that most people rejected Jesus' message, both among the rich and the poor. They came to hear him, to see him perform miracles, to hopefully get a free meal, and to delight in that they had possibly seen a prophet of the Lord up close (John 4:48).[29] To believe him, however, was a different matter. Believing meant facing the reality of their sinful lives and changing their priorities. Although Jesus called to all, regardless of their past sins or past attitudes toward the Lord (Matthew 9:10),[30] only a few believed. As Jesus pointed out, the way to salvation is narrow (Matthew 7:13,14).[31]

## Jesus' ministry—miracles

When the Lord wanted to get people's attention, he gave his spokesmen the ability to do miracles. Moses, Elijah, and Elisha are examples of prophets who were given limited power to perform miracles. On the other hand, Jesus had unlimited power to perform miracles whenever he desired in his ministry. The ones recorded in the Bible appear in Table 9-1. The prophet Isaiah said that this would be a sign of the Messiah (Isaiah 42:6,7),[32] and Jesus fulfilled that prophecy and thereby showed his divinity. He healed the sick, fed the hungry, raised the dead, and drove out demons (Matthew 11:4,5).[33] Obviously, this attracted people's attention, and many came to see him. If nothing else, it was good entertainment in a backwater of the Roman Empire. Yet the reader must be careful not to read more into the miracles than Scripture says about them. While Jesus is recorded several times as healing many sick people, these still were only a small proportion of the sick in Palestine. There are only two accounts of him feeding the hungry and only three accounts of him raising people from the dead. As the Lord God, he could have healed all the sick in the world, or at least in Pal-

---

[29]So Jesus said to him [a royal official with a sick son], "Unless you see signs and wonders you will not believe." (John 4:48)

[30]As Jesus reclined at table in the house, behold, many tax collectors and sinners came and were reclining with Jesus and his disciples. (Matthew 9:10)

[31][Jesus said,] "Enter by the narrow gate. For the gate is wide and the way is easy that leads to destruction, and those who enter by it are many. For the gate is narrow and the way is hard that leads to life, and those who find it are few." (Matthew 7:13,14)

[32]"I am the LORD; I have called you [the LORD's Servant = Christ] in righteousness; I will take you by the hand and keep you; I will give you as a covenant for the people, a light for the nations, to open the eyes that are blind, to bring out the prisoners from the dungeon, from the prison those who sit in darkness." (Isaiah 42:6,7)

[33]Jesus answered them, "Go and tell John what you hear and see: the blind receive their sight and the lame walk, lepers are cleansed and the deaf hear, and the dead are raised up, and the poor have good news preached to them." (Matthew 11:4,5)

estine, but he didn't. He could have commanded the fields and vineyards to bear bountiful fruit indefinitely, but he didn't. He could have started organizations to help the less fortunate, but he didn't do that either. While his miracles made the lives of a relatively few people better, they did not change the general status of the population. That was not their purpose.

The purpose of Jesus' miracles was to show people that he was the Servant of the Lord sent to cure their most pressing problem, their sin-infested hearts, and to restore them to spiritual life. Jesus used physical healing to symbolize this. He gave sight to the physically blind while he demonstrated his power to give sight to the spiritually blind (John 9:39).[34] He gave hearing to the physically deaf while he spoke words to give hearing to the spiritually deaf (Matthew 13:15).[35] He cleansed people of the leprosy of the flesh while he preached a message that would heal those who had diseases of the soul (Matthew 9:11,12).[36] He fed the people with bread for their stomachs while his words were bread for their souls (John 6:58).[37]

Some of the miracles had even deeper significance because they involved uncleanness according to the Mosaic Law, as well as physical issues. For example, a woman who had been suffering from bleeding for 12 years snuck up to Jesus to touch his cloak, desiring to be healed (Luke 8:43-48). For her to enter a crowd was forbidden, and touching Jesus would have made him unclean. She didn't want to be noticed, even after Jesus allowed her to be cured by touching him and thereby also removed her uncleanness. In the same way, Jesus must have shocked the people of Nain when he walked up and touched the bier of a corpse, because that would have made him, a rabbi, unclean (Luke 7:11-17). Yet when he raised the dead man to life, the cause of uncleanliness was gone. Jesus was showing that he had not only the power to cure the sick and raise the dead but also had the ability to remove the uncleanness of sin that separated humans from the Lord (Revelation 7:14).[38]

---

[34]Jesus said, "For judgment I came into this world, that those who do not see may see, and those who see may become blind." (John 9:39)

[35][Jesus said,] "This people's heart has grown dull, and with their ears they can barely hear, and their eyes they have closed, lest they should see with their eyes and hear with their ears and understand with their heart and turn, and I would heal them." (Matthew 13:15)

[36]When the Pharisees saw this, they said to his disciples, "Why does your teacher eat with tax collectors and sinners?" But when he [Jesus] heard it, he said, "Those who are well have no need of a physician, but those who are sick." (Matthew 9:11,12)

[37][Jesus said,] "This is the bread that came down from heaven, not like the bread the fathers ate, and died. Whoever feeds on this bread will live forever." (John 6:58)

[38]And he [the angel] said to me [apostle John], "These are the ones coming out of the great tribulation. They have washed their robes and made them white in the blood of the Lamb." (Revelation 7:14)

He himself was God, and when the unclean came to him, he made them clean. Removing sin and changing hearts were far greater miracles than multiplying a few loaves of bread to feed many people.

The miracles were a necessary part of Jesus' ministry, but they had limited benefit. Many of the people who saw them did not grasp their spiritual meaning because their hearts had become hardened. They believed that the Mosaic covenant guaranteed them certain benefits from the Lord, even though they did not keep their part of the bargain. They took the physical blessings that had been offered in that covenant as their due as children of Abraham, but they did not want to be concerned about the spiritual condition of their souls. Most of the Jewish people of Jesus' day missed the significance of the miracles because their attention was on themselves, not on the things of God. Sadly, it seems many Christian people today also miss the significance of Jesus' miracles, and for the same reason.

## TABLE 9-1—Recorded Miracles

| Topic | Title | Reference |
|---|---|---|
| Nature control | Water into wine | John 2:1-11 |
| Healing | Demon-possessed in synagogue | Mark 1:21-28; Luke 4:31-37 |
| Nature control | Huge catch of fish | Luke 5:4-11 |
| Healing | Man with leprosy | Matthew 8:1-4; Mark 1:40-44; Luke 5:12-14 |
| Healing | Roman centurion's servant | Matthew 8:5-13; Luke 7:1-10 |
| Healing | Peter's mother-in-law | Matthew 8:14-15; Mark 1:30-31; Luke 4:38-39 |
| Raising dead | Widow's son at Nain | Luke 7:11-17 |
| Nature control | Calming the storm | Matthew 8:23-27; Mark 4:37-41; Luke 8:22-25 |
| Healing | Two men possessed with devils | Matthew 8:28-34; Mark 5:1-15; Luke 8:27-39 |
| Healing | Man with palsy | Matthew 9:2-7; Mark 2:3-12; Luke 5:18-26 |
| Raising dead | Jairus' daughter | Matthew 9:18-26; Mark 5:21-43; Luke 8:40-56 |
| Healing | Woman with bleeding | Matthew 9:20-22; Mark 5:25-34; Luke 8:43-48 |
| Healing | Two blind men | Matthew 9:27-31 |

**Note:** Miracles are listed roughly in the order in which Jesus performed them. However, the four evangelists did not follow strict chronological order, so some may appear out of order.

## TABLE 9-1—Recorded Miracles *continued*

| Topic | Title | Reference |
|---|---|---|
| Healing | Mute, devil-possessed man | Matthew 9:32-33 |
| Healing | Nobleman's son at Capernaum | John 4:46-54 |
| Healing | Man at the pool of Bethesda | John 5:1-15 |
| Nature control | Feeding 5,000 | Matthew 14:14-21; Mark 6:30-44; Luke 9:10-17; John 6:1-14 |
| Nature control | Walking on water | Matthew 14:22-32; Mark 6:47-52; John 6:16-21 |
| Healing | Canaanite woman's daughter | Matthew 15:21-28; Mark 7:24-30 |
| Nature control | Feeding 4,000 | Matthew 15:32-39; Mark 8:1-9 |
| Healing | Blind man at Bethsaida | Mark 8:22-26 |
| Healing | Demon-possessed boy | Matthew 17:14-21; Mark 9:17-29; Luke 9:38-43 |
| Healing | Crippled woman | Luke 13:10-17 |
| Healing | Man with dropsy | Luke 14:1-4 |
| Nature control | Fish with coin | Matthew 17:24-27 |
| Healing | Ten men with leprosy | Luke 17:11-19 |
| Healing | Two blind men | Matthew 20:29-34; Mark 10:46-52; Luke 18:35-43 |
| Healing | Man born blind | John 9:1-41 |
| Nature control | Fig tree withers | Matthew 21:18-22; Mark 11:12-14,20-25 |
| Raising dead | Lazarus | John 11:1-44 |
| Healing | The high priest's servant | Luke 22:50-51 |
| Nature control | Huge catch of fish | John 21:1-11 |

**Note:** Miracles are listed roughly in the order in which Jesus performed them. However, the four evangelists did not follow strict chronological order, so some may appear out of order.

### Jesus' ministry—parables

To many people of his day, the numerous parables that Jesus told were the most perplexing part of his ministry, and they are often misunderstood today. To explain why he told them, he quoted the psalmist Asaph saying, "I will open my mouth in parables; I will utter what has been hidden since the foundation of the world" (Matthew 13:35). The parables were intended to teach spiritual lessons by using examples from the daily life of the people of the first century. Some of the parables are simple analogies or similes that are relatively easy to understand. Others involve deeper truths that take considerable study. Longer parables are listed in Table 9-2, and short parables and analogies are listed in Table 9-3.

Sometimes Jesus used parables to help his listeners understand spiritual things. For example, in the parable of the lost coin (Luke 15:8-10), Jesus teaches the people that souls are valuable to the Lord in the same way that a precious coin would be valuable to someone who only had a few of them. Because he was talking to lower-class people at the time, he wanted to convey to them that they also were valuable to the Lord and his angels. As the woman sought her lost coin, so the Lord through Jesus' ministry was seeking them. In this way, Jesus placed spiritual ideas into a context that even uneducated people could comprehend.

But Jesus also told parables to befuddle his hearers, while leaving them without excuse that they had never heard the gospel message (Matthew 13:13).[39] He did this when his hearers were not interested in the spiritual message because they felt they already knew everything they needed to know about the kingdom of God. He would then take something they should have known and present it in a parable so that they could gain a correct understanding by looking at the truth in a different way. For example, when he told the parable of the sower and the seeds (Mark 4:3-9), he wanted them to realize that simply because they had the Word of God being preached in their midst did not mean that they would all become faithful believers who would bear fruit acceptable to the Lord (2 Corinthians 3:14).[40] This parable was not even grasped by Jesus' disciples, so he had to explain it to them. To those who were self-satisfied with their religious knowledge, he gave no explanation so that the parable would serve as a witness against their hardened hearts that ignored the things of God (John 15:22).[41]

A full understanding of the parables by people today often takes more effort than was required by the people in Jesus' day. For example, when one reads the parable of the good Samaritan (Luke 10:25-37), one needs to know what first-century Jewish lawyers did, certain things about the Jewish ceremonial law, and what the relations were between Jews and Samaritans. All these things would have been known by those who first heard Jesus tell the

---

[39] [Jesus said,] "This is why I speak to them in parables, because seeing they do not see, and hearing they do not hear, nor do they understand." (Matthew 13:13)

[40] Their [the Jewish people's] minds were hardened. For to this day, when they read the old covenant, that same veil remains unlifted, because only through Christ is it taken away. (2 Corinthians 3:14)

[41] [Jesus said,] "If I had not come and spoken to them [the unbelieving Jews], they would not have been guilty of sin, but now they have no excuse for their sin." (John 15:22)

parable, but they are not known by most people today. The lawyer to whom Jesus told the parable could certainly have found good reasons in the ceremonial requirements of the Mosaic Law to justify the actions of the priest and the Levite who avoided helping the injured man. Yet he could not justify their ignoring the broader injunction of the law to love one's neighbor as oneself, which even a semi-pagan Samaritan felt compelled to obey. To learn the lessons that Jesus is teaching in his parables, the modern Christian has to be willing to invest the time needed to study them.

| TABLE 9-2—Major Parables | | |
|---|---|---|
| **Topic** | **Title** | **Reference** |
| Employment | The dishonest manager | Luke 16:1-12 |
| Employment | The generous employer | Matthew 20:1-16 |
| Employment | The master and servant | Luke 17:7-10 |
| Employment | The talents | Matthew 25:14-30; Luke 19:12-27 |
| Employment | The waiting servants | Matthew 24:45-51; Luke 12:42-46 |
| Employment | The wicked tenants | Matthew 21:33-41; Mark 12:1-9; Luke 20:9-16 |
| Hypocrisy | The children in the marketplace | Matthew 11:16-19; Luke 7:31-35 |
| Hypocrisy | The two sons | Matthew 21:28-32 |
| Ingratitude | The unworthy servant | Luke 14:7-11 |
| Ingratitude | The unmerciful servant | Matthew 18:23-35 |
| Ingratitude | The unwilling guests | Matthew 22:1-10; Luke 14:16-24 |
| Ingratitude | The wedding garment | Matthew 22:11-14 |
| Judgment | The barren fig tree | Luke 13:6-9 |
| Judgment | The weeds in the grain | Matthew 13:24-30 |
| Mercy | The good Samaritan | Luke 10:25-37* |
| Mercy | The prodigal son | Luke 15:11-32 |
| Ministry | The shepherd and the thief | John 10:1-18 |
| Ministry | The sower and the seeds | Matthew 13:3-9; Mark 4:3-9; Luke 8:5-8 |

* There is some question whether these are real accounts or parables. Jesus does not call them parables, and some of the literary structures common to Jesus' parables are missing.

| TABLE 9-2—Major Parables *continued* | | |
|---|---|---|
| **Topic** | **Title** | **Reference** |
| Persistence | The importunate neighbor | Luke 11:5-8 |
| Persistence | The persistent widow | Luke 18:1-8 |
| Watchfulness | The cleansed house | Matthew 12:43-45; Luke 11:24-26 |
| Watchfulness | The closed door | Luke 13:24-30 |
| Watchfulness | The doorkeeper | Mark 13:33-37 |
| Watchfulness | The ten virgins | Matthew 25:1-13 |
| Watchfulness | The waiting servants | Mark 13:33-37; Luke 12:35-38 |
| Wisdom/Folly | The Pharisee and the tax collector | Luke 18:9-14 |
| Wisdom/Folly | The rich fool | Luke 12:16-21 |
| Wisdom/Folly | The rich man and Lazarus | Luke 16:19-31* |
| Wisdom/Folly | The wise and foolish builder | Matthew 7:24-27; Luke 6:47-49 |

\* There is some question whether these are real accounts or parables. Jesus does not call them parables, and some of the literary structures common to Jesus' parables are missing.

| TABLE 9-3—Parables, Similes, and Analogies | | |
|---|---|---|
| **Topic** | **Title** | **Reference** |
| Judgment | The discarded salt | Matthew 5:13; Mark 9:50; Luke 14:34-35 |
| Judgment | The sheep and the goats | Matthew 25:31-33 |
| Judgment | The tree and its fruits | Matthew 7:16; Luke 6:43-49 |
| Judgment | The vultures and the carcass | Matthew 24:28; Luke 17:37 |
| Mercy | The son's request | Matthew 7:9-11; Luke 11:11-13 |
| Mercy | The two debtors | Luke 7:41-43 |
| Ministry | The bridegroom's attendants | Matthew 9:15a; Mark 2:18-20; Luke 5:34 |
| Ministry | The doctor and the sick | Matthew 9:12; Mark 2:17; Luke 5:31,32 |
| Ministry | The grain of wheat | John 12:23-26 |
| Ministry | The householder's treasure | Matthew 13:52 |

| Topic | Title | Reference |
|---|---|---|
| Ministry | The lamp | Matthew 5:14-16; Mark 4:21; Luke 8:16 |
| Ministry | The mustard seed | Matthew 13:31,32; Mark 4:30-32; Luke 13:18,19 |
| Ministry | The net | Matthew 13:47-50 |
| Persistence | The hidden treasure | Matthew 13:44 |
| Persistence | The lost coin | Luke 15:8-10 |
| Persistence | The lost sheep | Matthew 18:12-14; Luke 15:4-7 |
| Persistence | The pearl of great price | Matthew 13:45,46 |
| Providence | The birds of heaven | Matthew 6:26; Luke 12:24 |
| Providence | The flowers of the field | Matthew 6:28-30; Luke 12:27,28 |
| Providence | The seed growing unobserved | Mark 4:26-29 |
| Watchfulness | The budding fig tree | Matthew 24:32-35; Mark 13:28-31; Luke 21:19-31 |
| Watchfulness | The leaven | Matthew 13:33; Luke 13:20,21 |
| Watchfulness | The strong man bound | Matthew 12:29; Mark 3:27; Luke 11:21,22 |
| Watchfulness | The thief in the night | Matthew 24:42-44; Luke 12:39,40 |
| Watchfulness | The weather signs | Luke 12:54-56 |
| Wisdom/Folly | The body's lamp | Matthew 6:22,23; Luke 11:34-36 |
| Wisdom/Folly | The defendant | Matthew 5:25,26; Luke 12:57-59 |
| Wisdom/Folly | The divided realm | Mark 3:24-26; Luke 11:17-20 |
| Wisdom/Folly | The patch and the wineskins | Matthew 9:16,17; Mark 2:21,22; Luke 5:36-39 |
| Wisdom/Folly | The tower builder | Luke 14:28-30 |
| Wisdom/Folly | The warring king | Luke 14:31-33 |

TABLE 9-3—Parables, Similes, and Analogies *continued*

## Jesus' ministry—claim of deity

Jesus could have lived peaceably as an unconventional healer and a rustic teacher of morals if it had not been for two things he did. The first was his selective obedience to the "tradition of the elders" (Matthew 15:1,2).[42] This was a set of rules—some of which came from the ceremonial law that was part of the Mosaic covenant and the rest were rules that the Pharisees had drafted as a "hedge" to keep the people from offending the Lord in any way. Collectively, these were burdensome (Matthew 23:4).[43] The original ceremonial law had been given to keep the people separate until the time when the Messiah would come (Deuteronomy 18:15,16),[44] and the Messiah had arrived in the person of Jesus (Hebrews 3:3).[45] The Pharisaic rules were nothing but man-made rituals of the type that the prophet Isaiah had already condemned seven centuries earlier (Isaiah 29:13).[46] Jesus kept these traditions of the elders when they served a useful purpose in his ministry, but he did not let them prevent him from doing good to his fellow Jews (Mark 2:27).[47] This irritated the Pharisees, who felt that the rules were the most important part of the proper worship of the Lord. The Pharisees and their scribes feared that if Jesus' popularity grew, more and more people would abandon the traditions of the elders, and then the Pharisees, who excelled in keeping them, would lose the status that this gave them (John 11:48).[48]

The situation grew more intense when Jesus showed up in Jerusalem at the time of the feasts, because crowds of people would be there to hear him. Perhaps the religious leaders would have tolerated his irritating behavior had he stayed in Galilee, where there was a mixed population of Jews and Gentiles. When he came to Jerusalem, however, he did infuriating things like healing a blind man on the Sabbath (John 9:14) and driving merchants from the temple who had rented space from the religious leaders (Matthew

---

[42]Then Pharisees and scribes came to Jesus from Jerusalem and said, "Why do your disciples break the tradition of the elders?" (Matthew 15:1,2)

[43][Jesus said,] "They [the teachers of the law and the Pharisees] tie up heavy burdens, hard to bear, and lay them on people's shoulders, but they themselves are not willing to move them with their finger." (Matthew 23:4)

[44][Moses said,] "The LORD your God will raise up for you a prophet like me from among you, from your brothers—it is to him you shall listen—just as you desired of the LORD your God at Horeb on the day of the assembly, when you said, 'Let me not hear again the voice of the LORD my God or see this great fire any more, lest I die.'" (Deuteronomy 18:15,16)

[45]Jesus has been counted worthy of more glory than Moses—as much more glory as the builder of a house has more honor than the house itself. (Hebrews 3:3)

[46]The Lord said: "Because this people [the Jews] draw near with their mouth and honor me with their lips, while their hearts are far from me, and their fear of me is only a commandment taught by men." (Isaiah 29:13)

[47]He [Jesus] said to them [the Pharisees], "The Sabbath was made for man, not man for the Sabbath." (Mark 2:27)

[48][The Pharisees and chief priests said,] "If we let him [Jesus] go on like this, everyone will believe in him, and the Romans will come and take away both our place and our nation." (John 11:48)

21:12,13).[49] He was attacking them in their stronghold, and the religious establishment needed to deal with him or lose credibility with both the Jewish people and the Roman authorities. Jesus didn't back down, but he said that he had come "to bring a sword" (Matthew 10:34-39), a division between true and false worshipers of the Lord. He pointed out the inconsistency between the pious words and the less than pious actions of the teachers of the Law. He punctuated these charges with cries of "Scribes! Pharisees! Hypocrites!" (Matthew 23). This was outrageous behavior with which they had to deal. Who was this man who would dare to do such things to the religious leaders?

Who was he indeed? It was precisely in this regard that they could not ignore the second thing Jesus did; he claimed to be the equal of the Lord, that is, God the Father, whom they prided themselves in worshiping. That claim is already staked in the first verse of John's gospel: "In the beginning was the Word" (John 1:1). Jesus was the Son of God, the living Word. He had been with God the Father since before the beginning of the universe and was involved in the creation. John the Baptizer referred to him as "the Son of God" (John 1:32-34). Jesus confronted Nicodemus by telling him that his physical birth as a Jew was not enough to get him into the kingdom of heaven, but he needed to be spiritually reborn through believing in the Son of God. Hearing this would have incensed any Jewish religious leader; it struck at the heart of their belief of having a special arrangement with the Lord through Abraham and through the Mosaic covenant. If they had to repent and repudiate their lives of rules, they would be no better than the Gentiles or the Jewish lowlife. They considered this blasphemy and were convinced that a man who taught such things certainly could not be from God (John 9:16).[50]

The Jewish leaders tried to win the battle by appealing to their heroes of faith, Moses and Abraham. Jesus pointed out that they didn't follow Moses but circumvented his teachings by their own rules (Mark 7:8-13). He quoted Isaiah to condemn them (Isaiah 29:13). He pointed out that Moses had predicted him (Deuteronomy 18:15,16), and his miracles validated his claim (John 10:37,38).[51] He told them to go back and search the Old Testament Scriptures

---

[49] Jesus entered the temple and drove out all who sold and bought in the temple, and he overturned the tables of the money-changers and the seats of those who sold pigeons. He said to them, "It is written, 'My house shall be called a house of prayer,' but you make it a den of robbers." (Matthew 21:12,13)

[50] Some of the Pharisees said, "This man [Jesus] is not from God, for he does not keep the Sabbath." (John 9:16)

[51] [Jesus said,] "If I am not doing the works of my Father, then do not believe me; but if I do them, even though you do not believe me, believe the works, that you may know and understand that the Father is in me and I am in the Father." (John 10:37,38)

because they would find in them prophecies of his coming (John 5:39).[52] Jesus pointed out that they were nothing like their sainted father Abraham (John 8:39,40).[53] Abraham had believed God, but they wanted to kill Jesus because they did not want to hear God's message; therefore, they were not his children. Jesus then claimed to have existed before Abraham (John 8:58,59).[54] At this they were ready to stone him because he had again brought up the issue of his being God. Jesus did not stop his teaching, however, declaring himself to be the Son of God and to be one with God the Father (John 10:30).[55]

## Jesus' passion

After three years of Jesus' ministry, the Jewish religious leaders were at the end of their rope. Jesus had taken his claim that he was "the way" to salvation (John 14:6)[56] to the tax collectors, the prostitutes, the ceremonially unclean, and others engaged in gross sins. He had become well-known in both Judea and Galilee and might even have had some followers in Samaria (John 4:1-42). He had embarrassed the religious leaders, and his existence had almost certainly not escaped Roman attention. The situation was ripe if he was going to begin either a religious or political revolt. Either way, their positions would be threatened. They decided it was time to force Jesus to take unpopular positions and, by taking them, alienate some of his supporters no matter what he said. The Pharisees, the Sadducees, and the Herodians (i.e., King Herod's supporters) all sent people to him with trick questions about such things as the source of his authority (Matthew 21:23-27), paying taxes (Matthew 22:15-22), and marriage in heaven (Matthew 22:23-33), but their strategy failed. His answers further embarrassed them and strengthened his position with the people. The leaders decided they needed to kill him, but how (Matthew 26:3-5)?[57]

The religious leaders had planned to try to capture him after the Passover festival in some isolated place, but they had the good fortune of having one

---

[52] [Jesus said,] "You [the Jews] search the Scriptures because you think that in them you have eternal life; and it is they that bear witness about me." (John 5:39)

[53] They [some Jews] answered him, "Abraham is our father." Jesus said to them, "If you were Abraham's children, you would be doing the works Abraham did, but now you seek to kill me, a Man who has told you the truth that I heard from God. This is not what Abraham did." (John 8:39,40)

[54] Jesus said to them [the Jews], "Truly, truly, I say to you, before Abraham was, I am." So they picked up stones to throw at him, but Jesus hid himself and went out of the temple. (John 8:58,59)

[55] [Jesus said,] "I and the Father are one." (John 10:30)

[56] Jesus said to him [Thomas, his disciple], "I am the way, and the truth, and the life. No one comes to the Father except through me." (John 14:6)

[57] Then the chief priests and the elders of the people gathered in the palace of the high priest, whose name was Caiaphas, and plotted together in order to arrest Jesus by stealth and kill him. But they said, "Not during the feast, lest there be an uproar among the people." (Matthew 26:3-5)

of Jesus' disciples, Judas Iscariot,[58] agree to betray him to them (Matthew 26:14-16). Judas apparently had grown disillusioned with a "Messiah" who wasn't moving toward seizing power, and he decided to make some money on his way out of the group of Jesus' followers. Perhaps he had lost any personal feelings for Jesus, or perhaps he figured Jesus would elude capture as he had done so many times before. Once the plot was developed, Jesus knowingly walked into the trap prepared for him and did not try to escape (Matthew 26:46).[59] Judas became remorseful, which resulted in his committing suicide (Matthew 27:3-5).

Jesus, who had been predicting his capture and death for some time (Luke 18:31-33),[60] had begun his suffering before Judas ever appeared with his mob of temple officers (Luke 22:39-46). He knew what was coming, and he prayed in the Garden of Gethsemane to be released from the suffering or for the strength to endure it. He knew there would be no release, but his human nature groaned under the horror of what he had to do. Once they captured him, the Jewish leaders had to act fast (Matthew 26:57-68). They needed to get him executed before word got out about their actions and violence erupted in Jerusalem, which was packed with a huge number of pilgrims for the Passover festival. They held a secret and brutal nighttime trial, illegal under Jewish law, in order to convict him and then a formal sentencing at dawn to meet the letter of their law (Matthew 27:1,2). Unable to stone him under Roman law, they hustled him to the Roman governor, Pontius Pilate, for a quick death sentence.

Pilate was not eager to give them the verdict they wanted because of the haste with which they were proceeding (Luke 23:1-25). The Jewish leaders were being way too concerned about the welfare of the Roman state, and Jesus was not acting like a typical Jewish firebrand. Pilate was probably suspicious that they were trying to use him to get rid of religious opposition, and he didn't want to create more problems than he was solving. He therefore hustled Jesus off to King Herod, who ruled Galilee but was in Jerusalem for the Passover. Herod returned him just as quickly once he realized that

---

[58] There is a symbolism in biblical names that cannot be ignored. Jesus, who leads the spiritual Israel across the stream of death into the promised land of heaven, is the same name as Joshua, who led the physical Israel across the Jordan into the Promised Land of Canaan. Judas, who betrayed Jesus, is the same name as Judah, the father of the people who rejected Jesus.

[59] [Jesus said,] "Rise, let us be going; see, my betrayer is at hand." (Matthew 26:46)

[60] Taking the twelve, he [Jesus] said to them, "See, we are going up to Jerusalem, and everything that is written about the Son of Man by the prophets will be accomplished. For he will be delivered over to the Gentiles and will be mocked and shamefully treated and spit upon. And after flogging him, they will kill him, and on the third day he will rise." (Luke 18:31-33)

Jesus was not going to do any miracles for him. The interim gave the Jewish leaders time to raise a crowd demanding Jesus' crucifixion. Pilate realized this was a no-win situation (Matthew 27:24),[61] so he sentenced Jesus to death and got him out of the city before things got more complicated.

Yet neither the Jewish leaders nor Pilate were really in control of the situation. Jesus had ridden into Jerusalem the previous Sunday to fulfill the prophecy that the Jewish king would come to his people on a donkey (Zechariah 9:9)[62] and to mark the day before the Passover when the sacrificial lamb was traditionally set apart. Jesus' betrayal and sentencing had also followed prophecies. But the most important part of Jesus' passion, his atoning sacrifice for all humankind, was yet to come. On the day on which Jews sacrificed the Passover lamb, commemorating their deliverance from slavery in Egypt, Jesus was to provide a deliverance from a slavery far worse, the slavery of the human race to sin and death.

On Golgotha, the hill of crucifixion outside the city, prophecies continued to be fulfilled. He was cursed of God by being hung on wood to die (Deuteronomy 21:22,23).[63] He was crucified with the wicked and buried with the rich (Isaiah 53:9). His clothes were distributed and gambled over (Psalm 22:18).[64] None of his bones were broken (Psalm 34:20),[65] but he was pierced by nails and by a spear (Psalm 22:16; Zechariah 12:10). The ordeal was described by Isaiah seven hundred years before it happened when he wrote,

> Behold, my Servant shall act wisely; he shall be high and lifted up, and shall be exalted. As many were astonished at you—his appearance was so marred, beyond human semblance, and his form beyond that of the children of humankind—so shall he sprinkle many nations; kings shall shut their mouths because of him; for that which has not been told them they see, and that which they have not heard they understand. Who has believed what he has heard from us? And to whom has the arm of the Lord been revealed? For he grew up before him like a young plant, and

---

[61]When Pilate saw that he was gaining nothing, but rather that a riot was beginning, he took water and washed his hands before the crowd, saying, "I am innocent of this man's blood; see to it yourselves." (Matthew 27:24)

[62]Rejoice greatly, O daughter of Zion! Shout aloud, O daughter of Jerusalem! Behold, your King is coming to you; righteous and having salvation is he, humble and mounted on a donkey, on a colt, the foal of a donkey. (Zechariah 9:9)

[63][The LORD said,] "If a man has committed a crime punishable by death and he is put to death, and you hang him on a tree, his body shall not remain all night on the tree, but you shall bury him the same day, for a hanged man is cursed by God." (Deuteronomy 21:22,23)

[64]They divide my garments among them, and for my clothing they cast lots. (Psalm 22:18)

[65]He keeps all his bones; not one of them is broken. (Psalm 34:20)

like a root out of dry ground; he had no form or majesty that we should look at him, and no beauty that we should desire him. He was despised and rejected by men; a man of sorrows, and acquainted with grief; and as one from whom men hide their faces he was despised, and we esteemed him not. Surely he has borne our griefs and carried our sorrows; yet we esteemed him stricken, smitten by God, and afflicted. But he was pierced for our transgressions; he was crushed for our iniquities; upon him was the chastisement that brought us peace, and with his wounds we are healed. All we like sheep have gone astray; we have turned—every one— to his own way; and the LORD has laid on him the iniquity of us all. He was oppressed, and he was afflicted, yet he opened not his mouth; like a lamb that is led to the slaughter, and like a sheep that before its shearers is silent, so he opened not his mouth. By oppression and judgment he was taken away; and as for his generation, who considered that he was cut off out of the land of the living, stricken for the transgression of my people? And they made his grave with the wicked and with a rich man in his death, although he had done no violence, and there was no deceit in his mouth. Yet it was the will of the LORD to crush him; he has put him to grief; when his soul makes an offering for guilt, he shall see his offspring; he shall prolong his days; the will of the LORD shall prosper in his hand. Out of the anguish of his soul he shall see and be satisfied; by his knowl- edge shall the righteous one, my servant, make many to be accounted righteous, and he shall bear their iniquities. (Isaiah 52:13–53:11)

The ordeal was more than just the gruesome death, a man nailed to a cross. While Jesus was on the cross, God turned his eternal wrath on his Son so that he endured the punishments of hell. The agony was so great because God the Father had deserted his Son to face his justice. Jesus cried out in the agony of abandonment, using the words of a psalm, "My God, my God, why have you forsaken me?" (Psalm 22:1). But the end came, and Jesus died to the rejoicing of his enemies (Matthew 27:42).[66] Yet with his death, the curtain separating the Most Holy Place from the rest of the temple was torn in two (Matthew 27:51), signifying that the throne of God was no longer inaccessible to the people. The earthquake and the other signs accompany- ing Jesus' death caused even the hardened officer who oversaw the execution to realize this was not the death of any ordinary man (Matthew 27:51-54). Indeed, it wasn't; Jesus had endured the punishment for all the sins (1 John 1:7)[67] of all the human beings who had lived and ever would live (2 Cor-

---

[66] [The Jewish leaders said,] "He saved others; he cannot save himself." (Matthew 27:42)

[67] The blood of Jesus his Son cleanses us from all sin. (1 John 1:7)

inthians 5:15).[68] Humankind cannot understand the Lord's justice, but at Golgotha humankind can realize that it is anything but trivial. Without this there could have been no salvation for anyone. Redemption through Jesus' death will be discussed much more in chapter 14.

## The resurrection

But it was never in the Lord's plan that Jesus would stay physically dead. As Jesus had predicted (Matthew 16:21),[69] he rose on the third day after his crucifixion. Isaiah had prophesied that the Servant of the Lord would be victorious, writing, "Therefore I will give him a portion with the many, and he shall divide the spoil with the strong, because he poured out his soul to death and was numbered with the transgressors; yet he bore the sin of many and makes intercession for the transgressors" (Isaiah 53:12). He had overcome sin, death, and the powers of evil (1 Corinthians 15:55-57).[70] His disciples struggled to believe it (John 20:25),[71] and his enemies tried to hide the details (Matthew 28:13).[72] He began showing himself to groups of people, as many as five hundred at once (1 Corinthians 15:5-8), and continued teaching his disciples. He even reinstated brash but weak-kneed Peter into his followers (John 21:15-19).

Easter is the most joyous day in the year for Christians. He who had been "delivered up for our transgressions [had been] raised for our justification" (Romans 4:25). The head of the serpent had been crushed as the Lord had promised Adam and Eve (Genesis 3:15). Yet many people feel uncomfortable about Easter, because Easter shows that all the power is really in the Lord's hands. If what Jesus did is necessary to save someone, clearly no one can do that for himself or herself, so a person's salvation is out of his or her own hands. That does not sit well with people who want to have control of their destinies and to not be dependent upon anyone. As a result, in every

---

[68] He [Jesus, the Christ] died for all, that those who live might no longer live for themselves but for him who for their sake died and was raised. (2 Corinthians 5:15)

[69] From that time Jesus began to show his disciples that he must go to Jerusalem and suffer many things from the elders and chief priests and scribes, and be killed, and on the third day be raised. (Matthew 16:21)

[70] "O death, where is your victory? O death, where is your sting?" The sting of death is sin, and the power of sin is the law. But thanks be to God, who gives us the victory through our Lord Jesus Christ. (1 Corinthians 15:55-57)

[71] The other disciples told him [Thomas], "We have seen the Lord." But he said to them, "Unless I see in his hands the mark of the nails, and place my finger into the mark of the nails, and place my hand into his side, I will never believe." (John 20:25)

[72] [Jewish leaders said,] "Tell people, 'His [Jesus'] disciples came by night and stole him away while we were asleep.'" (Matthew 28:13)

generation there are people who try to explain away the physical resurrection of Jesus. A few of these stories are worth debunking.

**Claim:** Jesus was not really dead, but he had merely swooned and recovered in the cave.

**Reality:** Jewish leaders who had gone through a lot of effort to have Jesus killed would have insisted on proof that he was dead. Roman soldiers who performed crucifixions would have made sure Jesus was dead because they themselves would have been executed if a prisoner was allowed to escape alive. That blood and water poured from Jesus' side indicated that his blood had clotted, a certain sign of death.

**Claim:** His disciples stole his body.

**Reality:** His disciples were in mortal fear, and they had scattered when Jesus was arrested. Could these frightened men without military training have overpowered a squad of Roman soldiers? If they had, wouldn't the Romans have hunted them down and executed them as an example so people would not interfere with the Roman military?

**Claim:** A double was substituted for Jesus to pull off a resurrection plot.

**Reality:** Who would agree to be crucified for such a stunt? While the thugs sent to arrest Jesus might not have known him by sight, the Jewish religious leaders certainly did. They would hardly have gone through the effort of getting a man crucified if he were the wrong man.

**Claim:** The good feeling of Jesus' presence came alive in his disciples after his death, and they concocted the story of the resurrection to give credibility to that feeling.

**Reality:** Jesus' followers were uneducated men (Acts 4:13)[73] who, even after Jesus' resurrection, had trouble understanding his mission (Acts 1:6).[74] Could this fearful and befuddled band really have put together such a story to boldly proclaim in Jerusalem, when it might well have led to their own arrests and executions? Eventually, many of them did die for preaching about Jesus. Would they not rather have fled to Galilee, where they had spent so much time with Jesus, to put their lives back together? Yet this motley band suddenly began proclaiming a message with deep theological significance for which they were willing to die. The inspi-

---

[73] Now when they [the Jewish religious leaders] saw the boldness of Peter and John, and perceived that they were uneducated, common men, they were astonished. And they recognized that they had been with Jesus. (Acts 4:13)

[74] When they [his disciples] had come together, they asked him, "Lord, will you at this time restore the kingdom to Israel?" (Acts 1:6)

ration of Jesus' physical resurrection and the coming of the Holy Spirit upon them could explain such an occurrence, but it would not have been the product of just some warm feeling about Jesus in their hearts.

It is amazing what people will believe as long as it isn't in the Bible!

## Ascension

The time had come for the end of Jesus' earthly ministry. He had lived a life in perfect conformity to the will of the Lord God, he had died to pay for the sins of the world, and he had risen to show his victory over death and hell. Jesus left his disciples by ascending into the sky (Acts 1:9-11). He could have just disappeared, but a formal departing set the stage for a formal return, which he has promised will happen when he comes back to judge the world (Matthew 24:29-31). Before he left, he assured his disciples that he was still with them (Matthew 28:20),[75] although they would no longer be able to see him. He also promised that he would send the third member of the Trinity, the Holy Spirit, to teach and guide them to accomplish the work he was giving them to do (Acts 1:8).[76] Up until this point they had been in training, but the work of the kingdom of God was about to become their work. That work will be the subject of the next chapter.

---

[75] [Jesus said,] "Behold, I am with you always, to the end of the age." (Matthew 28:20)

[76] [Jesus said,] "You [his disciples] will receive power when the Holy Spirit has come upon you, and you will be my witnesses in Jerusalem and in all Judea and Samaria, and to the end of the earth." (Acts 1:8)

# CHAPTER 10

# The First-Century Church

At the end of Jesus' earthly ministry, even many people who had heard him speak and seen his miracles did not have a clear idea of why he had come to earth and what his message was. Their hearts were covered by a veil of false teachings that had developed in Judaism over the centuries (2 Corinthians 3:14).[1] They could not apply the Scriptures because the Scriptures had been presented to them by their teachers as a code of laws that they had to keep. The Old Testament Scriptures, however, also proclaim the gospel promises and prophecies of a Savior from sin (John 5:39,40),[2] but the people had stopped looking for them. Both Jesus' disciples and the Jewish people needed to have their eyes opened to see what they had previously missed (Luke 24:45).[3] That was about to happen.

## The church and its mission

To help them carry his message to the Jewish people and beyond to the Gentiles, Jesus promised his disciples that he would send the Holy Spirit, the third person of the Trinity (John 14:26).[4] The Holy Spirit would teach them

---

[1] Their [the Jewish people's] minds were hardened. For to this day, when they read the old covenant, that same veil remains unlifted, because only through Christ is it taken away. (2 Corinthians 3:14)

[2] [Jesus said,] "You [the Jews] search the Scriptures because you think that in them you have eternal life; and it is they that bear witness about me, yet you refuse to come to me that you may have life." (John 5:39,40)

[3] Then he [Jesus] opened their [two disciples'] minds to understand the Scriptures. (Luke 24:45)

[4] [Jesus said,] "The Helper, the Holy Spirit, whom the Father will send in my name, he will teach you [his disciples] all things and bring to your remembrance all that I have said to you." (John 14:26)

the correct understanding of the Scriptures and would change the hearts of some of those who heard them so that they too could believe the message of salvation (1 Corinthians 12:3).[5] The disciples and others whom they trained would become ambassadors, that is, proclaimers, to the people of the world (2 Corinthians 5:20).[6] The message was not to be their own to reshape as they saw fit, but it was the teachings given to them by the Holy Spirit. They were to preach the law, and they were to preach the gospel, and they were to preach no more than these (2 Timothy 4:2;[7] Galatians 1:8,9[8]). The organization that would bind them together in this effort would be the Christian church. The church would be comprised of all believers wherever they existed.

The workers of the church would be the messengers of the "new covenant," the covenant of free and full forgiveness of sins gained by Jesus Christ through his suffering, death, and resurrection (2 Corinthians 3:6).[9] It would differ from the "old covenant," which was discussed in chapter 7, because the old covenant was both a two-sided covenant and an earthly covenant. The Lord gave blessings in terms of land and prosperity, but the people had to obey a large set of laws, rules, and ordinances to keep their side of the covenant. When they failed, they had to seek reconciliation with the Lord through the work of the mediators of the covenant, namely, the priests who were the descendants of Aaron, and through the offering of sacrifices. Obedience and sacrifices were the required works of the old covenant (Deuteronomy 11:26-32). The new covenant was a one-sided covenant of grace in which the Lord did everything (Matthew 26:27,28).[10] It had been promised to Adam and Eve (Genesis 3:15), to Abraham (Genesis 18:18), and to David (2 Samuel 7:11-17), and now it had been put into effect. The Lord promised to forgive all sins without any works or mediation by any agent, living or dead (1 John 2:2).[11] Jesus had made the sacrifice necessary for the forgiveness of

---

[5] No one can say "Jesus is Lord" except in the Holy Spirit. (1 Corinthians 12:3)

[6] Therefore, we are ambassadors for Christ, God making his appeal through us. We implore you on behalf of Christ, be reconciled to God. (2 Corinthians 5:20)

[7] Preach the Word; be ready in season and out of season; reprove, rebuke, and exhort, with complete patience and teaching. (2 Timothy 4:2)

[8] Even if we or an angel from heaven should preach to you a gospel contrary to the one we preached to you, let him be accursed. As we have said before, so now I say again: If anyone is preaching to you a gospel contrary to the one you received, let him be accursed. (Galatians 1:8,9)

[9] Who has made us sufficient to be ministers of a new covenant, not of the letter but of the Spirit. For the letter kills, but the Spirit gives life. (2 Corinthians 3:6)

[10] [Jesus said,] "Drink of it, all of you [his disciples], for this is my blood of the covenant, which is poured out for many for the forgiveness of sins." (Matthew 26:27,28)

[11] He [Jesus] is the propitiation for our sins, and not for ours only but also for the sins of the whole world. (1 John 2:2)

sins, and he himself was the heavenly mediator who would speak to God the Father on behalf of those who believed his message (Hebrews 9:15).[12] The book of Hebrews explains this in great detail. Moreover, the new covenant granted permanent citizenship in the perfect kingdom of heaven, rather than merely in some temporary territory in an earthly realm. The mission of the church therefore was to proclaim this covenant, to get the news out.

## Missionary work among the Jews

Jesus was a Jew, a descendant of Judah and David. It was through the Jews that salvation had been promised to the world (John 4:22).[13] Jesus therefore started by preaching to the Jews and calling disciples from the Jews (Matthew 15:24).[14] His whole inner circle, containing the 12 disciples, was composed of Jews. Most of those whom the Bible mentions he encountered in his ministry were also Jews. While he did heal and preach to Gentiles, he did this only occasionally. When he commissioned his disciples to begin their mission work, he told them to start in Jerusalem (Luke 24:46,47).[15] His disciples, steeped in Jewish tradition and religious knowledge, were ideal for the task. Although most lacked formal education (Acts 4:13),[16] they had learned from Jesus and were guided by the Holy Spirit.

The missionary work to the Jews started with the outpouring of the Holy Spirit on Pentecost (Acts 2:1-12). Jews from all over the Roman Empire, and possibly from some places beyond, had gathered in Jerusalem for one of the three mandatory annual festivals for Jewish men. This was an ideal time to start the church. If Jews, who had some training in the Scriptures and who had some commitment to the old covenant, were gathered together in one place, they could be instructed in the new covenant and they could carry the message throughout the world. The nuclei for further efforts could be established in numerous communities. Peter preached the first sermon, and three thousand people who heard the message were moved by the Holy Spirit to

---

[12]Therefore he [Jesus] is the mediator of a new covenant, so that those who are called may receive the promised eternal inheritance, since a death has occurred that redeems them from the transgressions committed under the first covenant. (Hebrews 9:15)

[13][Jesus said,] "You [Samaritans] worship what you do not know; we [the Jews] worship what we know, for salvation is from the Jews." (John 4:22)

[14]He [Jesus] answered, "I was sent only to the lost sheep of the house of Israel." (Matthew 15:24)

[15]He [Jesus] said to them, "Thus it is written, that the Christ should suffer and on the third day rise from the dead, and that repentance and forgiveness of sins should be proclaimed in his name to all nations, beginning from Jerusalem." (Luke 24:46,47)

[16]Now when they [the Jewish religious leaders] saw the boldness of Peter and John, and perceived that they were uneducated, common men, they were astonished. (Acts 4:13)

join the Christian church (Acts 2:14-41). It was a remarkable start, and gains in Jerusalem were made quickly (Acts 2:47).[17]

During the next few months, the church continued to grow in Jerusalem, and the group was incredibly unified. The love of the Savior filled members' hearts. They met and worshiped together in a portion of the temple, as well as in individual homes (Acts 2:42-47). The church, however, soon faced two problems. First, the enthusiasm of the new members for the message caused them to establish a common treasury that would sustain those who had inadequate means. As this private welfare system grew, managing it became a burden on the original disciples, now called apostles,[18] so a system of deacons to handle food distribution was established (Acts 6:1-7). Second, the growing size of the movement, even without a dynamic figure such as Jesus, was becoming troubling to the Jewish religious hierarchy. They began threatening and punishing the church leaders (Acts 5:17-41). The apostles' teaching was having the desired effect, however, and the church members were becoming more knowledgeable in their faith.

The Jewish religious leaders concluded they needed to take firmer action against the church, so they seized Stephen, one of the deacons, and put him on trial. They were so incensed by a vision he saw during the trial that they took him outside the city and stoned him, despite the Roman prohibition of such an action (Acts 6:8–7:60). Following Stephen's stoning, the Jewish leaders launched a general persecution against the church, causing most of the church members to leave Jerusalem (Acts 8:2). This was a good development for the church because these people fled to Jewish settlements throughout the region, carrying the message of Jesus Christ with them (Acts 8:4). Soon small congregations were growing in a number of Jewish communities and even in Samaria.

The apostles realized that they needed to maintain a strong presence in Jerusalem because Jewish pilgrims came there from all over the world. They also needed to go out to the new congregations of the church that were being established to make sure they were teaching the Lord's message correctly. As a result, the apostles remained based in Jerusalem for some time, but they, and even the original deacons, were often on the missionary trail, giving support to places where Jews were becoming Christians (Acts 8:5-25). Some of the activities of the Jewish missionary efforts are described in the first half of the book of Acts, which was written by the physician Luke. These include missionary efforts by Peter, John, and Philip.

---

[17]The Lord added to their number [members of the church] day by day those who were being saved. (Acts 2:47)

[18]*Apostle* means "one who is sent" in Greek, while *disciple* means "one who learns."

As time passed, the situation in Jerusalem changed. The apostles were gone more and more on their missionary journeys. To the west, there was a significant Jewish settlement in Alexandria in northern Egypt. It was to this area that Jews had been fleeing since the time of Jeremiah (Jeremiah 43:1-7) and here where the Hebrew Old Testament had been translated into the Greek Septuagint. To the east, as far as the location of Babylon (1 Peter 5:13), there were Jewish communities composed of those who had never returned from the Babylonian captivity and those who had scattered out along the trade routes of the Fertile Crescent.[19] As a result, there were many Jewish settlements in what are now Egypt, Palestine, Jordan, Syria, and Iraq, where the Jewish missionary team based in Jerusalem would reach out and start congregations. Some nonbiblical accounts claim that they went much farther, but there is insufficient evidence to make any specific statements.

While this was happening, the situation in Jerusalem was evolving. With the apostles needing to travel to support mission work elsewhere, the leadership of the Jerusalem congregation fell to James (Acts 15:13), a brother of Jesus (Galatians 1:19). James had not been an early follower of his brother (John 7:5)[20] but had eventually joined the disciples and was left to manage the home base of the church. Two factions developed in the congregation. One faction began using the supposed imminent coming of Christ as an excuse to stop practicing the traditional care of the unfortunate that was a part of Jewish culture (Leviticus 19:9,10). James wrote the epistle of James to these people. The other party was zealous for the regulations of the Mosaic Law, and these people challenged even Peter and Paul over the nature of the gospel message (Acts 15:1).[21] The Jewish Sanhedrin had James executed in A.D. 62, and the Romans destroyed Jerusalem in A.D. 70, greatly reducing its importance as a center of Christianity. By that time most of the apostles had been martyred or scattered. The last of the apostles to die was John, who died in the area of Ephesus near the end of the first century.

## Missionary work among the Gentiles

The people who scattered from Jerusalem after Stephen was stoned spread the message of Christ and his salvation to fellow Jews in the communities

---

[19] The Fertile Crescent is a crescent-shaped area running north along the Mediterranean Sea, sweeping eastward to the upper Euphrates River and then down that river to the Persian Gulf.

[20] Not even his [Jesus'] brothers believed in him. (John 7:5)

[21] Some men came down from Judea [to Antioch in Syria] and were teaching the brothers, "Unless you are circumcised according to the custom of Moses, you cannot be saved." (Acts 15:1)

into which they fled. Some of these refugees went to Antioch in Syria, one of the largest cities in the Roman Empire. Here they began preaching about Jesus to the Gentiles as well (Acts 11:20),[22] probably starting with gentile converts to Judaism. When the church at Jerusalem learned of this, they sent missionary assistance (Acts 11:22). During the same timeframe, Saul of Tarsus, a Pharisee and a fanatical enemy of the Christian movement, was stopped dead in his tracks by a vision of the Lord Jesus Christ himself while on an expedition to arrest Christians in Damascus. The conversion of Saul (Acts 9:1-25) and his subsequent restudying of the Scriptures in light of this personal revelation eventually led to his being brought to Antioch by Barnabas, one of the missionaries sent there from Jerusalem (Acts 11:25,26). With a significant number of workers, the church in Antioch grew steadily. This congregation in Antioch was a key element in the Lord's plan for the growth of his church. Antioch would serve as the base for mission work among the Gentiles further to the west. It became a key contact point between these mission teams and the Jewish missionaries to the east. Eventually it grew into one of the five patriarchies of the early church.[23]

Missionary work in the Greek and Roman world presented different challenges from the work among the Semitic populations of the Fertile Crescent and Egypt. Jews in the Greco-Roman world had been much more Hellenized (i.e., acclimated to Greek culture) and mixed much more freely with the Gentiles. Few Gentiles knew anything about the Old Testament or the Jewish religion. Most of the people spoke Greek as their first or second language, rather than Aramaic or Hebrew. Greeks were impressed with knowledge and wisdom, and the Romans with strength and order. Missionaries to Asia Minor (i.e., Turkey) and Europe, therefore, had to be prepared to deal with these cultural differences. The first missionary team to the west consisted of Paul, Barnabas, and the evangelist Mark (Acts 13:4,5). They traveled into Asia Minor and made some progress. Their normal operating procedure was to find the Jews in the communities they entered and tell them about Jesus as the fulfillment of the Old Testament prophecies. Some Jews would believe, and the missionaries would make these a nucleus to reach out to the Gentiles. Unbelieving Jews often resented the missionaries and tried to get them driven out of town. When the missionaries left, they put their best students in charge of the congregations.

---

[22] There were some of them, men of Cyprus and Cyrene, who on coming to Antioch spoke to the Hellenists also, preaching the Lord Jesus. (Acts 11:20)

[23] The five patriarchies were Jerusalem, Antioch (Syria), Alexandria (Egypt), Rome, and Constantinople.

After Paul and Barnabas returned to Antioch, the missionary efforts to the Gentiles began to grow. Silas was added to the group, which split into two teams after a disagreement (Acts 15:39-41). Paul's team added Timothy, Titus, and Luke as frequent members and others as occasional traveling companions. In the growing group of workers were people who had been raised in the gentile world, even if they were Jews, or who had spent considerable time there previously. Some of them were Roman citizens (Acts 22:25),[24] which gave them more legal protection in their work. To facilitate their mission work among the Gentiles, Mark wrote an account of Jesus' life in Greek (gospel of Mark) and Paul wrote letters to numerous congregations so the gospel would not become distorted by word-of-mouth transmission and could be applied to local situations.

The missionary effort was soon faced with four challenges. First, unbelieving Jews were not happy with the arrival of the Christian missionaries, who were upsetting the status quo (Acts 17:5-9). Many of these Jews had semi-integrated into the gentile communities. They had business ties with Gentiles and had distorted the Jewish teachings enough to permit their behavior. If the Messiah had come, their world was going to be changed, and they did not like it. They instituted persecutions of the missionaries and those who joined them, often calling on gentile allies to leverage the government to join their efforts.

Second, both the paganism of the gentile subcultures and the ignorance of the Gentiles concerning the promise of the Savior forced the missionaries to do a lot of remedial education (Acts 20:31). The responses of the Gentiles varied from treating the missionaries as pagan gods (Acts 14:8-18) to scoffing at their teachings (Acts 17:32) to punishing them (Acts 16:22). The Greco-Roman society was as corrupt as present-day Western society, and most people did not want to hear about their sins.

Third, other Gentiles felt even more threatened. Those who made money from paganism saw their livelihoods in danger (Acts 19:23-41). Others felt these "blasphemers" would irritate their gods and bring misfortune on their nations. Some in the government viewed Jews in general as troublemakers and members of splinter Jewish sects as even worse troublemakers. They saw no reason for letting the Christians gain a foothold in their communities.

The worst problem for the missionaries to the Gentiles, however, was the efforts of nominally Jewish Christians to undermine the work with the

---

[24]Paul said to the centurion who was standing by, "Is it lawful for you to flog a man who is a Roman citizen and uncondemned?" (Acts 22:25)

Gentiles. This had begun already when Peter was challenged for going to the centurion Cornelius' house at the direction of the Lord (Acts 11:2,3).[25] It later flared up in Antioch, when people from the Jerusalem congregation arrived to demand circumcision of all the Gentiles (Acts 15:1-21). Although the Jerusalem church disavowed these teachings, Jews claiming to represent the "true" Christian movement in Judea, called Judaizers, entered numerous congregations in Asia Minor and Europe claiming that salvation required obedience to the laws of the Mosaic covenant or, at a minimum, circumcision (Galatians 1–2). Efforts to introduce phony specific works as a necessary condition for salvation have persisted in the church ever since.

The battle of the church against these challenges is documented in the Bible and in the writings of the early church fathers. It was only through the work of the Holy Spirit that faithful teachers were successful and that the Christian church survived. The Lord has been in charge even when things have seemed bleak.

## The church and its perpetuation

Jesus started the church with a small group of men whom he personally selected and trained. He gave them special powers through the Holy Spirit both to perform miracles—mostly those of healing—and to transmit his message through preaching and through writing the text of the New Testament for subsequent generations. St. Paul wrote of the church that it was "built on the foundation of the apostles and prophets, Christ Jesus himself being the cornerstone" (Ephesians 2:20). Yet the message—that is, the substance of the doctrine, which the apostles preached and which they recorded in the Bible—was never theirs to massage as they thought best. It was given to them by the Holy Spirit (2 Peter 1:21).[26] The structure of the ministry, however, was within their control. The church, for example, soon decided that it needed deacons to manage the physical activities of the church (Acts 6:1-6). St. Paul listed the qualifications for several of the ministry positions the church had established (Titus 1:5,6)[27] so that the church could choose

---

[25]When Peter went up to Jerusalem, the circumcision party criticized him, saying, "You went to uncircumcised men and ate with them." (Acts 11:2,3)

[26]No prophecy was ever produced by the will of man, but men spoke from God as they were carried along by the Holy Spirit. (2 Peter 1:21)

[27]Appoint elders in every town as I [Paul] directed you [Titus]—if anyone is above reproach, the husband of one wife, and his children are believers and not open to the charge of debauchery or insubordination. (Titus 1:5,6)

appropriate men to fill them. The apostles and their coworkers then worked
to train these people for service in the church.

There was naturally concern over how the church would function organi-
zationally once the apostles were gone, because they seemed indispensable
to it. They appointed men to serve as congregational leaders as they left one
mission field for another. For example, Paul asked Titus to appoint elders
for the congregations in Crete. In Jerusalem, the casting of lots (Acts 1:26)
and the public acclamation of the congregation (Acts 6:5) were used under
the apostles' guidance to place men into teaching and service positions. Yet
the Holy Spirit did not direct the apostles to establish a general procedure
to be used to fill vacant positions in the work of the church nor to create a
governing structure for the church. The Bible only states that the work of the
church is the work of the Lord and that those who do it are called by the Lord
(Romans 1:1).[28] The church was left with considerable latitude to determine
how to train and call workers to service. This was in marked contrast to the
ministry under the Mosaic covenant, where the form was specified in detail
and the men of each generation followed in the footsteps of their fathers,
performing the same rituals (Leviticus 1–9, 21–25).

As the church entered the second century A.D., some people felt uneasy
about the looseness in the church structure and wanted some way to guarantee smooth operations. With the death of the apostles, the church had lost its
"living" connection to the Lord. While it had the writings of these men, no
further questions could be asked of them. The canon of God's revelation was
closed. Who would be the court of last appeal on doctrinal issues? Who had
the final say on who was qualified for the ministry? With multiple congregations served by multiple pastors (bishops), some feared chaos might ensue,
so they pushed for a hierarchy to make certain that things were done in good
order. Unfortunately, this soon led to a political struggle for the position of
supreme bishop in each area.

While the efforts to gain power led to many local tussles over the calls
to be bishop of some of the larger parishes, the congregation in Rome gradually came to view this issue in terms of universal power over the entire
church. Being at the center of the Roman Empire had created a mind-set
of dominance among its members. The Roman congregation felt that the
whole church should naturally be guided by its bishop. It therefore created
the myth (1) that Christ had made Peter the head of the Christian church,
(2) that Peter had moved his ministry to Rome to run the church, and

---

[28] Paul, a servant of Christ Jesus, called to be an apostle, set apart for the gospel of God. (Romans 1:1)

(3) that Peter had made his successor bishops at Rome the perpetual head of the whole Christian church. It is a myth because none of the three parts is true, and it is important to look at why.

Those who appeal to Matthew 16:18[29] as a proof text that Jesus made Peter "the rock" on which the church stands lack an understanding of how first-century rabbis taught. After Peter had made a confession that Jesus was "the Christ, the Son of the living God" in verse 16, Jesus used Peter's name, which means "rock," to link to the real rock on which the church stands, namely, the confession that Peter had made. The Bible uses numerous plays on words (i.e., puns), which are not obvious in translation. By this statement, a first-century rabbi would have meant that when someone makes a statement that is rock solid, he is a rock. Five verses later, in Matthew 16:23,[30] Jesus calls Peter "Satan," the leader of the demons. Why? Because Peter had made a statement that advanced the cause of Satan. If Peter were literally the rock on which the church would be built, then he was also literally Satan, and Christ would have built his church on Satan. The evangelist Mark, who is generally believed to have been instructed by Peter, doesn't mention that Jesus called Peter a rock, only that he called him Satan (Mark 8:33). The Lord is not so foolish as to build his church on a sinful man when humans have a universal history of failure. Moreover, while Jesus gave the keys of the kingdom of heaven to Peter (Matthew 16:19), he also later gave them to all the disciples (John 20:23) and to the whole church (Matthew 18:18). Furthermore, Jesus warned his disciples not to call anyone "rabbi" or "father" in the church (Matthew 23:8,9),[31] since these titles would have implied a person was the highest authority in the church, not the Lord's Word. *Pope* literally means "father." Finally, if Peter had been named the head of the church, would not he, rather than Paul, have been given the task of writing most of the doctrinal books of the New Testament, thereby setting the theology of the church (compare Moses' position vis-à-vis the Israelites)? Knowing the history and the culture of the eras when the Bible was written is important to understanding the Bible.

The idea that Peter spent the bulk of his ministry in Rome is incompatible with the information given in the New Testament. He is only mentioned as

---

[29][Jesus said,] "I tell you, you are Peter, and on this rock I will build my church, and the gates of hell shall not prevail against it." (Matthew 16:18)

[30]He [Jesus] turned and said to Peter, "Get behind me, Satan! You are a hindrance to me. For you are not setting your mind on the things of God, but on the things of man." (Matthew 16:23)

[31][Jesus said,] "You are not to be called rabbi, for you have one teacher, and you are all brothers. And call no man your father on earth, for you have one Father, who is in heaven." (Matthew 23:8,9)

working in the Semitic mission fields and is never mentioned in relationship to Rome, even though many other people are mentioned in connection with Rome. Would not Luke, who recorded the early history of the church, have mentioned such an important event as Peter arriving in Rome to establish the church there? Near the end of his career, Peter associates himself with the church in Babylon (1 Peter 5:13).[32] The Catholic Church argues that "Babylon" is a code word for "Rome," but there is no textual evidence that Peter was writing in code. His only documented connection with Rome is that there were Jews from Rome at his first Pentecost sermon (Acts 2:10). Perhaps pilgrims from Rome consulted with him at Jewish feasts in Jerusalem and therefore regarded him as the founder of their congregation. If he ever did travel to Rome, it was only at the very end of his life, after the last of Paul's letters written from Rome.

There is no biblical support for the idea that the office of any apostle was to be passed on to subsequent generations. Apostles were called personally by Jesus to jump-start the church. While the apostles were able to perform miracles at times, this does not appear to have played as large a role in their ministry as it did in Jesus,' and it seems to have diminished as time passed. The gifts to perform various forms of ministry in all eras come only from the Holy Spirit, and he gives them to whom he pleases. The Bible says nothing about human beings having any control over the passing of these gifts from generation to generation. If they had such power, humans would have control over how the Lord God does his work.

The history of the church is beyond the scope of this book. Yet that history has been marred by exactly the same problems that plagued the nation of Israel. Those leading the church, just as those leading Israel, frequently have thought that they have better ideas than the Lord on how things should be done and what should be taught to the people. As a result, many people in the Christian church during its history have been Christians only in name, just as many people in Israel and Judah in the Old Testament were part of God's people only in name. The prophets pointed out that only a remnant would be saved from Old Testament Israel (Isaiah 10:22),[33] and the same is true of New Testament Israel, namely, the visible church (Matthew 22:14).[34] Those saved in the Old Testament times and those saved during the New Testament times are part of the true church,

---

[32] She who is at Babylon, who is likewise chosen, sends you greetings, and so does Mark, my son. (1 Peter 5:13)

[33] Though your people Israel be as the sand of the sea, only a remnant of them will return. (Isaiah 10:22)

[34] [Jesus said,] "Many are called, but few are chosen." (Matthew 22:14)

which is visible only to the Lord and will be revealed only on judgment day. In the words of the hymnist, let us pray, "With them numbered may we be, here and in eternity."[35] More about the church will be discussed in chapter 12.

---

[35]Refrain from "Blessed are the Sons of God," written by Augustus Toplady, 1776. Hymn 394 in Christian Worship.

CHAPTER 11

# End Times

After humankind fell into sin, the Lord carried out a plan of salvation for everyone, and Jesus sent forth his disciples to spread the message of this salvation to the whole world. But now what? When will this salvation come? Isn't it the same old world with the same old problems? When will things get better? These are all questions a person is likely to ask, and in the Bible the Lord has given us answers to such critical questions about his kingdom. There he tells us what will happen, but he often does not tell us when or how in as much detail as many people would like to know. Like Eve, we are curious about things that the Lord has decided we do not need to know.

The period of history we live in is called the New Testament Era, the era in which the new covenant in Jesus' blood is actively preached (1 Corinthians 11:25).[1] This era will end when Jesus returns to earth in visible form (Matthew 24:3).[2] The Bible says frequently that the time is short and that these are the last days (1 Corinthians 7:29),[3] but no more is given about the time of his return. In fact, Jesus himself says that no one knows the return date except God the Father (Mark 13:32).[4] Yet despite the fact that the date

---

[1] In the same way also he [Jesus] took the cup, after supper, saying, "This cup is the new covenant in my blood." (1 Corinthians 11:25)

[2] As he [Jesus] sat on the Mount of Olives, the disciples came to him privately, saying, "Tell us, when will these things be, and what will be the sign of your coming and of the end of the age?" (Matthew 24:3)

[3] This is what I mean, brothers: the appointed time has grown very short. (1 Corinthians 7:29)

[4] [Jesus said,] "Concerning that day or that hour, no one knows, not even the angels in heaven, nor the Son, but only the Father." (Mark 13:32)

has not been given, the sequence of events leading up to that day and on that day are presented in the Scriptures.

First, Jesus promised his disciples that he would return and judge all humankind (Matthew 25:31-46). This was important because it separated the reasons for his two comings. It clarified the situation. Many had a false conclusion from the Old Testament Scriptures, believing that when the Messiah came, he would set up an earthly kingdom and vanquish his physical enemies. Instead, Jesus, the Messiah, came the first time to vanquish his spiritual enemies (John 3:17).[5] He also promised to come again to set up his kingdom, which will be an eternal rather than an earthly kingdom (Matthew 25:31).[6] Therefore, one sees Jesus in his first coming as saying and doing those things necessary to call people to repentance, as well as personally suffering the punishment for the sins of the whole world. The second time he comes there will be no olive branch of forgiveness to the sinners, but rather there will be the gavel of the judge of the universe declaring verdicts on all who ever lived.

### The approaching judgment

Jesus said that as the earth moves toward its end at his return, a number of signs will occur (Matthew 24:4-12).[7] These will include signs in the earth, such as earthquakes, famines, and floods. They will include signs in the heavens, involving the sun, moon, and stars (Acts 2:19,20).[8] They will include signs among nations, such as wars, threats of wars, and rebellions. Finally, they will include signs within the human race, such as growing evil, people becoming fearful, and growing unbelief. While these signs seem significant, some will say that most of these signs happen all the time. So how can they be a reliable predictor of the future when they are so common? In fact, it is because they

---

[5] [Jesus said,] "God did not send his Son into the world to condemn the world, but in order that the world might be saved through him." (John 3:17)

[6] [Jesus said,] "When the Son of Man comes in his glory, and all the angels with him, then he will sit on his glorious throne." (Matthew 25:31)

[7] Jesus answered them, "See that no one leads you astray. For many will come in my name, saying, 'I am the Christ,' and they will lead many astray. And you will hear of wars and rumors of wars. See that you are not alarmed, for this must take place, but the end is not yet. For nation will rise against nation, and kingdom against kingdom, and there will be famines and earthquakes in various places. All these are but the beginning of the birth pains. Then they will deliver you up to tribulation and put you to death, and you will be hated by all nations for my name's sake. And then many will fall away and betray one another and hate one another. And many false prophets will arise and lead many astray. And because lawlessness will be increased, the love of many will grow cold." (Matthew 24:4-12)

[8] [Peter, quoting the Lord's words in Joel 2:30,31, said,] "And I will show wonders in the heavens above and signs on the earth below, blood, and fire, and vapor of smoke; the sun shall be turned to darkness and the moon to blood, before the day of the Lord comes, the great and magnificent day." (Acts 2:19,20)

are so common that they should remind believers that Jesus could return at any time. To unbelievers, these signs are just business as usual, the way the world is. Consequently, unbelievers will be completely shocked at Jesus' reappearing. Jesus himself warned of the need for believers to heed the signs of the times, lest they be caught unprepared (Matthew 16:3).[9]

The theme of being prepared for the return of Christ is presented in numerous ways in the New Testament. Jesus used parables to show that even in an earthly situation watchfulness is necessary (e.g., the parable of the ten virgins [Matthew 25:1-13]). In addition, he made direct warnings of the need to be alert (Matthew 24:36-44). The apostles also echoed this need for constant vigilance regarding the end of the world, as well as against Satan (1 Peter 4:7; 5:8). Finally, Revelation reminds us that the time of Jesus' return is not known, but it is rapidly approaching (Revelation 22:20).[10]

People might reasonably ask, "What if I die before Jesus returns again? Will I miss out on his second coming and salvation?" The answer to these questions has two parts. First, at death the soul separates from the body. While the body is buried, burned, or otherwise disposed of, the soul remains alive and is judged by the Lord, as will be discussed shortly. King Solomon wrote, "The dust returns to the earth as it was, and the spirit returns to God who gave it" (Ecclesiastes 12:7). In the story of the rich man and Lazarus (Luke 16:19-31), the soul of Lazarus immediately entered into heaven and the soul of the rich man immediately entered into hell. Jesus told the dying thief on the cross, "Truly, I say to you, today you will be with me in paradise" (Luke 23:43). St. Paul writes that he wants to "depart and be with Christ, for that is far better" (Philippians 1:23). In Revelation, the souls of the saints that have been beheaded are under the altar (Revelation 20:4). The Bible therefore teaches that the souls of those who die are immediately sent to their eternal homes. No one will be denied heaven or escape hell because he or she died too soon.

Second, Jesus told his disciples that there would be a general resurrection of the dead, both the good and the evil (John 5:28,29).[11] Such a resurrection had already been prophesied in the Old Testament (Daniel 12:2),[12]

---

[9] [Jesus said,] "In the morning, 'It will be stormy today, for the sky is red and threatening.' You [the Jewish people] know how to interpret the appearance of the sky, but you cannot interpret the signs of the times." (Matthew 16:3)

[10] He [Jesus] who testifies to these things says, "Surely I am coming soon." (Revelation 22:20)

[11] [Jesus said,] "Do not marvel at this, for an hour is coming when all who are in the tombs will hear his [Jesus'] voice and come out, those who have done good to the resurrection of life, and those who have done evil to the resurrection of judgment." (John 5:28,29)

[12] Many of those who sleep in the dust of the earth shall awake, some to everlasting life, and some to shame and everlasting contempt. (Daniel 12:2)

and the apostles also wrote about the same thing in their letters (1 Corinthians 15:52).[13] The idea that dead bodies will rise is hard for many people to accept. When someone dies, irreversible chemical processes occur, preventing the body from being restored to life. Moreover, general decay begins in the tissues of the body so that it soon does not have even the remnants of the internal organs necessary for life. Burning and other processes can speed up this decay, leaving little or nothing of the original body. Yet one should not underestimate the power of the Lord God Almighty. If he could create the universe out of nothing and if he can make spiritually dead souls become alive in Christ (Ephesians 2:4-7), he certainly can call back human bodies to life no matter what has happened to them since they died (Matthew 19:26).[14] A general resurrection of the dead will happen on judgment day.

### Judgment day

Judgment day will open with the return of Jesus Christ in heavenly glory on the clouds of the sky (Matthew 24:30).[15] This return will be sudden; there will be no opportunity to repent and change the verdict coming in the final judgment (Matthew 24:27).[16] Christ's return will be simultaneous all over the earth, so people will not be able to alert their friends in a "later time zone." His return will cause fear and panic among most of the people on earth (Luke 23:30).[17] Accompanying Jesus will be his holy angels, who will sort the people for judgment (Matthew 13:41-43). There will be the overwhelming sound of the trumpet, marking the end of all earthly activity (Matthew 24:31).[18] Everyone will drop their agendas and their plans for later in the day and go to be judged.

Those who have died in faith will be brought back to life first to stand before Jesus (1 Thessalonians 4:16).[19] Then will follow the living believers

---

[13] In a moment, in the twinkling of an eye, at the last trumpet. For the trumpet will sound, and the dead will be raised imperishable, and we shall be changed. (1 Corinthians 15:52)

[14] Jesus looked at them and said, "With man this is impossible, but with God all things are possible." (Matthew 19:26)

[15] [Jesus said,] "They will see the Son of Man coming on the clouds of heaven with power and great glory." (Matthew 24:30)

[16] [Jesus said,] "As the lightning comes from the east and shines as far as the west, so will be the coming of the Son of Man." (Matthew 24:27)

[17] [Jesus said,] "Then they [the unbelievers] will begin to say to the mountains, 'Fall on us,' and to the hills, 'Cover us.'" (Luke 23:30)

[18] [Jesus said,] "He [Jesus himself] will send out his angels with a loud trumpet call, and they will gather his elect from the four winds, from one end of heaven to the other." (Matthew 24:31)

[19] The dead in Christ will rise first. (1 Thessalonians 4:16)

and, lastly, the unbelievers, living and dead (1 Thessalonians 4:17). The books of the deeds of each person will be opened, at least figuratively, and what is there will be used to judge each individual (Revelation 20:12).[20] For the believers, there will be nothing on the pages set aside for the recording of their sins. These will all have been washed clean by the blood of the Lamb (Revelation 7:14).[21] The judge, Jesus, will be satisfied and will then turn to the pages of good works done in faith in response to the love of the Lord (Matthew 25:34-40). These will be duly tallied, and the degrees of glory will be assigned.[22] For the unbelievers, the pages set aside for the recording of their sins will be crammed with their vile deeds and their acts of rebellion against the Lord (Ecclesiastes 7:20;[23] John 3:36[24]). The judge will be enraged and assign degrees of punishment based on the number and type of sins each individual has done (Luke 12:47,48).[25] The pages of good works will be empty because unbelievers have done nothing in response to faith but only for their own purposes (Hebrews 11:6).[26] The final sorting of believers from the unbelievers, figuratively, the sheep from the goats (Matthew 25:32), will be performed. Jesus will then pronounce his formal sentence over the two groups, sending the believers to eternal life with him and the unbelievers to hell (Matthew 25:46).

One should not think that the judgment will be a long process of endless waiting, like a visit to the department of motor vehicles. The Lord is capable of judging each case individually, yet simultaneously. One must not probe more deeply into the act of judgment than the glimpses of it that the Scriptures give us. We will not be in a position to raise points of procedure or to bring in our own evidence to present or to have expert witnesses to testify on

---

[20] I [John] saw the dead, great and small, standing before the throne, and books were opened. Then another book was opened, which is the book of life. And the dead were judged by what was written in the books, according to what they had done. (Revelation 20:12)

[21] They have washed their robes and made them white in the blood of the Lamb. (Revelation 7:14)

[22] While all the people in heaven will have the same joy and blessedness, by his grace the Lord will grant some people more glory within this perfect realm. We do not understand how this will work, but we know it will not cause the sin of jealousy. Likewise, while all impenitent sinners will experience terrible punishment in hell, some will be given even worse punishment based on the opportunities they had to repent and didn't. (Matthew 10:14,15; 11:20-24; Luke 12:47,48; 19:17,19)

[23] Surely there is not a righteous man on earth who does good and never sins. (Ecclesiastes 7:20)

[24] [John the Baptizer said,] "Whoever believes in the Son has eternal life; whoever does not [believe in] the Son shall not see life, but the wrath of God remains on him." (John 3:36)

[25] [Jesus said,] "That servant who knew his master's will but did not get ready or act according to his will, will receive a severe beating. But the one who did not know, and did what deserved a beating, will receive a light beating." (Luke 12:47,48)

[26] Without faith it is impossible to please him, for whoever would draw near to God must believe that he exists and that he rewards those who seek him. (Hebrews 11:6)

our behalf. The Lord knows everything, and there will be no miscarriages of justice. The only thing necessary for a person to be saved is faith that Jesus died for all of his or her sins and has given him or her his righteousness (Romans 3:22-24).[27] All those who believe this is true will not only repent of all their sins but also repudiate everything about themselves, whether good or evil, and rely completely on him. He will be their "pearl of great value" (Matthew 13:46), their most valuable possession. If a man tries to bribe a judge with his money to let him off despite the crimes he has committed, he will go to jail for an even longer sentence. Imagine what will happen to anyone who tries to bribe the Lord with "worthless" good works to let him or her off despite the sins he or she has committed!

## Hell

Hell is a place of torment originally prepared for Satan and those angels who followed him into rebellion against the Lord (2 Peter 2:4).[28] When humankind fell into sin, humankind earned a similar punishment (Matthew 25:41).[29] Hell, in common expressions, is often referred to in a manner implying it is somewhere inside the earth, somewhere downward. Yet this is because heaven is thought of as being upward, so hell, being the opposite of heaven, is considered to be in the opposite direction. The location of hell is not given in the Bible, and it is better for people to spend their time trying to avoid going there than in speculating where it is. In any event, hell is not a place that one can reach from the physical universe (Luke 16:26). It is not in the realm of time but rather the realm of eternity. Therefore, the punishment of those in hell will last forever (Mark 9:47,48).[30]

There is nothing funny about hell, and joking about it only makes something that is intolerable seem like it can be managed by those sent there. That is very wishful thinking. The Bible describes hell as a place of intense suffering (Matthew 8:12;[31] Matthew 13:42). Both the souls and the bodies of people

---

[27] The righteousness of God is through faith in Jesus Christ for all who believe. For there is no distinction: for all have sinned and fall short of the glory of God, and are justified by his grace as a gift, through the redemption that is in Christ Jesus. (Romans 3:22-24)

[28] God did not spare angels when they sinned, but cast them into hell and committed them to chains of gloomy darkness to be kept until the judgment. (2 Peter 2:4)

[29] [Jesus said,] "Then he [Jesus himself] will say to those on his left, 'Depart from me, you cursed, into the eternal fire prepared for the devil and his angels.'" (Matthew 25:41)

[30] [Jesus said,] "If your eye causes you to sin, tear it out. It is better for you to enter the kingdom of God with one eye than with two eyes to be thrown into hell, 'where their worm does not die and the fire is not quenched.'" (Mark 9:47,48)

[31] [Jesus said,] "In that place there will be weeping and gnashing of teeth." (Matthew 8:12)

sent there will suffer continually, but the Lord has not told us the details of the suffering that will be inflicted, and we need not speculate. What the Bible does say is that there will be no relief, no breaks to catch one's breath, and no mercy from the Lord (Revelation 20:10).[32] In fact, the complete absence of the Lord and of the hope that he might yet intervene will make the suffering all the worse. Everyone will be in complete despair, including the demons, who will no longer be able to do anything to frustrate the Lord's plans.

Many people have the feeling that hell cannot be real. They view it as a threat that the Lord is holding over people's heads to make them shape up. They argue that, in the end, the Lord is loving and will let everyone into heaven. But the Lord does not threaten people with hell; he promises it to those who do not accept Jesus Christ as the way of salvation. That is why Jesus himself, more than any other person in the Bible, talks about people being condemned to hell. If hell is not going to be the punishment of most people, then the Lord is lying to humankind, which means that he is no different from us and therefore has no right to judge us. The Lord does not lie, so it is a dangerous delusion to think that what he tells us is anything but the truth (Numbers 23:19).[33]

Those who accept that the Lord will punish evil but do not like that the punishment is eternal have tried to reshape his punishment in one of two ways. Some argue that the punishment will only last for a fixed time, and then those in hell will be completely annihilated. There is no biblical support for this idea (Isaiah 66:24).[34] Others argue that the Lord will only punish the really bad people eternally, but the rest will be allowed to endure a fixed term of punishment based on the amount of their sins and then they will be allowed to enter heaven. The Bible clearly states that one cannot cross between hell and heaven (Luke 16:26).[35] Purgatory is one scheme of limited punishment. It was originally restricted to Roman Catholics in good standing in their church, but the idea has developed in recent years that people from other religions who try hard to live a good life might also be allowed

---

[32] The devil who had deceived them was thrown into the lake of fire and sulfur where the beast and the false prophet were, and they will be tormented day and night forever and ever. (Revelation 20:10)

[33] [The Lord said,] "God is not man, that he should lie, or a son of man, that he should change his mind. Has he said, and will he not do it? Or has he spoken, and will he not fulfill it?" (Numbers 23:19)

[34] [The Lord said,] "They [generic they] shall go out and look on the dead bodies of the men who have rebelled against me. For their worm shall not die, their fire shall not be quenched, and they shall be an abhorrence to all flesh." (Isaiah 66:24)

[35] [Jesus, quoting Father Abraham:] "Besides all this, between us and you a great chasm has been fixed, in order that those who would pass from here to you may not be able, and none may cross from there to us." (Luke 16:26)

to use this route to reach heaven. The idea that one can get into heaven by suffering a degree of punishment for one's sins is merely another work-righteousness scheme, with part of the scheme coming into play only after a person's death. It denies salvation is by grace alone; it is therefore synergistic[36] and will take people to hell and not heaven. A just God is not going to renege on punishing those who do not accept his means of salvation. Trying to finesse the Lord is the height of stupidity (Hebrews 10:30,31).[37]

## Heaven

The Hebrews used their word for heaven in three ways, much as we do today. The lower heaven was the atmosphere up to the level where the clouds float. The middle heaven was where the sun, moon, and stars travel. The third, or upper, heaven was where the Lord and his heavenly hosts dwelled. Certainly, the atmosphere and "outer space" constitute two levels of the physical domain which can be called heaven. The place where the Lord exists, however, is not in the physical universe; it is in the realm of eternity. The "third heaven," therefore, is a place independent of our time and space where the Lord dwells and where Jesus has prepared a place for us (2 Corinthians 12:2,3).[38] As with everything else about the Lord, his dwelling place is beyond our ability to describe and is nothing like the cartoons one sees in the press. It is the place that John saw in his visions in Revelation.

In Revelation chapters 21–22, the Bible gives us picture descriptions of what heaven is like. It is described as having gates that are each single pearls and streets that are of gold. It has no sources of light but the Lord, and there is no night. There is a river of life and trees along it that are always bearing fruit. Precious stones form the bases of the walls, and the heavenly city is very large in size. All these are but visions of what heaven really is like, because we do not have the frame of reference yet to fully appreciate it. Speculating about heaven serves little purpose; we will have to wait to see it.

What we will do in heaven has always been a topic for discussion. We know that we will sing and praise the Lord (Psalm 84:4; Revelation

---

[36]When two different organisms work together for their mutual benefit to accomplish what neither can do by itself, it is called synergism. Theology is synergistic if it requires both the work of God and man to achieve salvation.

[37]We know him who said, "Vengeance is mine; I will repay." And again, "The Lord will judge his people." It is a fearful thing to fall into the hands of the living God. (Hebrews 10:30,31)

[38]I know a man in Christ who fourteen years ago was caught up to the third heaven—whether in the body or out of the body I do not know, God knows. And I know that this man was caught up into paradise. (2 Corinthians 12:2,3)

15:2,3), but heaven should not be thought of as one long choir practice. The Lord will have activities that will keep us busy and happy for endless time (2 Timothy 2:12). We know that we will have glorified bodies that cannot decay or suffer want of any kind (Revelation 21:4).[39] We do not know at what physical age these bodies will appear. How we will recognize one another and what we will talk about are things the Lord did not think it necessary for us to know beforehand. There will be no sin and no temptation. What we will eat and drink is unknown (Luke 22:29,30).[40] We know that Jesus ate after his resurrection and that there will be fruit trees in heaven. And despite what it says in a well-known, beer-drinking song, perhaps there will even be beer! We don't know whether there will be animals, such as pets, in heaven.

All the details about heaven may excite our curiosity because we do not yet know them. What we do know, however, is far more important than what we don't know. We will be with the Lord continually, enjoying his presence in a perfect world (Matthew 25:46). All the strife that we endured will be behind us. Heaven is compared to a wedding banquet (Revelation 19:6-9) because that is a time of great happiness with which almost everyone has had some experience, regardless of which time period they have lived in. Living Christians need to keep their focus on the permanent joy of heaven so they do not become enamored with the things of this world and lose the heavenly prize (Philippians 3:12-14).

## False teachings about the end times

The Lord promised to give the land of Canaan to Abraham's descendants as their homeland. After the Lord led them out of Egypt and before he brought them into Canaan, however, he established a covenant with them that required them to keep all of his ordinances in order to remain in the Promised Land and receive his blessing. If they failed to obey his commandments and ordinances, then he would evict them from the land and punish them severely (Deuteronomy 28:15-68). And, in fact, they did disobey his laws and rebelled against him countless times. Finally, he did expel them from the land but eventually brought back a remnant of the people from Babylon to continue his plan of salvation.

---

[39] [A loud voice from the throne of God said,] "He will wipe away every tear from their eyes, and death shall be no more, neither shall there be mourning, nor crying, nor pain anymore, for the former things have passed away." (Revelation 21:4)

[40] [Jesus said,] "I assign to you, as my Father assigned to me, a kingdom, that you may eat and drink at my table in my kingdom and sit on thrones judging the twelve tribes of Israel." (Luke 22:29,30)

The Jews, however, never stopped dreaming about the high point of their history, the united kingdom under David and Solomon and the temple that Solomon had built for the Lord. The Messiah that had been promised to save them from their sins became associated in their thinking with the restoration of the kingdom of Israel as the home of the Jews and as the dominant force in the world. When the Messiah did come, some of the Jews, including Jesus' own disciples, expected that he would establish that earthly kingdom. Jesus emphatically denied that he was going to establish an earthly kingdom (John 18:36).[41] Despite this, even until the time Jesus ascended into heaven his disciples entertained this hope (Acts 1:6). After the coming of the Holy Spirit on Pentecost, however, they realized that they were to call people to repentance so that they could live in a heavenly, not an earthly, kingdom.

Some of the Jews in the early church never gave up on the idea of an earthly kingdom being established when Jesus returned. They had the desire to have physical power over their enemies, at least for a time on this earth. Eventually, these ideas became associated with the prophecies of Revelation 20 (see discussion in chapter 3), and the concept of a thousand-year period on earth in which Christians would dominate was developed. This "millennium" was not accepted as doctrine by either the Eastern or Western branch of the Christian church and fell into disfavor for centuries. It was revived, however, after the Lutheran Reformation by those who wanted their earthly deeds to have some lasting importance. They dug out prophesies meant to describe the heavenly paradise and attached them to an imagined earthly reign of Christ. Because these Bible verses do not apply to a millennium, however, there is great disagreement among those who argue that a millennium will occur.

There are a number of issues to consider. Will Christ return before the millennium period, as the premillennialists claim, or after it, as the postmillennialists claim? Will the enemies of Christ be given a second chance to repent during this period? Will there be a formal period of tribulation? If so, will this be before or at the end of the millennium? What about the battle of Armageddon? Any answers to these and other questions about the millennium that people attempt to draw from the Bible are pure fantasy because the timeline for the end of the world that the Bible gives does not include a millennium. The millennial period during which Satan is bound is the New Testament Era, as discussed in chapter 3.

---

[41]Jesus answered, "My kingdom is not of this world. If my kingdom were of this world, my servants would have been fighting, that I might not be delivered over to the Jews. But my kingdom is not from the world." (John 18:36)

A concept associated with the millennium is the "rapture." The Bible says that at the time of the return of Christ, a separation will occur between the believers and the unbelievers (Matthew 24:38-41).[42] They may regularly be standing side by side, the same to human eyes. At the sudden return of Christ, however, one will be taken to be with the group of saints, and the other will be left with the unbelievers. Those who believe in some form of millennialism believe that this separation will occur before judgment day in preparation for the millennium occurring, despite what the Bible says. They envision cars suddenly without drivers and pitchers without catchers. The concept of a separation before judgment day, however, is something that is read into the Scriptures and is not compatible with the context in which these verses are written.

Another effort by humans to inflate their own importance is the recurring effort to determine the date when Jesus will return. Jesus said that no one knows the date and the time except the heavenly Father himself (Matthew 24:36). Jesus did not even permit himself to know it while he was here on earth. Nevertheless, people over the centuries have dug through the various symbolic numbers, particularly in Daniel and Revelation, to set dates for the return, which strangely enough often are only a few months or years in the future from when they are living. This is clear evidence that such a person is trying to gain a name for himself as a prophet, ignoring the clear words of Jesus. Some, such as the Jehovah's Witnesses, have been embarrassed so often by their failures that they have declared Jesus has already returned invisibly and will reveal himself openly at a future date.

The second coming of Jesus is a major doctrine of the Christian church. It is the end of the story that began in Genesis with the creation of the world and the fall into sin. The story ends with the glorification of those restored to their original relationship with the Lord and with the destruction of the creation as we know it. Therefore, it is important not to become discouraged that Jesus has not yet returned, even though much time has passed (2 Peter 3:3-7).[43] It is equally important not to be led astray by false prophets of the

---

[42] [Jesus said,] "As in those days before the flood they were eating and drinking, marrying and giving in marriage, until the day when Noah entered the ark, and they were unaware until the flood came and swept them all away, so will be the coming of the Son of Man. Then two men will be in the field; one will be taken and one left. Two women will be grinding at the mill; one will be taken and one left." (Matthew 24:38-41)

[43] Knowing this first of all, that scoffers will come in the last days with scoffing, following their own sinful desires. They will say, "Where is the promise of his coming? For ever since the fathers fell asleep, all things are continuing as they were from the beginning of creation." For they deliberately overlook this fact, that the heavens existed long ago, and the earth was formed out of water and through water

end times, whom Jesus specifically warned against (Matthew 24:23-27).[44] We must always be ready but not be so eager that we become foolish. Those interested in a deeper study of the end times should consult the book by that name written by Thomas Nass.[45]

## Feelings about the end times

The approaching end of the world, like our approaching death, is naturally a source of apprehension because it means drastic change. Although we may alternately love our situation in the world or hate the world in general, we have come to know the world and feel a certain comfort in it. Death or the coming of Christ will put an end to our time in this world, and the thought of that causes discomfort. We have no choice in the matter, no matter how many civil rights we may feel we are entitled to. The Lord God will assert himself, and our powerlessness will be undeniable.

This situation may be annoying and even terrifying to someone who does not believe in Christ. Facing the judgment of the Lord is not something one will get a chance to redo if it doesn't go well the first time. Even for the nominal Christian who anticipates putting his good works down to offset at least some of his sins, there has to be a feeling of apprehension lest his offered payment will be too small. Alas, we know from the Scriptures that it will certainly be too small. It is therefore imperative that we do not fall into the chasm of unbelief or the quicksand of synergism.

For those who rely completely on Christ for their salvation, the verdict is effectively in already. The Lord is not going to cast his dear children away. Death or judgment day is our passage into heaven. Jesus has promised it, and who can contradict him? Will Jesus as our judge be talked out of our salvation, which he paid for with his blood, by Satan and his lies? St. Paul writes, "Who shall bring any charge against God's elect? It is God who justifies. Who is to condemn? Christ Jesus is the one who died—more than that,

---

by the Word of God, and that by means of these the world that then existed was deluged with water and perished. But by the same Word the heavens and earth that now exist are stored up for fire, being kept until the day of judgment and destruction of the ungodly. (2 Peter 3:3-7)

[44][Jesus said,] "If anyone says to you, 'Look, here is the Christ!' or 'There he is!' do not believe it. For false christs and false prophets will arise and perform great signs and wonders, so as to lead astray, if possible, even the elect. See, I have told you beforehand. So, if they say to you, 'Look, he is in the wilderness,' do not go out. If they say, 'Look, he is in the inner rooms,' do not believe it. For as the lightning comes from the east and shines as far as the west, so will be the coming of the Son of Man." (Matthew 24:23-27)

[45]Thomas P. Nass, *End Times,* People's Bible Teachings series (Milwaukee: Northwestern Publishing House, 2011).

who was raised—who is at the right hand of God, who indeed is interceding for us" (Romans 8:33,34). The thought of the coming of the end of all things is therefore both comforting and joyful for those who put their faith in Christ alone. In the end, all evil will be destroyed and will never disturb us again. All pain and suffering and uncertainty will be gone. In the end, the Lord wins, and we win. In the words of Job, "I know that my Redeemer lives, and at the last he will stand upon the earth. And after my skin has been thus destroyed, yet in my flesh I shall see God, whom I shall see for myself, and my eyes shall behold, and not another" (Job 19:25-27).

# Plan of Salvation—Theological View

In section III we looked at the historical account of the Lord's interaction with humankind, as well as what he has told us about the future, that is, the end times. In this section we will move into God's chair, so to speak, and look at the way he views his relationship with humankind. This will naturally be limited because the Lord has not told us many things about himself, so we will need to be careful not to fill in details he has not revealed to us. Even from the limited view that we have, however, we will see how the many puzzle pieces of our lives on earth fit into the Lord's plan.

In reading these chapters, it is important to remember what a dominating being the Lord is. Readers may want to skim through chapter 4 again to refresh their memories on the extraordinariness of the Lord. The Lord is not bound by anything physical. He is not bound by human values (Isaiah 45:9).[1] He has created the whole framework in which we live. He has established all the reference points according to which we view the things of this world and by which we make decisions.

---

[1] [The LORD said,] "Does the clay say to him who forms it, 'What are you making?' or 'Your work has no handles'?" (Isaiah 45:9)

Although we may think that we have devised something clever, it is only because the Lord has put the right things into the right place at the right time when we are in the right frame of mind so that we could even consider a matter. We can never outthink the Lord.

As we look at the world from God's view in the next five chapters, we need to be prepared to accept that what we learn will not always sit well with our reason. There will be things we will not be able to grasp and things we will not be able to reconcile with one another. The Lord is so much greater than we are that his "foolishness" far exceeds our wisdom (1 Corinthians 1:25).[2] We must therefore work at understanding the Lord as well as we are able from what he has told us and believing what he says without putting our own spin on it. We must not deny something just because our reason tells us it cannot be if it is what the Lord has said. Salvation comes through faith, not through works or reason (2 Corinthians 5:6,7).[3]

---

[2]The foolishness of God is wiser than men, and the weakness of God is stronger than men. (1 Corinthians 1:25)

[3]We are always of good courage. We know that while we are at home in the body we are away from the Lord, for we walk by faith, not by sight. (2 Corinthians 5:6,7)

# CHAPTER 12

# Kingdom of God

In the 21st century, most kings hold only ceremonial positions rather than positions of real power. Today, kings do a lot of formal activities for their nations, like opening parliaments, dedicating important buildings, and appearing at diplomatic events in fancy garb. In the time period during which the Bible was written, kings had real power, life-or-death power, over everyone in their kingdoms. What they said was the way it would be, and few survived long by defying a king. To help us understand the Lord, the Bible represents the Lord as such a king—in fact, as more powerful than such a king. He is called the "King of kings and Lord of lords" (Revelation 19:16).[1] In other words, the same absolute power that kings at one time had over their subjects the Lord always had and has now and forever over all rulers and all their subjects. Absolutely nothing can happen at any level without his personal approval that the event fits with his plan for the universe. While powerful kings have almost completely disappeared from the earth, the Lord and his power remain the same as they have ever been (1 Chronicles 29:11).[2] His form of government will never change, and he does not accept our objections to his rule (Isaiah 40:13-15).[3]

---

[1] On his robe and on his thigh he has a name written, King of kings and Lord of lords. (Revelation 19:16)

[2] [David said,] "Yours, O Lord, is the greatness and the power and the glory and the victory and the majesty, for all that is in the heavens and in the earth is yours. Yours is the kingdom, O Lord, and you are exalted as head above all." (1 Chronicles 29:11)

[3] Who has measured the Spirit of the Lord, or what man shows him his counsel? Whom did he consult, and who made him understand? Who taught him the path of justice, and taught him knowledge,

## The Lord's kingdom(s)

When people hear the phrase "kingdom of God," too many think of a utopian society on earth where Jesus or God reigns in visible form. Often this is referred to as the "millennium," but whatever it is called, a utopian kingdom of God in this world is a fantasy. Jesus said, "The kingdom of God is not coming in ways that can be observed, nor will they say, 'Look, here it is!' or 'There!' for behold, the kingdom of God is in the midst of you" (Luke 17:20,21). The kingdom of God is wherever the Lord is working, that is, exercising his kingly power, and he is always working for the benefit of his elect.[4] To aid in our understanding of the ways in which he works, we often divide the Lord's work into several different kingdoms, even though from the Lord's viewpoint it is all one kingdom. Before we can look at these, however, we must recognize there is a realm (i.e., a domain) called "eternity," where only the Lord resides. We know almost nothing about this realm except that it exists independent of our time and space, because the Lord created our time and space. It is in this realm of eternity that all the internal actions of the Godhead occur, of which we know only a few, for example, the Father begetting the Son. The Lord is sometimes called the "hidden God" because we cannot approach him or comprehend him who dwells "in unapproachable light" (1 Timothy 6:15,16).[5] Because the working of this realm has not been revealed to us, it need not concern us. Certainly, it is a mystery to us now, and perhaps it will remain so even when we see the Lord in his heavenly kingdom.

The first of the kingdoms into which we divide the Lord's work is his kingdom of power. This kingdom, which includes the whole physical universe, is a realm where everything obeys his commands because he rules it by his almighty power. The Lord's relationship to the universe was introduced in chapter 6. The second kingdom is his kingdom of grace (i.e., his spiritual kingdom), the realm in which he rules through the means of grace and the work of the Holy Spirit on human hearts. The Christian church, which was briefly discussed in chapter 10, is the visible manifestation of the Lord's work in the kingdom of grace. Finally, there is the Lord's kingdom of glory (i.e., his heavenly or eternal kingdom), the kingdom he has prom-

---

and showed him the way of understanding? Behold, the nations are like a drop from a bucket, and are accounted as the dust on the scales. (Isaiah 40:13-15)

[4] John Schaller, "The Kingdom of God," in *The Wauwatosa Theology*, Vol. III (Milwaukee: Northwestern Publishing House, 1997), pp. 13-50.

[5] He who is the blessed and only Sovereign, the King of kings and Lord of lords, who alone has immortality, who dwells in unapproachable light, whom no one has ever seen or can see. To him be honor and eternal dominion. Amen. (1 Timothy 6:15,16)

ised to all believers. Note that the latter is not the same as the realm of eternity in which the Lord dwells, because even in heaven no one will have the attributes of the Lord or his understanding. He is the God who has created all things, even the heavenly kingdom, and we are not. As we look at these kingdoms, we must recognize that the kingdom of power exists solely for the support of the kingdom of grace and that the kingdom of grace exists solely for the purpose of preparing people for the kingdom of glory. The first two kingdoms of God will disappear in their current forms, but the kingdom of glory will last forever.

## Kingdom of power

The Lord's kingdom of power extends over everything that exists, whether visible or invisible; whether matter, antimatter, energy, or spirit; whether animate or inanimate; whether simple or complex. It governs all that we can discern with our senses, things we can only measure with our instrumentation, and things that are beyond our capabilities to probe. The Lord's management of the kingdom of power is essential for our lives because we live in the physical universe that can often be a hostile environment. Careless, and even seemingly innocent, actions can result in serious harm to individuals, to entire species, and to whole ecological systems. Because the Lord is actively reigning over the physical universe, the believer does not need to fear (Psalm 91:9,10).[6]

The Lord manages his physical realm through both direct and delegated power. In chapter 6 the concept of the Lord figuratively having two hands was introduced, one working through natural "laws" and the other working by his direct intervention in situations through "miracles." No matter how he controls the physical universe, it is he who controls it (Isaiah 43:13).[7] That is what the kingdom of power is all about. There are no accidents or unexpected results (Jeremiah 1:4,5).[8] The Lord knows everything that will happen, when it will happen, and how to make sure that it happens, even when that means taking advantage of the choices of the living creatures he created. He is more than the director of the production being performed on the stage of the physical universe. He is the master technician who

---

[6]Because you have made the LORD your dwelling place—the Most High, who is my refuge—no evil shall be allowed to befall you, no plague come near your tent. (Psalm 91:9,10)

[7][The LORD said,] "Also henceforth I am he; there is none who can deliver from my hand; I work, and who can turn it back?" (Isaiah 43:13)

[8]The word of the LORD came to me, saying, "Before I formed you in the womb I knew you, and before you were born I consecrated you; I appointed you a prophet to the nations." (Jeremiah 1:4,5)

makes sure that everything is functioning properly and the stage master who makes sure that everything and everyone is in precisely the right place to give the performance that he desires. When the creatures to whom he gave wills of their own challenge his control of a situation, he knows their motives and their intentions, and he arranges events so his, not their, will establishes the final results (Proverbs 16:33).[9]

Some question the Lord's control of the physical universe because there is so much human suffering and misery in it. "If the Lord is in control," they ask, "why doesn't he prevent earthquakes, floods, tidal waves, and hurricanes? Why does he allow famine, drought, and disease?" Surely, reason argues, if the Lord is good and has the power to prevent the bad things from happening, he would do so. Yet we must remember that the Lord didn't want any of these troubles that plague humankind to happen. He created the world to be perfect (Genesis 1:31),[10] and he permitted no natural disasters. Moreover, the Lord warned Adam and Eve not to eat of the tree of the knowledge of good and evil, and that if they did, they would certainly die (Genesis 2:17).[11] When they did eat of the forbidden fruit, the Lord could have killed them right there, as if the fruit of the tree had been highly toxic. Instead, he extended their lives, but he cursed the ground because they had destroyed the harmony he had created (Genesis 3:17).[12] All the natural disasters that occur are a result of this cursing of the earth on account of human sins. They are the alternative punishment to immediate death, just as the ancient Greek courts used to give exile as the alternative punishment for a death sentence. Humankind certainly has not improved in any way to justify the removal of the curse. The Lord doesn't owe anything good to those who continue to be disobedient to his will, yet in his mercy he gives most of us plenty of good things (Matthew 5:45).[13] Due to people's sinfulness, natural disasters should be expected to be the standard rather than the exception in this world. The earth belongs to the Lord (Psalm 24:1),[14] and people are his tenants who are

---

[9] [Solomon said,] "The lot is cast into the lap, but its every decision is from the LORD." (Proverbs 16:33)

[10] God saw everything that he had made, and behold, it was very good. And there was evening and there was morning, the sixth day. (Genesis 1:31)

[11] [The LORD said,] "Of the tree of the knowledge of good and evil you shall not eat, for in the day that you eat of it you shall surely die." (Genesis 2:17)

[12] To Adam he [the LORD] said, "Because you have listened to the voice of your wife and have eaten of the tree of which I commanded you, 'You shall not eat of it,' cursed is the ground because of you; in pain you shall eat of it all the days of your life." (Genesis 3:17)

[13] [Jesus said,] "For he [God the Father] makes his sun rise on the evil and on the good, and sends rain on the just and on the unjust." (Matthew 5:45)

[14] [David said,] "The earth is the LORD's and the fullness thereof, the world and those who dwell therein." (Psalm 24:1)

not managing it well (Leviticus 25:23).[15] They have no basis for complaint if the conditions are less than ideal, because they aren't ideal either.

Due to the sinfulness of humankind, the Lord needs to govern the people as well as to control their environment through the kingdom of power, lest they destroy each other. He does this by creating governing authorities (Romans 13:1,2).[16] In New Testament times, governing authorities are often collectively referred to as the "state," in contrast to the "church." The purpose of the state is to manage interactions among people, regardless of their religious affiliations. The rules of the state are not intended to make people morally better but rather to make them behave legally by use of force and incentives. Through the state the Lord offers people protection for their lives and properties, providing them a stable environment in which to live and work (Romans 13:3,4).[17] Through the state he provides people with ways to organize their economic activities, grants tax incentives, and gives subsidies to promote the general welfare. Through the state the Lord provides for certain freedoms that are guaranteed through legal processes. Through the state he provides protection against invasion by foreign nations and against revolutions by the disgruntled. Through the state he encourages acts of civic righteousness and neighbors working together for the common good. The state is sometimes referred to as the "left hand of God" because, while necessary for good order, it does not represent the Lord's primary interest in humans.

While many people believe that democracy is the only proper form of government, the Lord endorses no specific form of government. Most governments are really of mixed form. Even when a king is the primary ruler, he often has to deal with a parliament and judges who are not appointed by him. In democracies, courts often overturn the work of democratically elected bodies when they feel it endangers the general welfare of the country. There are often families or religious leaders who have a significant influence on the government, no matter what its official form is. Finally, good government is not based on its formal type but on whether it carries out the tasks of governing honestly and with due concern for the citizens of the country.

---

[15] [The LORD said,] "The land shall not be sold in perpetuity, for the land is mine. For you are strangers and sojourners with me." (Leviticus 25:23)

[16] Let every person be subject to the governing authorities. For there is no authority except from God, and those that exist have been instituted by God. Therefore whoever resists the authorities resists what God has appointed, and those who resist will incur judgment. (Romans 13:1,2)

[17] Rulers are not a terror to good conduct, but to bad. Would you have no fear of the one who is in authority? Then do what is good, and you will receive his approval, for he is God's servant for your good. But if you do wrong, be afraid, for he does not bear the sword in vain. For he is the servant of God, an avenger who carries out God's wrath on the wrongdoer. (Romans 13:3,4)

Unfortunately, all governments are run by sinful human beings, many of whom often place themselves, their families, and their friends ahead of the interests of the people as a whole. Some countries are more corrupt than others, and some rulers do not take seriously their obligations to work for the good of their citizens. Sometimes the governing process breaks down into disorder or civil strife. When things are not going well, it is important to realize that the Lord God is still in control. The Bible calls for obedience to rulers and not for rebellion—either active or passive—against them, so long as they do not prevent the teaching of the Word of the Lord in its truth and purity. Bad governments, like natural disasters, are used by the Lord for his purposes. Even bad governments are his servants to accomplish his purpose (1 Samuel 24:10),[18] and he will punish them for their evil at the time he deems to be appropriate.

The only situation in which Lutherans may disobey their government is when that government requires them to do things that are against biblical teachings (Acts 5:29).[19] This might include killing the innocent, indiscriminate destruction of property, sexual immorality, or brutality. The most common reason to disobey governmental authorities, however, is when they insist that the church teach contrary to the Bible for the benefit of the state or that the church support state activities that violate biblical teachings. Note well that a government violating the civil rights (human rights) of people is not, in itself, a reason to disobey the government, that is, to engage in rebellion or in acts of civil disobedience.

Whether the Lord is controlling the physical entities that he created in the universe or is managing the governments that he established within nations, his real goal is not improving the universe or even keeping it going for its own sake. He is not interested in creating a physical or economic paradise on earth. If he were, he could make that happen instantly. The physical universe is but a stage whose sole purpose for existence is to provide a setting for the Lord to save his elect. Therefore, those who set their hearts on the things of this world are not in tune with the Lord's program. While the Lord expects people to be good stewards of the things he has given them to manage, they are not to become devoted to them (Matthew 6:19-21).[20] The Lord's activities in his

---

[18] [David said,] "Some told me to kill you, but I spared you. I said, 'I will not put out my hand against my lord, for he is the LORD's anointed.'" (1 Samuel 24:10)

[19] Peter and the apostles answered, "We must obey God rather than men." (Acts 5:29)

[20] [Jesus said,] "Do not lay up for yourselves treasures on earth, where moth and rust destroy and where thieves break in and steal, but lay up for yourselves treasures in heaven, where neither moth nor rust destroys and where thieves do not break in and steal. For where your treasure is, there your heart will be also." (Matthew 6:19-21)

kingdom of power as we now know it will only continue until the kingdom of grace has fully populated the invisible church with his elect.

## Kingdom of grace

The Lord's real interest in his creation is in those creatures to which he originally gave freedom of choice, namely, humankind and the angels. While the rest of creation will be destroyed, these two species will remain. The issue with the angels has already been resolved because they have been judged, either into eternal bliss to serve the Lord or into eternal punishment for rebelling against the Lord. The situation with the human race is different. All its members have, by nature, been his enemies since the time when Adam and Eve sinned. Unless they repent and turn to Christ as their only means of salvation, they will receive eternal punishment for their lives of sin, just like the demons. As a result, the Lord's focus is now on the actions that he must take to save his elect, those whom he chose from eternity to believe in his Son. This is the sole purpose of all his activities in his kingdom of grace. (The Lord's election to salvation will be discussed in the next chapter.)

The kingdom of grace produces and sustains the "invisible church." It is invisible because no person can tell who is a member of this church and who is not. Only the Lord can see into the hearts of people, so only he knows who really believes in the message of the gospel. Belonging to a congregation or parish of some nominally Christian church body does not automatically make one a member of the invisible church, because many churchgoers have a distorted view of the gospel and are, in fact, idolaters, worshiping gods created by their own minds and hands. The words of Jesus that "many are called, but few are chosen" (Matthew 22:14) should continually be ringing in people's ears. It is critical that people learn the correct message of the gospel and that they do not merely sleepwalk through their religious life. Church membership and a moral life are necessary signs that someone is a member of the invisible church, but these are not sufficient evidence.

The invisible church was already present with Adam and Eve because they believed the promise of a deliverer who would crush the head of Satan (Genesis 4:1).[21] It was present with the patriarchs of Israel to whom the Lord gave the promise of the land of Canaan and to whom he renewed the promise of the deliverer (Genesis 15:6).[22] It was present in the nation of Israel and later in the nation of Judah during the era of the Old Testament

---

[21] Now Adam knew Eve his wife, and she conceived and bore Cain, saying, "I have gotten a man with the help of the LORD." (Genesis 4:1)

[22] He [Abraham] believed the LORD, and he counted it to him as righteousness. (Genesis 15:6)

(Psalm 51:9,10).[23] Because the invisible church was present, however, did not mean that most of the people belonged to it. In fact, very few people were members of the invisible church during most time periods in the history of the Israelites. Even when the nations of Israel and Judah appeared to be serving the Lord, only a few people did. The Lord preserved the Israelites as a nation because of this small number of true believers and because he was using Israel as the vehicle to carry out his plan of salvation for humankind. To grasp how few were saved, one needs only to look at times when the Lord gave the exact number of those who believed. Only eight people were saved from the flood (1 Peter 3:20). Only two out of six hundred thousand men of military age were permitted to enter the land of Canaan after their rebellion, although more may have later repented (Numbers 14:30). The Lord referred to the Israelites as a "stiff-necked people" (Exodus 33:5)[24] who were always rebelling against him. At the time of Elijah, the Lord said he still had seven thousand faithful in the Northern Kingdom of Israel (1 Kings 19:18), out of more than one hundred times that number of citizens (that is, less than one percent believed). The number of people who returned from the Babylonian captivity was small (Ezra 2:64,65) compared to the number who had inhabited the land at David's time, and many of these people quickly intermarried with their pagan neighbors (Ezra 10). In chapter 8 we saw how the Lord tried in numerous ways to teach the people to follow him, but they refused again and again. That the Lord endured such unfaithful behavior by so many for so long to save so few shows how gracious he really is. When the Jews of Jesus' time boasted about their faithfulness to the Lord, the God of the old covenant, Jesus justly called them hypocrites (Mark 7:6-8).[25] They were faithful to their man-made, reengineered form of religious service, but their service was actually for the building of the kingdom of Satan, not the kingdom of the Lord.

The Christian church in the New Testament has replaced the Hebrew people of the old covenant as the visible evidence of the Lord's work and rule in the kingdom of grace (Ephesians 2:11-22). Forty years after Jesus died and rose, the Lord obliterated the remnants of the Jewish nation. Its

---

[23] [David said,] "Hide your face from my sins, and blot out all my iniquities. Create in me a clean heart, O God, and renew a right spirit within me." (Psalm 51:9,10)

[24] The LORD had said to Moses, "Say to the people of Israel, 'You are a stiff-necked people.'" (Exodus 33:5)

[25] He [Jesus] said to them [the Pharisees and teachers of the Law], "Well did Isaiah prophesy of you hypocrites, as it is written, 'This people honors me with their lips, but their heart is far from me; in vain do they worship me, teaching as doctrines the commandments of men.' You leave the commandment of God and hold to the tradition of men." (Mark 7:6-8)

worship under the old covenant ceased. Judaism then reinvented itself through the teachings of the rabbis and the development of the *Mishnah*[26] and the *Talmud*.[27] Judaism is no longer a saving religion because it is no longer the religion of the Scriptures. The visible Christian churches, moreover, are not the same as the invisible church, which has only a small fraction of the membership of these churches. Already at the time of the apostles, there were people trying to take the Christian church into a different direction from that set by Jesus Christ and from those he had personally called to write the New Testament of the Bible (Galatians 1:6;[28] 2 Peter 3:16[29]). The number of leaders during the history of the church who have believed that they have received special directions from the Lord to take the church away from its biblical foundation has been large, and more keep coming. Sadly, the old false doctrines are often merely stated in new ways today and continue to draw crowds who follow the pied pipers proclaiming them.

It is natural to ask why the Lord doesn't do something about the heresies that have troubled the visible Christian church and have led so many people astray. How can he, the almighty King, claim to love his followers and yet leave so many false teachers afoot to lead people to eternal destruction? There are three things that affect the answer to this question. First, while the Lord commissioned the office of the ministry as guided by the Holy Spirit to spread his teachings, he did not remove the ability to sin from those in that office. People can sin by teaching false doctrine in the same way that they can sin by stealing, lying, or murdering. All people, even church leaders, are prone to listen to their own sinful hearts and the demons as well as to the Lord. When they do not restrict their teachings to what agrees with the sure standard, the Bible, they fall into error. St. Paul sternly warns against teaching falsely (Galatians 1:8).[30] Yet if the Lord struck dead someone every time he made a theological mistake, as for example Aaron's sons (Leviti-

---

[26]The Mishnah is the written form of the Jewish Oral Law, which Jesus attacked in Matthew 15:1-9 as only the work of men.

[27]The Talmud is the written collection of senior rabbis' comments on and applications of the Hebrew Scriptures (Old Testament), and it includes the Mishnah. The Babylonian Talmud (22 volumes) is regarded as the most authoritative.

[28]I am astonished that you are so quickly deserting him who called you in the grace of Christ and are turning to a different gospel. (Galatians 1:6)

[29]There are some things in them [Paul's letters] that are hard to understand, which the ignorant and unstable twist to their own destruction, as they do the other Scriptures. (2 Peter 3:16)

[30]But even if we or an angel from heaven should preach to you a gospel contrary to the one we preached to you, let him be accursed. (Galatians 1:8)

cus 10:1,2),[31] the clergy of the church would rapidly be depopulated. Even faithful teachers occasionally make errors and have to be reminded to study the Scriptures. Certainly, the Lord does not want errors in his church, but because he has chosen to work through sinful humans rather than perfect beings like the holy angels, false teachings will occur.[32] It is because the Lord loves people that he has given them the opportunity to work with him in the great task of sharing his saving message with the world (1 Corinthians 3:9).[33] He also holds those whom he calls to teach to a higher standard than others (Ezekiel 3:16-21).

Second, while the Lord wants all people to be saved, he does not want them to deceive themselves by merely holding membership in a congrega-tion without accepting his message—yet many do. Throughout history, even in times of persecution, numerous people joined churches for reasons other than to repent and to receive the free gift of salvation. Some have sought status, like the Pharisees, by belonging to a prominent congregation. Some have wanted to feel good morally by being involved in churchly activities. Some have sought sanctification by association. Some have sought business advantage. Some have seen the church as a sanctified social outlet. Some have become members to please family and friends. No matter how "good" church members appear to be, the Lord searches the hearts of all to see whether they are still self-centered or whether they have repudiated them-selves to follow him alone. Large numbers of people are lost because, in real-ity, they want to be saved on their own terms and view church membership as a way to bind the Lord to their own agendas (Luke 11:37-52).

Finally, the Lord has continued to work in many congregations and church bodies that have sunk deep into theological error and whose official doctrinal positions can harm or even destroy saving faith. He works through the readings of sections of Scripture that are done at worship services. These words from the Bible are backed by the power of the Holy Spirit. Even if the readings are not explained correctly or at all by the minister, it is possible for the Holy Spirit to bring faith into, and keep it within, people's hearts (Romans 10:17).[34] Obviously, when false doctrine is taught alongside correct biblical doctrine, people more easily become confused and acquire a false faith, a

---

[31] Now Nadab and Abihu, the sons of Aaron, each took his censer and put fire in it and laid incense on it and offered unauthorized fire before the LORD, which he had not commanded them. And fire came out from before the LORD and consumed them, and they died before the LORD. (Leviticus 10:1,2)

[32] For the discussion of the perfection of the angels, see chapter 19.

[33] We are God's fellow workers. (1 Corinthians 3:9)

[34] Faith comes from hearing, and hearing through the word of Christ. (Romans 10:17)

faith that minimizes sin and/or gives redeeming status to human works. Sometimes the Holy Spirit opens the eyes of people trained in churches steeped in error, and they realize what has happened and return to the teachings of the Scriptures. Martin Luther had a PhD in the Holy Scriptures, and he was teaching at the University of Wittenberg when he realized that what he was teaching was not the message of the Bible at all but commentaries on commentaries on commentaries that had long ago strayed from the meaning of the biblical text. He therefore turned to the Scriptures themselves, rather than the works of fallible men, so as to proclaim the Word of God correctly.

The kingdom of grace, working through the visible church even with its many divisions, exists only for the purpose of converting the elect and preparing them for the kingdom of glory (2 Timothy 4:2-4).[35] In reality, it is only the elect who have the Great Commission to preach the gospel throughout the world. The rest of the members of the visible church bumble along for their own purposes, but they are used by the Lord to accomplish his plan for the building of his invisible church, even though they themselves will eventually be lost through unbelief (Matthew 7:21-23).[36] No matter how bad or good things look, the Lord is always in full control (Romans 8:28).[37] Through the kingdom of grace he daily blesses those whom he has chosen and strengthens their faith. He guards and protects them through ways that they often do not understand or appreciate but that he deems best for them. The elect will have to struggle against the demons, against worldly lusts, and against their own cravings (Acts 14:22). They will be ridiculed, persecuted, and perhaps even killed for their faith. The Lord knows all of this is necessary so that the members of the invisible church will abandon the temptations of this sinful world for the firm vision of heaven and will not look back at them as Lot's wife did (Genesis 19:26).[38]

To help the members of the invisible church understand the workings of the kingdom of grace better, Jesus used various illustrations to describe

---

[35]Preach the word; be ready in season and out of season; reprove, rebuke, and exhort, with complete patience and teaching. For the time is coming when people will not endure sound teaching, but having itching ears they will accumulate for themselves teachers to suit their own passions, and will turn away from listening to the truth and wander off into myths. (2 Timothy 4:2-4)

[36][Jesus said,] "Not everyone who says to me, 'Lord, Lord,' will enter the kingdom of heaven, but the one who does the will of my Father who is in heaven. On that day many will say to me, 'Lord, Lord, did we not prophesy in your name, and cast out demons in your name, and do many mighty works in your name?' And then will I declare to them, 'I never knew you; depart from me, you workers of lawlessness.'" (Matthew 7:21-23)

[37]We know that for those who love God all things work together for good, for those who are called according to his purpose. (Romans 8:28)

[38]Lot's wife, behind him, looked back, and she became a pillar of salt. (Genesis 19:26)

it. In these he often used the phrases "the kingdom of God" or "the kingdom of heaven" to identify it. He referred to the world as a field in which
both wheat (true believers) and weeds (false believers) grow. Because for a
long time they look very similar, they cannot be separated until the time of
harvest, lest the wheat be destroyed in the process (Matthew 13:24-30). He
called the kingdom of grace "the narrow gate" and the "straight path" (Matthew 7:13,14).[39] It is the road the Bible prescribes even though the worldly
superhighway next to it is more appealing to most. Jesus compared the
kingdom of grace to a businessman who gives his servants money to manage while he is gone (Matthew 25:14-30). He then pointed out that those
who are dedicated to him will use the opportunities the Lord gives them for
service. Jesus also compared the kingdom of heaven to attendants waiting
for the arrival of the bridegroom at a wedding. The bridesmaids who were
prepared with the oil of faith in their lamps became part of the wedding
party (i.e., the invisible church), while those who weren't prepared because
they allowed their faith to dwindle were excluded (Matthew 25:1-13). The
kingdom of grace is maintained by the work of the Holy Spirit, which will
be discussed in chapter 16.

### Kingdom of glory

When Jesus returns on judgment day, the universe as we know it will disappear (2 Peter 3:10).[40] In its place there will be a new heaven and a new
earth, the home of God's elect (2 Peter 3:11-13). The kingdom of power will
be reconstituted to serve the kingdom of glory. The members of the invisible
church will be ushered before the judgment throne to receive their rewards
in this new realm. The kingdom of grace, having served its purpose of sus-
taining the faithful with the necessities of spiritual life, will be dissolved into
the kingdom of glory. The kingdom of glory, the blessed home of God's elect,
will be established as the Lord's eternal kingdom.

Heaven was briefly discussed in chapter 11, in reference to the end times.
More detailed descriptions are available,[41] but no one can be very knowledgeable about heaven. The Bible tells us very little. Anything beyond what

---

[39][Jesus said,] "Enter by the narrow gate. For the gate is wide and the way is easy that leads to destruction, and those who enter by it are many. For the gate is narrow and the way is hard that leads to life, and
those who find it are few." (Matthew 7:13,14)

[40]The day of the Lord will come like a thief, and then the heavens will pass away with a roar, and the
heavenly bodies will be burned up and dissolved, and the earth and the works that are done on it will
be exposed. (2 Peter 3:10)

[41]Brian R. Keller, *Heaven and Hell*, People's Bible Teachings series (Milwaukee: Northwestern Publishing House, 2007).

it says is speculative. Nevertheless, there are several things worth reiterating as we look forward to the kingdom of glory.

From the Lord's point of view, the current age in which we live is the prelude to the kingdom of glory. Because he has given us this age, some things in it are important, for the Lord is not a frivolous God. On the other hand, because the demons and sinful humankind have corrupted the world, many things in the world are not important, and some are even dangerous. The Lord wants believers in Christ to keep focused on the important things that will reach their culmination in the kingdom of glory. He wants his followers to use the things in the physical world, but he does not want people to become attached to them. For example, through his kingdom of power, the Lord makes it possible for most people to work to earn their livings, and he expects them to do so (2 Thessalonians 3:10).[42] Yet he makes it clear that food should not be an end in itself (1 Corinthians 6:13).[43] People cannot have their hearts set on things in the physical world and at the same time be focused on the kingdom of glory. This is what Jesus was saying when he told the people they could not serve both God and money (Matthew 6:24). The possessions of this world and the recognition by this world pass away with the world. "The paths of glory lead but to the grave."[44] They do not lead to the *kingdom of glory.*

The Lord does not want the church to misuse its position as it works in the kingdom of grace. This occurs when the church seeks the glory of this world for itself and its members and, as a result, the means of grace are watered down or shoved out of the central position in the church. For example, preaching law and gospel is essential, but merely preaching "about the law" and "about the gospel" does not allow either to be effective. It is a much easier thing to do and doesn't offend anyone, but it accomplishes nothing. Liturgy can be the beautiful setting that holds the precious gem of God's Word, or it can instead be something people mumble through because it is expected, even though they do not understand what it means (1 Corinthians 14:19).[45] It might as well be in Latin. In the same way, hymns that are not understood are doing nothing but filling time in the service. When the

---

[42] Even when we were with you, we would give you this command: If anyone is not willing to work, let him not eat. (2 Thessalonians 3:10)

[43] "Food is meant for the stomach and the stomach for food"—and God will destroy both one and the other. (1 Corinthians 6:13)

[44] From the poem "Elegy Written in a Country Churchyard" by Thomas Gray, 1751.

[45] In church I would rather speak five words with my mind in order to instruct others, than ten thousand words in a tongue. (1 Corinthians 14:19)

mechanics of worship or other church programs become what the church is known for, instead of being known for the message of free salvation through Christ, God's grace is misused. The kingdom of grace is about the Lord's marvelous works, not about ours. Because people's time of grace is short and the kingdom of glory is rapidly approaching, it is essential not to get sidetracked by style but rather to be willing to sacrifice style for substance.

While the kingdom of power serves everyone and the kingdom of grace reaches out to everyone, the kingdom of glory is only for those who have "washed their robes and made them white in the blood of the Lamb" (Revelation 7:14). There are only two verdicts on judgment day, the kingdom of glory or hell, and hell is a dungeon, not a kingdom (Matthew 25:31-45). Hell is a place of pure misery and no hope. It is a damning fallacy to think there is a place of limited punishment or of second chances. The Bible says nothing of these. Therefore, while we do not know most of the details about heaven, we do know enough about it and about its alternative that we should want to be completely focused on entering the kingdom of glory. Nothing else really matters, so why should it trouble us? Our hearts and our minds should long to be with the Lord.

CHAPTER 13

# Predestination

To discuss the Lord's view of his plan of salvation for humankind, we need to start before the existence of everything we know. It was before he created the space, time, and materials of our universe that the Lord was making the plans and decisions, in whatever manner he does that, concerning what would happen in the world that he would create (Psalm 90:2).[1] We do not know the way the Lord thinks (1 Corinthians 2:16),[2] so we must be careful not to draw conclusions about the reasons why he did things in the manner in which he did. We must instead accept the information he gives us without twisting it to fit our human reasoning. Our best efforts to grasp how and why the Lord acts are limited, so our explanations remain tentative until we receive a full revelation in heaven (1 Peter 3:15).[3]

## Foreknowledge

The extent of the Lord's knowledge was introduced in chapter 4. To put it as simply as it can be put, he knows everything—everything that was, is, will be, or could be. When the Lord contemplated the universe that he

---

[1] [Moses said,] "Before the mountains were brought forth, or ever you had formed the earth and the world, from everlasting to everlasting you are God." (Psalm 90:2)

[2] [Paul, quoting Isaiah, said,] "Who has understood the mind of the Lord so as to instruct him?" (1 Corinthians 2:16)

[3] In your hearts honor Christ the Lord as holy, always being prepared to make a defense to anyone who asks you for a reason for the hope that is in you. (1 Peter 3:15)

would create, he had the whole picture of it in his mind. A number of scenarios, which is beyond our ability to imagine much less grasp, was a part of the picture that he saw. This complex gestalt was his foreknowledge. It was a knowledge that was exact. It was not some hazy representation of the future as if seen through a dirty window or a heavy fog. It was as tangible as reality. Like a computer simulation in which numerous parameters can be changed to see the effects on the results, so also the Lord's understanding of his intended creatures existed in his mind. But the mind of the Lord could perform analyses beyond what any possible computer built by humans will ever accomplish. It is this foreknowledge that is presented in the Scriptures (Acts 2:23;[4] 1 Peter 1:2;[5] 1 Peter 1:20,21[6]).

This foreknowledge was not like someone reading the script of a movie and therefore knowing the plot when she views it with her friends. It was an unfathomable interactive setting up of the coming creation so that it would accomplish the Lord's goals, while still allowing the creatures to whom he would give the freedom of choice the ability to use their powers as they pleased. It was an approach only the Lord would have chosen. It would be like the owner of a large company giving complete freedom in decision-making to his employees, but he knows every employee's mode of thinking so well that, by arranging the order in which the decisions needed to be made and the circumstances in which they needed to be made, he would end up with the employees doing precisely what was necessary to accomplish his desires. No business owner would follow such a course of action because something, probably many things, would almost certainly go wrong. Yet the Lord's foreknowledge is so thorough and his power so great and yet so precise that he did the equivalent of this example with the whole human race. The Lord's foreknowledge implies his guidance of, as well as his envisioning of, what will happen (Matthew 10:29,30).[7]

## Universal love for humankind

In his decision to create humankind, the Lord loved all of humankind. It was his fervent desire that all humankind would remain in prefect har-

---

[4] [Peter said,] "This Jesus, delivered up according to the definite plan and foreknowledge of God, you crucified and killed by the hands of lawless men." (Acts 2:23)

[5] According to the foreknowledge of God the Father, in the sanctification of the Spirit, for obedience to Jesus Christ and for sprinkling with his blood. (1 Peter 1:2)

[6] He [God the Son] was foreknown before the foundation of the world but was made manifest in the last times for the sake of you who through him are believers in God, who raised him from the dead and gave him glory, so that your faith and hope are in God. (1 Peter 1:20,21)

[7] [Jesus said,] "Are not two sparrows sold for a penny? And not one of them will fall to the ground apart from your Father. But even the hairs of your head are all numbered." (Matthew 10:29,30)

mony with his will and would live in his presence forever (1 Timothy 2:2-4).[8] To reach this goal, he created humans in his own image (Genesis 1:26,27), with his will already planted in the human heart. Humans were fully capable of retaining that image and also behaving in accordance with what the Lord desired. Because humankind understood the benefits of doing things the Lord's way, it was not burdensome labor but something that humans delighted in doing (Psalm 40:8).[9] Adam and Eve were completely content in what they were doing to maintain the Garden of Eden. Yet because the Lord wanted their obedience to be free and not forced, he gave them the ability to choose to continue to obey or to choose an easy way to exit their relationship with him (Genesis 2:17). They chose the latter option (Genesis 3:6), and the Lord could no longer have the close relationship to them that he wanted because they had become rebels who contaminated his creation (2 Thessalonians 1:9).[10] The Lord's justice cannot tolerate sin, and he must punish it with his full wrath (Psalm 1:5,6).[11] It is an attribute of the Lord that, like all his attributes, is essential to his essence.

Mercy is also an attribute that is essential to the Lord's essence. He cannot look at a creature of his own creation doomed to eternal punishment and not be moved (Isaiah 49:15,16).[12] The situation of the angels, each of whom had its fate completely in its own control because all of them were created at the same time, did not elicit the same feelings of mercy from the Lord as did humankind's situation. Because the first two people had sinned, their descendants, who would not have a direct choice in the matter, would also be corrupted and would be sinful rebels against the Lord (Psalm 51:5).[13] The longer the world continued, the larger the mass of humanity headed for hell would be. Foreknowing this, the Lord devised a plan of salvation to save all humankind (John 3:16). Not one person would have to be punished for his or her sins, but everyone would be able to escape from hell because the Lord

---

[8] That we may lead a peaceful and quiet life, godly and dignified in every way. This is good, and it is pleasing in the sight of God our Savior, who desires all people to be saved and to come to the knowledge of the truth. (1 Timothy 2:2-4)

[9] [David said,] "I delight to do your will, O my God; your law is within my heart." (Psalm 40:8)

[10] They will suffer the punishment of eternal destruction, away from the presence of the Lord and from the glory of his might. (2 Thessalonians 1:9)

[11] Therefore the wicked will not stand in the judgment, nor sinners in the congregation of the righteous; for the LORD knows the way of the righteous, but the way of the wicked will perish. (Psalm 1:5,6)

[12] [The LORD said,] "Can a woman forget her nursing child, that she should have no compassion on the son of her womb? Even these may forget, yet I will not forget you. Behold, I have engraved you on the palms of my hands." (Isaiah 49:15,16)

[13] [David said,] "Behold, I was brought forth in iniquity, and in sin did my mother conceive me." (Psalm 51:5)

would offer a substitute to be punished in their place. Already before Eve reached for the piece of fruit, the whole plan was developed (Romans 11:2),[14] and the Lord presented the promise of it to Adam and Eve on the same day that they sinned (Genesis 3:15).

As the Lord had promised, so he acted (Galatians 4:4,5).[15] He sent his Son—the second person of the Trinity—to take on a human nature, to live the life that people should have lived, and to die the atoning death necessary for the guilt of their sins. Through this payment, which will be discussed in chapter 15, every person who will ever exist was granted a full remission of sins. It is the greatest news that has ever been proclaimed. So great was the Lord's love for humankind and the Lord's mercy.

In his mercy, the Lord went even further in his effort to save each individual from eternal damnation. He sent out messengers and commissioned them to tell the people of the world about their sins and the Lord's salvation (Matthew 28:19,20).[16] He told his messengers of the urgency of their message (John 9:4).[17] Alas, many messengers garbled the message, and most people over the centuries who have heard it have been unwilling to accept it at face value. They have rejected it or changed it to their own liking. In truth, no one by their own thinking and analyzing can accept the message because it seems like nonsense (1 Corinthians 12:3).[18] The Lord, therefore, did yet another thing to save at least some.

### Election (predestination)

In the internal counsels of the Lord in eternity (1 Corinthians 2:7),[19] he elected (i.e., selected) those whom he would bring to faith as part of his plan of salvation, and he decreed that they would be saved (John 10:28).[20] This was an internal act of the Lord, and therefore we do not understand it.

---

[14] God has not rejected his people whom he foreknew. (Romans 11:2)

[15] When the fullness of time had come, God sent forth his Son, born of a woman, born under the law, to redeem those who were under the law, so that we might receive adoption as sons. (Galatians 4:4,5)

[16] [Jesus said,] "Go therefore and make disciples of all nations, baptizing them in the name of the Father and of the Son and of the Holy Spirit, teaching them to observe all that I have commanded you." (Matthew 28:19,20)

[17] [Jesus said,] "We must work the works of him who sent me while it is day; night is coming, when no one can work." (John 9:4)

[18] No one can say "Jesus is Lord" except in the Holy Spirit. (1 Corinthians 12:3)

[19] We impart a secret and hidden wisdom of God, which God decreed before the ages for our glory. (1 Corinthians 2:7)

[20] [Jesus said,] "I give them eternal life, and they will never perish, and no one will snatch them out of my hand." (John 10:28)

We know that the election was not arbitrary because the Lord is a purposeful being (Deuteronomy 32:39).[21] We know that it was not based on what people would do (Romans 9:11)[22] because that would make it dependent on the actions (works) of people. The Lord has made clear that all the actions of people are evil in his sight and that he is not dependent on his creatures for direction in his decision-making (Romans 11:34,35).[23] He elected only some (Exodus 33:19),[24] and he elected them because of his grace and because Christ died to redeem humankind (Romans 3:24).[25] We cannot go beyond this because it has not been revealed to us.

We do know, however, that the Lord's predestination was not just choosing names and letting it go at that. No, he developed a complete plan of salvation for each person he elected to save. He decided on all the detailed events and agents that would be used in the process of bringing each one to faith and of preserving that faith (Romans 8:29,30).[26] He then used his power to set the course of the events of the world so that the plan for each person would be carried out. Regardless of the complexities needed to reach each one of the elect with the message and to change that person's heart to accept the message, the Lord gave the right commands to his creation to make every plan happen. Because the Lord has gone through the necessary planning and action to save each of the elect, nothing can cause them to eventually be lost (John 10:27-29).[27] Who can steal anything from the hand of the Lord? When he decides something *will* happen, it is impossible for it not to happen. This should comfort all believers with the certainty of their salvation, because it is in the Lord's hands and not theirs.

---

[21] [The Lord said,] "I kill and I make alive; I wound and I heal; and there is none that can deliver out of my hand." (Deuteronomy 32:39)

[22] Though they [Esau and Jacob] were not yet born and had done nothing either good or bad—in order that God's purpose of election might continue, not because of works but because of him who calls. (Romans 9:11)

[23] "Who has known the mind of the Lord, or who has been his counselor? Or who has given a gift to him that he might be repaid?" (Romans 11:34,35)

[24] He [the Lord] said, "I will make all my goodness pass before you and will proclaim before you my name 'The LORD.' And I will be gracious to whom I will be gracious, and will show mercy on whom I will show mercy." (Exodus 33:19)

[25] [All] are justified by his grace as a gift, through the redemption that is in Christ Jesus. (Romans 3:24)

[26] Those whom he foreknew he also predestined to be conformed to the image of his Son, in order that he might be the firstborn among many brothers. And those whom he predestined he also called, and those whom he called he also justified, and those whom he justified he also glorified. (Romans 8:29,30)

[27] [Jesus said,] "My sheep hear my voice, and I know them, and they follow me. I give them eternal life, and they will never perish, and no one will snatch them out of my hand. My Father, who has given them to me, is greater than all, and no one is able to snatch them out of the Father's hand." (John 10:27-29)

## Election errors

Although the mechanism of election is beyond our comprehension, that some have been elected to eternal life is a clear concept in the Scriptures. Despite this, there are three factors that cause many people to object to the doctrine. The first of these is fairness. It doesn't seem fair that the Lord chose some and not others. How could a loving God do that? We need to look at this from God's perspective to give an answer. First, the Lord will not accept humans imposing their morality on him (Isaiah 45:9-12).[28] People cannot set up a bunch of hoops through which they think the ideal God should jump before they allow him to be God. In a contest between helpless humans and the Lord God Almighty, who is going to win? Refusing to believe in the Lord unless he does things our way is like jumping off the top of the Empire State Building to protest gravity. Moreover, the Lord has given everyone ample chances for eternal life. He made humankind sinless, he gives people consciences to remind them that they are accountable for their actions, and he sent his Son to pay for the guilt of all the sins of every individual. Those who fail to seek the Lord and his salvation have no right to complain of ill treatment. That type of argument would not even be accepted in a human court of law.

The second issue that causes concern for some people is their feeling that they ought to be able to apply human logic to the things of God. From the Lord's perspective, all human logic is filled with fallacies when applied to his eternal things.

*Election fallacy 1:* If the Lord chose some to be saved, then he must have chosen the rest to be damned. This is called double predestination. Yet the Bible does not say that he did this, rather it says that he wants everyone to be saved (Ezekiel 33:11).[29] Therefore, there is no eternal decree that individual unbelievers must go to hell. Unbelievers will, however, go there as a consequence of their sins, but that decree will not happen until their deaths or the final judgment (Matthew 25:41).[30]

---

[28] [The LORD said,] "Woe to him who strives with him who formed him, a pot among earthen pots! Does the clay say to him who forms it, 'What are you making?' or 'Your work has no handles'? Woe to him who says to a father, 'What are you begetting?' or to a woman, 'With what are you in labor?'" Thus says the LORD, the Holy One of Israel, and the one who formed him: "Ask me of things to come; will you command me concerning my children and the work of my hands? I made the earth and created man on it; it was my hands that stretched out the heavens, and I commanded all their host." (Isaiah 45:9-12)

[29] "Say to them, As I live, declares the LORD God, I have no pleasure in the death of the wicked, but that the wicked turn from his way and live." (Ezekiel 33:11)

[30] [Jesus said,] "Then he will say to those on his left, 'Depart from me, you cursed, into the eternal fire prepared for the devil and his angels.'" (Matthew 25:41)

*Election fallacy 2:* Since Jesus' dying for those who would be damned would serve no purpose, he died only for the elect. This is called limited atonement. Yet the Bible says that Jesus died to forgive the guilt of the sins of all people who ever lived (Romans 5:18,19).[31] This is called "universal atonement." Such an action might seem worthless to us, but it is an essential part of how the Lord views fairness.

*Election fallacy 3:* If those who are going to heaven and those who are going to hell were determined before the creation of the world, then everything must have been preordained and people are like actors following a script as they move through life. Even the fall into sin was scripted by the Lord. He therefore is the author of everything, including sin. Yet the Bible says that the Lord hates sin and does not tolerate it (James 1:13,14).[32] It also says that the Lord gave humankind and the angels the ability to choose to serve him or to rebel (1 Kings 18:21).[33] That would not be true if man were merely following a script.

*Election fallacy 4:* Because it is certain that those who are predestined will be saved, they are converted by "irresistible grace" when they hear the saving message. Stated otherwise, the Holy Spirit cannot fail to convert them. If this were true, then clearly the Lord would not be trying to convert all who hear the saving message because they would be unable to resist if the Holy Spirit tried to convert them. But as discussed above, the Lord does want all people to be saved (Ezekiel 33:11). The Bible says that when the Lord operates through means, such as the means of grace, rather than directly by his almighty power, then people can resist his efforts (Acts 7:51).[34] Why he is successful with some but not with others is part of the ways of God that he chose not to reveal to us.

Trying to apply human logic to the hidden things of the Lord is the height of folly. Alas, these are all errors taught by Calvinism.

Finally, some people find the idea that the Lord predestined people without any input from them to be arbitrary and abhorrent. They therefore

[31] Therefore, as one trespass led to condemnation for all men, so one act of righteousness leads to justification and life for all men. For as by the one man's disobedience the many were made sinners, so by the one man's obedience the many will be made righteous. (Romans 5:18,19)

[32] Let no one say when he is tempted, "I am being tempted by God," for God cannot be tempted with evil, and he himself tempts no one. But each person is tempted when he is lured and enticed by his own desire. (James 1:13,14)

[33] Elijah came near to all the people and said, "How long will you go limping between two different opinions? If the LORD is God, follow him; but if Baal, then follow him." (1 Kings 18:21)

[34] [Stephen, a deacon filled with the Holy Spirit, said,] "You stiff-necked people, uncircumcised in heart and ears, you always resist the Holy Spirit. As your fathers did, so do you." (Acts 7:51)

reason that the Lord must have used his foreknowledge in some way to dis-cern who would or who could believe, and then he must have predestined them because of their faith (*intuitu fidei*), rather than predestining them so that they would come to faith. Men like Phillip Melanchthon felt that conversion, and ultimately election, must have had a human component as well as a divine component. While they disagree in how they present their arguments, all who hold this position believe that in some way all people are not the same in their sinful nature. Some argue that certain people are less resistant to the work of the Holy Spirit. Others claim certain people behave better because they resist temptation better. Others believe that certain people seek the true God more fervently. Still others assert some people will make a "decision for Christ" when given the opportunity, while the rest will not. Regardless of how the argument is developed, however, it always comes down to certain people doing something that gets them into the proper position to be predestined and saved. People's salvation there-fore ultimately depends on themselves. Yet the Bible says that people are by nature spiritually dead (Ephesians 2:1)[35] and therefore can do nothing for themselves (1 Corinthians 12:3).[36] They must be reborn through water and the Holy Spirit (John 3:5)[37] to be alive in Christ. Their coming to faith is no more their own work than being physically conceived and born is the work of a baby.

## Summary

St. Paul summarized the doctrine of predestination best when he wrote, "Those whom he foreknew he also predestined to be conformed to the image of his Son. . . . And those whom he predestined he also called, and those whom he called he also justified, and those whom he justified he also glorified" (Romans 8:29,30). In this series, everything is the work of the Lord; none of it is the work of humans. The Lord's plan of salvation is all the Lord's work, and that should be comforting because we cannot mess it up. And being totally depraved by nature, we would mess it up. However, we are foolish to fear the Lord's predestination simply because we cannot log-ically understand everything about it. When we have doubts or fears about our predestination, God's Word always points us to the forgiveness of all our sins earned by the suffering, death, and resurrection of Jesus Christ that

---

[35] You were dead in the trespasses and sins. (Ephesians 2:1)

[36] No one can say "Jesus is Lord" except in the Holy Spirit. (1 Corinthians 12:3)

[37] Jesus answered him, "Truly, truly, I say to you, unless one is born of water and the spirit, he cannot enter the kingdom of God." (John 3:5)

saves; full forgiveness and salvation is available to everyone who believes (see chapter 15). The teaching of predestination in the Bible is meant to reassure believers that their salvation is securely in the Lord's hands. Nothing can take our salvation away from us, so we must pray to the Lord that he will strengthen our faith so that we do not foolishly walk away from his free gift.

CHAPTER 14

# Law

In his perfect realm of eternity, the Lord foresaw the whole history of the universe that he was about to create. He elected some to be saved, as we have seen in the previous chapter, and he planned the actions he would take to make certain that they were saved. To the human mind, this is strange behavior. If the Lord foresaw that angels and humankind would spoil his perfect world, why did he create them? Why didn't he do things differently so that there would be no possibility of sin or imperfections occurring? These are questions that we cannot answer because the Lord, the only being who knows the answers, has not revealed them to us (Jeremiah 33:2,3).[1] Rather, he has left us to marvel at his incredible love for humankind, a humankind that has so deeply offended him.

To the Lord who is perfect, perfection is his intrinsic goal in all his works (Deuteronomy 32:3,4).[2] He wanted his creation to be the perfect reflection of his perfection and therefore to operate according to his will (Matthew 5:48).[3] In fact, his will and his perfection are two of his attributes that cannot be separated. When it came to the inanimate things of his crea-

---

[1] "Thus says the LORD who made the earth, the LORD who formed it to establish it—the LORD is his name: Call to me and I will answer you, and will tell you great and hidden things that you have not known." (Jeremiah 33:2,3)

[2] [Song of Moses:] "I will proclaim the name of the LORD; ascribe greatness to our God! The Rock, his work is perfect, for all his ways are justice. A God of faithfulness and without iniquity, just and upright is he." (Deuteronomy 32:3,4)

[3] [Jesus said,] "You therefore must be perfect, as your heavenly Father is perfect." (Matthew 5:48)

tion, the Lord could directly maintain perfection by his direction of every object, regardless of size, to conform to his will (Psalm 33:7).[4] When it came to creatures to which he had not given freedom to choose, he could bend their wills to always perform in a manner to perfectly fulfill his will (Psalm 104:27-29).[5] In the cases of angels and people, however, to whom he gave freedom to choose, he needed to somehow make them aware of his will so that they could obey it. We do not know how he placed his will into the angels when he created them because he has not told us. And because there is nothing we can do to or for the angels, there is no reason for us to know except idle curiosity. We do know that some angels did not respect the Lord's will and rebelled. As a result, they incurred his eternal wrath (2 Peter 2:4).[6] The rest had their freedom to choose removed from them and the will of the Lord instilled within them in such a manner that they cannot disobey him and sin (1 Timothy 5:21).[7]

The Lord has revealed that he created man in his own image (Genesis 1:26,27). This certainly was not a physical image, because God is a spirit (John 4:24). Rather, the Lord gave humans the inherent knowledge they needed to use their freedom to choose to be both perfect and willing servants of the Lord. Like a perfect plane mirror produces an image that exactly represents the object in front of it, so people were to reflect the perfection of the Lord who created them. Part of this image of the Lord was the moral law written into people's hearts. That law was the perfect internal picture of the Lord's will, which the conscience could reliably use to tell each person whether what he or she might do was consistent with the perfection that the Lord demanded of all his creation. Humans knew their role and were inspired by the greatness of the Lord to follow with joy the guidance of their consciences in all things (Psalm 1:1,2).[8]

In addition to the internal standard of behavior that the Lord gave humankind, he also gave humankind several external commands. For

---

[4]He gathers the waters of the sea as a heap; he puts the deeps in storehouses. (Psalm 33:7)

[5]These all [the animals] look to you, to give them their food in due season. When you give it to them, they gather it up; when you open your hand, they are filled with good things. When you hide your face, they are dismayed; when you take away their breath, they die and return to their dust. (Psalm 104:27-29)

[6]God did not spare angels when they sinned, but cast them into hell and committed them to chains of gloomy darkness to be kept until the judgment. (2 Peter 2:4)

[7]In the presence of God and of Christ Jesus and of the elect angels I charge you to keep these rules without prejudging, doing nothing from partiality. (1 Timothy 5:21)

[8]Blessed is the man [whose] delight is in the law of the LORD, and on his law he meditates day and night. (Psalm 1:1,2)

example, he commanded humankind to procreate and to rule over his creation (Genesis 1:28).[9] He also commanded Adam and Eve not to eat of the tree of the knowledge of good and evil, with the promise that they would die if they ate of it (Genesis 2:17). This command was external because it was not part of the moral law in the human heart, but it was an additional command for the purpose of allowing people to show their willing obedience to their Creator-God. Both internal and external commands were from the Lord, and therefore both were perfect. Unfortunately, Eve and Adam did not grasp this equality of commands and saw a way to gain independence of action to go along with their freedom to choose (Genesis 3:6). To the Lord, disobedience was disobedience and an affront to his divine essence. The status of Adam and Eve sank in his sight when they sinned, going from dearly beloved children to accursed rebels (Isaiah 13:9).[10]

The Lord foresaw that sin could not be contained to external commandments. The demons would work tirelessly to distort the remnants of the Lord's will written in people's hearts (Genesis 6:5).[11] The human conscience, bound to this internal law, could only inaccurately guide people's behaviors from this corrupted source. Once a person believed that he or she could disobey the Lord and continue to live in this world, that person would only look for more and more opportunities to expand this perceived freedom and would fall deeper and deeper into depravity (Matthew 15:19).[12] With each person seeking his own good, there would be conflict and hostility among people. It started with Adam accusing Eve (Genesis 3:12),[13] and it has continued to this day. The Lord knew that humankind would be destructive to itself and his whole creation (Matthew 24:6,7), so he inflicted punishments upon humankind, everything short of immediate extermination.

The Lord's punishment of Adam and Eve was indeed the death that he had promised them, even though they did not physically die immediately (Genesis 3:16-24). He threw them out of the Garden of Eden and pre-

---

[9]God blessed them [Adam and Eve]. And God said to them, "Be fruitful and multiply and fill the earth and subdue it, and have dominion over the fish of the sea and over the birds of the heavens and over every living thing that moves on the earth." (Genesis 1:28)

[10]Behold, the day of the LORD comes, cruel, with wrath and fierce anger, to make the land a desolation and to destroy its sinners from it. (Isaiah 13:9)

[11]The LORD saw that the wickedness of man was great in the earth, and that every intention of the thoughts of his heart was only evil continually. (Genesis 6:5)

[12][Jesus said,] "Out of the heart come evil thoughts, murder, adultery, sexual immorality, theft, false witness, slander." (Matthew 15:19)

[13]The man [Adam] said, "The woman [Eve] whom you gave to be with me, she gave me fruit of the tree, and I ate." (Genesis 3:12)

vented them from eating from the tree of life. They no longer had direct access to him. He assured them that they would physically die, and their bodies return to the ground. Finally, he cursed the earth because of their sin. They would see how evil sin was by having to experience its temporal consequences. They would no longer be rulers but would have to compete with the rest of God's creatures for the necessities of life. The earth would never again be a paradise humankind could enjoy. Wherever sinful people existed, there the vile fruits of sinning would also be. Worst of all, physical death would lead only to eternal punishment for people, based on the sins that they had committed while living (Matthew 25:41-46).

The Lord knew that after people sinned, his perfect law in their hearts would become progressively marred. The internal standard would become unreliable. The Lord responded by giving humankind an external standard based on the Ten Commandments (Exodus 20:1-17). This law was first given to Moses on two stone tablets, representing people's obligation to the Lord (the first table of the law) and their obligation to their fellow humans (the second table of the law). As detailed in Exodus, Leviticus, Numbers, and Deuteronomy, the external moral law consisted of more than just the few lines of the Ten Commandments themselves. These were only the overview. Even the details, however, were not complete, because the law involved viewing everything that humankind might do from the Lord's perspective. The fulfilling of the law requires a perfect love for the Lord and a perfect love for one's fellow humans, and these were no longer possible for anyone to have (Matthew 22:37-40).[14] The Lord understood this situation well, and all people also needed to be led to understand it so that they would not imagine that they could please the Lord by their own actions.

### The curb

The Lord uses his moral law in three ways. The first is in dealing with the gross immorality in this world. Because their internal sense of right and wrong has been corrupted by sin, pewople try to devise their own rules for what is acceptable behavior (Isaiah 5:20).[15] They then create gods that permit them to do these actions and maybe even consider their sinful actions to be a service to these gods (Psalm 115:4-8). Sadly, sometimes they use the

---

[14]He [Jesus] said to him [a lawyer of the Pharisees], "You shall love the Lord your God with all your heart and with all your soul and with all your mind. This is the great and first commandment. And a second is like it: You shall love your neighbor as yourself. On these two commandments depend all the Law and the Prophets." (Matthew 22:37-40)

[15]Woe to those who call evil good and good evil. (Isaiah 5:20)

name of the Lord to cover their idolatry by attaching his name to what they worship, but this gains them only worse punishment in hell for blasphemy (2 Peter 2:1).[16] False standards cannot be used to justify sin.

The Lord has commissioned his church to preach the law so that people will know his standards of behavior and fear his wrath (Romans 3:20).[17] When people hear the demands of the law, they resent them because they feel that their freedom of choice is being curtailed. The preaching of the law causes the corrupted copy of the law in their hearts to receive a buffing, that is, it is like removing some of the corrosion from a metal surface. Their consciences then accuse them of their sinful actions (Acts 2:37).[18] To avoid the Lord's wrath, they often refine their actions in an effort to silence their consciences. People even try to get their consciences to commend them by doing more than they feel the law has a right to require. They imagine that such willing and superior deeds will offset their sins before the Lord. Such behavior does not meet the Lord's perfect standard and therefore is not God-pleasing, as Jesus pointed out in the parable of the Pharisee and the tax collector (Luke 18:9-14).

The curbing of humankind's sinful pursuits because of the promptings of conscience, however, does have a beneficial effect in the Lord's management of his physical kingdom. Deeds of the sinful heart meant to silence conscience are called civic righteousness. This means these have earthly benefit for one's fellow people and the society in which a person lives (Proverbs 14:34).[19] Such deeds might include obeying the laws of the nation, giving to charities, and helping one's neighbors. Certainly, these things have a positive place in the current age. On the other hand, they do not fulfill the obligation to obey the Lord even though he does desire these things (1 Corinthians 13:1-3). This is because they are done from selfish motivations, ranging from silencing their consciences to gaining status in the world.

## The mirror

While the law does curb gross immorality and in the process makes civilized society possible, this response to the law is inadequate to move people

---

[16]False prophets also arose among the people, just as there will be false teachers among you, who will secretly bring in destructive heresies, even denying the Master who bought them, bringing upon themselves swift destruction. (2 Peter 2:1)

[17]By works of the law no human being will be justified in his sight, since through the law comes knowledge of sin. (Romans 3:20)

[18]When they [those hearing Peter preach on Pentecost] heard this they were cut to the heart, and said to Peter and the rest of the apostles, "Brothers, what shall we do?" (Acts 2:37)

[19][Solomon said,] "Righteousness exalts a nation, but sin is a reproach to any people." (Proverbs 14:34)

to face their real problem—their utter sinfulness before the Lord. For this to happen, the law must be skillfully applied to each person's particular situation. Only when people see just how sinful their actions are do they realize what deep trouble they are in. They see how hopeless the task of correcting their actions is, and they tremble at the harsh reality that they must make restitution for previous sins. When used for this purpose, the law is a mirror.

While preaching the law as a curb frightens people, whether they admit it or not, people can evade it to some extent by taking actions to mollify their consciences and to pass themselves off to their fellow citizens as being law-abiding. Preaching the law as a mirror, as Jesus did in his sermon against the scribes and Pharisees (Matthew 23:13-36), gives people no such place to hide. It shows them that some of their favorite activities are sinful. It points out that their thoughts are less than pure and that they secretly love evil (Psalm 44:20,21).[20] It confronts them with their condescending attitudes toward those they despise or think less worthy than themselves (James 2:1-13). It tells them of their smugness, of their love of gossip, and of their dishonesty with themselves and others (Deuteronomy 25:13,14).[21] It accuses them of loveless words, careless speech, and outright lies (Zechariah 8:16,17).[22] It shows that even their supposed good deeds are driven by sinful motives (1 Samuel 16:7).[23] It illustrates the dark and hidden places of their hearts and reveals what they thought even God would not know about (Psalm 69:5).[24] It leaves them naked before the Lord with no place to hide.

Naturally, people do not want to hear the law preached as a mirror. They may tolerate it preached as a curb to some extent, particularly when directed against things they find easy to avoid. But when the law is preached as a mirror, people want the preachers to shut up or to be shut up by government authorities or by public opinion. Yet it is only when the law is preached as a mirror that people understand that there is no hope of saving themselves.

---

[20] [The sons of Korah said,] "If we had forgotten the name of our God or spread out our hands to a foreign god, would not God discover this? For he knows the secrets of the heart." (Psalm 44:20,21)

[21] [The LORD said,] "You shall not have in your bag two kinds of weights, a large and a small. You shall not have in your house two kinds of measures, a large and a small." [large for buying, small for selling] (Deuteronomy 25:13,14)

[22] [The Lord said,] "These are the things that you shall do: Speak the truth to one another; render in your gates judgments that are true and make for peace; do not devise evil in your hearts against one another, and love no false oath, for all these things I hate, declares the LORD." (Zechariah 8:16,17)

[23] The LORD said to Samuel, "Do not look on his [the oldest of Jesse's sons] appearance or on the height of his stature, because I have rejected him. For the LORD sees not as man sees: man looks on the outward appearance, but the LORD looks on the heart." (1 Samuel 16:7)

[24] [David said,] "O God, you know my folly; the wrongs I have done are not hidden from you." (Psalm 69:5)

It is only then they will despair of their own efforts and accept the gospel (Psalm 19:12,13),[25] which will be discussed in the next chapter.

## The guide

But what happens when people repent of their sins and believe the gospel? Does the law have any purpose then? Some claim that it doesn't. These people are called antinomians. They claim that the new person, who is created when the gospel is believed, so desires to do God's will that preaching the law to these people is actually a hindrance to faith, because they are saved by faith, not by works.

There are three problems with this argument. First, as long as Christians live on this earth, they will continue to have within themselves a sinful nature, as well as a new nature that wants to serve the Lord (Romans 7:22,23).[26] The old nature wants to again assert control through gross sinning. People need to hear the law to keep the old nature in check. The law must continue to produce the fear that faith can be lost and that the damning consequences for sin will follow (Mark 16:16).[27] The law as a curb is necessary to curb the actions of the old nature. Second, because everyone continues to sin, falling often to temptation, everyone needs to see the gravity of those sins so that they will abandon them and flee to Christ for forgiveness (Psalm 51:3).[28] In the same way that people look into a mirror daily to see whether their faces are clean, so they must regularly look into the mirror of the law to see whether their consciences are clean. The more they study God's law, the more stains of sin they will find for which they need Christ's cleansing blood. Third, when the new nature is formed within a person, it is like a child being born (1 Corinthians 3:2).[29] It is desirous of pleasing the Lord, but it does not know how. It must be trained in what is pleasing and what is not so that it does not make up its own rules and think that such rules lead to God-pleasing actions. The preaching of the law gives believers the information that they need to be faithful servants. This is called using the law as a guide. The more people understand the nature of the Lord and of his will as expressed in the law, the better they can serve the

---

[25][David said,] "Who can discern his errors? Declare me innocent from hidden faults. Keep back your servant also from presumptuous sins; let them not have dominion over me!" (Psalm 19:12,13)

[26]I delight in the law of God, in my inner being, but I see in my members another law waging war against the law of my mind and making me captive to the law of sin that dwells in my members. (Romans 7:22,23)

[27][Jesus said,] "Whoever believes and is baptized will be saved, but whoever does not believe will be condemned." (Mark 16:16)

[28][David said,] "I know my transgressions, and my sin is ever before me." (Psalm 51:3)

[29]I fed you with milk, not solid food, for you were not ready for it. (1 Corinthians 3:2)

Lord (Psalm 119:105).[30] Such service does nothing to gain salvation, but it is
the service that every Christian wants to give in grateful thanks for what Jesus
has done for him or her.

## Preaching the law

The law does not save (Galatians 3:21,22).[31] It does not help even a little
bit. Placing any reliance on the law is a ticket to hell (James 2:10).[32] Yet the
preaching of the law is essential to salvation. The law must be preached to
show people how terrible their sins are. If they do not believe that their sins
are horrible or if they do not despise themselves for committing them, then
they will cling to many of their sins (1 Samuel 15:1-23). They will only part
with some of their wickedness, and they will argue that the rest of the things
they do are not so bad and may even be pretty good. To have a saving faith,
one must repudiate everything about oneself, not only what one thinks is
bad but also whatever one thinks is good (Matthew 16:24).[33] That is because
without Christ, there is no good in anyone. That is what the teaching of total
depravity is all about (Genesis 8:21).[34] To say, "I'm not by nature totally bad,"
is equivalent to saying, "I have a guaranteed ticket to hell," because it means
the person is planning to put some of his or her worthless works on the table
before the Lord at the judgment. Human works, regardless of how good the
doer thinks they are, would stink up heaven, and people who insist on trying
to bring them along will not be allowed in (Isaiah 64:6).[35]

The preaching of the law as a mirror must precede the proclamation of
the gospel or the gospel has little value (Luke 7:47).[36] You cannot be thank-
ful for salvation unless you realize how desperately you need salvation. You
cannot produce good works that are pleasing before the Lord if your heart
has not been completely changed by the love that Christ has shown to you

---

[30]Your Word is a lamp to my feet and a light to my path. (Psalm 119:105)

[31]Is the law then contrary to the promises of God? Certainly not! For if a law had been given that
could give life, then righteousness would indeed be by the law. But the Scripture imprisoned everything under sin, so that the promise by faith in Jesus Christ might be given to those who believe.
(Galatians 3:21,22)

[32]Whoever keeps the whole law but fails in one point has become guilty of all of it. (James 2:10)

[33]Jesus told his disciples, "If anyone would come after me, let him deny himself and take up his cross
and follow me." (Matthew 16:24)

[34]The LORD said in his heart, "I will never again curse the ground because of man, for the intention of
man's heart is evil from his youth." (Genesis 8:21)

[35]We have all become like one who is unclean, and all our righteous deeds are like a polluted garment.
(Isaiah 64:6)

[36][Jesus said,] "He who is forgiven little, loves little." (Luke 7:47)

and all humankind (1 Corinthians 6:9-11).[37] Only the law can create the need that only the gospel can fill. If a person believes that Christ is not the complete answer, then that person does not have a saving faith in Christ. Anyone who believes that to be saved involves some of his or her deeds plus some of Christ's redemptive work has a faith that is synergistic, and that will lead to damnation. The Lord does not want a share of our love and commitment; he wants all of it (Revelation 3:15,16).[38] The preaching of the law, therefore, must never leave room for human efforts and "reformed living" as viable options for "getting right with God."

While the above might seem to be pretty clear, the preaching of the law has another constraint. When improperly preached, the law can cause despair in those who believe in Christ. While believers in Christ continue to be sinners, they are forgiven sinners. Believers must always be reassured that no matter how terrible their sins, they have all been forgiven (Isaiah 1:18).[39] If that gospel assurance is not given, then the demons will use the preaching of the law to work such despair that people will feel that not even Christ can save them. Avoiding this pitfall in preaching the law is critical. Yet, on the other hand, one cannot make forgiveness appear so trivial, so cheap, that the unrepentant also believe that they have it if they merely endure the lambasting of the preaching of the law. It takes wisdom that only the Lord can give to preach the law properly. More about law and gospel preaching will be discussed in the next chapter.

### The law and human governments

If the law of the Lord is so good that it would make the world perfect if only everyone obeyed it, it might seem that people should lobby their governments to establish the law given by the Lord as their national law code. In fact, some people do such lobbying, particularly people who believe in some form of a millennium (see chapter 11). Many governments actually do use most of the Ten Commandments in their laws, although in somewhat

---

[37]Do you not know that the unrighteous will not inherit the kingdom of God? Do not be deceived: neither the sexually immoral, nor idolaters, nor adulterers, nor men who practice homosexuality, nor thieves, nor the greedy, nor drunkards, nor revilers, nor swindlers will inherit the kingdom of God. And such were some of you. But you were washed, you were sanctified, you were justified in the name of the Lord Jesus Christ and by the Spirit of our God. (1 Corinthians 6:9-11)

[38][Jesus said,] "I know your works: you are neither cold nor hot. Would that you were either cold or hot! So, because you are lukewarm, and neither hot nor cold, I will spit you out of my mouth." (Revelation 3:15,16)

[39]"Come now, let us reason together, says the LORD: though your sins are like scarlet, they shall be as white as snow; though they are red like crimson, they shall become like wool." (Isaiah 1:18)

altered form. This is because these commandments, although greatly tarnished by sin, remain written onto all human hearts. Despite this, it would be foolish for any government to adopt the law as it is presented in the Bible. Using the law as a governing standard only works when the law is obeyed out of love for the Lord God.

The states of Israel and of Judah in the Old Testament did have the law as given in the Bible as their national law code, but great problems still remained. The people were sinful, and they tried to leverage the law to their own advantage. Enforcement was haphazard because it required people to treat everyone fairly, and many people did not apply it with the same severity to family and friends as they applied it to others. Some judges were dishonest and took bribes. In short, it took force to make the people obey it, and people frequently rebelled. No set of laws will ever create perfect justice in a sinful world, and as a result, there will never be peace in the world even with the best laws in place (Matthew 24:6).[40] Because civic righteousness does not save, it is not the message that the church was sent to preach. The church must be very careful not to become distracted by wasting its efforts trying to reform the state.

## Summary

The Lord gave humans the moral law as an external standard to replace the internal standard given at creation, which had become corrupted by sin. The purposes of the law are to restrain evil behavior by the threat of punishment (curb), to help people to see their sins so they repent of them and despair of their own works (mirror), and to show the believer in Christ how to please the Lord (guide). The law cannot save because it cannot be kept perfectly, yet it must be preached to prepare the way for the gospel.

---

[40] [Jesus said,] "You will hear of wars and rumors of wars. See that you are not alarmed, for this must take place, but the end is not yet." (Matthew 24:6)

CHAPTER 15

# Gospel

The word *gospel* comes from an Old English word meaning "good tidings." This meaning is derived from the Greek word *euangelion*. The news that there is salvation for humankind is extremely good tidings because the law of the Lord left humankind in a horrible predicament. Once again, it was the Lord who showed his power and his love to bring about the gospel.

## The need and the plan

When the Lord foresaw from eternity that people would fail miserably at obeying his will, he readied a plan of salvation to rescue humankind from its hopeless plight. The Lord developed his plan so that it relied completely on himself and not at all on humankind, for he foresaw that humankind was wholly unreliable in spiritual things (Ephesians 1:9,10).[1] According to his plan, the Lord would establish a payment for sins that would meet his divine justice (1 John 2:2)[2] and would develop the righteousness in respect to his divine will for humankind that humankind itself had failed to produce (Philippians 1:10,11).[3] Because both his justice and his will are perfect, his

---

[1] According to his [God the Father's] purpose, which he set forth in Christ as a plan for the fullness of time, to unite all things in him, things in heaven and things on earth. (Ephesians 1:9,10)

[2] He [Jesus] is the propitiation for our sins, and not for ours only but also for the sins of the whole world. (1 John 2:2)

[3] That you [the reader] may approve what is excellent, and so be pure and blameless for the day of Christ, filled with the fruit of righteousness that comes through Jesus Christ, to the glory and praise of God. (Philippians 1:10,11)

plan would involve the only being who could perfectly carry out such a plan, namely, himself. Through this plan, the Lord's great love for humankind was demonstrated already before creation. Rather than creating humankind without the freedom to choose whether to obey or to disobey, destroying people immediately when they sinned, or sentencing them irrevocably to eternal damnation for their transgressions, he committed himself to do for humankind what humankind could not do in order to save its members.

## God's commitment

Human conflict with the will of the Lord occurred quickly after humans were created in the image of God (Genesis 1:26,27). When humankind lost that image through sinning, the Lord had his plan of salvation ready. The Lord's first step was to obligate himself to his plan by announcing it to Adam and Eve (Genesis 3:15). The Lord placed himself on the hook to perform what was necessary to effect salvation for the very people who had so bitterly disappointed him by disobeying his simple command not to eat of the fruit of a tree. It was as if a great king vowed to place himself in debt to save the lives of vile rebels. This is what the Lord of lords and King of kings, the great God, the Almighty, did for a feeble and fickle species he had made from the dust.

## The training with the law

The Lord's second step was to let humankind demonstrate conclusively that its corroded internal standard would not work. It didn't take long to accomplish this (Genesis 6:5),[4] as discussed in chapter 7. Following this colossal human failure, the Lord gave the law (i.e., his will) as an external standard, and humankind demonstrated that it could not meet that standard either (Ezekiel 20:13),[5] as shown in chapter 8. The Lord acted in this way because he had given humankind the freedom to choose whether to follow his will. Therefore, he wanted to convince humankind that it needed his plan of salvation and could not work things out for itself. Humankind has been a slow learner, and even today most people cannot grasp the magnitude of their sins and the ineffectiveness of their own

---

[4] The LORD saw that the wickedness of man was great in the earth, and that every intention of the thoughts of his heart was only evil continually. (Genesis 6:5)

[5] [The LORD said,] "They [the Israelites on the way to Canaan] did not walk in my statutes but rejected my rules, by which, if a person does them, he shall live; and my Sabbaths they greatly profaned." (Ezekiel 20:13)

efforts (Isaiah 6:10).[6] The record of humankind's overwhelming failure is well-documented in human history, but people do not want to see it.

## The fulfillment

When the Lord judged that the time was right, he took the third step in his plan. He sent his Son to obtain the forgiveness of sins that humankind so desperately needed (Galatians 4:4,5).[7] As usual, the Lord's action did not make sense to the human mind. The Lord is almighty and fills his whole creation (Jeremiah 23:24),[8] and therefore all the persons of the Godhead are also almighty and fill the whole creation. But the Son, the second person of the Trinity, took upon himself a human nature, a nature that is very limited in its power and in the space it can occupy (1 Peter 1:24).[9] Yet the Son did this in a way so that he was truly God and also truly human. Moreover, the Father and the Holy Spirit, who are of the same essence as the Son, did not assume a human nature. This is beyond the ability of any person to comprehend. Human mathematics and human science cannot create a model in which such a situation could occur. People shake their heads and doubt, and the Lord laughs (Psalm 2:4).[10]

The Lord furthermore brought about this incarnation in a fantastic way. He made a virgin pregnant so that the human component of the Savior came only from her, by the power of the Holy Spirit (Luke 1:35).[11] Thus, he created a human male embryo without a human father, an impossibility according to human science. With only one human parent, the Lord shielded the embryo from the original sin of humankind's first father, disobedient Adam, so that the child conceived was sinless (Hebrews 4:15).[12] The name of the child, designated by God the Father, was Jesus, which

---

[6][The LORD said,] "Make the heart of this people dull, and their ears heavy, and blind their eyes; lest they see with their eyes, and hear with their ears, and understand with their hearts, and turn and be healed." (Isaiah 6:10)

[7]When the fullness of time had come, God sent forth his Son, born of woman, born under the law, to redeem those who were under the law, so that we might receive adoption as sons. (Galatians 4:4,5)

[8]"Do I not fill heaven and earth? declares the LORD." (Jeremiah 23:24)

[9]All flesh is like grass and all its glory like the flower of grass. The grass withers, and the flower falls. (1 Peter 1:24)

[10]He who sits in the heavens laughs; the Lord holds them in derision. (Psalm 2:4)

[11]The angel answered her [the virgin Mary], "The Holy Spirit will come upon you, and the power of the Most High will overshadow you; therefore the child to be born will be called holy—the Son of God." (Luke 1:35)

[12]We do not have a high priest who is unable to sympathize with our weaknesses, but one [Jesus] who in every respect has been tempted as we are, yet without sin. (Hebrews 4:15)

means "the Lord saves" (Matthew 1:21).[13] Jesus was therefore a restarting
of the human race in God's image, as the human race had been before
sin (Romans 5:18,19).[14] This action was critical to the Lord's plan so that
Jesus would not have a sin-corrupted beginning. The Lord further put
the virgin into humble circumstances so that his Son would receive no
undue attention (Luke 2:7), and he rescued him when Herod sought his
life (Matthew 2:13-18).

But what was this newborn Jesus like as a person? On one hand, he was a
tiny baby, helplessly lying on his mother's lap. On the other hand, he was the
almighty God, filling the whole universe (Isaiah 9:6).[15] Again the human
mind is faced with a situation it cannot grasp. If Jesus was really truly God
and truly man, then he had to meet both the human and the divine conditions. The attributes of his divine nature were the same as those of God.
The attributes of his human nature were the same as any other male human
on earth. If he was really one person, the natures had to be inseparably
united with each other; they could not go off to do individual functions or
he would have been a fraud. He would just have used his divine power to
create a human form to move around like a chess piece without any iden-
tity of its own. Yet the Bible says that Jesus was truly a human being with
a human body (Luke 24:39)[16] and a human soul (Matthew 26:38).[17] He
would hardly have needed a birth just to create a human form for himself;
he had created such forms for various appearances recorded in the Old Testament (e.g., Judges 6:11-27; 13:2-25). Jesus was indeed the Son of Man,
just as he was the Son of God.

The answer to the riddle of the one person with two natures is only partially revealed in the Scriptures. Jesus always had the full powers of the
Godhead available to him to use as he willed, but he only used them when
necessary to carry out his saving mission. He did miracles, he healed the
sick, and he read people's thoughts—but he did these things only when it

---

[13][The Lord said,] "She [Mary] will bear a son, and you [Joseph] shall call his name Jesus, for he will save his people from their sins." (Matthew 1:21)

[14]Therefore, as one trespass led to condemnation for all men, so one act of righteousness leads to justifi- cation and life for all men. For as by the one man's [Adam's] disobedience the many were made sinners, so by the one man's [Jesus'] obedience the many will be made righteous. (Romans 5:18,19)

[15]To us a child is born, to us a son is given; and the government shall be upon his shoulder, and his name shall be called Wonderful Counselor, Mighty God, Everlasting Father, Prince of Peace. (Isaiah 9:6)

[16][Jesus said,] "See my hands and my feet, that it is I myself. Touch me, and see. For a spirit does not have flesh and bones as you see that I have." (Luke 24:39)

[17]Then he [Jesus] said to them [his disciples Peter, James, and John], "My soul is very sorrowful, even to death; remain here, and watch with me." (Matthew 26:38)

served his purpose here on earth. This limited use of his divine powers is referred to as his state of humiliation (Philippians 2:5-7).[18] He entered into this state at the time of his birth and remained in it until the time of his resurrection from the dead. While in this state, however, he continued to be the almighty God and was in control of every particle in the universe (Malachi 3:6).[19] Moreover, both natures were present everywhere in the universe because they were one person. Jesus could be seen on earth because his human nature could occupy physical space. In addition, because his divine nature was completely present everywhere, as discussed in chapter 4, his human nature also was completely present everywhere and still is until this day (Matthew 28:20).[20] It is a power that the Lord God has and that Jesus' divine nature bestowed on (communicated to) his human nature.[21] This situation did not make the human nature less human, but it allowed Jesus to function as one person. How this could be has not been revealed to us, and therefore we do not need to understand it for salvation. We only need to believe it, as we believe everything else the Lord has made known to us.

## Active and passive obedience

The reason that Jesus needed to be fully human was so that he could take the place of each member of the human race under the law of God (Galatians 4:4,5). As we have seen, the law was given to humankind to show people how to live in accordance with the Lord's will. The obedience to that law was to generate the righteousness necessary to please the Lord and to cause him to declare a person to be a "good and faithful servant" (Matthew 25:21). People had proven hopelessly inadequate at producing such righteousness (Isaiah 64:6),[22] so if it was to be generated, Jesus would have to do it for them. Moreover, because the law was given to humans, Jesus had to be human and therefore subject to the same temptations that humans suffered in order to accomplish this. If this had not been the case, then the righteousness would not have been earned under the law (Hebrews 2:17)[23] and would therefore

---

[18]Have this mind among yourselves, which is yours in Christ Jesus, who, though he had the form of God, did not count equality with God a thing to be grasped [flaunted,] but emptied himself, by taking the form of a servant, being born in the likeness of men. (Philippians 2:5-7)

[19]"I the LORD do not change." (Malachi 3:6)

[20][Jesus said,] "Behold, I am with you always, to the end of the age." (Matthew 28:20)

[21]Harlyn J. Kuschel, *Christ,* People's Bible Teachings series (Milwaukee: Northwestern Publishing House, 2006).

[22]All our righteous deeds are like a polluted garment. (Isaiah 64:6)

[23]He [Jesus] had to be made like his brothers in every respect, so that he might become a merciful and faithful high priest in the service of God, to make propitiation for the sins of the people. (Hebrews 2:17)

be phony. This part of Jesus' ministry is called his active obedience, because he actively worked to fulfill the law.

People, however, cannot accept this righteousness as long as they have sin clinging to them (1 Corinthians 2:14).[24] Even if they could, the guilt of humankind's sin prevents anyone from coming into the presence of the Lord to present even a gift of perfect righteousness (Leviticus 16:11-14). Everyone has been totally contaminated by the stain and stench of sin and therefore is not welcome in the holy chambers of the Lord. Until the guilt of their sins is removed, people have no destination other than hell (Zephaniah 1:18).[25] But guilt means punishment, and the punishment for sins is so great that no one can bear it (Matthew 13:41,42;[26] Isaiah 66:24[27]). Therefore, Jesus also had to show "passive obedience" to God by enduring the punishment for the sins of the world (Acts 8:32),[28] just as a prisoner before the court must passively accept the sentence of the judge. This punishment was hideous and had to be endured by both the body and the soul, just as the punishment of hell is of both the body and the soul. While the world saw only the terrible suffering of a man being crucified when Jesus died, the heavenly Father saw the far worse suffering of someone bearing the punishment for the sins of the entire human race (Hebrews 9:26).[29] Jesus was driven to cry, "My God, my God, why have you forsaken me?" as he endured the wrath of his Father for the guilt of humankind's sins (Matthew 27:46). We cannot understand the magnitude of this suffering, how it removed the guilt of our sins, or how Jesus endured it. We do not need to understand the mechanics; we need to believe the Scriptures that his sufferings and death succeeded in removing the guilt of all the sins of all the people who have lived, are living, or will live in this world.

---

[24]The natural person does not accept the things of the Spirit of God, for they are folly to him, and he is not able to understand them because they are spiritually discerned. (1 Corinthians 2:14)

[25]Neither their silver nor their gold shall be able to deliver them on the day of the wrath of the LORD. In the fire of his jealousy, all the earth shall be consumed; for a full and sudden end he will make of all the inhabitants of the earth. (Zephaniah 1:18)

[26][Jesus said,] "The Son of Man will send his angels, and they will gather out of his kingdom all [the offenses] and all law-breakers, and throw them into the fiery furnace. In that place there will be weeping and gnashing of teeth." (Matthew 13:41,42)

[27][The LORD said,] "They [generic they] shall go out and look on the dead bodies of the men who have rebelled against me. For their worm shall not die, their fire shall not be quenched, and they shall be an abhorrence to all flesh." (Isaiah 66:24)

[28]"Like a sheep he [the Servant of the Lord = Jesus] was led to the slaughter and like a lamb before its shearer is silent, so he opens not his mouth." (Acts 8:32)

[29]As it is, he [Jesus] has appeared once for all at the end of the ages to put away sin by the sacrifice of himself. (Hebrews 9:26)

Because the passive obedience of Jesus removed the guilt of the human race, God the Father has declared everyone to be forgiven in Christ (2 Corinthians 5:19).[30] In the courtroom of the Lord, all debts have been paid, and there are no charges remaining for anyone to face. Everyone has been declared not guilty, that is, justified before God (Titus 3:7).[31] This is called objective justification because it is fully accomplished. There is nothing more to be done by anyone to enter heaven. As a result, when Jesus came forth from the grave, he was no longer the humble servant striving to win salvation for humankind but the conquering hero who had accomplished the task (Philippians 2:9-11).[32] While he was still both true God and true man, his state of humiliation was completed and he returned to his former glory in what is called his state of exaltation. When he ascended to heaven, this act was only to create a formal parting from his disciples until judgment day. He continues to be fully present in both his natures throughout the entire universe.

With Jesus' return to heaven, the third and most critical step of the Lord's plan of salvation for humankind was completed. The whole plan relied solely on the Lord's grace. There was absolutely no reliance on any contribution by man (Romans 11:6).[33] Humans only helped to carry it out in the passive sense that the Lord used their inherent sinfulness to accomplish Jesus' suffering and death (Acts 2:23).[34] The envy of the religious leaders led them to want Jesus' death (John 11:48).[35] Judas' greed led him to betray Jesus (John 12:6).[36] The cowardliness of the disciples left Jesus to suffer alone, completing a task they really couldn't help with anyway (Mark 14:50).[37] Pontius

---

[30] In Christ God was reconciling the world to himself, not counting their trespasses against them, and entrusting to us the message of reconciliation. (2 Corinthians 5:19)

[31] So that being justified by his [the Lord's] grace we might become heirs according to the hope of eternal life. (Titus 3:7)

[32] Therefore God has highly exalted him and bestowed on him the name that is above every name, so that at the name of Jesus every knee should bow, in heaven and on earth and under the earth, and every tongue confess that Jesus Christ is Lord, to the glory of God the Father. (Philippians 2:9-11)

[33] If it is by grace, it is no longer on the basis of works; otherwise grace would no longer be grace. (Romans 11:6)

[34] [Peter said,] "This Jesus, delivered up according to the definite plan and foreknowledge of God, you crucified and killed by the hands of lawless men." (Acts 2:23)

[35] [The chief priests and the Pharisees said,] "If we let him go on like this, everyone will believe in him, and the Romans will come and take away both our place and our nation." (John 11:48)

[36] He [Judas] said this, not because he cared about the poor, but because he was a thief, and having charge of the moneybag he used to help himself to what was put into it. (John 12:6)

[37] They all [Jesus' disciples] left him and fled. (Mark 14:50)

Pilate caved in to the mob (Matthew 27:24).[38] The soldiers gambled over Jesus' clothes (Luke 23:34). Everything happened the way it did—and it happened in the way in which it had been prophesied—because the Lord knew what people would do when given the appropriate opportunity (Mark 14:49).[39] He gave them the chance to do what their evil hearts wanted, and they carried out their evil intents in such a manner that the Lord's plan was carried out precisely as he wanted (Proverbs 16:33).[40] It was solely grace, that favorable attitude of the Lord toward humankind, that led him to do everything needed for their salvation.

## By grace, through faith

No person can earn the Lord's grace (Mark 8:36,37).[41] The Lord needs nothing from us; he has and owns everything (Psalm 50:12).[42] Certainly he does not need people to "impress" him with their worthless deeds. He knows what every person is like and that each is individually as spiritually rotten by nature as the next (1 John 1:10).[43] No one can climb out of the cesspool of sin in which he is drowning to present himself as a worthy candidate for admission to heaven. With free salvation available to all because of objective justification, it becomes ours only through faith (Acts 16:30,31).[44] If the demands of the law do not scare a person into utter despair of ever keeping them or if the incomprehensibly precious gift of the gospel does not cause a person to believe God's unconditional promise of it, then that person justly forfeits God's free gospel gift (Matthew 23:37,38). Because our salvation does not depend on our efforts to keep the law, no deeds of any person can contribute to salvation. Who can be so brave as to say to the Lord, "You did not do enough to save me; I must do more"? Salvation is therefore by grace through faith; no good works are required, and none are accepted (Ephesians 2:8,9).[45]

---

[38]When Pilate saw that he was gaining nothing, but rather that a tumult was beginning, he took water and washed his hands before the crowd, saying, "I am innocent of this man's blood; see to it yourselves." (Matthew 27:24)

[39][Jesus said,] "Day after day I was with you in the temple teaching, and you did not seize me. But let the Scriptures be fulfilled." (Mark 14:49)

[40][Solomon said,] "The lot is cast into the lap, but its every decision is from the LORD." (Proverbs 16:33)

[41][Jesus said,] "What does it profit a man to gain the whole world and forfeit his soul? For what can a man give in return for his soul?" (Mark 8:36,37)

[42][The Lord said,] "If I were hungry, I would not tell you, for the world and its fullness are mine." (Psalm 50:12)

[43]If we say we have not sinned, we make him [Jesus] a liar, and his word is not in us. (1 John 1:10)

[44]Then he [the jailer] brought them [Paul and Silas] out and said, "Sirs, what must I do to be saved?" And they said, "Believe in the Lord Jesus, and you will be saved, you and your household." (Acts 16:30,31)

[45]By grace you [believers] have been saved through faith. And this is not your own doing; it is the gift of God, not a result of works, so that no one may boast. (Ephesians 2:8,9)

While they are both the Word of the Lord, the law and the gospel could not be more different. The law says, "Do this, don't do this, and if you perform everything perfectly, you will be saved." The demands of the law are like being told to swim, completely unaided, across the Pacific Ocean from Seattle to Sydney to gain heaven. Such a task is incomprehensibly hard. The gospel, on the other hand, makes no demands but rather says, "All has been done for you. Enter." The Lord has made the gospel so sweet that it is incredible that anyone would not gladly accept it. Yet the vast majority of people have rejected or will reject it because of human pride (Romans 10:3).[46] If on the first day of the NFL season, the league representatives gave the Super Bowl trophy for the season to one team before the first play was run, who would want such a trophy? There would be no sport in being declared the winner without competing. Many people view eternal salvation in the same way. The gospel seems too easy, but here again human wisdom is deceived. Accepting the gospel indeed gives free entry into heaven, but it also totally changes the person who accepts it. The person is no longer self-centered and an enemy of the Lord. To prevent defections from his kingdom, Satan has developed many tricks to convince people they should be true to themselves and do it their own way. All these "individual lanes to success" make the highway to hell very broad indeed (Matthew 7:13).[47]

## The great exchange

The gospel can be summarized in terms of a great exchange. Sinners give Christ all the guilt of their sins, and he has atoned for the guilt of these sins by his passive obedience on the cross. In exchange, Christ gives sinners the righteousness that he earned by his active obedience to the law. No better deal has ever been offered (2 Corinthians 5:21).[48] When people realize the value of the deal, it changes the course of their lives. They no longer want to be doing the things that the mob is headed for hell is doing. They instead want to cling to the Lord who saved them by studying his Word, by thanking and praising him, and by spreading the glory of his plan of salvation by words and actions. What are the things of this world when there is the Lord?

Martin Luther referred to the righteousness earned for us by Christ and that alone is of value before the Lord as a foreign righteousness. We do not

---

[46]For, being ignorant of the righteousness of God, and seeking to establish their own, they [the Israelites] did not submit to God's righteousness. (Romans 10:3)

[47][Jesus said,] "The gate is wide and the way is easy [broad] that leads to destruction, and those who enter by it are many." (Matthew 7:13)

[48]For our sake he [God the Father] made him [Jesus, his Son] to be sin who knew no sin, so that in him [Jesus] we might become the righteousness of God. (2 Corinthians 5:21)

get it through anything we do, but we receive it wholly as a gift from another. While it is sometimes also called the righteousness of God, it is not that righteousness with which the Lord himself is righteous. That righteousness is beyond human comprehension and imitation. It is rather that righteousness the Lord credits to us for Christ's sake. It is the righteousness that the Pharisees could not produce no matter how much they strove to perfectly perform God's law and their man-made rules (Matthew 5:20),[49] yet it is a righteousness that even a little child can have through the faith formed in Baptism. The Lord indeed hides his gospel from the wise and reveals it to babes (Luke 10:21).[50]

---

[49] [Jesus said,] "I tell you [those listening to the Sermon on the Mount], unless your righteousness exceeds that of the scribes and Pharisees, you will never enter the kingdom of heaven." (Matthew 5:20)

[50] In that same hour he [Jesus] rejoiced in the Holy Spirit and said, "I thank you, Father, Lord of heaven and earth, that you have hidden these things from the wise and understanding and revealed them to little children; yes, Father, for such was your gracious will." (Luke 10:21)

CHAPTER 16

# Work of the Holy Spirit

The Lord's plan of salvation did not end with objective justification. If it had, all of humankind would still have been lost. To be saved, people must apply the objective justification earned by Christ to themselves so that it becomes theirs. In other words, they need to believe the message of the gospel of the Lord's free grace (Isaiah 55:1).[1] Free food, no matter how plentiful, does not do a starving woman any good if she does not eat it. Merely knowing about it is not enough. Neither would it help her if she believed in principle that the food would benefit her, but she did not actually eat it. In the same way, free salvation does not benefit anyone who does not accept it and rejoice to have it. One must take it to oneself as one's dearest treasure, because it certainly is (Mark 8:36,37).[2] Everything else will be used up, will be given away, will rot, or will be left to another at one's death (Isaiah 40:8).[3] Only the justification offered through Christ can be taken out of this world by a dying person, and a person must take it along in order to enter heaven.

The grim reality is that people by their own powers are incapable of accepting the generous offer of free salvation (1 Corinthians 2:14).[4]

---

[1] [The LORD said,] "Come, everyone who thirsts, come to the waters; and he who has no money, come, buy and eat! Come, buy wine and milk without money and without price." (Isaiah 55:1)

[2] [Jesus said,] "What does it profit a man to gain the whole world and forfeit his soul? For what can a man give in return for his soul?" (Mark 8:36,37)

[3] The grass withers, the flower fades, but the word of our God will stand forever. (Isaiah 40:8)

[4] The natural person does not accept the things of the Spirit of God, for they are folly to him, and he is not able to understand them because they are spiritually discerned. (1 Corinthians 2:14)

Humankind has been totally corrupted by sin, and that corruption causes people to be completely self-centered. While they inherently want for themselves anything that they view as good, they cannot view the Lord's plan of salvation in that way. Instead, people see the Lord accusing them of sin through the preaching of his law, and they do not like it (Luke 4:16-30). If the law beats them down so that they despair of meeting its demands, they would rather sulk and suffer (Genesis 4:4,5).[5] They will even torture themselves in an effort to force the Lord to feel sorry for them and to relent of his punishment of them, even though they have no intention of sincerely repenting of their sins and permanently repudiating them (Matthew 6:16).[6] In the utmost agony of soul, they still see themselves as their own savior because they want to see things in no other way. They have too much pride to do anything else.

## Conversion

The fourth step in the Lord's plan of salvation is to create faith in people's hearts, which is called conversion.[7] To accomplish conversion, the Lord works through both the law and the gospel. How the law is preached to the sinner is important, however. If it is preached as a curb, then it will reduce the amount of evil in people's actions, but it will not cause them to repent of their sins (Matthew 19:18-20).[8] This is because they will not be stung by the law condemning them personally, but they will view the law as applying mostly to others. If they do feel it pressing them on some issue, they will alter their behavior to escape direct condemnation and still continue to do pretty much as they please. They will also dismiss the accusations of the law if they can find others whose conduct is worse than theirs (Luke 18:11).[9] Many adopt a "middle of the pack" philosophy. They tell themselves that the Lord will not condemn everyone, so if they are not worse than others in their behavior, the

---

[5] The LORD had regard for Abel and his offering, but for Cain and his offering he had no regard. So Cain was very angry, and his face fell. (Genesis 4:4,5)

[6] [Jesus said,] "When you fast, do not look gloomy like the hypocrites, for they disfigure their faces that their fasting may be seen by others." (Matthew 6:16)

[7] Steps after humans sinned: the Lord's obligating himself to humankind to send a Savior, his demonstrating to humankind that it could not save itself, his sending the Savior, and, lastly, his converting people to believe in the Savior.

[8] He [a young man] said to him, "Which ones [commandments]?" And Jesus said, "You shall not murder, You shall not commit adultery, You shall not steal, You shall not bear false witness, Honor your father and mother, and, You shall love your neighbor as yourself." The young man said to him, "All these I have kept. What do I still lack?" (Matthew 19:18-20)

[9] [Jesus said,] "The Pharisee, standing by himself, prayed thus: 'God, I thank you that I am not like other men, extortioners, unjust, adulterers, or even like this tax collector.'" (Luke 18:11)

Lord will have to give them a place in heaven (Psalm 50:16,17).[10] Such people are not on the road to repentance. Governments use the principles contained in the law in their civil law codes in order to control the behavior of people in society, but their efforts certainly do not lead to anyone being saved.

To be an effective tool in conversion, the law must be preached as a mirror (James 1:23,24).[11] Moreover, it must be presented as a perfect mirror, showing every wrinkle and blemish in a person's behavior. People must see the absolute hideousness of their behavior and that there is not even one good thread in the tapestry of their character. Such preaching starts with a forceful description of the almighty nature of the Lord, a God who can and does demand conformity to his rules (Deuteronomy 5:32).[12] It points out people's actual sins, that is, real sins—not just sin in a general sense. It shows people that they have spiritual deficiencies in places in which they didn't realize they were accountable before the Lord (1 Chronicles 28:9,10).[13] The mirror of the law convicts them of the wrong deeds they do but also of the supposedly good deeds they do for the wrong reasons (Isaiah 64:6).[14] It holds them accountable for their words, their profanity, their hateful speech, and their gossip (James 1:26).[15] It reminds them of their secret thoughts by which they enjoy the sins they would like to perform in actual deeds but are too afraid of punishment to publicly commit (Matthew 15:19,20).[16] It leaves them not only spiritually naked before the Lord but also completely transparent to his penetrating vision. The law shows how lengthy the indictment will be that will be brought against them on judgment day (2 Peter 2:9,10),[17] and it makes clear that there is no way that the record can be cleared by

---

[10]To the wicked God says: "What right have you to recite my statutes or take my covenant on your lips? For you hate discipline, and you cast my words behind you." (Psalm 50:16,17)

[11]If anyone is a hearer of the word and not a doer, he is like a man who looks intently at his natural face in a mirror. For he looks at himself and goes away and at once forgets what he was like. (James 1:23,24)

[12][The LORD said,] "You shall be careful therefore to do as the LORD your God has commanded you. You shall not turn aside to the right hand or to the left." (Deuteronomy 5:32)

[13]"The LORD searches all hearts and understands every plan and thought. If you seek him, he will be found by you, but if you forsake him, he will cast you off forever." (1 Chronicles 28:9,10)

[14]We have all become like one who is unclean, and all our righteous deeds are like a polluted garment. (Isaiah 64:6)

[15]If anyone thinks he is religious and does not bridle his tongue but deceives his heart, this person's religion is worthless. (James 1:26)

[16][Jesus said,] "Out of the heart come evil thoughts, murder, adultery, sexual immorality, theft, false witness, slander. These are what defile a person." (Matthew 15:19,20)

[17]The Lord knows how to rescue the godly from trials, and to keep the unrighteous under punishment until the day of judgment, and especially those who indulge in the lust of defiling passion and despise authority. (2 Peter 2:9,10)

remedial actions (Matthew 16:26).[18] Correct preaching of the law as a mirror brings nothing but despair.

If the Lord's message were only the mirror of the law, humankind's situation would be grim indeed. People would only see impending and unavoidable doom. The most hardened might say, "Let us eat, drink, and be merry because we will soon suffer regardless." Most, however, would deny what the mirror showed them, would try to create some fantasized escape plan, or would utterly despair. And it is despair that the Lord wants the sinner to feel. A mere feeling of remorse is not good enough. Remorse is sorrow for having done something that got one into trouble, not repudiation of the deed itself. Only when a person is in despair will they give up on self-help and be ready to ask, "How can I be saved?" It is only then that the answer of the gospel can be given: "You can do nothing! Everything necessary for your salvation has already been done by Jesus Christ. Believe the message and live." This is the response that Paul and Silas gave to the jailer at Philippi when he feared that his life would be forfeited if prisoners escaped during an earthquake (Acts 16:25-34).

Sadly, the only response to this announcement that sinful humans are capable of by nature is: "It is too good to be true; therefore, it is not true. I am not so gullible as to believe it." This is because the human heart is spiritually dead (1 Corinthians 2:14).[19] Just as a dead person cannot respond to the greatest of financial offers, so the spiritually dead heart cannot accept the gospel. Humankind's corrupted ability to choose to do the Lord's will can now only choose to do evil and never choose anything that is spiritually good (Genesis 6:5).[20] Yet the Holy Spirit does not let a person's refusal to accept the gospel go unchallenged. Instead, he brings the message into the dead heart, and the heart changes (Colossians 2:13,14).[21] It becomes alive and believes the message. A new saint is born. It is only the Holy Spirit who can effect the necessary change to make the human heart accept the message (1 Corinthians 12:3).[22] In the same way that people are not in the least bit

---

[18][Jesus said,] "What shall a man give in return for his soul?" (Matthew 16:26)

[19]The natural person does not accept the things of the Spirit of God, for they are folly to him, and he is not able to understand them because they are spiritually discerned. (1 Corinthians 2:14)

[20]The LORD saw that the wickedness of man was great in the earth, and that every intention of the thoughts of his heart was only evil continually. (Genesis 6:5)

[21]You, who were dead in your trespasses and the uncircumcision of your flesh, God made alive together with him, having forgiven us all our trespasses, by canceling the record of debt that stood against us with its legal demands. This he set aside, nailing it to the cross. (Colossians 2:13,14)

[22]I want you to understand that no one speaking in the Spirit of God ever says "Jesus is accursed!" and no one can say "Jesus is Lord" except in the Holy Spirit. (1 Corinthians 12:3)

responsible for their physical conception and birth, so they are not in the least bit responsible for their election to faith and their spiritual birth. With the creation of the new person within the sinner, the sinner can truly repent of his or her sins and repudiate the phony good works that had in the past been the source of such pride (Matthew 16:24).[23] This is called subjective justification because a person, a "subject," has accepted the message and applied it to himself through faith (Romans 6:11).[24] By grace, through faith, the person is now an heir of heaven (Titus 3:7).[25]

Alas, in most cases the process of rebirthing a sinner into a saint fails (Matthew 13:18-23).[26] There are various reasons. Often people refuse to see how devastating their sins really are. Many are too self-centered to be willing to accept the help of the Lord but instead want to work out their salvation without him. Others fight and defeat the Holy Spirit's efforts to create the new person within them. Still others quickly choose to go back to their sinful life once faith has been implanted in their hearts (2 Peter 2:22).[27] Why some believe and others do not believe is known only by the Lord. If the conversion effort succeeds, the work of the Holy Spirit is solely responsible (1 Corinthians 12:3);[28] if it fails, the fault lies solely with the person involved (Acts 7:51).[29] This is because when the Lord works through means, such as his Word as given in the Bible and the sacraments,[30] his efforts can be thwarted by humans. When the Lord acts directly, nothing can resist him, as we saw in chapter 4.

---

[23] Then Jesus told his disciples, "If anyone would come after me, let him deny himself and take up his cross and follow me." (Matthew 16:24)

[24] You also must consider yourselves dead to sin and alive to God in Christ Jesus. (Romans 6:11)

[25] So that being justified by his grace we might become heirs according to the hope of eternal life. (Titus 3:7)

[26] [Jesus said,] "Hear then the parable of the sower: When anyone hears the word of the kingdom and does not understand it, the evil one comes and snatches away what has been sown in his heart. This is what was sown along the path. As for what was sown on rocky ground, this is the one who hears the word and immediately receives it with joy, yet he has no root in himself, but endures for a while, and when tribulation or persecution arises on account of the word, immediately he falls away. As for what was sown among thorns, this is the one who hears the word, but the cares of the world and the deceitfulness of riches choke the word, and it proves unfruitful. As for what was sown on good soil, this is the one who hears the word and understands it. He indeed bears fruit and yields, in one case a hundredfold, in another sixty, and in another thirty." (Matthew 13:18-23)

[27] What the true proverb says has happened to them: "The dog returns to its own vomit, and the sow, after washing herself, returns to wallow in the mire." (2 Peter 2:22)

[28] No one can say "Jesus is Lord" except in the Holy Spirit. (1 Corinthians 12:3)

[29] "You stiff-necked people, uncircumcised in heart and ears, you always resist the Holy Spirit." (Acts 7:51)

[30] The Word of God (i.e., the Scriptures) and the sacraments (i.e., Holy Baptism and Holy Communion) are called the means of grace because it is through these means that faith is worked and strengthened within people. More about the sacraments will be discussed in chapter 17.

## Errors related to faith and conversion

It is only natural that human beings do not like to do things the Lord's way, and this includes issues involving faith and conversion. Because people do not like to hear about their sins, some church bodies have adopted "gospel-first" evangelism. Rather than first telling people they are sinners in need of a Savior, they tell people what marvelous things Jesus has done for them and how loving he is. But people who do not feel the guilt of their sins upon their hearts are not likely to be too enthusiastic about a salvation plan they don't realize they need (Luke 7:47).[31] It would be like trying to sell parkas to people in the Amazon jungle. Invariably, other inducements must be given to make people want to come into the church and stay there, and the church soon becomes involved in the social gospel, that is, helping people with their economic and social needs instead of their spiritual needs, as the Lord commissioned the church to do (Matthew 28:19,20).[32] Although these churches claim that they do preach the law eventually, they often preach it only as a guide or dilute it so as not to frighten away their members. This approach has become common in the mainline Protestant churches. Without the preaching of the law as a mirror, people do not repent and are not saved (Matthew 12:34,35).[33] The message of God's love is an important message, but it is intended only for those who grieve over their sins.

Pentecostal and many Evangelical church bodies preach the law as a mirror and duly bring people to feel despair over their sins, but they have the wrong remedy. Their remedy is not the gospel but the law as a guide. They give the people rules and procedures to address their sinful condition. They emphasize preparing one's heart so as to be able to make a decision for Christ. This approach has been called Pietism because its goal is to induce people to live more pious lives and therefore be worthy of Christ's forgiveness. Church bodies do this because they do not accept the biblical teaching that the sinful nature also includes sinful thoughts and sinful longings of the heart, so they concentrate only on sinful deeds. The spiritually dead heart, however, can never make a decision about anything any more than a physically dead body can, nor can it produce works that are good in the sight of

---

[31][Jesus said,] "He who is forgiven little, loves little." (Luke 7:47)

[32][Jesus said,] "Go therefore and make disciples of all nations, baptizing them in the name of the Father and of the Son and of the Holy Spirit, teaching them to observe all that I have commanded you. And behold, I am with you always, to the end of the age." (Matthew 28:19,20)

[33][Jesus said,] "You brood of vipers! How can you speak good, when you are evil? For out of the abundance of the heart the mouth speaks. The good person out of his good treasure brings forth good, and the evil person out of his evil treasure brings forth evil." (Matthew 12:34,35)

God (Romans 3:20).[34] Their teaching that conversion is a process in which the person participates rather than an event effected by the Holy Spirit (Ephesians 2:4-6)[35] leaves people in doubt about their salvation. They must always wonder whether they have become pious enough to believe. Without a firm reliance on the gospel, there can be no salvation.

Mega churches also often preach a law-law approach to salvation. They preach the law as a curb against the evils of society and the law as a guide for Christian living. They view Jesus as a new lawgiver, looking to such sections of the Bible as the Sermon on the Mount (Matthew 5–7). They urge people to ask, "What would Jesus do?" (WWJD) and encourage people to read religious self-help books to become effective in their lives and therefore more like Christ. While this may make members of such churches good friends and great neighbors, it leaves them relying on themselves to become "savable." The amount of gospel, which is the power of the Lord for salvation, that members of these churches hear is often only a shadow of what is presented in the Scriptures. This leaves the souls of the members often spiritually starving. Consider this approach in light of what Isaiah wrote: "Come now, let us reason together, says the LORD: though your sins are like scarlet, they shall be as white as snow; though they are red like crimson, they shall become like wool" (Isaiah 1:18). Contrast it to what Jesus said: "Come to me, all who labor and are heavy laden, and I will give you rest. Take my yoke upon you, and learn from me, for I am gentle and lowly in heart, and you will find rest for your souls. For my yoke is easy, and my burden is light" (Matthew 11:28-30).

The law cannot bring about conversion, which is solely the work of the Lord (John 6:29).[36] The "third use" of the law (i.e., as a guide) is intended only for those who already believe (John 15:5,6).[37] Some unbelievers will respond to the preaching of the law as a guide by modifying their behavior. They think such efforts at living a better life will impress the Lord and earn good marks in the ledger he keeps of their good and bad deeds. Good works offsetting sins has been a false teaching that has plagued the Christian

---

[34] By works of the law no human being will be justified in his sight, since through the law comes knowledge of sin. (Romans 3:20)

[35] God, being rich in mercy, because of the great love with which he loved us, even when we were dead in our trespasses, made us alive together with Christ—by grace you have been saved—and raised us up with him and seated us with him in the heavenly places in Christ Jesus. (Ephesians 2:4-6)

[36] Jesus answered them, "This is the work of God, that you believe in him whom he has sent." (John 6:29)

[37] [Jesus said,] "Whoever abides in me and I in him, he it is that bears much fruit, for apart from me you can do nothing. If anyone does not abide in me he is thrown away like a branch and withers; and the branches are gathered, thrown into the fire, and burned." (John 15:5,6)

church from the time of the apostles, but the lead weights of sins cannot be offset by the canary feathers of good works (Micah 6:7).[38] Moreover, it is a damning deception that living an outwardly Christian life leads to salvation, which Jesus pointed out in the parable of the Pharisee and the tax collector (Luke 18:9-14). It is a quid pro quo approach, one in which something is gained in exchange for something else. Sadly, the whole Roman Catholic sacramental system is based on a payment of this nature to offset the punishment for one's sins through good works, masses, and indulgences.

The quid pro quo approach to paying for sins quickly degenerates into trying to appease the Lord with one's own approaches to repentance. The Catholic Church, for example, decided to make repentance easier for its members by changing the requirements to obtain forgiveness. Rather than demanding *contrition*, the deep sorrow for sinning against the Lord and a promise to strive to refrain from such sinning in the future, it agreed to accept *attrition*, the mere regret of having committed the sin and a hope to repudiate the sin at a future time that is more opportune.[39] In other words, one can receive provisional forgiveness on the promise of hoping to be contrite sometime in the future. This encourages Catholics to try to bargain with the Lord, pledging to do some good works (at least, "good" in their opinion) to offset sins that they have done or want to do. Unfortunately, it is not only Catholics who try to wheel and deal with God. Many Protestants, including some Lutherans, try to offer good behavior to the Lord in exchange for physical blessings, even if they realize that they cannot bargain over the forgiveness of sins. For the creature to pull up his chair at the table across from the Creator and to offer to give the Creator what is already his is blasphemy (Isaiah 29:16).[40] In all things we are only supplicants, seeking the Lord's mercy, not equals demanding what is due us (Job 41:11).[41]

Any effort to bring human works into the salvation process, whether it be in justification or in conversion, is called synergism. It is an effort to harness the mighty elephant (the Lord) together with the weak cricket (humans) to pull the wagon that represents our salvation to the heavenly granary. The

---

[38] [The Lord states what is folly.] "Will the Lord be pleased with thousands of rams, with ten thousands of rivers of oil? Shall I give my firstborn for my transgression, the fruit of my body for the sin of my soul?" (Micah 6:7)

[39] *Catechism of the Catholic Church*, sec. 1453.

[40] You turn things upside down! Shall the potter be regarded as the clay, that the thing made should say of its maker, "He did not make me"; or the thing formed say of him who formed it, "He has no understanding"? (Isaiah 29:16)

[41] [The Lord said,] "Who has first given to me, that I should repay him? Whatever is under the whole heaven is mine." (Job 41:11)

efforts that we put in to get the cricket to do his share of the pulling will only delay our arrival until it is too late, and we will find the door shut (see parable of the ten virgins, Matthew 25:1-13). Synergism appeals to our sinful nature because it allows us to keep something of our own. If our repentance is to be true, we must not only have sorrow for our sins but must also reject anything within us that appears good to us. All our good works are contaminated by sin and therefore cannot be brought into the presence of the Lord (Isaiah 64:6).[42] It is only the righteousness that Christ gives us that can be presented before the Lord (Romans 3:21,22).[43] Therefore, everything about us must be discarded. This includes any way in which we think that we contributed to our conversion. It was not that we were less sinful or less resistant or more reasonable; our conversion was wholly due to the grace of the Lord (Ephesians 2:8,9).[44] The trap of synergism will always be before us while we are here on earth, and we must pray diligently to the Lord that he would keep us from falling into it and being lost (1 Corinthians 10:12).[45]

## Keeping the faith

Although the Holy Spirit works faith in our hearts, that faith is ours to lose. Although we could do nothing to create spiritual life within us because we were spiritually dead, once we are spiritually alive, we can do things to keep ourselves spiritually alive. The parallel with physical life is often used in the Scriptures to encourage us to be persistent in the use of the means of grace (studying the Bible and receiving Holy Communion) to strengthen our faith (Acts 17:11).[46] It also encourages us to flee those places where we would be tempted to sin (Psalm 1:1,2).[47] Satan is eager to regain all those whom he has lost from his kingdom by constantly prowling after Christians, offering them all sorts of "hot deals." While the Lord promises to assist us so that we do not fall to the enticements of the demons, that help cannot come

---

[42]We have all become like one who is unclean, and all our righteous deeds are like a polluted garment. (Isaiah 64:6)

[43]Now the righteousness of God has been manifested apart from the law, although the Law and the Prophets bear witness to it—the righteousness of God through faith in Jesus Christ for all who believe. (Romans 3:21,22)

[44]By grace you have been saved through faith. And this is not your own doing; it is the gift of God, not a result of works, so that no one may boast. (Ephesians 2:8,9)

[45]Therefore let anyone who thinks that he stands take heed lest he fall. (1 Corinthians 10:12)

[46]These Jews [in Berea] were nobler than those in Thessalonica; they received the word with all eagerness, examining the Scriptures daily to see if these things were so. (Acts 17:11)

[47]Blessed is the man who walks not in the counsel of the wicked, nor stands in the way of sinners, nor sits in the seat of scoffers; but his delight is in the law [teachings] of the LORD, and on his [teachings] he meditates day and night. (Psalm 1:1,2)

if we cut our lifeline to the means of grace and rely on our own inadequate strength to keep us in the saving faith (Proverbs 3:5).[48]

One of the great mistakes of John Calvin was his teaching that "once in faith, always in faith." While he correctly believed that the Lord would save all his elect and that nothing could take them out of the Lord's hand, he sometimes tried to use human reason to understand the hidden things of God. We do not understand how our faith can be in danger if we are predestined and therefore guaranteed salvation. Yet the Lord clearly says that both are true (1 Peter 5:8;[49] John 10:27,28[50]), and we should accept these statements without doubting him. Calvin tried to solve the dilemma by claiming that those who were predestined to hell (another of his errors) could never truly believe, even if they were apparently faithful members of the church. Similarly, Calvin said that once someone predestined to salvation came to faith, that person could not fall away from faith, even temporarily, no matter how vile his actions might become for a while. Consequently, Calvin denied that someone could be converted, fall away, and be converted again, even though the Bible issues numerous appeals to those who have fallen from the faith to return (Psalm 51:13).[51] We must ever guard ourselves from trying to explain the things of God that he has not revealed to us, lest we deceive ourselves and lose our faith.

### Sanctification

The word *sanctification* comes from a Greek word meaning "to make holy." People are made holy before the Lord when they are brought to faith in Jesus Christ. They are declared righteous because he has atoned for their sins through his suffering, death, and resurrection (passive obedience) and because his righteous life (active obedience) is credited to them as their own righteousness. This is sometimes labeled "sanctification in the narrower sense." Through the conversion process, the Holy Spirit gives the believers citizenship in the kingdom of heaven (Philippians 3:20)[52] and creates a new person in each of

---

[48]Trust in the LORD with all your heart, and do not lean on your own understanding. (Proverbs 3:5)

[49]Be sober-minded; be watchful. Your adversary the devil prowls around like a roaring lion, seeking someone to devour. (1 Peter 5:8)

[50][Jesus said,] "My sheep hear my voice, and I know them, and they follow me. I give them eternal life, and they will never perish, and no one will snatch them out of my hand." (John 10:27,28)

[51][After he himself repented and returned to faith in the Lord, David wrote,] "Then I will teach transgressors your ways, and sinners will return to you." (Psalm 51:13)

[52]Our citizenship is in heaven, and from it [heaven] we await a Savior, the Lord Jesus Christ. (Philippians 3:20)

them (2 Corinthians 5:17)[53] who wants to live a life that is pleasing to the Lord. At this point the believers are already saints (i.e., holy ones) in the eyes of the Lord (Ephesians 1:1).[54] Yet he is not ready to take them out of this world. There is still one more part to his plan before they can leave the church militant (i.e., the earthly church) for the church triumphant (the church in heaven).

The Lord did not choose to bring people into his heavenly kingdom as we might have done it. He could have sent his holy angels out with the message of salvation so that it always would have been presented completely correctly. He could have taken people to heaven as soon as they believed to prevent them from having an opportunity to fall back into a life of sin. At the very least, he could have given his believers special powers so that they would not have to suffer in this world after they abandoned this world in a spiritual sense. The Lord's wisdom led him to take a different approach. He tries the faith of the believers by leaving them in the world for a while and asking them to remain faithful to him (Revelation 2:10).[55]

While his believers remain in the church militant, Jesus prays for them, as he did in his High Priestly Prayer (John 17). He sends the Holy Spirit to help them (John 14:16,17),[56] and the Spirit works to strengthen their faith so that they remain faithful (John 14:26).[57] Every day Christians are under assault by the forces of evil. While the new person in us wants to serve the Lord, the old person in us (i.e., old Adam) wants to continue sinning (Romans 7:18,19).[58] The demons have all sorts of arguments to justify rebelling against the Lord, and they seek to attack us at our weakest points (1 Timothy 6:9).[59] The world around us is full of sinful activities that offer us the ability to be our own person and enjoy ourselves (Galatians 5:18-21).[60] The people of the world even taunt us for not joining with them. Jesus

---

[53]If anyone is in Christ, he is a new creation. The old has passed away; behold, the new has come. (2 Corinthians 5:17)

[54]Paul, an apostle of Christ Jesus by the will of God, to the saints who are in Ephesus, and are faithful in Christ Jesus. (Ephesians 1:1)

[55][Jesus said,] "Be faithful unto death, and I will give you the crown of life." (Revelation 2:10)

[56][Jesus said,] "I will ask the Father, and he will give you another Helper, to be with you forever, even the Spirit of truth." (John 14:16,17)

[57][Jesus said,] "He [the Holy Spirit] will teach you all things and bring to your remembrance all that I have said to you." (John 14:26)

[58]I know that nothing good dwells in me, that is, in my flesh. For I have the desire to do what is right, but not the ability to carry it out. For I do not do the good I want, but the evil I do not want is what I keep on doing. (Romans 7:18,19)

[59]Those who desire to be rich fall into temptation, into a snare, into many senseless and harmful desires that plunge people into ruin and destruction. (1 Timothy 6:9)

[60]If you are led by the Spirit, you are not under the law. Now the works of the flesh are evident: sex-

calls on each of his disciples to "take up his cross and follow me" (Matthew 16:24). The Christian life is a life under the cross. The Holy Spirit works to help us persevere. First, he daily assures us that our worst problem has been solved by reminding us that our sins have been forgiven (1 Timothy 6:6-8).[61] He comforts us through the words of the Bible, assuring us that we are not facing anything that others have not faced before us (1 Corinthians 10:13).[62] He also uses the Bible to increase our knowledge so that we are not so easily duped by Satan and so we can sort out sinful activities from those that please the Lord (Galatians 5:16,17).[63] He helps us formulate prayers (Romans 8:26).[64] He works behind the scenes to frustrate the plans of the demons and to bring comfort into the lives of his believers (Psalm 91:11,12).[65] He gives us successes to build our resolve and failures to strengthen our reliance on the Lord rather than ourselves. In all ways through his spiritual gifts (Galatians 5:22,23)[66] he seeks to build up his faithful for the struggles we will face until we are called home to the Lord. This is labeled "sanctification in the broader sense."

As Christians, we are not our own people; we are the Lord's servants and soldiers (1 Corinthians 7:22,23).[67] The Lord's intention for his followers, therefore, is not merely to survive in this world. He wants us to have the opportunity to become fellow workers with him in proclaiming his message of repentance and redemption through Jesus Christ (Matthew 28:19,20). To accomplish this, he needs to take weak human beings, who are ignorant and

---

ual immorality, impurity, sensuality, idolatry, sorcery, enmity, strife, jealousy, fits of anger, rivalries, dissensions, divisions, envy, drunkenness, orgies, and things like these. I warn you, as I warned you before, that those who do such things will not inherit the kingdom of God. (Galatians 5:18-21)

[61]Godliness with contentment is great gain, for we brought nothing into the world, and we cannot take anything out of the world. But if we have food and clothing, with these we will be content. (1 Timothy 6:6-8)

[62]No temptation has overtaken you that is not common to man. God is faithful, and he will not let you be tempted beyond your ability, but with the temptation he will also provide the way of escape, that you may be able to endure it. (1 Corinthians 10:13)

[63]I say, walk by the Spirit, and you will not gratify the desires of the flesh. For the desires of the flesh are against the Spirit, and the desires of the Spirit are against the flesh, for these are opposed to each other, to keep you from doing the things you want to do. (Galatians 5:16,17)

[64]The Spirit helps us in our weakness. For we do not know what to pray for as we ought, but the Spirit himself intercedes for us with groanings too deep for words. (Romans 8:26)

[65]He [the Lord] will command his angels concerning you to guard you in all your ways. On their hands they will bear you up, lest you strike your foot against a stone. (Psalm 91:11,12)

[66]The fruit of the Spirit is love, joy, peace, patience, kindness, goodness, faithfulness, gentleness, self-control. (Galatians 5:22,23)

[67]He who was free when called is a bondservant of Christ. You were bought with a price. (1 Corinthians 7:22,23)

prone to err, and remold them into his messengers. The Holy Spirit therefore continues to work in us to build our faith so we are arrayed with the whole armor of God (Ephesians 6:10-18). He gives us the gifts we need to make us useful in the work of spreading the message of salvation throughout the world (Romans 12:6-8).[68] His followers are to be ambassadors of his truth (2 Corinthians 5:20)[69] to a world that relishes lies and flattery. We are not in a physical battle in which territory can be seized and the enemies routed (Ephesians 6:12).[70] The demons never grow weary or become worn down. The fight will be continuous while Christians live. When the struggle seems overwhelming, the Holy Spirit assures us that the victory is certain because nothing can separate us from the love of God (Romans 8:31-39). The Lord sees all of human history, and he controls every atom of the universe. While unbelieving fools may reign here, only saints reign in heaven. But no Christian should despise unbelievers, for all Christians were unbelievers before the Holy Spirit called us and made our souls alive in Christ (1 Corinthians 6:9-11).[71] Instead, the Lord wants all his followers to spread his message so that more may hear it.

---

[68]Having gifts that differ according to the grace given to us, let us use them: if prophecy, in proportion to our faith; if service, in our serving; the one who teaches, in his teaching; the one who exhorts, in his exhortation; the one who contributes, in generosity; the one who leads, with zeal; the one who does acts of mercy, with cheerfulness. (Romans 12:6-8)

[69]Therefore, we are ambassadors for Christ, God making his appeal through us. We implore you on behalf of Christ, be reconciled to God. (2 Corinthians 5:20)

[70]We do not wrestle against flesh and blood, but against the rulers, against the authorities, against the cosmic powers over this present darkness, against the spiritual forces of evil in the heavenly places. (Ephesians 6:12)

[71]Do you not know that the unrighteous will not inherit the kingdom of God? Do not be deceived: neither the sexually immoral, nor idolaters, nor adulterers, nor men who practice homosexuality, nor thieves, nor the greedy, nor drunkards, nor revilers, nor swindlers will inherit the kingdom of God. And such were some of you. But you were washed, you were sanctified, you were justified in the name of the Lord Jesus Christ and by the Spirit of our God. (1 Corinthians 6:9-11)

# Life in the Church

Once people have been brought to faith in Christ, they are no longer orphans left to fend for themselves in a hostile world (1 Peter 2:10).[1] Instead, they are members of the holy Christian church, the invisible body of all believers who are both in the world and in heaven (Romans 12:5).[2] They are almost always also members of a visible congregation and a church body. It is in the visible church that they need to grow in faith and knowledge and to work in the Lord's kingdom of grace here on earth (Acts 2:42).[3] Both their growth and their work are important to the individual Christians and also to the Lord's plan for the salvation of other people. Each follower of Christ will want to take advantage of the opportunities for spiritual growth and for service in the congregation to which he or she belongs (Ephesians 6:10-20). Each believer also needs to evaluate whether that congregation teaches the doctrines of the Bible faithfully and to seek another congregation or church body if it doesn't,

---

[1] Once you were not a people, but now you are God's people; once you had not received mercy, but now you have received mercy. (1 Peter 2:10)

[2] We, though many, are one body in Christ, and individually members one of another. (Romans 12:5)

[3] They devoted themselves to the apostles' teaching and the fellowship, to the breaking of bread and the prayers. (Acts 2:42)

so as not to place his or her soul in danger of losing its saving faith (1 John 4:1).[4]

After coming to faith in Christ, moreover, each person remains a citizen of a nation in this world and of its subdivisions. Citizenship gives each person, including each Christian, certain privileges and also certain responsibilities (Romans 13:5-7).[5] The laws of the nations are not identical to the Lord's moral law. Sometimes these laws permit what the Lord forbids, and sometimes they place restrictions on what the Lord allows. As Lutherans, we obey the laws of the state except when they conflict with the commands of the Lord, as will be discussed in chapter 18. Furthermore, we try to be good citizens, not just residents in the area in which we live, having no concern for others or for our government (Jeremiah 29:7).[6]

It is the intent of this section to put these topics into perspective rather than to explore them in detail. The goal is to cover the key theological points. These should serve as a guide to Christian living and as a basis for further study.

---

[4] Do not believe every spirit, but test the spirits to see whether they are from God, for many false prophets have gone out into the world. (1 John 4:1)

[5] One must be in subjection, not only to avoid God's wrath but also for the sake of conscience. For because of this you also pay taxes, for the authorities are ministers of God, attending to this very thing. Pay to all what is owed to them: taxes to whom taxes are owed, revenue to whom revenue is owed, respect to whom respect is owed, honor to whom honor is owed. (Romans 13:5-7)

[6] Seek the welfare of the city where I [the LORD] have sent you into exile, and pray to the LORD on its behalf, for in its welfare you will find your welfare. (Jeremiah 29:7)

# CHAPTER 17

# Mission of the Church

In his or her local congregation, a Lutheran finds many things happening. The purpose of these activities is to further the kingdom of grace. Each activity has its place, and if carried out properly, they all fit together like the gears of a machine to produce useful work. St. Paul compares them to the organs of the human body (1 Corinthians 12:14-26). All parts of the body are important, and therefore no part should despise any of the other parts. Through the activities of the local congregation, strong members are given opportunities to serve their Lord, weak members are strengthened in their faith, poor members are given assistance and purpose in life, and nonmembers are acquainted with the gospel of salvation.

## Preaching

Jesus gave the Great Commission to his church, that is, the commission to proclaim to all people the way of salvation (Matthew 28:19,20).[1] In worship services, the Lutheran pastor generally does this by explaining a selection from the Scriptures (i.e., a text) so that the hearers can understand the message of the Lord. This is what Jesus did when he was given the scroll of the book of Isaiah to read and expound upon in the synagogue in Nazareth (Luke 4:16-22). The pastor does not talk about a topic merely because

---

[1] [Jesus said,] "Go therefore and make disciples of all nations, baptizing them in the name of the Father and of the Son and of the Holy Spirit, teaching them to observe all that I have commanded you. And behold, I am with you always, to the end of the age." (Matthew 28:19,20)

he finds it interesting but rather chooses a topic on which the Bible gives information for the spiritual health of the members. If a pastor's sermons are not anchored in the Scriptures, then they are worthless for salvation (Galatians 1:8).[2]

To explain the Scriptures and to apply them, the preacher gives the hearers the context of the biblical text he has chosen. He informs his listeners of the circumstances in which the writer or the speaker of the words produced them and of the nature of the original audience. How the words are to be understood depends on why they were first written or spoken. The pastor may also need to explain the historical context of the issue the writer was addressing. For example, understanding what Jesus said sometimes requires knowing something about the ceremonial cleanliness laws of the Jews (Mark 7:3,4).[3] In another case, understanding a portion of one of Paul's letters might require knowledge of the situation in the city and in the congregation to which he was writing.

The Lutheran preacher next turns to the text itself. In the text there might be linguistic artifacts that make understanding it more challenging. For example, Greek is written with heavy use of participial construction, which is often translated into English merely by the word *and*. Yet the participles often indicate a progression that is important to a good understanding of the text. For example, a literal translation of Matthew 28:19 is "Therefore as you go, make disciples," while most Bible translations have "Go therefore and make disciples." All the writers of the New Testament were Jews. Sometimes Hebraic ways of representing thoughts were used within their Greek writing style, and these can cause misunderstandings if directly translated into English. For example, in Romans 5:18,19 Paul used the word "all" to indicate that all were lost and all have been redeemed, but in the next verse he used "many" to indicate that many were lost and many have been redeemed. Paul was used to the Hebrew usage of "all" and "many" together to indicate every one of a large number, and he wrote these two verses as a typical Hebrew couplet, even though he was writing in Greek. Lutheran pastors have been trained to recognize these language features and can point them out to their listeners when such information is needed to understand the scriptural message.

---

[2]Even if we or an angel from heaven should preach to you a gospel contrary to the one we preached to you, let him be accursed. (Galatians 1:8)

[3]The Pharisees and all the Jews do not eat unless they wash their hands properly, holding to the tradition of the elders, and when they come from the marketplace, they do not eat unless they wash. And there are many other traditions that they observe, such as the washing of cups and pots and copper vessels and dining couches. (Mark 7:3,4)

The main emphasis in the sermon, however, must be the preaching of the law and the gospel. Sometimes the law and/or the gospel jump out of the text and hit the hearer with a clear and unmistakable meaning (Romans 3:23,24).[4] In many cases, however, the law and the gospel are a part of the overall fabric of the section of the Scriptures from which the text is taken. How the law applies to the situation that led to the production of the text may need to be explained. The law may sometimes seem to be only a curb or only a guide, and the preacher may need to go beyond these easier applications and preach how the text acts as a mirror of the sins of the people sitting in front of him. Because the text is part of the message of the Lord's plan of salvation, it was aimed at people who were deplorable sinners from the very time it was first produced (Jeremiah 17:23).[5] The hearers in the pew need to see themselves in a way that they cannot but recognize that they have totally depraved hearts.

But the Lutheran preacher will not stop with the law. He will go on to talk about the Lord's great love in his rescue of humankind through the work of Jesus Christ. He will assure those who recognize their sins and repent of them that there is complete forgiveness for them (1 John 1:9).[6] The sinners' stained robes have been washed white in the blood of the Lamb of God (Revelation 7:14).[7] Even in times of deepest sorrow, this message of great joy is proclaimed. The preacher will also warn his hearers that this precious gift of salvation is not for those who only go through the motions but in their hearts want to cling to their favorite sins (1 John 1:8).[8] The gift of salvation is so great that it changes hearts and makes people want to serve the Lord by learning his Word, telling it to others, and helping their neighbors. The preacher makes the law most bitter so that the gospel will be most sweet (Luke 7:47).[9] [10]

---

[4] All have sinned and fall short of the glory of God, and are justified by his grace as a gift, through the redemption that is in Christ Jesus. (Romans 3:23,24)

[5] Yet they [the people of Judah] did not listen or incline their ear, but stiffened their neck, that they might not hear and receive instruction. (Jeremiah 17:23)

[6] If we confess our sins, he [the Lord] is faithful and just to forgive us our sins and to cleanse us from all unrighteousness. (1 John 1:9)

[7] They [the believers] have washed their robes and made them white in the blood of the Lamb. (Revelation 7:14)

[8] If we say we have no sin, we deceive ourselves, and the truth is not in us. (1 John 1:8)

[9] [Jesus said,] "He who is forgiven little, loves little." (Luke 7:47)

[10] While Lutheran pastors do speak from the pulpit about applications of their texts to Christian living, this is seldom a major part of their sermons because members of the congregation need the ability to learn about sanctification in their lives in settings where discussion is possible. This is better handled in a teaching, rather than a preaching, environment.

## Teaching

A sermon is a short explanation and exhortation based on a small portion of the Bible. To grow in faith, people need a much greater exposure to the Bible on a regular basis (Deuteronomy 6:6-10). To give its members an opportunity to study the Scriptures more deeply, Lutheran congregations frequently conduct one or more Bible classes during the week. It is difficult to teach one Bible class that will benefit every person in a congregation, even every adult in a congregation. This is because the scriptural knowledge and maturity of the members may differ greatly based on their age, their past schooling, and the amount of personal Bible study they have done (1 Corinthians 3:2).[11] Because organized Bible study is effective at building people's faith, it is essential that it be done well (2 Timothy 3:16,17).[12] It needs to be more than Sunday school for adults, and it should take people deeper into the teachings of the Bible.

Because of the tremendous spiritual comfort gained from Bible study and the importance of such study in resisting the allurements of Satan, every adult Christian should try to regularly participate in at least one organized Bible class each week. The choice of Bible classes should be based on what is available and on what each individual thinks would best help him or her to grow spiritually. General Bible classes have some value for all members, but those who have studied God's Word more diligently or for a longer time will gain less from such classes. These people should consider more challenging classes on biblical topics, on specific doctrines, or on books of the Bible. Regardless of the format or the depth of the class, learning depends on people actively being involved in the class, such as by taking notes in their Bibles and by thinking or reading about the discussed material outside of class. A reliable study Bible that gives background and commentary can greatly aid Bible study because it gives useful information to help understand the verses.[13]

Formal Bible classes are not enough to become knowledgeable about the Bible. It greatly benefits every Christian to engage daily in some form of personal Bible study (Psalm 1:1,2).[14] One often can get devotional books

---

[11] I fed you with milk, not solid food, for you were not ready for it. And even now you are not yet ready. (1 Corinthians 3:2)

[12] All Scripture is breathed out by God and profitable for teaching, for reproof, for correction, and for training in righteousness, that the man of God may be complete, equipped for every good work. (2 Timothy 3:16,17)

[13] As of the writing of this book, the most reliable study Bible available is *The Lutheran Study Bible* (St. Louis: Concordia Publishing House, 2009).

[14] Blessed is the man who walks not in the counsel of the wicked, nor stands in the way of sinners, nor sits in the seat of scoffers; but his delight is in the law of the LORD, and on his law he meditates day and night. (Psalm 1:1,2)

from the national church body to guide simple daily devotions.[15] Schedules are available to help people who want to read through the Bible in one year or three years. Topical books can be obtained from national Lutheran publishers such as Northwestern Publishing House. It is always advisable for members to consult their pastors, however, before obtaining books from sources such as general religious bookstores, because they sell a wide variety of books of varying theological soundness. Regardless of the format of the daily devotions, it is important for all of us to have them to grow in faith (Isaiah 55:11).[16] Daily devotions are more important than our favorite television programs, browsing the internet, or athletic events. If there are multiple members in a household, having devotions together is good for strengthening the bond of faith among the members of our households (Colossians 3:16).[17]

A major purpose of studying the Bible is so each of us can teach others. The "others" might be our children (Proverbs 22:6),[18] grandchildren, other relatives, or friends. We might even teach Sunday school or a Bible class in our congregations. Teaching is what the Great Commission is all about, and it is a commission for every member of the Christian church.

## Evangelism

The Great Commission, in fact, drives the Christian church. The goal is to reach everyone in the world with the message that although all have sinned, all can also be saved (Luke 24:46,47).[19] It is not the complexity of the message that is the problem, but rather that Satan and his demons want to prevent people from hearing and believing the message (Matthew 13:19).[20] It is therefore necessary for the church not only to be persistent in its efforts at spreading the message, but it also needs to use methods that will allow

[15]Northwestern Publishing House publishes a daily devotion series called *Meditations Daily Devotional*.

[16][The LORD said,] "So shall my word be that goes out from my mouth; it shall not return to me empty, but it shall accomplish that which I purpose, and shall succeed in the thing for which I sent it." (Isaiah 55:11)

[17]Let the word of Christ dwell in you richly, teaching and admonishing one another in all wisdom, singing psalms and hymns and spiritual songs, with thankfulness in your hearts to God. (Colossians 3:16)

[18]Train up a child in the way he should go; even when he is old he will not depart from it. (Proverbs 22:6)

[19][Jesus said,] "Thus it is written, that the Christ should suffer and on the third day rise from the dead, and that repentance and forgiveness of sins should be proclaimed in his name to all nations, beginning from Jerusalem." (Luke 24:46,47)

[20][Jesus said,] "When anyone hears the word of the kingdom and does not understand it, the evil one comes and snatches away what has been sown in his heart." (Matthew 13:19)

the message to get past the cultural and personal filters people employ that prevent it from being understood (1 Corinthians 9:20-22).[21]

Everyone has a mind-set that is formed by culture and experience. Each culture has developed its own approaches to dealing with the world by creating either physical or virtual idols, that is, phony gods (Joshua 24:15).[22] When the Lord is mentioned and when Christians try to teach others about sin and grace, those hearing the message use their mental image of what a god should be like to try to grasp the nature of the Lord. When he does not fit with that image, they are likely either to only accept those things about him that fit their preconceived notions or to reject him outright as unworthy of being a deity (1 Corinthians 2:14).[23] Either approach prevents a correct faith in the Lord from being formed; therefore, the people are not saved. An evangelist needs to get around such cultural blocks by using elements within a culture to gain a hearing and give the Holy Spirit an opportunity to change hearts and minds. Paul faced the same problems, going all the way from people thinking that he himself was a god in Lystra (Acts 14:8-18) to having to preach about "an unknown god" in Athens (Acts 17:22-34). The struggle can be difficult and sometimes bears little visible fruit.

Effective evangelists always stick to the message. People must be led to realize how serious their sins are through the preaching of the law, because their sins are numerous and are committed against the almighty God. The gospel must be preached even if it is ridiculed, rejected, or ignored (2 Timothy 4:3,4).[24] When people are brought into the church through other means, the nature of the church itself changes. If the church's focus is merely on making this world a better place to live, for example, it becomes viewed in those terms. There is a wide variety of ways to get people through the front door of the church, and even to keep them in the church, that have nothing to do with their repenting of their sins and believing in Christ as their Savior

---

[21] To the Jews I became as a Jew, in order to win Jews. To those under the law I became as one under the law (though not being myself under the law) that I might win those under the law. To those outside the law I became as one outside the law (not being outside the law of God but under the law of Christ) that I might win those outside the law. To the weak I became weak, that I might win the weak. I have become all things to all people, that by all means I might save some. (1 Corinthians 9:20-22)

[22] [Joshua said,] "If it is evil in your eyes to serve the LORD, choose this day whom you will serve, whether the gods your fathers served in the region beyond the River, or the gods of the Amorites in whose land you dwell. But as for me and my house, we will serve the LORD." (Joshua 24:15)

[23] The natural person does not accept the things of the Spirit of God, for they are folly to him, and he is not able to understand them because they are spiritually discerned. (1 Corinthians 2:14)

[24] The time is coming when people will not endure sound teaching, but having itching ears they will accumulate for themselves teachers to suit their own passions, and will turn away from listening to the truth and wander off into myths. (2 Timothy 4:3,4)

from sin. A church can even become the "right place to be" in a community without the biblical purpose of the church being mentioned in anything but vague terms (2 Corinthians 11:13).[25] Real evangelism isn't interested in merely collecting people; it is interested in changing hearts, and only the Holy Spirit can do this through the preaching of the gospel after the people's hearts have been prepared by the law (2 Timothy 4:2).[26]

Once people have become interested in the message they have heard, they must be trained in that message and retained in the church family. Pastors, and sometimes trained laypeople, teach classes for new members to familiarize them with the doctrines of the Scriptures. This needs to be done in enough detail so that people will understand these teachings before they join the congregation. Although people must keep learning throughout their whole lives so their faith does not wither and die, there is a certain level of understanding that is needed so that people are not joining the church under false assumptions. New members often require extra assistance to become faithful attendees who continue to hear the Word of the Lord and to grow, and such help can be provided through an assimilation program. Through it, new members are taught about the various organizations and programs of the congregation and how they serve its overall mission. They are urged to become part of organized Bible studies, are taught how to establish a routine of daily personal and family devotions, and are shown how they can serve in the congregation's program. If there is no assimilation process, the evangelism effort will not be very effective.

## Worship services

The preaching of a biblical message on Sunday mornings or other times is included in what is called a worship service. Lutheran worship centers on the Lord's service to us rather than our service to him. Lutherans typically view a worship service as having two principal components: what we offer to God and what he gives to us. We offer to God our prayers, our offerings, our hymns, and the confession of our faith and our sins. God gives to us his Word, his sacraments, his absolution, and a sermon by his minister. Good worship services balance these things but always gives God's serving us predominance. To ensure such a balance, Lutheran worship uses liturgies, and therefore Lutheran worship is called "liturgical." Liturgies came into use

---

[25] Such men are false apostles, deceitful workmen, disguising themselves as apostles of Christ. (2 Corinthians 11:13)

[26] Preach the word; be ready in season and out of season; reprove, rebuke, and exhort, with complete patience and teaching. (2 Timothy 4:2)

already in the second century A.D., and they are intended to be the setting holding the gem that is the Word of the Lord. The Bible does not require Christians to use a liturgy for worship, and it has not prescribed a liturgy as it did for the Old Testament covenant people of Israel (see Leviticus). Rather, it states only that all things should be done in good order so that people understand the message of the Scriptures (1 Corinthians 14:40).[27]

The original Lutheran liturgy was adapted from the liturgy being used in the Roman Catholic Church at the time of the Reformation. Martin Luther wanted to cause as little disruption as possible in the conducting of the worship service so that the common people would not become disturbed by the changes. Those things that were not biblically sound were removed, but changes were not made for the sake of change. The most obvious change was that the liturgy was translated from Latin into the language of the people (German) so that they could understand it. The major addition to the liturgy was the singing of hymns by the congregation (1 Chronicles 16:23).[28]

Lutheran liturgies commonly start with a hymn sung by the congregation and include two or more additional congregational hymns during the service. These hymns may be hymns of general praise, or they may be related to the sermon, the season of the church year, or some other special event (e.g., the beginning or the end of the service, Holy Baptism, or Holy Communion). The most important thing about the hymns chosen is that they are doctrinally sound and clear, as members are effectively confessing their faith when they sing the hymns. Hymns should be singable by ordinary congregational members. Ideally, hymns should be easy for the people to remember and have melodies that stick in people's minds. Luther wanted the doctrines of the church in the hymns so that people would be reminded of them whenever the melodies came into their minds. What people sing and pray—that is what they believe.

After the initial hymn, worship services generally include the following: statements by the pastor and responses by the congregation, prayers, a general confession of sins by the congregation followed by an absolution by the pastor, a confession of faith using one of the three creeds of the Christian church, psalms, readings from the Bible, a sermon, and a final blessing by the pastor. In addition, Holy Communion, discussed below, may also be celebrated as part of the worship service. Except for the readings[29] and the ser-

---

[27] All things should be done decently and in order. (1 Corinthians 14:40)

[28] Sing to the LORD, all the earth! Tell of his salvation from day to day. (1 Chronicles 16:23)

[29] In a few congregations, some of the scriptural readings are sung.

mon, all parts of the service may be sung instead of being spoken, depending on the liturgy and the singing skills of the pastor. Sometimes a cantor or liturgist leads the congregation in parts of the liturgy. Services often have additional music provided by instrumentalists and/or vocal choirs. This additional music is meant to help carry the theme of the service and establish the mood of worship.

The center of all Lutheran services is the reading and preaching of the Word of the Lord. The Word is generally first presented in a series of readings—an Old Testament lesson, a selection from a New Testament epistle, and a section from one of the four gospels. These readings are commonly taken from an established series of readings called a pericope (pronounced pe-ric-oh-pee), or lectionary. The purpose of the pericope is to cover all areas of biblical teaching during the church year,[30] referred to as "the whole counsel of God." Pericope is also related to the events of the church year. There are a number of lectionaries available, and pastors often use different ones in different years to increase the amount of the Bible to which the congregation is exposed over a period of time. Sometimes a pastor will choose other readings, such as for special events like a church anniversary or if he wants to do a sermon series[31] that he feels would benefit the congregation. The readings are usually followed some time later in the service by the sermon, as was discussed above.

Worship services may be simple or complex, but it is important for people to realize that worship is a human activity. While it should not be done in a slipshod manner, as if it doesn't matter to the Lord whether we care what we are doing or not, we gain no merit from how well we perform it. The critical part of the service is what the Lord does for us. He gives us his Word for our spiritual growth, his forgiveness for our sins, his ear for our prayers, and his blessing for our lives. When these are present, all worship is truly divine worship.

## Holy Baptism

To become a member of the holy Christian church, a person must be brought to faith by the Holy Spirit (John 3:3).[32] Because all people are sin-

---

[30]The church year begins with the Advent season, which starts four Sundays before Christmas, and continues through the season of the end times, which is completed about the end of November.

[31]A sermon series is a group of sermons preached on consecutive Sundays over a broader topic, such as the Ten Commandments.

[32]Jesus answered him, "Truly, truly, I say to you, unless one is born again he cannot see the kingdom of God." (John 3:3)

ners from the time they are in the womb (Psalm 51:5),[33] it is imperative that all people go through such a conversion by the Holy Spirit. In a general sense, we know how the Holy Spirit converts adults through their hearing of the law and the gospel (Romans 10:17).[34] He changes their hearts through this message. While we cannot look into people's hearts to see if they really believe the message of the Scriptures, we can at least hear their lips confess that they hold such a belief (Romans 10:9),[35] and they are admitted into membership in a local congregation based on that confession. But how does the Holy Spirit convert children? It would seem that we cannot be sure of what a child believes or whether a child can believe. How can we know whether they believe the saving message and should therefore be considered part of the local congregation or they do not believe and therefore should be excluded from the congregation?

The Scripture answers this question for us. Jesus commanded his followers to teach and baptize "all nations" (Matthew 28:19). If an adult claims to believe the message of salvation by God's grace through faith, then the Lutheran church baptizes that person as commanded by Jesus. The Bible also promises that Holy Baptism saves through the washing away of sin and the creation of a new person in the heart of the person baptized (Titus 3:5;[36] 1 Peter 3:21[37]). If Holy Baptism has this power in an adult, it certainly has the same power in children, regardless of age. Baptizing a child therefore creates the faith that is necessary to become a member of the holy Christian church, even if the child is not able to confess that faith in a manner adults can understand. Therefore, baptized children can be members of a local congregation.

If this seems like we are making a large jump to a conclusion, it is only because we overvalue reason in the conversion of adults. In reality, we do not know how an adult can be converted and believe, because adults are no different than infants by nature. Both are totally self-centered and are enemies of the Lord. Neither has any interest in repudiating their selfishness (Genesis 8:21).[38]

---

[33][David said,] "Behold, I was brought forth in iniquity, and in sin did my mother conceive me." (Psalm 51:5)

[34]Faith comes from hearing, and hearing through the word of Christ. (Romans 10:17)

[35]If you confess with your mouth that Jesus is Lord and believe in your heart that God raised him from the dead, you will be saved. (Romans 10:9)

[36]He saved us, not because of works done by us in righteousness, but according to his own mercy, by the washing of regeneration and renewal of the Holy Spirit. (Titus 3:5)

[37]Baptism, which corresponds to this [Noah being saved through the water of the flood], now saves you, not as a removal of dirt from the body but as an appeal to God for a good conscience, through the resurrection of Jesus Christ. (1 Peter 3:21)

[38][The Lord said,] "The intention of man's heart is evil from his youth." (Genesis 8:21)

Neither can comprehend accepting the forgiveness of sins nor contribute to the formation of a new person within their hearts (Romans 8:5).[39] While an adult can grasp the message of the Bible by reason, he or she will always reject it using that same reason (1 Corinthians 2:14).[40] The message of the Bible is not reasonable, so it is not with the intellect that an adult grasps the message but with the heart (Romans 10:10),[41] which can only be changed by the Holy Spirit (1 Corinthians 12:3).[42] While adults may be able to articulate their faith once it is formed, they still do not understand it (2 Corinthians 9:15).[43] In this way, an adult is no different from a child. In the same way that a person does not have to be able to explain the way the human body works to be physically alive, so a person does not have to be able to explain how faith is formed and exists in the heart to be spiritually alive. Jesus, in fact, demands that everyone have the faith of a little child, because a little child is willing to accept what he or she cannot understand (Matthew 18:3).[44] To refuse to baptize infants and young children when the Bible says that Holy Baptism works faith is to expose them to the risk of death as unbelievers before they can grasp enough to verbally assent to the saving message of the Scriptures (1 Peter 3:21).

The Lutheran church has historically called Holy Baptism a sacrament. Like the other Christian sacrament, the Lord's Supper, Baptism (1) was instituted by Christ himself, (2) includes the use of an earthly element (water) connected with God's Word, and (3) offers and gives the forgiveness of sins. Because Holy Baptism works the forgiveness of sins—a necessary step in conversion as well as a general blessing—it is also referred to as a *means of grace*.[45]

Any Christian can baptize another person, although pastors usually do the baptizing as representatives of the whole Christian church. In reality, it is the Holy Spirit that performs the Holy Baptism, and the person applying

---

[39]Those who live according to the flesh set their minds on the things of the flesh. (Romans 8:5)

[40]The natural person does not accept the things of the Spirit of God, for they are folly to him, and he is not able to understand them because they are spiritually discerned. (1 Corinthians 2:14)

[41]With the heart one believes and is justified, and with the mouth one confesses and is saved. (Romans 10:10)

[42]No one can say "Jesus is Lord" except in the Holy Spirit. (2 Corinthians 12:3)

[43]Thanks be to God for his inexpressible gift! (1 Corinthians 9:15)

[44][Jesus said,] "Truly, I say to you, unless you turn and become like children, you will never enter the kingdom of heaven." (Matthew 18:3)

[45]*Means of grace* is a term developed by the church for any method by which the Lord shows his grace to us. Through these means he gives us the forgiveness of sins and strengthens our faith. The means of grace are Baptism, Holy Communion, and his Word, particularly the gospel in the form of the absolution of our sins.

the water and speaking the words is only a human agent. Therefore, the genuineness of the faith of the pastor or of another person doing the baptizing has no effect on the validity of the Holy Baptism. The human agent merely applies water in some manner to the person being baptized and says, "I baptize you in the name of the Father, and of the Son, and of the Holy Spirit." With these words and this action, the Holy Spirit creates or strengthens faith in the person's heart. Without the Word of God, the application of water is a meaningless washing, but with the Word of God, it is the power of the Lord himself accomplishing what he has promised.

Lutheran congregations accept as valid the baptisms performed by the members of any church body that confesses the Trinity. The Greek word used in the New Testament for baptizing means "to wash with water." The word does not require immersion of the object being washed (Mark 7:4)[46] but does permit it. Holy Baptism may therefore be carried out by the application of water in any manner.

### Holy Communion

The other sacrament in the Lutheran church is Holy Communion, also commonly called the Lord's Supper, the Sacrament of the Altar, or the Eucharist. On the evening on which Jesus was subsequently betrayed and taken away to be crucified, he used the celebration of the Jewish Passover to institute a new "means of grace," that is, Holy Communion (Mark 14:22-25). In the Lutheran church, Holy Communion is called a sacrament because, like Baptism, it was instituted by Christ, it includes the use of earthly elements (bread and wine) that are connected with Christ's words, and it offers and gives the forgiveness of sins. Like Holy Baptism, Holy Communion strengthens faith as well as forgives sins.

To establish the sacrament, Jesus took some of the foods used in the Passover and blessed them with specific words. Taking and blessing the bread, he said, "Take, eat; this is my body" (Matthew 26:26). Taking and blessing the cup, he said, "Drink of it, all of you, for this is my blood of the covenant, which is poured out for many for the forgiveness of sins" (Matthew 26:27,28). It is these original words of Jesus that consecrate the bread and the wine used in the sacrament for all times. When the presiding minister says these words in a service where Holy Communion is being celebrated, he is not performing some kind of magic act where through his own powers he causes the bread

---

[46]When they [Pharisees] come from the marketplace, they do not eat unless they wash. And there are many other traditions that they observe, such as the washing of cups and pots and copper vessels and dining couches. (Mark 7:4)

and the wine to also become Jesus' body and blood. Instead, the minister is merely acting as the visible agent for what Jesus is doing, namely, combining his body and blood with the bread and wine.

Those receiving the sacrament are, therefore, meeting Jesus personally by eating his body and drinking his blood, which are present in, with, and under the bread and wine of the sacrament (1 Corinthians 10:16).[47] Jesus is no longer a foreigner, a God that is far away, but he comes to his children to be an integral part of them (1 Corinthians 10:17).[48] It is an encounter like none other we will experience. It is his personal assurance that we are forgiven no matter how bad our sins are and that the believing communicant is really God's dear child.

The Lutheran doctrinal position on Holy Communion is called the real presence because we believe that the Lord's body and blood are really present when we take the bread and wine. We believe this because Jesus said, "This is my body" (Luke 22:19). The word *is* is present in each of the four places where the words of institution are mentioned in the Greek New Testament. This is not a requirement in Greek, because *is* is often understood, but its presence here adds emphasis. On the other hand, the presence of bread and wine is also indicated by the Scriptures, for it includes them in the eating and drinking process (1 Corinthians 11:27).[49]

The Roman Catholic Church views Holy Communion as a sacrifice as well as a sacrament. It claims that the priest changes the bread and wine permanently into the body and blood of Christ (called transubstantiation) and then offers them to God the Father as a "bloodless" sacrifice for the sins of the living and the dead. Alas, no command to do this exists in the Bible. Instead, the New Testament writers point out that Christ's sacrifice for sin was sufficient and that no further sacrifice for sin is needed (Hebrews 7:27).[50] His body and blood are present in the sacrament only for the purpose of being received by the communicant because that is the purpose he assigned to these elements. We dare go no further than Christ went since we have no word of God to do so.

---

[47]The cup of blessing that we bless, is it not a participation in the blood of Christ? The bread that we break, is it not a participation in the body of Christ? (1 Corinthians 10:16)

[48]Because there is one bread, we who are many are one body, for we all partake of the one bread. (1 Corinthians 10:17)

[49]Whoever, therefore, eats the bread or drinks the cup of the Lord in an unworthy manner will be guilty concerning the body and blood of the Lord. (1 Corinthians 11:27)

[50]He [Jesus] has no need, like those high priests, to offer sacrifices daily, first for his own sins and then for those of the people, since he did this once for all when he offered up himself. (Hebrews 7:27)

Some have argued that Jesus' body and blood cannot really be present because he is seated at the right hand of God the Father (Colossians 3:1),[51] and as a result, the bread and wine merely represent Christ's body and blood. They believe that his human nature is confined to that one location and cannot be all over the world to be present in Holy Communion. As discussed in chapter 15, however, where Christ's divine nature is, his human nature must also be or he would not be one person. The nonbiblical Calvinistic argument that "the finite cannot contain the infinite" not only distorts the person of Christ but also robs the Christian of the assurance that Jesus personally gives to him or to her the forgiveness of sins in the sacrament. If Jesus wanted us to believe that the bread and wine merely represented his body and blood, he would have indicated that he was using figurative language, as he did in some of his other teachings (John 2:18-22). We must never pare back the Scriptures to say only what we regard as reasonable.

## The call and the ministry

The work of the church is the responsibility of everyone in the church, because all members are called on to use their talents for the Lord (Romans 12:6-8).[52] Much of the work in the church is the type of work that is necessary in any organization for good order and to make it function effectively. Volunteers and paid staff function as secretaries and janitors; they serve lunches and help the infirm. Some of the work of the church, however, directly involves the teaching and preaching of the Word of God, conducting worship services, administering the sacraments, and giving spiritual counsel. These tasks collectively are called the "ministry of the word" (Acts 6:4).[53] While each Christian has a responsibility to do these things on a personal level (Acts 11:20),[54] when they are done in the name of the church, they are done by men and women who are "called" (Romans 1:1)[55] for that purpose by the local congregation or other body with the responsibility for church activities of a particular type. (Note: A "call" differs from

---

[51] If then you have been raised with Christ, seek the things that are above, where Christ is, seated at the right hand of God. (Colossians 3:1)

[52] Having gifts that differ according to the grace given to us, let us use them: if prophecy, in proportion to our faith; if service, in our serving; the one who teaches, in his teaching; the one who exhorts, in his exhortation; the one who contributes, in generosity; the one who leads, with zeal; the one who does acts of mercy, with cheerfulness. (Romans 12:6-8)

[53] [The apostles said,] "We will devote ourselves to prayer and to the ministry of the word." (Acts 6:4)

[54] There were some of them, men of Cyprus and Cyrene, who on coming to Antioch spoke to the Hellenists [Greek-speaking Gentiles] also, preaching the Lord Jesus. (Acts 11:20)

[55] Paul, a servant of Christ Jesus, called to be an apostle, set apart for the gospel of God. (Romans 1:1)

"ordination" in the Lutheran church. Men who are ordained are those who have been trained and have dedicated themselves to the preaching ministry. A call is a particular set of ministerial or teaching tasks for which the person holding the call is responsible.)

A particular call to the ministry gives specific responsibilities to the person called (Romans 11:13)[56] and may be for a limited period of time (e.g., district president, vicar) or an indefinite period of time (e.g., pastor of a congregation). When the call is issued by a congregation, a synod, or a governing board, it is a call from the Lord to serve in the duties that are part of the call (Ephesians 4:4-6).[57] In effect, while the person may receive a salary from a congregation or a subgroup in a church body, the real overseer of the person is the Lord himself. The person's obligation is to meet the conditions of the call in accordance with his or her abilities and with faithfulness to the Scriptures. It is the call that gives someone the authority to act, not anything inherent in the person or in an earned degree or in a certification given by a church body or by a secular authority (1 Corinthians 4:3,4).[58] Therefore, before a person is called, it is necessary that the organization (e.g., congregation, institution, mission board) issuing the call determine that the person has the necessary training and skills to carry out the call and that the person's lifestyle is consistent with being a representative of the Lord's church (1 Timothy 3:1-13). People who have such calls are said to be in the "public ministry."

People in the public ministry act on behalf of the organization that has called them. A pastor preaches the Word of God, administers the sacraments, teaches confirmands,[59] and reaches out to the lost. These things are part of his call. A teacher teaches a class in the congregation's parochial school. A pastor or an elder ministers to someone who is sick in a hospital on behalf of the congregation. These are examples of the public ministry in action. Actions in the public ministry always come as a result of a call, whether a physical document describing the duties or a verbal request from

---

[56]Now I am speaking to you Gentiles. Inasmuch then as I am an apostle to the Gentiles. (Romans 11:13)

[57]There is one body and one Spirit—just as you were called to the one hope that belongs to your call—one Lord, one faith, one baptism, one God and Father of all, who is over all and through all and in all. (Ephesians 4:4-6)

[58]With me it is a very small thing that I should be judged by you or by any human court. In fact, I do not even judge myself. For I am not aware of anything against myself, but I am not thereby acquitted. It is the Lord who judges me. (1 Corinthians 4:3,4)

[59]A confirmand is someone receiving instruction in the doctrines of the Bible before he or she is confirmed.

someone who has the authority to issue such a request. Those who have not been called must not take it upon themselves to act for a congregation (Ezekiel 13:6).[60] As individual Christians, however, because of the Great Commission, they can teach the doctrines of the Bible to fellow members and to unbelievers, visit the sick, or conduct devotions within their own homes.

Because the call makes the person holding the call an agent of the Lord, it is essential that everyone in the congregation supports the person in carrying out his or her call (Hebrews 13:17).[61] Pastors and teachers are not political leaders who can be criticized publicly at will (1 Timothy 5:19).[62] If there is a concern about someone's work quality or work ethic, that concern is a matter that must be handled through private discussions and helpful suggestions. If the person is having trouble meeting the demands of the call, then efforts need to be made to help the person or to call the person to a different position. If the workload specified in a call decreases or financial support disappears, calls may be terminated because the conditions that prompted the call have changed, but this is infrequent. As servants of the Lord, called workers are not to be hired and fired as if they were employees of a secular organization.

### Church discipline

It is wonderful for us to worship with those with whom we share the same beliefs about the Lord. The demons are not pleased when this happens, and they strive to create conflict in the church by introducing false doctrines and leading people into sinful lives. They know that once planted, false doctrines and open sinfulness will spread and corrupt the faith of the members (1 Corinthians 5:6).[63] To address this problem, Christ has given to his church a power called the office of the keys.[64] It is through this "office" that the church forgives (the "loosing key") and and refuses to forgive sins (the "binding key") (John 20:23),[65] but it is not an arbitrary power. When some-

---

[60][The LORD said,] "They have seen false visions and lying divinations. They say, 'Declares the LORD,' when the LORD has not sent them, and yet they expect him to fulfill their word." (Ezekiel 13:6)

[61]Obey your leaders and submit to them, for they are keeping watch over your souls, as those who will have to give an account. Let them do this with joy and not with groaning, for that would be of no advantage to you. (Hebrews 13:17)

[62]Do not admit a charge against an elder except on the evidence of two or three witnesses. (1 Timothy 5:19)

[63]Your boasting is not good. Do you not know that a little leaven leavens the whole lump? (1 Corinthians 5:6)

[64]David P. Kuske, Luther's Catechism, 3rd ed. (Milwaukee: Northwestern Publishing House, 1998), pp. 262-271.

[65][Jesus said,] "If you [his disciples] forgive the sins of any, they are forgiven them; if you withhold forgiveness from any, it is withheld." (John 20:23)

one confesses his or her sins to a pastor or some other member of a congregation, it is the responsibility of the person hearing this private confession to announce the Lord's absolution of the person from the guilt for his or her sins (2 Samuel 12:13).[66] Unless the confession is clearly phony, it must be taken as sincere, and absolution must be announced because the Lord has already forgiven all sins (1 John 1:9).[67] If a person refuses to recognize and confess one or more sins that he or she has committed, then the one dealing with the person must tell him or her that the sin or sins are not forgiven because of the impenitence (1 John 1:10).[68] In performing these actions, the church is the messenger, not the master.

In dealing with the sins of members within a congregation, the horribleness of the sins is irrelevant. Jesus has atoned for the guilt of all sins, both big and small (1 John 1:7).[69] To the Lord there is no difference between the serial killer and the gossiper; there is no hierarchy of sin. Sin is sin, and every sinner deserves to be sent to hell for his or her sins (James 2:10).[70] The issue in church discipline is always the willingness of a person to acknowledge the sin he or she has committed and to repent of it. Repentance means having a genuine sorrow for offending the Lord by disobeying him and having a resolve not to repeat the sin (John 5:14).[71] It involves throwing oneself completely on the Lord's mercy and not offering either excuses or bribery to escape the consequences of the sin (Matthew 16:26).[72]

In accordance with the Lord's call to repentance (Matthew 4:17),[73] the church has established a procedure for dealing with most sins committed by church members. This procedure is through the general confession of sins in the worship service. Here people acknowledge that they have been sinners from their mother's womb (Psalm 51:5)[74] and that they regularly sin

---

[66]David said to Nathan, "I have sinned against the LORD." And Nathan said to David, "The LORD also has put away your sin; you shall not die." (2 Samuel 12:13)

[67]If we confess our sins, he is faithful and just to forgive us our sins and to cleanse us from all unrighteousness. (1 John 1:9)

[68]If we say we have not sinned, we make him [the Lord] a liar, and his word is not in us. (1 John 1:10)

[69]The blood of Jesus his Son cleanses us from all sin. (1 John 1:7)

[70]Whoever keeps the whole law but fails in one point has become accountable for all of it. (James 2:10)

[71]Afterward Jesus found him in the temple and said to him, "See, you are well! Sin no more, that nothing worse may happen to you." (John 5:14)

[72][Jesus said,] "What will it profit a man if he gains the whole world and forfeits his soul? Or what shall a man give in return for his soul?" (Matthew 16:26)

[73]From that time Jesus began to preach, saying, "Repent, for the kingdom of heaven is at hand." (Matthew 4:17)

[74][David said,] "Behold, I was brought forth in iniquity, and in sin did my mother conceive me." (Psalm 51:5)

against the Lord in thought, word, and deed—both through sinful actions committed and through loving actions omitted with malice. "From king to peasant," all stand next to one another in the same condition before the Lord and confess their unworthiness. It is impossible for anyone to be aware of all their faults (Psalm 19:12),[75] so this general confession covers all the sins that people have committed, and the pastor announces the Lord's absolution to them. This absolution, because it is God's Word, is also a means of grace because it forgives sins.

There is, of course, the expectation that in saying the general confession, each person is sincerely repentant of his or her sins. If some people are not sincere because there are certain sins of which they refuse to repent, then the absolution does not apply to them because their confession is hypocritical (Acts 5:1-11). If these sins to which they cling become publically known, then intervention by the members of the congregation needs to occur. There are three types of sins that commonly require an intervention by the pastor, by the elders, and/or by fellow congregation members. These are the profession of false doctrine (e.g., claiming Jesus did not become God until his baptism), gross public sin (e.g., drunkenness or adultery), and sins that show a careless attitude toward the moral law (e.g., habitually stealing supplies from work).

Because all sins are faith-destroying, the Bible says that action must be taken as soon as it is realized that a church member is guilty of continuing in a sin of one of these types (Matthew 18:15-18). Whoever discovers the sin of a brother or sister in Christ must talk with the person and point out the sin to him or her. If the person repents, he or she is given unconditional forgiveness, and the matter is dropped. If the first person can make no progress with the sinner, then one or two additional people must be asked to join the discussion to show the urgency of repenting of the sin. If that fails, then the matter is brought to the spiritual leaders of the congregation and finally to the whole congregation. The Lord offers forgiveness for all sins, but the impenitent person has turned his back on God's forgiveness and therefore does not receive it. If there is no repentance, then the person must be excommunicated[76] from the church to show the person how grievous his or her sin really is. This is the last act of love the church can formally perform, although any Christian can still try to witness to the person. In summary, it is impenitence that leads to excommunication, not the nature of the sin itself.

---

[75] [David said,] "Who can discern his errors? Declare me innocent from hidden faults." (Psalm 19:12)

[76] Excommunication removes a person from a local congregation and its church body. The person is treated as an unbeliever because the person has refused to repent or be instructed from the Scriptures.

While church discipline is primarily directed toward the unrepentant sinner, it is also essential for the teaching of the rest of the congregation. If unrepentant sinners are allowed to remain in the church, then their sins will soon be imitated by others. False doctrine held by one will soon become false doctrine held by many. Gross sins by one will influence others to do the same. When people develop a careless attitude toward sin, soon more and more sins become part of their lives. The yeast of unrepented sin soon works its way through a congregation, causing others to sin and divisions to occur among the members. Actively practicing church discipline is therefore essential to the health of a congregation.

## Church fellowship

Even if the spiritual leaders are faithful in maintaining sound doctrine and practice within a congregation, they still have to deal with people who are not members of their congregation but who want to worship at it, join it, or work with it. How can the leaders be sure that these people will not undermine their efforts to maintain a healthy spiritual environment for the current members? This topic is called church fellowship.

The Lutheran church, in the tradition of Christ and his apostles, proclaims the Word of the Lord to everyone. All are invited and welcomed in a Lutheran congregation and can worship there, as long as they do not disturb the worship of others. Nonmembers who attend remain merely guest worshipers, however, and are excluded from other religious activities, such as attending Communion, leading worship, or singing in the choir, unless they request to join the congregation.[77] At that point the pastor and/or the elders evaluate their religious beliefs to see that they are the same as those of the congregation. If the people are weak on biblical or doctrinal knowledge, they will be asked to take a new-member information class before they are allowed to join. This allows the pastor to evaluate their understanding of the basic doctrines and their dedication to them.

To prevent everyone who applies for membership in a congregation from having to go through such a procedure, congregations band together to form church bodies and synods. In such church bodies, a standard of doctrine is set with the agreement of all the congregations that are part of the church body. Because of this, if someone is a member of one of the congregations

---

[77]Members of other Lutheran congregations that are "in fellowship" with one another (that is, they believe and confess the same teachings) are invited to receive Communion as guest worshipers. Those guests will want to introduce themselves in person to the pastor before the service begins and speak to him about receiving Holy Communion.

in a church body, they can move their membership to another congregation within that church body without having to go through the new-member procedure. The congregations in a church body are said to be "in fellowship" with one another. Pastors, teachers, and members can flow among the member congregations without having to go through "colloquy," which is the formal name for the process of examining people's beliefs.

Sometimes several church bodies desire to work together. Under what conditions can this happen? Between any two church bodies, there are three situations that can exist. First, they might completely agree in doctrine and practice even though they are not one organization.[78] They might remain separate, for example, because their members speak, or once spoke, different languages. If there is a recognized agreement on doctrine and practice, then the church bodies can work together and members can flow between the congregations of the church bodies with minimal difficulty. Pastors from one of the two bodies can preach in the congregations of the other body. This is called altar-and-pulpit fellowship. A different situation exists when two church bodies have similar goals but do not have complete doctrinal agreement. In this case, members wishing to transfer between the church bodies might still have to undergo colloquy and receive some training if there is a lack of understanding of the doctrinal position of their new church home. There cannot be joint worship services, joint devotions, sharing of Holy Communion, or joint mission work between members of such church bodies, although some sharing of expertise between members might occur (e.g., consultation on Bible translations, music workshops, etc.). Finally, sometimes church bodies differ enough in their doctrine and practice that they cannot work together on any religious activities.

When church bodies are not in altar-and-pulpit fellowship, it does not mean that one church body is judging the faith of the individual members of the other church body. It means that one church body cannot be sure of what the nature of the faith of the members of the other church body is because they do not hold a common standard of belief. To practice fellowship under such circumstances would undermine the ability of the congregations in both church bodies to maintain church discipline. While this may sometimes be inconvenient when friends or family cannot commune together, the Bible warns against working and worshiping with those who teach false doctrine (Romans 16:17).[79]

---

[78] To "agree in practice" means to accept one another's practices as scriptural even if they are not identical.

[79] I appeal to you, brothers, to watch out for those who cause divisions and create obstacles contrary to the doctrine that you have been taught; avoid them. (Romans 16:17)

## Prayer

The Bible claims that all members of the church are "priests," that is, there is a priesthood of all believers (1 Peter 2:9).[80] This means that each member of the invisible church can directly approach the throne of God because his or her sins have been forgiven and because he or she has received the righteousness of Christ. It is no longer necessary to have an earthly intermediary (see chapter 8) because Jesus Christ, the heavenly intermediary, will act as everyone's intercessor (1 Timothy 2:5,6).[81] His sacrifice covers all sins so that the believer is free to make requests. Prayer to the Lord by believers is possible because of what Jesus has done.

Jesus commanded all of his followers to pray and has promised them that God the Father will hear and answer prayers addressed to him in faith (Matthew 6:6).[82] Both the command and the promise are important. The command reminds us that we are not self-sufficient (Psalm 145:15,16).[83] The Lord has done great things for his people, and he wants to hear from them (1 Thessalonians 5:16-18).[84] The command should also cause believers to assess their needs, both spiritual and physical. In the process they will realize how much the Lord has given to them. Prayer helps to put perceived needs into the proper perspective. Paul said, "If we have food and clothing, with these we will be content" (1 Timothy 6:8). While we may want many things in addition, Jesus' promise assures us that when we come before our heavenly Father, he will give us what we really need (Matthew 6:31-33).[85] The Lord will not neglect those whom he has redeemed; in fact, he often gives us much more than we need just because he loves us. He would bless us even more, except that we often do not ask or we have asked for sinful reasons (James 4:2,3).[86]

---

[80]You are a chosen race, a royal priesthood, a holy nation, a people for his own possession, that you may proclaim the excellencies of him who called you out of darkness into his marvelous light. (1 Peter 2:9)

[81]There is one God, and there is one Mediator between God and men, the man Christ Jesus, who gave himself as a ransom for all, which is the testimony given at the proper time. (1 Timothy 2:5,6)

[82][Jesus said,] "When you pray, go into your room and shut the door and pray to your Father who is in secret. And your Father who sees in secret will reward you." (Matthew 6:6)

[83][David said,] "The eyes of all look to you, and you give them their food in due season. You open your hand; you satisfy the desire of every living thing." (Psalm 145:15,16)

[84]Rejoice always, pray without ceasing, give thanks in all circumstances; for this is the will of God in Christ Jesus for you. (1 Thessalonians 5:16-18)

[85][Jesus said,] "Therefore do not be anxious, saying, 'What shall we eat?' or 'What shall we drink?' or 'What shall we wear?' For the Gentiles seek after all these things, and your heavenly Father knows that you need them all. But seek first the kingdom of God and his righteousness, and all these things will be added to you." (Matthew 6:31-33)

[86]You do not have, because you do not ask. You ask and do not receive, because you ask wrongly, to spend it on your passions. (James 4:2,3)

Because it is only through the forgiveness of sins that Christ has won for us that we can approach the throne of the Father at all, we should always pray in Jesus' name (John 15:16),[87] even though we might not end every prayer with "in Jesus' name, Amen." No one else has the credentials with the Father to aid us in any way. Neither the dead nor the angels have been appointed as mediators between his people and the Lord. The Lord demands that prayer be addressed to him alone (Isaiah 8:19).[88] He is never too busy to hear the prayers of believers (Psalm 50:15)[89] but is functionally deaf to the prayers addressed to other beings or offered without faith (1 Samuel 28:6).[90]

In addition to asking for things, we should use prayer to review our own hearts and recognize our own spiritual inadequacies (Psalm 130:1-4).[91] The Lord is not interested in hearing from us how well we think we have kept his commandments or how well we have used the gifts he has given us (Luke 18:11,12).[92] He knows that we have not kept his commandments and that we have frequently misused the gifts he has given us. He also is not interested in bargaining with us for blessings in exchange for our service to him that is his due anyway (1 Timothy 6:7).[93] Where he has promised spiritual blessings, we can be bold in asking for the promised gifts, but when we seek physical blessings, he wants us to come as supplicants, relying on his grace to care for us (James 4:6,7).[94] Moreover, we should not concentrate our prayers on ourselves, but we should pray for those the Lord has given us as family, friends, coworkers, and fellow members of the church (Galatians 6:10).[95] We ought also to pray for those whom the

---

[87] [Jesus said,] "Whatever you ask the Father in my name, he [will] give it to you." (John 15:16)

[88] When they say to you, "Inquire of the mediums and the necromancers who chirp and mutter," should not a people inquire of their God? Should they inquire of the dead on behalf of the living? (Isaiah 8:19)

[89] [The Lord said,] "Call upon me in the day of trouble; I will deliver you, and you shall glorify me." (Psalm 50:15)

[90] When Saul inquired of the LORD, the LORD did not answer him, either by dreams, or by Urim, or by prophets. (1 Samuel 28:6)

[91] Out of the depths I cry to you, O LORD! O Lord, hear my voice! Let your ears be attentive to the voice of my pleas for mercy! If you, O LORD, should mark iniquities, O Lord, who could stand? But with you there is forgiveness, that you may be feared. (Psalm 130:1-4)

[92] [Jesus said,] "The Pharisee, standing by himself, prayed thus: 'God, I thank you that I am not like other men, extortioners, unjust, adulterers, or even like this tax collector. I fast twice a week; I give tithes of all that I get.'" (Luke 18:11,12)

[93] We brought nothing into the world, and we cannot take anything out of the world. (1 Timothy 6:7)

[94] Therefore it says, "God opposes the proud, but gives grace to the humble." Submit yourselves therefore to God. (James 4:6,7)

[95] So then, as we have opportunity, let us do good to everyone, and especially to those who are of the household of faith. (Galatians 6:10)

Lord has put into positions of authority and even to pray for our enemies (1 Timothy 2:1,2).[96]

While prayer is an important part of a believer's life, prayer is not a means of grace. The means of grace bring the Lord's favor to his people through the forgiveness of their sins and the strengthening of their faith. People should pray for these spiritual gifts, but they do not receive them through the act of praying. Prayer goes in the other direction. It puts people's needs before the Lord. In response to prayer, the Lord will give physical blessings, but he will also use the means of grace to aid the believer spiritually. Prayer strengthens faith only through bringing the Lord's promises into focus as we lay out the joys and sorrows of our lives before the only One who can give genuine help.

## Stewardship

After the Lord created Adam and Eve, he assigned them as caretakers of the Garden of Eden (Genesis 2:15).[97] A caretaker is a steward, that is, he takes care of property that belongs to another. He has duties for which he is accountable to the owner of the property. When Adam and Eve disobeyed the Lord and fell into sin, they lost their position and responsibilities within the Garden of Eden, and they then had to fend for themselves in a harsher environment (Genesis 3:17-24). Property does not belong to anyone permanently, as everyone must yield it at death, if not before; therefore, all people are only stewards of the gifts that the Lord gives to them while they are living. The Lord made this clear to the Israelites when he gave them the land of Canaan (Leviticus 25:23).[98] All of us will have to give an account on judgment day of how we used all the gifts and talents that the Lord gave to us (Luke 12:48).[99]

The resources that the Lord gives to us are frequently divided into three categories: time, talents (special abilities), and treasure (physical resources). We use all these resources to live in this world, and it is these resources that we also need to use to support the church so it can carry out its mission. As part of the Old Testament covenant, the Lord specified how much was to

---

[96]First of all, then, I urge that supplications, prayers, intercessions, and thanksgivings be made for all people, for kings and all who are in high positions, that we may lead a peaceful and quiet life, godly and dignified in every way. (1 Timothy 2:1,2)

[97]The LORD God took the man and put him in the Garden of Eden to work it and keep it. (Genesis 2:15)

[98][The LORD said,] "The land shall not be sold in perpetuity, for the land is mine. For you are strangers and sojourners with me." (Leviticus 25:23)

[99][Jesus said,] "Everyone to whom much was given, of him much will be required, and from him to whom they entrusted much, they will demand the more." (Luke 12:48)

be given for the temple and the various offerings and how frequently all the male Israelites had to appear to worship him (rules are scattered throughout Leviticus and Numbers). No such regulations are given to the New Testament church. Instead, each of us who believes in the gift of salvation through Jesus Christ is to devote his or her whole life to the Lord because he redeemed us from the bondage of sin (2 Corinthians 8:3-5).[100] How we balance our work for the kingdom of grace with our work in our various activities in the physical kingdom is something we need to decide after asking the Lord for guidance.

While money is needed to permit the church to function, the donations of time and talents are also critical. There never seems to be enough time for all the tasks that are demanding our attention. Yet someday those tasks involving worldly things will be meaningless, but the souls gained through the work we do for the kingdom of grace will have eternal meaning (Matthew 6:31-33). Those who have particular talents needed for the various church activities should consider who gave them these talents and not use them only for doing things that will soon be in the landfill (Romans 12:6-8).[101] Just as the human body cannot fully function if each of its parts does not contribute what it has the ability to do, so also the church cannot thrive without its members doing what they are gifted to do.

Failing to plan is planning to fail, both in the physical world and in the use of our talents in the church. All of us in a congregation need to assess and plan how we, both individually and collectively, can give of what the Lord has given us in terms of our time, talents, and treasures so that the Lord's work can be done (1 Corinthians 12:4-6).[102] That donation might be serving as a church officer, teaching Sunday school, singing in a choir, or being helpful hands in various projects. It might involve working extra hours to increase church contributions. It might involve assisting others so that they can become better stewards of their resources in the service of the Lord. In all the work of stewardship, we can only give what the Lord has first given

---

[100] Of their [the Macedonians] own accord, begging us earnestly for the favor of taking part in the relief of the saints—and this, not as we expected, but they gave themselves first to the Lord and then by the will of God to us. (2 Corinthians 8:3-5)

[101] Having gifts that differ according to the grace given to us, let us use them: if prophecy, in proportion to our faith; if service, in our serving; the one who teaches, in his teaching; the one who exhorts, in his exhortation; the one who contributes, in generosity; the one who leads, with zeal; the one who does acts of mercy, with cheerfulness. (Romans 12:6-8)

[102] There are varieties of gifts, but the same Spirit; and there are varieties of service, but the same Lord; and there are varieties of activities, but it is the same God who empowers them all in everyone. (1 Corinthians 12:4-6)

us. The Lord must be given the glory for whatever he gives his people the privilege of doing (1 Corinthians 10:31).[103]

## Adiaphora

There are many matters about which the Bible does not give us specific instructions. Such matters are called adiaphora (singular: adiaphoron). Where the Bible has not spoken, the church cannot establish doctrine, although it can establish temporary rules to maintain good order. For example, the church cannot declare specific days to be fast days or to be days of compulsory worship attendance because the Bible does not give any commands on these matters and forbids establishing any (Colossians 2:16).[104] Lutheran congregations have no dietary laws, restricting what members can eat or when they can eat it, for the same reason (Colossians 2:20-23). On such matters, we as members are free to serve the Lord as directed by our enlightened consciences; these are matters of "Christian freedom." Christian freedom should not be confused with the American ideas of personal freedom. We are always bound to serve the Lord in everything that we do and to be concerned with the welfare of our neighbors as well as our personal desires, as discussed in the next chapter. In addition, congregations can establish rules for their members to preserve good order in matters where numerous people are involved, such as using particular liturgies for worship on particular Sundays. Christian freedom is neither a license for chaos nor a permit to commit sinful acts.

Next, just because something is mentioned in the Bible does not mean it is required for all believers at all times. For example, the Mosaic Law required that all blasphemers be stoned (Leviticus 24:16).[105] The New Testament church does not have a command to do that. In another example, Gideon asked for two physical signs from the Lord that he would give him victory (Judges 6:36-40). This does not mean that we have the ability to ask for physical signs from the Lord whenever we need to make a decision. Some things recorded in the Bible are prescriptive; that is, the Lord commands or forbids that they be done. Other things are merely descriptive; that is, they happened the way the Bible described, but there is no command to do

---

[103]Whether you eat or drink, or whatever you do, do all to the glory of God. (1 Corinthians 10:31)

[104]Therefore let no one pass judgment on you in questions of food and drink, or with regard to a festival or a new moon or a Sabbath. (Colossians 2:16)

[105][The Lord said,] "Whoever blasphemes the name of the LORD shall surely be put to death. All the congregation shall stone him. The sojourner as well as the native, when he blasphemes the Name, shall be put to death." (Leviticus 24:16)

likewise and there may even be a prohibition against doing likewise. Judas committed suicide after betraying Jesus (Matthew 27:5). That is no reason for us to kill ourselves if we have committed horrible sins, however, because Jesus died to gain us forgiveness.

## Congregational organization

The Bible gives us some information about how several of the congregations in the early church carried out their work, but it gives us no specific directions about how congregations should be organized. Therefore, this is an adiaphoron. Lutheran congregations are legal corporations within the states in which they exist and have constitutions and bylaws. They typically hold meetings of the voters in the congregation several times each year to consider important matters and elect a church council to handle the rest of the business of the congregation. In addition, they often establish boards to handle specific tasks, such as elders' work, education, evangelism, stewardship, church maintenance, and long-term planning. Some of these groups may be specified in the congregation's constitution, while others are ad hoc. How members for these boards are chosen and whether the boards have overlapping membership with the church council vary from congregation to congregation.

Congregations usually also have special-purpose groups. Groups for women, men, young adults, teens, mission workers, and mothers with young children are common. Bowling and softball leagues exist in some congregations. All these kinds of groups are under the general supervision of the church council, a particular board, and/or the pastor. These groups are created and disbanded based on need and interest of the members.

CHAPTER 18

# Civil Estates

The Lord's kingdom of glory is an eternal kingdom. Those things related to that kingdom can never change, because they are part of the Lord's unchanging will (Hebrews 6:17).[1] The kingdom of power and the kingdom of grace are temporal kingdoms, that is, they exist only in this world. Unlike the Lord's eternal things, some things in these two kingdoms can change, depending on the physical and political circumstances (Hebrews 7:12).[2] Those things related to the kingdom of grace were discussed in the last chapter. In this chapter we will look at how we, as followers of Christ, are to live in the secular world, which is part of the Lord's kingdom of power. This is necessary because as well as being members of a local congregation, we are also citizens of some earthly nation (some people belong to more than one). Sometimes we visit other nations. Each nation has its own laws, and the subdivisions of those nations—such as cities, states, counties, and provinces—may have additional regulations. People living and traveling in them must be aware of and obey such laws. In whatever location we Lutherans find ourselves, we want to be good citizens by the standards of that place because our Lord asks us to be such (Jeremiah 29:7).[3]

---

[1] When God desired to show more convincingly to the heirs of the promise the unchangeable character of his purpose, he guaranteed it with an oath. (Hebrews 6:17)

[2] When there is a change in the priesthood, there is necessarily a change in the law as well. (Hebrews 7:12)

[3] But seek the welfare of the city where I have sent you into exile, and pray to the LORD on its behalf, for in its welfare you will find your welfare. (Jeremiah 29:7)

## Church and state

The relationship between the Lord's church and the various political entities has changed during the history of the world. Whatever its form, this relationship has been guided by the Lord to accomplish his plan of salvation. We do not know what kind of governing structure the Lord would have set up in the world if humankind had not fallen into sin. With only Adam and Eve present, marriage was an adequate governing structure for humankind. Once our first parents had sinned, however, some structure was needed, because every person thereafter was a self-centered sinner.

The primary structure of early government was patriarchal, extending the authority of the father in the family structure, which the Lord gave Adam, to the generations of his descendants. Each father (patriarch) ruled his family and his extended family, and this still serves as a method of government in parts of the world today (Genesis 36:15,16).[4] It is a structure of which the Lord approved and which he used in the Old Testament (Numbers 1:16).[5] Patriarchy has been neither mandated nor prohibited in the New Testament, but respect for parents (Ephesians 6:1-3) and elders (seniors) (1 Timothy 5:1)[6] is the will of the Lord. We have no information about the governments before the flood, although we do know that cities were established (Genesis 4:17). Immediately after the flood, the same pattern of governing seems to have continued.

The first mention in the Scriptures of another governmental structure is when the Bible identifies cities ruled by kings (Genesis 10:10). Most of these were relatively small settlements. The governmental structure was probably initially an expansion of the extended family structure to include a whole clan, of which the clan patriarch was the "king." The clans arising from the sons of Jacob were organized in this fashion. As clans got bigger, there were subclans and sub-subclans. In some parts of the world, the clan structure is still dominant today.

When the Lord rescued his people from Egypt, he established a the-ocracy. He gave Israel its civil law code, which was administered through judges chosen from the senior members of each tribe and of its subdivisions. When there were difficult questions about the application of a law or when

---

[4]These are the chiefs of the sons of Esau. The sons of Eliphaz the firstborn of Esau: the chiefs Teman, Omar, Zepho, Kenaz, Korah, Gatam, and Amalek; these are the chiefs of Eliphaz in the land of Edom; these are the sons of Adah. (Genesis 36:15,16)

[5]These were the ones chosen from the congregation, the chiefs of their ancestral tribes, the heads of the clans of Israel. (Numbers 1:16)

[6]Do not rebuke an older man but encourage him as you would a father. (1 Timothy 5:1)

something unexpected occurred, the high priest had the means to get a decision from the Lord himself, namely, the Urim and Thummim[7] (Exodus 28:30; Numbers 27:21). Resistance to the established rule in Israel led to exile or death (Exodus 12:15).[8] When the nation of Israel was distressed by its neighbors, the Lord himself appointed judges to rescue them and point them to the correct way of living (Judges 2:16).[9] Under the Mosaic Law, the church and the state were united.

Church and state remained united, at least in theory, once the Israelites demanded a king, and the Lord began to give them kings (1 Samuel 9:15,16).[10] The kings, however, were often more interested in using religion for their own purposes rather than for the benefit of the souls of their subjects. Kings and their favorites frequently introduced idolatry, and insincere worship became more the rule rather than the exception (Isaiah 29:13).[11] Because of this, the Lord led other nations to destroy both Israel and Judah, forcing the Israelites into captivity within nations where their religion was not the religion of the state (Jeremiah 22:8,9).[12] Efforts to reestablish a church-state alliance among the Jews were made after they returned from the Babylonian captivity, but these were of limited success. With the fall of Jerusalem in 70 A.D., the Jews were reduced to a culture and religion, but for many centuries they no longer had a state.

Although the Christian church began in the Roman Empire, it did not attempt to establish an attachment to the Roman state or to the Jewish aspirations for an independent Israel. The Roman government was not asked to enforce the beliefs of the church; in fact, it often tried to suppress them. The church had no power to influence the government. It could enforce its rules only upon its own members but only as long as they were willing to remain members of the church. This was by the Lord's design. Jesus and the apostles worked to separate the New Testament church from the state

---

[7] We do not know of what the Urim and Thummim consisted or how they were used.

[8] [The Lord said,] "On the first day you shall remove leaven out of your houses, for if anyone eats what is leavened, from the first day until the seventh day, that person shall be cut off from Israel." (Exodus 12:15)

[9] Then the LORD raised up judges, who saved them out of the hand of those who plundered them. (Judges 2:16)

[10] The LORD had revealed to Samuel: "Tomorrow about this time I will send to you a man from the land of Benjamin, and you shall anoint him to be prince over my people Israel." (1 Samuel 9:15,16)

[11] The Lord said: "... this people draw near with their mouth and honor me with their lips, while their hearts are far from me." (Isaiah 29:13)

[12] [The LORD said,] "Many nations will pass by this city, and every man will say to his neighbor, 'Why has the LORD dealt thus with this great city?' And they will answer, 'Because they have forsaken the covenant of the LORD their God and worshiped other gods and served them.'" (Jeremiah 22:8,9)

(Matthew 22:21).[13] They taught how Christians were to behave toward the authority of the state (Romans 13:1-7), as well as toward their non-Christian neighbors (1 Corinthians 5:9,10)[14] and even their enemies (Matthew 5:44,45).[15] After Constantine became the Roman emperor, an alliance between the church and the Roman government was established, but it was seldom harmonious. The church and the state tried to leverage each other throughout the centuries. When the territory of the Roman Empire was divided among other nations, the struggles between the church and the governments of these other nations continued. Civil rulers have tried to control church leaders, and church leaders have tried to control civil rulers. It is a game that still goes on, even beneath the cloak of 21st-century secularism. Civil rulers often want to appear to have the endorsement of some popular religious movements for their programs. Many religious leaders want legal clout to force people to follow their teachings.

The Lutheran Reformation led to an effort to reestablish the separate roles of church and state as presented in the New Testament. It wanted the state to govern its citizens but not attempt to impose religious or moral standards upon them. The legitimate interests of the state are in legality (Romans 13:3,4),[16] not morality. The government can do nothing to help its citizens in eternity, so it should not interfere with their worship of supernatural beings. It should regulate religious practice only to the extent necessary for public safety and good order in the community. Moreover, it should neither include religious activities, such as prayers and Scripture readings, in its public gatherings or schools, nor expect church endorsement of its policies and practices. Governmentally endorsed religious activities violate fellowship principles because no one knows what all the rest of the people in a crowd believe or whether they even nominally worship the same god (Daniel 3).

As Lutherans, we serve Christ by being good citizens of the nations and their subdivisions in which we reside and by being law-abiding when we visit

---

[13] Then he [Jesus] said to them, "Therefore render to Caesar the things that are Caesar's, and to God the things that are God's." (Matthew 22:21)

[14] I wrote to you in my letter not to associate with sexually immoral people—not at all meaning the sexually immoral of this world, or the greedy and swindlers, or idolaters, since then you would need to go out of the world. (1 Corinthians 5:9,10)

[15] [Jesus said,] "I say to you, Love your enemies and pray for those who persecute you, so that you may be sons of your Father who is in heaven." (Matthew 5:44,45)

[16] Would you have no fear of the one who is in authority? Then do what is good, and you will receive his approval, for he is God's servant for your good. But if you do wrong, be afraid, for he does not bear the sword in vain. For he is the servant of God, an avenger who carries out God's wrath on the wrongdoer. (Romans 13:3,4)

other countries. We obey the laws, pay taxes, serve on juries, and even fight in just wars, all as presented in Romans chapter 13. Lutherans are not rebellious toward governments, nor do we engage in civil disobedience. We build rather than destroy. We respect the legal rights of others and attempt to live peacefully with our neighbors (Romans 12:18).[17] Lutherans participate in governing activities to the extent it is permitted, and we can serve in public office. We understand that while the politics within a nation may, at times, be troubling, the Lord ultimately controls the course of events (Proverbs 16:33).[18] We know that we are only strangers here and that our real citizenship is in heaven (Philippians 3:20).[19]

On the other hand, we Lutherans do not try to deify the role of the state. While we work to improve the local situation, we do not believe that governments will ever solve many of the problems in the world, because the Lord has said that the problems will continue until judgment day (Matthew 24:6-12). We do not believe in trying to use the state to impose our religious views on others, because we know that faith comes through the preaching of the Word of God (1 Corinthians 1:21).[20] We Lutherans work to carry out the Great Commission in the area in which we live but outside of the framework of the state. We pray for the welfare of the nation in which we reside (1 Timothy 2:1-4), but we never give a religious stamp of approval to its activities. It is a balancing act to be both mission-minded and respectful of others' civil liberties.

It should be noted that while the Bible does say the governing powers are ordained by God, it does not dictate any particular form of government. The Bible does not establish a "divine right of kings," but it also does not establish a "divine mandate for democracy." From the time of Moses to the Babylonian captivity, the government of Israel was a theocracy—first under a prophet, then under judges, and finally under kings. The Lord calls on his people to be good citizens whether the form of government is a monarchy, an oligarchy, a dictatorship, or a democracy. At the time Jesus lived and the New Testament was written, the people lived in an empire where equality did not exist among the people, yet neither Jesus nor the apostles called for anything other than obedience to the government.

---

[17] If possible, so far as it depends on you, live peaceably with all. (Romans 12:18)

[18] [Solomon said,] "The lot is cast into the lap, but its every decision is from the LORD." (Proverbs 16:33)

[19] Our citizenship is in heaven, and from it we await a Savior, the Lord Jesus Christ. (Philippians 3:20)

[20] Since, in the wisdom of God, the world did not know God through wisdom, it pleased God through the folly of what we preach to save those who believe. (1 Corinthians 1:21)

## Marriage and sex

In a world that is filled with lust and that is drunk with the idea of romance, the followers of Christ must be aware of what the Bible does and does not say about marriage and sexual relations. It is best to start at the beginning of the Bible to see what the Lord's plan was and how humans degraded it along the way.

Based on how the Lord established marriage (Genesis 2:18-24) and on Jesus' words (Matthew 22:30),[21] we know that marriage is a temporal institution,[22] in the same way governments, employment, and civic organizations are temporal institutions. These institutions have all in one way or another been established by the Lord and are important in this life, but they do not carry over into eternity. In the first chapter of the Bible, we learn that man and woman are to procreate, that is, to fill the earth with people (Genesis 1:28).[23] Maleness and femaleness are therefore an important part of the Lord's plan in this world because they are necessary to populate it, but they are not necessary in eternity because no additional people will be born in heaven or in hell. In Genesis chapter 2, the Lord notes that he created a woman to be with the man that he had created so that the man would not be alone. He knew this was important to human life on earth, but it will not be necessary in heaven where there will be close fellowship among all the saints. They will all be spiritually united with the Lord, and loneliness will never occur. In hell everyone will be spiritually alone and hateful of everyone else because of their own sufferings (Matthew 13:41,42).[24] Misery will not love company. Both procreation and companionship are themes that the Lord wants in marriage.

Let us start with the theme of companionship. The Lord created only one human being out of the dust of the ground (Genesis 2:7).[25] He created the second human from the first, and the rest have come from this pair. All humans have indeed but one root. They are all related. Before Eve was

---

[21] [Jesus said,] "For in the resurrection they neither marry nor are given in marriage, but are like angels in heaven." (Matthew 22:30)

[22] A temporal institution is one that only affects a person while the person is living on earth, and that effect ends when the person dies.

[23] And God blessed them. And God said to them, "Be fruitful and multiply and fill the earth and subdue it, and have dominion over the fish of the sea and over the birds of the heavens and over every living thing that moves on the earth." (Genesis 1:28)

[24] [Jesus said,] "The Son of Man will send his angels, and they will gather out of his kingdom all causes of sin and all law-breakers, and throw them into the fiery furnace. In that place there will be weeping and gnashing of teeth." (Matthew 13:41,42)

[25] The LORD God formed the man of the dust from the ground and breathed into his nostrils the breath of life, and the man became a living creature. (Genesis 2:7)

formed, what would become Eve was part of Adam (Genesis 2:21,22).[26] After she was created, the Lord declared them to be "one flesh" (Genesis 2:24).[27] They should therefore function as if they were of one purpose rather than two people contracted together, each with their own agenda. This verse was cited by Jesus to condemn divorce (Mark 10:2-9). A wife should be as much a part of a man psychologically as his right arm is physically, and he should desire to divorce her as little as he would desire his right arm to be chopped off from him at the shoulder (Ephesians 5:28,29).[28] Marriage is that important to the Lord.

The companionship between man and woman received a severe blow when Eve ate of the forbidden fruit and gave some to Adam also (Genesis 3:6).[29] Adam was quick to blame Eve for the sin, and their life of companionship was never the same thereafter (Genesis 3:12).[30] The Lord cursed Eve by giving her pain in childbirth and by changing her relationship to her husband. While she had been designated as his "helper" (Genesis 2:18) from before her formation, her subjection to her husband, who was now a sinner, would be harder to bear (Genesis 3:16).[31] He cursed Adam with a hostile environment in which to earn a living (Genesis 3:17-19) and gave him the chief responsibility for the sin (1 Corinthians 15:22).[32] Eventually, a woman would be a privileged participant in the birth of the Savior, but there would be no human father (Luke 1:34,35).[33] After the coming of

---

[26]The LORD God caused a deep sleep to fall upon the man, and while he slept took one of his ribs and closed up its place with flesh. And the rib that the LORD God had taken from the man he made into a woman and brought her to the man. (Genesis 2:21,22)

[27]A man shall leave his father and his mother and hold fast to his wife, and they shall become one flesh. (Genesis 2:24) (Note: One cannot be certain from the text whether the Lord made this statement at this time or whether Moses made it as a divinely inspired explanation in writing his narrative. That it is the Lord who does the joining together in marriage is clear from Jesus' quotation of this verse and his declaration, "What therefore God has joined together, let not man separate" [Matthew 19:6].)

[28]Husbands should love their wives as their own bodies. He who loves his wife loves himself. For no one ever hated his own flesh, but nourishes and cherishes it, just as Christ does the church. (Ephesians 5:28,29)

[29]When the woman saw that the tree was good for food, and that it was a delight to the eyes, and that the tree was to be desired to make one wise, she took of its fruit and ate, and she also gave some to her husband who was with her, and he ate. (Genesis 3:6)

[30]The man said, "The woman whom you gave to be with me, she gave me fruit of the tree, and I ate." (Genesis 3:12)

[31]To the woman he [the LORD] said, "I will surely multiply your pain in childbearing; in pain you shall bring forth children. Your desire shall be for your husband, and he shall rule over you." (Genesis 3:16)

[32]As in Adam all die, so also in Christ shall all be made alive. (1 Corinthians 15:22)

[33]Mary said to the angel [Gabriel], "How will this be, since I am a virgin?" And the angel answered her, "The Holy Spirit will come upon you, and the power of the Most High will overshadow you; therefore the child to be born will be called holy—the Son of God." (Luke 1:34,35)

the Savior, St. Paul would remind both men and women what their roles in marriage should be. Marriage was to reflect Christ's love for his church and the church's obedience to him, even though marriage is an earthly institution corrupted by sin (Ephesians 5:22-33).

The procreation theme was also severely impacted by the fall into sin. There were no children born before the fall, so we have no benchmark of how the Lord expected children to be born and raised. Procreation involves sexual union, and the Lord needed to provide exterior commandments concerning sexual activities once the image of God had been lost from the heart by the first sin. He wanted children to be the product of a stable relationship where the father would play an instrumental role in raising the children to adulthood (Ephesians 6:4;[34] Proverbs 22:6[35]). He therefore placed sexual relations inside the context of the "one flesh" union he established in Genesis 2:24 (1 Corinthians 6:15–7:6).

To understand the Lord's commands about sexual relations and marriage, one must be familiar with the definition of several terms as they are used in the Bible. *Adultery* occurred when a man had consensual sexual intercourse with a woman married or betrothed to another man. The Mosaic Law prescribed stoning of both the man and the woman (Deuteronomy 22:22-24). If the woman did not consent to intercourse, then their intercourse would be treated as rape, and the man alone would be stoned (Deuteronomy 22:25-27). *Fornication* occurred when a man had consensual sexual intercourse with an unbetrothed woman, and the punishment was that he had to marry her and could never divorce her (Deuteronomy 22:28,29). The marital status of the man was irrelevant, so a married man could be forced to take another wife if he had sexual relations with an unmarried woman. This rule did not apply if the woman was a prostitute (i.e., sold sexual relations for money), because prostitution also was a violation of the Law (Leviticus 19:29). A *concubine* was a genuine wife but one who had a lower social status and whose children were not automatically heirs of their father's estate. Her husband, however, did have a lifelong commitment to her (Genesis 25:5,6).[36] Concubines were often slaves of the man who was sexually involved with them, women with a history of impro-

---

[34]Fathers, do not provoke your children to anger, but bring them up in the discipline and instruction of the Lord. (Ephesians 6:4)

[35][Solomon said,] "Train up a child in the way he should go; even when he is old he will not depart from it." (Proverbs 22:6)

[36]Abraham gave all he had to Isaac. But to the sons of his concubines Abraham gave gifts, and while he was still living he sent them away from his son Isaac, eastward to the east country. (Genesis 25:5,6)

prieties and divorces, or commoners married to a king. Concubines had special rules protecting them (Exodus 21:7-11).[37]

In Old Testament times two major factors, in addition to sexual desire, governed the drive for people to get married. First, men wanted to maintain their names into future generations by having sons (Numbers 27:6-11). Property ownership passed primarily from fathers to sons. If a man had only daughters, they had to marry within his tribe so his land would not be lost to another tribe (Numbers 36:12). If he died before he had children, then his brother or near male relative would have to marry his widow, and her first son would assume the original husband's lineage and property (Deuteronomy 25:5,6).[38] This "law of the levirate" was the basis of Boaz marrying Ruth, for example (Ruth 4). The second major factor driving marriage was the belief that every woman had the right to bear children. Failing to bear legitimate children was regarded as the ultimate shame for a woman (Genesis 30:23).[39] This meant that she had the right to a husband, and her father, or another relative if her father was dead, was responsible for securing a husband for her. Because not all men could afford wives or were interested in having them, a father might choose for his daughter to marry a man who already had a wife and could afford another. Frequent warfare encouraged polygyny, due to the lack of available single men. Men had the obligation to support their wife or wives (1 Timothy 5:8). Isaiah predicted a situation so desperate that seven women would seek to marry one man and would even be willing to pay their own expenses so they would not have to live in disgrace because they had not borne legitimate children (Isaiah 4:1).

Divorce was not part of the Lord's original plan. In the perfect world he created, men and women would get along in complete harmony and would not sin against each other. When sin caused disharmony, the Lord dealt with that disharmony in an effort to contain the damage and encourage compliance with his will. The Lord allowed a man to divorce his wife under the Mosaic covenant if he had married her with the consent of her father and if he found that she had some terrible character flaw that had been kept

---

[37] The term for a man having multiple wives is polygyny. Polyandry, a woman having multiple husbands, was not permitted because a woman would have been stoned as an adulteress if she had sexual relations with a second man.

[38] [Moses said,] "If brothers dwell together, and one of them dies and has no son, the wife of the dead man shall not be married outside the family to a stranger. Her husband's brother shall go in to her and take her as his wife and perform the duty of a husband's brother to her. And the first son whom she bears shall succeed to the name of his dead brother, that his name may not be blotted out of Israel." (Deuteronomy 25:5,6)

[39] She [Rachel] conceived and bore a son and said, "God has taken away my reproach." (Genesis 30:23)

secret during the marriage negotiation (Deuteronomy 24:1).[40] The husband lost the bride price in the process, so it was not a cheap option. The
Lord further restricted the likelihood of divorce by preventing a man or a
woman from subsequently marrying any of their spouse's extended family,
who would be the people in the best position to create trouble between
husband and wife (Leviticus 18:6-17). Fathers were also prevented from
marrying less desirable daughters off as part of a package deal (Leviticus
18:18), as Laban had to Jacob (Genesis 29:21-30). When divorce became
more common among the Jews and was done for frivolous reasons, the
prophet Malachi stated the Lord's displeasure with it (Malachi 2:13-16). In
the New Testament, Jesus condemned divorce as violating the Lord's will
(Matthew 19:3-9). Divorce always involves sin on the part of one or both of
the spouses. The Lutheran church therefore recognizes divorce only if one
spouse destroys the marriage by failing to take his or her marriage vows
seriously. This could be willful physical or emotional desertion (i.e., one
party effectively ending the marriage), or it could be flagrant adultery that
makes reconciliation impossible, even if there is repentance. As with the
lopping off of one's arm at the shoulder, it should be done only in the most
grievous situations.

It is clear from the Mosaic Law that the Lord wants sexual relations only
within a heterosexual marriage. The Mosaic Law imposed the death pen-
alty for homosexual relations (Leviticus 20:13)[41] and adultery (Leviticus
20:10),[42] and it required marriage when fornication was committed (Exodus
22:16).[43] The Hebrew word *thoevah* used by the Lord to describe such sexual
misconduct means that he regards such behavior as abhorrent, offensive to
his very essence. St. Paul lists adultery, fornication, and homosexual acts as
sins that will keep people out of heaven if they are not repented of (1 Corinthians 6:9,10).[44] Therefore, it is incompatible with the Christian faith to have

---

[40][Moses said,] "When a man takes a wife and marries her, if then she finds no favor in his eyes because he has found some indecency in her, and he writes her a certificate of divorce and puts it in her hand and sends her out of his house, and she departs out of his house." (Deuteronomy 24:1)

[41][The LORD said,] "If a man lies with a male as with a woman, both of them have committed an abomination; they shall surely be put to death; their blood is upon them." (Leviticus 20:13)

[42][The LORD said,] "If a man commits adultery with the wife of his neighbor, both the adulterer and the adulteress shall surely be put to death." (Leviticus 20:10)

[43][The LORD said,] "If a man seduces a virgin who is not betrothed and lies with her, he shall give the bride-price for her and make her his wife." (Exodus 22:16)

[44]Do you not know that the unrighteous will not inherit the kingdom of God? Do not be deceived: neither the sexually immoral, nor idolaters, nor adulterers, nor men who practice homosexuality, nor thieves, nor the greedy, nor drunkards, nor revilers, nor swindlers will inherit the kingdom of God. (1 Corinthians 6:9,10)

casual sexual relations, practice homosexuality, or live together with someone with sexual contact without a lifelong commitment (Hebrews 13:4).[45]
The Lord, however, requires much more under his law; he requires clean
thoughts and speech in relation to sexual matters (Matthew 5:28).[46] Therefore, impious sexual comments and jokes, pornography, entertainment and
novels that sexually excite, as well as lustful fantasizing are all inappropriate
because they move sexual pleasure outside of marriage, where the Lord has
placed it (Matthew 15:19,20).[47] All these are temptations of the demons, and
like all temptations, they must be resisted. Moreover, to say that God made
someone to have particular sexual desires is blasphemous (James 1:13,14).[48]
All humans are totally depraved and tempted to disobey the Lord's will
(Genesis 6:5).[49] It is just the manner in which we are most subject to temptation that differs. There are no exemptions from doing the Lord's will just
because of the way we feel about ourselves or others.

While people getting married and having children were central to the
Lord's plan for the nation of Israel (to create a people who would produce
the Savior and who would be the initial missionary force to spread the news
about the Savior), the Lord has given an alternative in the New Testament.
It is still proper for men and women to marry and to raise children. The
command of Genesis 1:28 has not been set aside, and the moral law has not
changed. Because of the great urgency of spreading the message of salvation throughout the world, however, the Lord has given people who have
the gift of remaining celibate the permission to do so, as long as they use the
extra time and resources they gain from not being married to serve the Lord
(1 Corinthians 7:32-34). Gaining wealth, indulging your desire for personal
freedom, and living only for yourself are not biblically acceptable reasons
for failing to marry (1 Timothy 6:10).[50] On the other hand, the early church
overemphasized this alternative and claimed it was superior to marriage.

---

[45]Let marriage be held in honor among all, and let the marriage bed be undefiled, for God will judge the sexually immoral and adulterous. (Hebrews 13:4)

[46][Jesus said,] "I say to you that everyone who looks at a woman with lustful intent has already commit-ted adultery with her in his heart." (Matthew 5:28)

[47][Jesus said,] "Out of the heart come evil thoughts, murder, adultery, sexual immorality, theft, false witness, slander. These are what defile a person." (Matthew 15:19,20)

[48]Let no one say when he is tempted, "I am being tempted by God," for God cannot be tempted with evil, and he himself tempts no one. But each person is tempted when he is lured and enticed by his own desire. (James 1:13,14)

[49]The LORD saw that the wickedness of man was great in the earth, and that every intention of the thoughts of his heart was only evil continually. (Genesis 6:5)

[50]The love of money is a root of all kinds of evils. It is through this craving that some have wandered away from the faith and pierced themselves with many pangs. (1 Timothy 6:10)

This was never so. Paul encouraged those who had been given an aptitude for celibacy to remain unmarried, but he urged men who had not been given this aptitude and younger women to marry and have children (1 Corinthians 7:8,9).[51] The kingdom is also spread in this way.

In today's world there is plenty of bad advice about marriage. Yet having a successful marriage is not a Herculean task if one enters marriage with the right intentions. First, a couple needs to marry with the purpose of serving the Lord (Joshua 24:15).[52] Second, both members of the couple must share a common plan for their life together and a commitment to each other's welfare that is as strong as to their own welfare (Ephesians 5:28).[53] The common plan may change when the Lord gives different circumstances than expected, but it must remain a common plan, not two individual plans. Regular, if not daily, family devotions help to build the Lord into the marriage, and he is an incredible glue (Matthew 18:20).[54] If people are too busy for family devotions, then the god they are worshiping is unlikely to be the Lord, who demands first place in our lives (Deuteronomy 6:4-9). While romantic love can add interest to life, it is the mundane things that are done in selfless love by each spouse for the other spouse that make a marriage work. As an old Amish saying goes, "Kissing don't last; cooking do." Getting married earlier in life rather than later and having children while young are good ideas if one has the opportunity to do so. It is more important for children to see the unity of their parents working together as the family faces the challenges of establishing itself than to see the expensive toys and the bigger house that they will then assume is their right to have.

Some might ask whether a marriage certificate from the state is really necessary for marriage. During the history of the world, there has not always been the same answer to that question. In many places in the past, and in a few places today, marriage was regarded as a private thing in which the government took no role. For a thousand years of Christian church history, from the fifth century to the time of the Reformation, it was the church that kept the official marriage records, and state registration of marriages was separate, if it existed at all. Births, baptisms, marriages, and deaths were all overseen by the church rather than the state (i.e., civil governments). After

---

[51] To the unmarried and the widows I say that it is good for them to remain single as I am. But if they cannot exercise self-control, they should marry. For it is better to marry than to burn with passion. (1 Corinthians 7:8,9)

[52] [Joshua said,] "As for me and my house, we will serve the LORD." (Joshua 24:15)

[53] Husbands should love their wives as their own bodies. (Ephesians 5:28)

[54] [Jesus said,] "Where two or three are gathered in my name, there am I among them." (Matthew 18:20)

the Reformation, Protestants sought to move the registration of marriages out of the hands of the Roman Catholic Church and into the realm of the state. The various church bodies went along, for the most part, with the regulations that the state established for marriage and generally recognized marriages if the state did. This practice is now troubled because the states and nations of the world have allowed so much unscriptural divorce and remarriage and are now granting marital status to same-sex couples. Recognition of a marriage by the state does not guarantee that the marriage is scriptural and therefore a marriage before the Lord. Because it is the Lord who actually effects marriage (Matthew 19:6),[55] it is the church's responsibility to recognize a marriage if it believes that the marriage is a lifelong commitment before the Lord. The Lutheran church therefore follows the practice of recognizing a marriage if it is scripturally permissible and when there are the public vows necessary for state registry of the marriage. Pastors are licensed to act as agents of the state to legally establish marriages, but they bless marriages as agents of the church. The underlying scriptural principle remains unchanged. Consent makes the marriage—not romantic love or any other kind of love but rather a commitment to live together as husband and wife by two people who are free to make such a commitment and are willing to do it in a public way. A marriage is regarded as a Christian marriage if the purpose of the marriage is to serve the Lord.

Because marriage is a temporal institution, it is in competition with other temporal institutions within a person's life. In these competitions, marriage does not always win (1 Corinthians 7:34).[56] For example, a person might be called to jury duty or to military service, causing the activities of marriage to be put on hold. A person might be sent on a business trip or might have to work a different shift, interfering with a couple's time together. An emergency might keep someone from a romantic dinner. The activities of marriage have to be scheduled around civic duties, employment, organizational commitments, and even church activities. All of these things are also temporal gifts from the Lord and must be treated with respect, the same as marriage must be treated with respect. It is imperative, however, that marital unity not be sacrificed to gain advantages in other venues, because that is not the Lord's will for marriage (Ephesians 5:22-29). The marital partnership must not be left to flounder if a spouse desires to achieve

---

[55][Jesus said,] "They are no longer two but one flesh. What therefore God has joined together, let not man separate." (Matthew 19:6)

[56]The unmarried or betrothed woman is anxious about the things of the Lord, how to be holy in body and spirit. But the married woman is anxious about worldly things, how to please her husband. (1 Corinthians 7:34)

greatness elsewhere, because that would be despising a gift from the Lord (Proverbs 31:10).[57]

## Work and employment

The Lord assigned work to Adam on the sixth day of creation (Genesis 2:15),[58] and people have been working ever since. In the beginning the work was pleasant, but after Adam had sinned, the Lord cursed the ground and work often became difficult (Genesis 3:17-19). The struggle to acquire the necessities for survival became a part of everyone's daily activities. Humankind had to gather food, to find or build shelters, and to make clothing. This struggle is one of the ways in which sin makes life unpleasant.

Initially, everyone was living hand-to-mouth. People needed to find food and water each day. Gradually, they learned how to store food and take advantage of the seasons of the year to produce food for longer time periods. Yet storage was primitive, and many other creatures were interested in their stores of food. Floods and droughts added to their misery. Over time, people invented simple tools to aid in the growing and preserving of food (Genesis 4:22).[59] After the flood, the Lord officially added meat to people's diets (Genesis 9:3),[60] although it may have been eaten before that time by some. As people found better ways to do things, some became rich and could pay or force others to do the work necessary for their personal survival.

While numerous inventions and social covenants have made life easier in many parts of the world, work is still an important part of life for most people. The Lord wants it that way. He provides for all his creatures (Psalm 145:15,16),[61] but he often provides for each of us through our own efforts. Work is service to the Lord, and none of us has a right to stop serving the Lord (2 Thessalonians 3:10).[62] If we become wealthy enough so that we do not have to work for our own livelihood, we have ample opportunities to serve the Lord in his church and to help the less fortunate people in this world. Even those of us who have physical limitations need to look for what

---

[57]An excellent wife who can find? She is far more precious than jewels. (Proverbs 31:10)

[58]The LORD God took the man and put him in the Garden of Eden to work it and keep it. (Genesis 2:15)

[59]Zillah also bore Tubal-Cain; he was the forger of all instruments of bronze and iron. (Genesis 4:22)

[60][The LORD said,] "Every moving thing that lives shall be food for you. And as I gave you the green plants, I give you everything." (Genesis 9:3)

[61][David said to the Lord,] "The eyes of all look to you, and you give them their food in due season. You open Your hand; you satisfy the desire of every living thing." (Psalm 145:15,16)

[62]Even when we were with you, we would give you this command: If anyone is not willing to work, let him not eat. (2 Thessalonians 3:10)

we can do for as long as we can do it. Sometimes "they also serve who only stand and wait."[63] None of us has the right to retire from the service of the Lord and still expect the Lord to look after us.

On the other hand, work should not overrun our lives (Matthew 6:31-33).[64] Nothing we accomplish in this world (Matthew 16:26)[65] will lengthen the history of the world by even one second. Because all our work is service to the Lord, we should not act like the world depends on us, nor should we seek glory from it (Luke 12:18-21). Whether we succeed or we fail, we know that the will of the Lord will be accomplished. We should work with the ability that the Lord has given us, not for our own glory but so that the glory of his love shines through our actions (Matthew 5:16).[66]

As faithful Lutherans, therefore, we put work into perspective. We work to the extent that we need to work so as to meet the responsibilities the Lord has given us. We provide for ourselves and for those whom the Lord has given us to care for (1 Timothy 5:8).[67] We consider not only the present but also the future so that we are no more of a burden on others than circumstances dictate. Yet we must be careful to consider what things are necessities for us and what things are merely desires. People become rich when they can buy everything that they want, and they become richer much quicker if they are content with less (Proverbs 30:8,9).[68] There is no commandment against having more than the minimum in this life. Such things are blessings from the Lord (Job 42:12).[69] Nevertheless, we need to balance our service to the Lord against our desire for comfort and luxury. It is a matter of Christian freedom, as will be discussed shortly.

---

[63] A famous line from a poem by John Milton ("On His Blindness," 1655), written as he finally reconciled himself to his loss of sight.

[64] [Jesus said,] "Therefore do not be anxious, saying, 'What shall we eat?' or 'What shall we drink?' or 'What shall we wear?' For the Gentiles seek after all these things, and your heavenly Father knows that you need them all. But seek first the kingdom of God and his righteousness, and all these things will be added to you." (Matthew 6:31-33)

[65] [Jesus said,] "What will it profit a man if he gains the whole world and forfeits his soul? Or what shall a man give in return for his soul?" (Matthew 16:26)

[66] [Jesus said,] "In the same way, let your light shine before others, so that they may see your good works and give glory to your Father who is in heaven." (Matthew 5:16)

[67] If anyone does not provide for his relatives, and especially for members of his household, he has denied the faith and is worse than an unbeliever. (1 Timothy 5:8)

[68] [Agur said,] "Remove far from me falsehood and lying; give me neither poverty nor riches; feed me with the food that is needful for me, lest I be full and deny you and say, 'Who is the LORD?' or lest I be poor and steal and profane the name of my God." (Proverbs 30:8,9)

[69] The LORD blessed the latter days of Job more than his beginning. And he had 14,000 sheep, 6,000 camels, 1,000 yoke of oxen, and 1,000 female donkeys. (Job 42:12)

Therefore, as we who are Lutherans plan our futures, we will strive to avoid falling into the two ditches that would lead us away from Christ.[70] On one hand, we do not want to commit ourselves to driving so hard for success that we have no time to also serve the Lord and to study his Word. Fame and money will give no comfort in hell (Matthew 19:23).[71] On the other hand, we do not wish to plan and work so haphazardly or lazily that we are forced to live off the work of others or are crushed by a load of foolishly incurred debt (Proverbs 22:7).[72] Our planning always needs to start with how we will serve the Lord, and then we must wrap career, family and other activities around that. This means considering not only what we like to do but how our choice of occupation will affect other choices that we will need to make. When the focus is kept on our service to Christ, whether in church work or in secular employment, the Lord will cause other things to fall into place (Romans 8:28).[73]

In our employment we as Lutherans should always work diligently and honestly, as if we were working for the Lord himself (Colossians 3:23).[74] Because we know that the Lord will bless us, we will neither try to gain unfair advantage nor shortchange either our employer or our customers. If we feel that our job is forcing us to compromise our obedience to the moral law, we will seek employment elsewhere. When faced with disappointment, we will always seek comfort from the Lord, knowing that the Lord knows the needs and shares in the sufferings of all his children (Hebrews 2:17,18).[75] In the hassle of the struggle for survival, the knowledge that our salvation is sure can carry us through many trials.

## Social responsibility

As Lutherans and followers of Christ, we need to have a heartfelt concern for the less fortunate (James 1:27).[76] Already in the Mosaic Law, provisions

---

[70]Daniel M. Deutschlander, *The Narrow Lutheran Middle* (Milwaukee: Northwestern Publishing House, 2011).

[71]And Jesus said to his disciples, "Truly, I say to you, only with difficulty will a rich person enter the kingdom of heaven." (Matthew 19:23)

[72][Solomon said,] "The rich rules over the poor, and the borrower is the slave of the lender." (Proverbs 22:7)

[73]We know that for those who love God all things work together for good, for those who are called according to his purpose. (Romans 8:28)

[74]Whatever you do, work heartily, as for the Lord and not for men. (Colossians 3:23)

[75]Therefore he had to be made like his brothers in every respect, so that he might become a merciful and faithful high priest in the service of God, to make propitiation for the sins of the people. For because he himself has suffered when tempted, he is able to help those who are being tempted. (Hebrews 2:17,18)

[76]Religion that is pure and undefiled before God, the Father, is this: to visit orphans and widows in their affliction, and to keep oneself unstained from the world. (James 1:27)

were made for the care of the orphans, the widows, and the foreigners. For example, when fields of grain were harvested, any grain that remained in the field after the first gathering was to be left for these less fortunate (Deuteronomy 24:19-22). Ruth gleaned in the field of Boaz to find grain for her mother-in-law and for herself under this regulation (Ruth 2). When trees and grapevines were harvested, they were not to be re-harvested to find those pieces of fruit that had been missed or were slow at ripening. Special offerings of the crops were set aside for the poor (Deuteronomy 14:28,29). When the people failed to supply these gifts to the poor, the prophets called on them to account for their sins (Isaiah 1:23).[77]

The same pattern of loving concern was followed in the early church. The new converts in Jerusalem, perhaps believing that Jesus' second coming was imminent, were willing to sell all their property to help the poor, assuming that they would soon have no need of property (Acts 4:32-37). As time passed and as people realized that earthly goods would continue to be needed, they began to be less eager to help the poor, not even willing to follow the previous practice of the Mosaic Law. The epistle of James addresses this stinginess. Collections for needy Christians were taken when famines occurred. Paul discusses one such collection that was taken in Greece to help the Christians in Judea (2 Corinthians 8–9). Concern for the poor is mentioned often in the New Testament (Galatians 2:10).[78] The church continued this practice of helping the poor during the following centuries.

We Lutherans today continue to have a responsibility to help the poor and the less fortunate. Although state welfare programs have assumed much of the burden of providing the basic necessities for the poor and the chronically ill, that does not change the Lord's will that we help those who are, for whatever reason, less fortunate. We will want to look on all people as Jesus looks upon us. What we have, he has given to us (1 Corinthians 4:7).[79] It is ours to use but not to hog. Yet, like Jesus, we need not jump at every opportunity to help (Mark 14:7).[80] Jesus did miracles when it was appropriate, and he didn't do them when they would have served no purpose in his ministry

---

[77][The LORD said,] "Your princes are rebels and companions of thieves. Everyone loves a bribe and runs after gifts. They do not bring justice to the fatherless, and the widow's cause does not come to them." (Isaiah 1:23)

[78]Only, they asked us to remember the poor, the very thing I was eager to do. (Galatians 2:10)

[79]What do you have that you did not receive? If then you received it, why do you boast as if you did not receive it? (1 Corinthians 4:7)

[80]You always have the poor with you, and whenever you want, you can do good for them. (Mark 14:7)

(Matthew 13:58).[81] The maxim of doing what is in front of us and letting others do what is in front of them often is the best advice, but reaching out to help elsewhere when it can make a difference should not be ignored.

The natural resources of the world, the production of our factories, and the global environment are also gifts from the Lord. We should neither despise them nor allow them to remain unused. These things exist for our benefit, our use, and our pleasure, but unless the Lord returns, we will pass them on to others. Here, the Golden Rule is good counsel to us as believers in Christ living in the world (Matthew 7:12).[82] We should desire to leave the world to our descendants no worse than we received it from previous generations. We have no fixed ordinances about these things. Sincere people may differ in what they think is good stewardship of what we have been given. Each should act according to the dictates of his or her own conscience as enlightened by the Scriptures so that all things are done to the glory of the Lord (1 Corinthians 10:31).[83]

One way in which we can serve our fellow human beings is through volunteering with civic organizations that make the community a better place to live and work. Such groups help to feed the poor, clean up highways, give concerts, or run historical sites. This type of work is not specially mandated by the Scriptures, but it is a way to show our love and concern for the members of our community and it might even open opportunities to spread the gospel. As in all things, we who are followers of Christ need to balance the good done by such volunteer work with the other responsibilities that the Lord has given us, in particular, the responsibility to study God's Word and spread its message.

## Christian freedom

The Mosaic Law was the guardian slave that forced the Israelites (Galatians 3:24)[84] to learn the ways of the Lord. When one is in school, one is not free but is subject to the direction of others. Christ's first coming has freed his followers from the stipulations of the law (Galatians 3:25,26).[85] Instead of living under law, the members of his church live under grace. St. Paul

---

[81]He [Jesus] did not do many mighty works there, because of their unbelief. (Matthew 13:58)

[82][Jesus said,] "Whatever you wish that others would do to you, do also to them, for this is the Law and the Prophets." (Matthew 7:12 [The Golden Rule])

[83]Whether you eat or drink, or whatever you do, do all to the glory of God. (1 Corinthians 10:31)

[84]The law was our guardian until Christ came, in order that we might be justified by faith. (Galatians 3:24)

[85]Now that faith has come, we are no longer under a guardian, for in Christ Jesus you are all sons of God, through faith. (Galatians 3:25,26)

warns people not to put themselves back under the Mosaic Law or any other moralistic law, because we are not saved through the observance of some legal code (Galatians 3:11-13).[86]

It would seem that Paul's statements would fall right in with the American idea of personal freedom. According to this idea, people should be allowed to do anything they please, and they should be restricted as little as they have to be. If something is not harmful to anyone other than those involved, then it should be permissible and even legally supported. After all, the Declaration of Independence lists the "pursuit of happiness" as one of man's inalienable rights. It seems that everyone from the political far left to the political far right agrees with this idea, at least as long as the requirements they want to impose on others are not eliminated. Many people on the Christian left have also come to accept to a large extent the idea that the pursuit of happiness is a basic human right.

However, St. Paul definitely did not have this type of freedom in mind when he wrote about Christian freedom. Paul was rather addressing freedom from legalism, where the purpose of the law is perverted by an effort to define it in all imaginable cases. For example, laws in this world never cover all possible situations, and the spirit of the law often differs from the wording. This is why so many cases end up in court. Even the Mosaic Law suffered from this problem because it could not possibly list the appropriate action for every situation that might occur (Ezra 2:63).[87] Jesus often confronted his religious opponents on their emphasis of the letter over the spirit (Mark 2:27),[88] but he never denied the importance of following the law and not improvising one's own nuances to make it more palatable. Jesus did not come to start a revolution but rather to save humankind. Part of that effort involved demonstrating how people were to serve the Lord, not by a code but from a heart filled with love for the Lord. As redeemed children of God, we Lutherans will naturally want to serve the Lord; therefore, no law is needed to coerce unwilling obedience from us. On the other hand, Christian freedom is not a license to do evil (1 Peter 2:16).[89]

---

[86]Now it is evident that no one is justified before God by the law, for "The righteous shall live by faith." But the law is not of faith, rather "The one who does them shall live by them." Christ redeemed us from the curse of the law by becoming a curse for us—for it is written, "Cursed is everyone who is hanged on a tree." (Galatians 3:11-13)

[87]The governor told them that they were not to partake of the most holy food, until there should be a priest to consult Urim and Thummim. (Ezra 2:63)

[88]He [Jesus] said to them, "The Sabbath was made for man, not man for the Sabbath." (Mark 2:27)

[89]Live as people who are free, not using your freedom as a cover-up for evil, but living as servants of

In his treatise *On the Freedom of a Christian*, Luther wrote, "A Christian is a perfectly free lord of all, subject to none. A Christian is a perfectly dutiful servant of all, subject to all."[90] This is the essence of Christian freedom. Obedience is not required for salvation, so a Christian can choose to do as he (or she) wills, following the course he desires (Colossians 2:16).[91] In this way he is a lord, subject to no one. But a Christian, because his heart has been changed by the Holy Spirit, will want to serve the Lord and his fellow people in all that he does (1 Peter 2:17).[92] He will not build his life around the "big I," but he will consider how his actions will affect others around him and will adjust them to reflect the love of Christ in his life (Philippians 2:5-7).[93] In this way, he is a dutiful servant of all. As Lutherans, therefore, we believe that Christian freedom is the freedom to serve, not the freedom to indulge. (See the section on God's law as a guide for our Christian living, pp. 201,202.)

God. (1 Peter 2:16)

[90]Martin Luther, *On the Freedom of a Christian, Luther's Works,* American Edition, Vol. 31 (Philadelphia Fortress Press, 1957), pp. 327-377.

[91]Therefore let no one pass judgment on you in questions of food and drink, or with regard to a festival or a new moon or a Sabbath. (Colossians 2:16)

[92]Honor everyone. Love the brotherhood. Fear God. Honor the emperor. (1 Peter 2:17)

[93]Have this mind among yourselves, which is yours in Christ Jesus, who, though he was in the form of God, did not count equality with God a thing to be grasped [flaunted,] but emptied himself, by taking the form of a servant, being born in the likeness of men. (Philippians 2:5-7)

CHAPTER 19

# Saints, Angels, and Demons

The purpose of this chapter is to discuss three topics that are commonly misunderstood. Because they are frequently the subject of conversations and cartoons, it is important that they be correctly understood from a biblical perspective. Failure to do so can undermine a proper understanding of Christianity and can even lead to idolatry.

## Saints

Saints are holy ones, which is what the Greek word translated as "saints" really means. The term first appears in the Old Testament in 2 Chronicles 6:41[1] and in Psalm 16:3.[2] Saints are mentioned a number of times in Psalms and in the book of Daniel. They are mentioned frequently in Acts and the epistles (e.g., Romans 15:25[3]). In almost all cases, the word *saints* refers to living people.

If all people are sinners, how can any of them be called saints? They can as a direct result of subjective justification, which was discussed in chapter 16. When a person believes that Jesus Christ suffered and died for his or her sins and repents, that person has all guilt removed and is covered with

---

[1][Solomon prayed,] "Let your priests, O LORD God, be clothed with salvation, and let your saints rejoice in your goodness." (2 Chronicles 6:41)

[2][David said,] "As for the saints in the land, they are the excellent ones, in whom is all my delight." (Psalm 16:3)

[3]At present, however, I am going to Jerusalem bringing aid to the saints. (Romans 15:25)

the righteousness that Jesus earned through his active obedience in perfectly keeping God's law (Romans 3:21-25). Because the person no longer has any guilt of sin but instead has Christ's righteousness, the person is therefore holy in God's sight. This is why Paul could begin his letters to the members of various congregations by writing, "To the saints who are at" (e.g., Colossians 1:1; Ephesians 1:1). While people remain sinners in this world due to the imperfections in their actions, they are perfect before the Lord because none of the guilt of their sins is counted against them. And being holy before God, they will enter heaven when they die or when the Lord returns.

The term *saint* is misused in common speech in two ways. First, it is used to describe someone who does many actions of civic righteousness or who suffers an unusual amount of pain or misfortune without complaint. By human standards, this person seems to be ideal. This is the type of person that those unfamiliar with biblical teachings think is certain to be saved because they are so "godlike" in their lives. On the other hand, the phrase "he's no saint" is applied to someone who has numerous or serious character flaws. Human judgment, however, has no impact on the Lord, who looks at the heart and not at externals (1 Samuel 16:7).[4] The Pharisees were the "perfect" people of Jesus' time, yet he rejected most of them (Luke 18:9-14). Instead, he selected to be his disciples some people whose pasts were anything but perfect. Consider Matthew, a member of the dishonorable profession of tax collector (Matthew 9:9-13).

The other misuse of the term *saint* is that employed by the Roman Catholic Church and some other church bodies. From early Christian times, those who died martyr's deaths were honored in the churches. On the anniversaries of their births or deaths, their local congregations and perhaps the congregations in the vicinity would mention their names during worship services and would sometimes hold vigils to remind people of their sacrifices in the cause of Christ. They were held up as examples to inspire others. After Christianity became the state religion of the Roman Empire, the church was overwhelmed by new members and could no longer adequately train them in all the doctrines of the church. Therefore, more and more pagan customs entered the church, at least among the laity. The Greeks and Romans had worshiped many gods and heroes. It was natural for them to want a larger group of beings to venerate than just the Lord himself. Grad-

---

[4]The LORD said to Samuel, "Do not look on his [the oldest son of Jesse's] appearance or on the height of his stature, because I have rejected him. For the LORD sees not as man sees: man looks on the outward appearance, but the LORD looks on the heart." (1 Samuel 16:7)

ually, the church compromised by allowing their martyred heroes to fill the roles that the Roman gods had held in the past. Martyred heroes became associated with all kinds of human activities, such as travel, farming, fishing, and childbearing. People moved from honoring the past Christian heroes to looking to them as intercessors before God. Because each area had its own heroes, the Roman church decided that it had to gain control over the situation by officially designating who could and who couldn't be venerated and prayed to as intercessors. This led to the practice of the Roman church canonizing people based on specific criteria. The Roman church currently uses a detailed process that evaluates various aspects of a person's life before canonization, including requiring the performance of "verifiable" miracles.

The Roman church practice of creating saints is thoroughly unscriptural. First, it is the Lord who creates saints because he can see into people's hearts—the church can see only the outward life. The Lord never gave his church the right or power to do this. The Roman church is, in effect, claiming that it can reach into eternity, the Lord's realm, and establish its will there. Second, based on their public confessions of faith, it is likely that many of the "saints" canonized in recent history by the Roman church are not in heaven at all. Many of them were idolaters, praying to creations of the Roman church in addition to God. Third, the veneration of anyone or anything in addition to, or instead of, the Lord is idolatry and can only undermine saving faith (Matthew 4:10).[5] The Lord has declared that he will not share credit for his works with anyone (Isaiah 42:8).[6] Is it then wrong to use the title "Saint" for people such as the apostles and early church fathers? For the apostles and biblical writers, it is certainly permissible, because the Lord has clearly approved them. For others, it is best to identify them by name and location of their work rather than applying an indiscriminate endorsement of the genuineness of their faith by calling them saints.

## Angels

To a limited extent, angels have been discussed previously in this book. This section will summarize in one place what the Bible tells us about angels. It is relatively short because the information given in the Bible about angels is limited and not organized for our deeper study. Speculation serves no good purpose.

---

[5] Then Jesus said to him, "Be gone, Satan! For it is written, 'You shall worship the Lord your God and him only shall you serve.'" (Matthew 4:10)

[6] "I am the LORD; that is my name; my glory I give to no other." (Isaiah 42:8)

Origin:        All the angels were created sometime during creation week, because the Lord finished his whole creation by the end of the sixth day (Genesis 2:1,2).[7] They were mentioned as the Lord's agents already in Genesis 3:24,[8] where the type of angel was designated as cherubim. They were working among God's people by the time of Abraham (Genesis 19:1).[9] Because angels are created beings, they had a beginning, but they will never cease to exist (Luke 20:36).[10]

Substance:     Angels are spirits (Hebrews 1:14)[11] with no physical component (Luke 24:39).[12] They can, however, assume human form to carry out their duties (John 20:12).[13] In the Bible, when they took on visible form so that they could be seen by people, they normally did not have wings (Hebrews 13:2),[14] but sometimes they did have wings in visions (Ezekiel 1:23).[15] Being spirits, they do not procreate, so the number of angels never increases (Matthew 22:30).[16]

Types:         There are various divisions among the angelic creatures, of which the Bible mentions some but perhaps not all. Those mentioned are archangel (1 Thessalonians 4:16),[17] cherubim

---

[7]Thus the heavens and the earth were finished, and all the host of them. And on the seventh day God finished his work that he had done, and he rested on the seventh day from all his work that he had done. (Genesis 2:1,2)

[8]He [the LORD] drove out the man [Adam], and at the east of the garden of Eden he placed the cherubim and a flaming sword that turned every way to guard the way to the tree of life. (Genesis 3:24)

[9]The two angels [in human form] came to Sodom in the evening, and Lot was sitting in the gate of Sodom. (Genesis 19:1)

[10][Jesus said,] "They [the saints in heaven] cannot die anymore, because they are equal to angels and are sons of God, being sons of the resurrection." (Luke 20:36)

[11]Are they [the holy angels] not all ministering spirits sent out to serve for the sake of those who are to inherit salvation? (Hebrews 1:14)

[12][Jesus said,] "See my hands and my feet, that it is I myself. Touch me, and see. For a spirit does not have flesh and bones as you see that I have." (Luke 24:39)

[13]She [Mary Magdalene] saw two angels in white, sitting where the body of Jesus had lain, one at the head and one at the feet. (John 20:12)

[14]Do not neglect to show hospitality to strangers, for thereby some have entertained angels unawares. (Hebrews 13:2)

[15]Under the expanse their [the living creatures'] wings were stretched out straight, one toward another. And each creature had two wings covering its body. (Ezekiel 1:23)

[16][Jesus said,] "In the resurrection they [the saints in heaven] neither marry nor are given in marriage, but are like angels in heaven." (Matthew 22:30)

[17]The Lord himself will descend from heaven with a cry of command, with the voice of an archangel, and with the sound of the trumpet of God. And the dead in Christ will rise first. (1 Thessalonians 4:16)

(Genesis 3:24), seraphim (Isaiah 6:2),[18] and living creatures (Revelation 19:4).[19] Some attributes of angels seen in visions are very different from those of terrestrial creatures. Angels exist in large numbers, but the number is not given in the Bible (Matthew 26:53).[20] The types of angels and the duties of the various types are not listed in any detail in the Scriptures.

Personality:   Angels have names (Luke 1:19).[21] They are rational, can rejoice (Luke 15:10),[22] and can be curious (1 Peter 1:12).[23] Although their knowledge may be great, it is limited (Matthew 24:36).[24] The angels delight in singing praises to the Lord (Isaiah 6:3).[25]

Properties:    Angels are very powerful (2 Kings 19:35),[26] but they are not almighty because they cannot challenge the Lord (Hebrews 1:3,4).[27] At their creation, they were given the ability to choose between good and evil. Some of them rebelled against the Lord and were then cast out of his service and condemned to spend eternity in hell (2 Peter 2:4).[28] After

---

[18] Above him [the LORD] stood the seraphim. Each had six wings: with two he covered his face, and with two he covered his feet, and with two he flew. (Isaiah 6:2)

[19] The twenty-four elders and the four living creatures fell down and worshiped God who was seated on the throne, saying, "Amen. Hallelujah!" (Revelation 19:4)

[20] [Jesus said,] "Do you think that I cannot appeal to my Father, and he will at once send me more than twelve legions of angels?" (Matthew 26:53)

[21] The angel answered him [Zachariah, the priest], "I am Gabriel. I stand in the presence of God, and I was sent to speak to you and to bring you this good news." (Luke 1:19)

[22] [Jesus said,] "Just so, I tell you, there is joy before the angels of God over one sinner who repents." (Luke 15:10)

[23] It was revealed to them [the prophets of the Old Testament] that they were serving not themselves but you, in the things that have now been announced to you through those who preached the good news to you by the Holy Spirit sent from heaven, things into which angels long to look. (1 Peter 1:12)

[24] [Jesus said,] "Concerning that day and hour no one knows, not even the angels of heaven, nor the Son, but the Father only." (Matthew 24:36)

[25] One [angel] called to another and said: "Holy, holy, holy is the LORD of hosts; the whole earth is full of his glory!" (Isaiah 6:3)

[26] That night the angel of the LORD went out and struck down 185,000 in the camp of the Assyrians. (2 Kings 19:35)

[27] He [Jesus] is the radiance of the glory of God and the exact imprint of his nature, and he upholds the universe by the word of his power. After making purification for sins, he sat down at the right hand of the Majesty on high, having become as much superior to angels as the name he has inherited is more excellent than theirs. (Hebrews 1:3,4)

[28] God did not spare angels when they sinned, but cast them into hell and committed them to chains of gloomy darkness to be kept until the judgment. (2 Peter 2:4)

that, the remaining angels were "confirmed in their bliss" so that they no longer had the ability to act against the Lord. These are referred to as "the elect" (1 Timothy 5:21).[29] They will remain holy and return with Christ on judgment day (Mark 8:38).[30] The angels are glorious because they are holy; therefore, they can perfectly reflect the radiance and glory of the Lord whom they serve (Acts 6:15).[31]

Purpose:    The purpose of the angels is to carry out assignments made by the Lord (Psalm 103:20).[32] Sometimes they guide people and help them prosper (Genesis 24:7).[33] Sometimes their assignments are delivering messages (Luke 1:13).[34] The word for angel and messenger is the same in Hebrew and Greek, so the context indicates whether it is speaking of a heavenly or earthly agent. Angels protect believers (Psalm 91:11,12).[35] Children get special attention from angels (Matthew 18:10).[36] Sometimes angels are assigned to fight evil (Acts 12:23).[37] In all their actions, they are always faithful servants, never masters or decision-makers with independent authority.

There are numerous false ideas about angels. Being in dread of the Lord God Almighty as he is described in the Bible, many people try to find some

---

[29]In the presence of God and of Christ Jesus and of the elect angels I charge you to keep these rules without prejudging, doing nothing from partiality. (1 Timothy 5:21)

[30][Jesus said,] "Whoever is ashamed of me and of my words in this adulterous and sinful generation, of him will the Son of Man also be ashamed when he comes in the glory of his Father with the holy angels." (Mark 8:38)

[31]Gazing at him [Stephen], all who sat in the council saw that his face was like the face of an angel. (Acts 6:15)

[32][David said,] "Bless the LORD, O you his angels, you mighty ones who do his word, obeying the voice of his word!" (Psalm 103:20)

[33][Abraham said,] "The LORD, the God of heaven, who took me from my father's house and from the land of my kindred, and who spoke to me and swore to me, 'To your offspring I will give this land,' he will send his angel before you, and you shall take a wife for my son from there." (Genesis 24:7)

[34]The angel [Gabriel] said to him, "Do not be afraid, Zechariah, for your prayer has been heard, and your wife Elizabeth will bear you a son, and you shall call his name John." (Luke 1:13)

[35]He [the Lord] will command his angels concerning you to guard you in all your ways. On their hands they will bear you up, lest you strike your foot against a stone. (Psalm 91:11,12)

[36][Jesus said,] "See that you [generic you] do not despise one of these little ones. For I tell you that in heaven their angels always see the face of my Father who is in heaven." (Matthew 18:10)

[37]Immediately an angel of the Lord struck him [King Herod] down, because he did not give God the glory, and he was eaten by worms and breathed his last. (Acts 12:23)

way to improve their situation relative to the supernatural world. They create idols of the mind to which they can give their devotion in order to get a favorable verdict on their prayers and their lives. The misuse of saints for this purpose was discussed in the previous section. Other people create their own god to which they assign some of the names and attributes of the Lord in the hopes of duping the Lord into thinking that they are worshiping him. Attempting to use the holy angels as pseudo-deities is yet another means some people employ to get around dealing with a God whom they do not want to please or listen to. These are a few of the common false ideas that are popular:

*Everyone has a guardian angel:* The Lord does use angels to protect the members of his visible church (Psalm 91:11), but how he does this is not described in the Scriptures. One angel may be watching multiple people, or angels may be dispatched as the Lord sees fit, while he personally does most of the work of protecting his followers. That one angel is constantly assigned to the same person cannot be shown from the Scriptures. Moreover, credit should not be given to guardian angels for one's protection because, if angels are involved, they are only there as agents of God (Colossians 2:18).[38] All praise and thanks must go to the Lord (Matthew 4:10).[39]

*Angels sit on people's shoulders to tell them what is the right thing to do:* This is not correct. It is the conscience that, based on the law written in a person's heart, has the responsibility to warn a person against sinful actions, not the angels (Romans 2:15).[40]

*Angels can become personally or emotionally involved with humans:* Angels are perfect servants of the Lord (Psalm 103:20).[41] They are not physically or emotionally attracted to individual people. They are never influenced by people but only and always follow the commands of the Lord.

*One can pray to angels for help:* Praying to angels is idolatry (Exodus 20:4-6). They do not have the ability to answer prayer because that would mean they were listening to someone in addition to the Lord. Such an action would constitute rebellion, of which the holy

---

[38] Let no one disqualify you, insisting on asceticism and worship of angels. (Colossians 2:18)

[39] [Jesus quoting Scripture:] "You shall worship the Lord your God and him only shall you serve." (Matthew 4:10)

[40] They [the Gentiles] show that the work of the law is written on their hearts, while their conscience also bears witness, and their conflicting thoughts accuse or even excuse them. (Romans 2:15)

[41] [David said,] "Bless the LORD, O you his angels, you mighty ones who do his word, obeying the voice of his word!" (Psalm 103:20)

angels are no longer capable. All prayers must be directed to the Lord (Psalm 50:15).[42]

*Angels are female:* Because angels do not reproduce, there is no need for them to have gender. The only two angels mentioned by name (i.e., Gabriel [Luke 1:19] and Michael [Jude 9]) have what we today consider to be male names. Angels are almost always called men when they take on human form.

*Angels are cute and chubby cherubs:* Picturing angels as cute or out-of-shape is dangerous sentimentality. Angels are powerful beings (2 Thessalonians 1:7,8)[43] without physical bodies. While the Lord might allow them to appear in any form, depending on their mission, it is disrespectful of the Lord to picture his faithful servants in a cutesy fashion.

*People become angels when they die:* The holy angels were a separate creation of the Lord. They were never sinful humans, but they have always been perfect servants of the Lord. When believers die, their souls go to heaven until judgment day (Ecclesiastes 12:7).[44] At that time, the souls rejoin the bodies to spend eternity in heaven with the Lord as humans, not as angels (John 5:28,29).[45]

The Bible sometimes refers to the Son of God, the second person of the Trinity, as "the angel of the Lord" (Exodus 3:2-6) before he became incarnate through Mary. Because *angel* and *messenger* are the same word in the Old Testament and because there is no capitalization in Hebrew, we have to judge what is meant by the context. This means that in the narrative the "angel" does something that only the Lord can do or accepts praise that no angel would dare accept. The Son became the Messenger of the Lord to carry out the intent of the Trinity in person rather than sending a servant. In these cases, this angel was naturally all-powerful, being the Lord himself.

---

[42][The LORD said,] "Call upon me in the day of trouble; I will deliver you, and you shall glorify me." (Psalm 50:15)

[43]When the Lord Jesus is revealed from heaven with his mighty angels in flaming fire, inflicting vengeance on those who do not know God and on those who do not obey the gospel of our Lord Jesus. (2 Thessalonians 1:7,8)

[44][Solomon said,] "The dust returns to the earth as it was, and the spirit returns to God who gave it." (Ecclesiastes 12:7)

[45][Jesus said,] "Do not marvel at this, for an hour is coming when all who are in the tombs will hear his [Jesus' returning on judgment day] voice and come out, those who have done good to the resurrection of life, and those who have done evil to the resurrection of judgment." (John 5:28,29)

## Demons

The demons, or devils, are angels, just like the holy angels that serve the Lord continually. They are the same type of being, created at the same time. They were created without sin, but they decided that they did not need to be subservient to the Lord. They disobeyed him (1 John 3:8),[46] but they could not resist the power of the Lord, who sent the rest of the angels to oust them from heaven (Revelation 12:7-9). How many angels or what percentage of the total angels revolted is not known, but it is a large number. Even when these demons possessed a single individual, sometimes many were involved (Mark 5:9).[47]

The reaction of the Lord was more than just to throw the rebellious angels out of heaven. He did not give them a way of salvation as he did humankind (Hebrews 2:16).[48] Instead, he judged them immediately and cast them into hell to await the final sentencing, when their imprisonment will be made permanent (2 Peter 2:4).[49] Their final punishment will last forever (Revelation 20:10).[50]

According to non-biblical tradition, the angel who led the revolt was named Lucifer (which means "light bearer"), but the Bible usually refers to him as "Satan" (which means "accuser") (Job 1:9-11), "Beelzebul" (Matthew 12:24), "the evil one" (Matthew 13:19), or "the devil" (Matthew 4:1). He is also referred to as "the serpent" and "the dragon" (Revelation 20:2), because it was in the form of a serpent that he tempted Eve (Genesis 3:1-7). The angels who joined him are called "demons" (Matthew 8:16) or "unclean spirits" (Mark 1:27).

Satan knew from personal experience that the Lord hated sin and would not tolerate it in his creatures. The temptation of Eve was the beginning of an effort by Satan and the demons to force the Lord to condemn humans, the crown of his creation, to eternal punishment. Satan's demonic hosts have ever since been violent enemies of humankind (1 Peter 5:8).[51] They are

---

[46]Whoever makes a practice of sinning is of the devil, for the devil has been sinning from the beginning. (1 John 3:8)

[47]Jesus asked him [a demon-possessed man], "What is your name?" He replied, "My name is Legion, for we are many." (Mark 5:9)

[48]Surely it is not angels that he [the Lord] helps, but he helps the offspring of Abraham. (Hebrews 2:16)

[49]God did not spare angels when they sinned, but cast them into hell and committed them to chains of gloomy darkness to be kept until the judgment. (2 Peter 2:4)

[50]The devil who had deceived them [the people of the earth] was thrown into the lake of fire and sulfur where the beast and the false prophet were, and they will be tormented day and night forever and ever. (Revelation 20:10)

[51]Be sober-minded; be watchful. Your adversary the devil prowls around like a roaring lion, seeking someone to devour. (1 Peter 5:8)

continually trying to undermine the faith of people who cling to Jesus for salvation, so believers must be at all times on their guard by studying the Scriptures (Ephesians 6:11,12).[52] The demons try to prevent God's Word from taking root in human hearts (Matthew 13:19).[53] Satan targets the great and the small, always seeking a way to destroy a soul (John 13:2).[54] He is vicious in pursuit of human prey, like a dog on a long chain, because he knows his time is short (Revelation 12:12).[55] Even Jesus experienced the cleverness of Satan's temptations (Luke 4:1-13).

Everyone falls to Satan's temptations, as did Adam and Eve, but the Lord provides assistance. He does this passively by limiting what Satan can do to people, because even Satan can do nothing unless the Lord permits it (Job 1:12).[56] The Lord also actively guards the faith of his elect (John 10:28).[57] Finally, the Lord will rescue his faithful to the safety of heaven, while sending those whom the demons have misled into rebellion against the Lord to hell to join them (Matthew 25:41).[58]

The demons do not just work through direct temptations, inciting people to disobey the moral law. One of their favorite attack methods is to turn the things of the world into idols, which take people away from actively serving the Lord (1 Timothy 6:10).[59] The world has many things that can be used to lure people away from Christ, and the demons choose the ones to which each person is most susceptible. They also try to use people's interest in the supernatural, whether it be "lucky socks," horoscopes, palm reading,

---

[52] Put on the whole armor of God, that you may be able to stand against the schemes of the devil. For we do not wrestle against flesh and blood, but against the rulers, against the authorities, against the cosmic powers over this present darkness, against the spiritual forces of evil in the heavenly places. (Ephesians 6:11,12)

[53] [Jesus said,] "When anyone hears the word of the kingdom and does not understand it, the evil one comes and snatches away what has been sown in his heart." (Matthew 13:19)

[54] The devil had already put it into the heart of Judas Iscariot, Simon's son, to betray him [Jesus]. (John 13:2)

[55] [A voice in heaven said loudly,] "But woe to you, O earth and sea, for the devil has come down to you in great wrath, because he knows that his time is short!" (Revelation 12:12)

[56] The LORD said to Satan, "Behold, all that he has is in your hand. Only against him do not stretch out your hand." (Job 1:12)

[57] [Jesus said,] "I give them [Jesus' followers] eternal life, and they will never perish, and no one will snatch them out of my hand." (John 10:28)

[58] [Jesus said,] "Then he [Jesus as judge] will say to those on his left [the unbelievers], 'Depart from me, you cursed, into the eternal fire prepared for the devil and his angels.'" (Matthew 25:41)

[59] The love of money is a root of all kinds of evils. It is through this craving that some have wandered away from the faith and pierced themselves with many pangs. (1 Timothy 6:10)

contact with the dead, or things even more devilish.[60] The Bible warns against getting involved with any of these directly or through human agents who have sold out to the devil (Deuteronomy 18:10-12).[61] Whether occult activities appear to be just fun or whether they are undertaken in seriousness, the demons are waiting to pounce on the person who puts his or her soul at risk. The demons are always alert for every opportunity to replace people's faith with doubt. They do not play fair, so they should not be given any opportunities to work their temptations on us (John 8:44).[62]

---

[60] Siegbert W. Becker, *Wizards That Peep* (Milwaukee: Northwestern Publishing House, 1978).

[61] [Moses said,] "There shall not be found among you anyone who burns his son or his daughter as an offering, anyone who practices divination or tells fortunes or interprets omens, or a sorcerer or a charmer or a medium or a necromancer or one who inquires of the dead, for whoever does these things is an abomination to the LORD." (Deuteronomy 18:10-12)

[62] [Jesus said,] "He [Satan] was a murderer from the beginning, and does not stand in the truth, because there is no truth in him. When he lies, he speaks out of his own character, for he is a liar and the father of lies." (John 8:44)

# Epilogue

In the end, the only thing that will matter is whether a person believes the gospel of Jesus Christ as it is presented in the Bible or whether that person is worshiping something of his or her own creation. It is easy to create idols out of material things in the world, out of friendships, out of causes, and even out of things in the church. The Lord God Almighty challenges us to know him by studying his Word and by dedicating our whole lives to his service rather than serving idols. Being a Lutheran is not for people who merely want to feel good about themselves, because there is, by nature, nothing within ourselves about which to feel good. Instead, the Lord calls for us to put all our trust in him, whether he gives us joys or sorrows. Not ourselves but the Lord must dominate everything about us, because he has given us every good thing that we have. Most important, he has given us the certainty of our salvation because Jesus has already paid for the guilt of all of our sins. It is from this that real happiness comes. When we fail to live up to his standards, as guilty children we need to rush to confess our sins to him, to accept his forgiveness, and to start again to serve him. It is an endless cycle until he calls us home from this place of heartache and temptation to his kingdom of glory.

Until then, let us stand firm in our faith and in his teachings and let us give all glory to the Lord.

# For Further Reading

Bainton, Roland. *Here I Stand*. New York: Abingdon Press, 1950.

Deutschlander, Daniel M. *The Narrow Lutheran Middle*. Milwaukee: Northwestern Publishing House, 2011.

Deutschlander, Daniel M. *The Theology of the Cross*. Milwaukee: Northwestern Publishing House, 2008.

Engelbrecht, Edward A., ed. *Lutheran Bible Companion,* Vols. 1 & 2. St. Louis: Concordia Publishing House, 2014.

Engelbrecht, Edward A., ed. *The Lutheran Study Bible*. St. Louis: Concordia Publishing House, 2009.

Keller, Brian R. *Bible*. Milwaukee: Northwestern Publishing House, 2002.

Kuske, David P. *Biblical Interpretation: The Only Right Way*. Milwaukee: Northwestern Publishing House, 1995.

Kuske, David P. Luther's Catechism, 3rd ed., Northwestern Publishing House, Milwaukee, 1998.

Lange, Lyle W., ed. *Our Great Heritage,* Vols. I-III. Milwaukee: Northwestern Publishing House, 1991.

McClain, Paul T., ed. *Concordia: The Lutheran Confessions,* 2nd ed. St. Louis: Concordia Publishing House, 2006.

Nass, Thomas P. *End Times*. Milwaukee: Northwestern Publishing House, 2011.

Pieper, Francis. *Christian Dogmatics,* Vols. I-IV. St. Louis: Concordia Publishing House, 1950.

# Scripture Index

## Genesis

1–68, 69
1:2—60
1:24—69
1:26—55, 57, 85
1:26,27—39, 187, 196, 206
1:27—69
1:28—85, 197, 262, 267
1:31—69, 174
2—69, 262
2:1,2—280
2:7—85, 262
2:8,9—85
2:15—85, 253, 270
2:17—86, 174, 187, 197
2:18—263
2:18-24—262
2:21,22—263
2:21-23—85
2:24—263, 264
3—68, 69, 70
3:1-7—285
3:4,5—86
3:6—187, 197, 263
3:9-13—86
3:12—197, 263
3:15—11, 35, 87, 93, 118, 139, 144, 188, 206
3:16—263
3:16-19—86
3:16-24—197
3:17–174
3:17,18—70
3:17-19—263, 270
3:17-24—253
3:22—58
3:24—280, 281
4:1—87, 177

4:1-16—88
4:4,5—216
4:17—258
4:19-24—89
4:22—270
4:26—12
5—12
5:21-24—90
6–8—70
6:1-3—89
6:5—24, 197, 206, 218, 267
6:5,6—89
6:5-7—12
6:8—90
6:9—90
6:9–8:19—12, 77
6:11-22—90
6:12—118
7:1-9—90
7:13—91
8:21—82, 93, 202, 240
8:22—50, 77
9:1—91
9:3—90, 270
9:8-17—91
9:13-16—90
9:20-27—91
10—91
10:10—258
11:1-9—51
11:4—91
11:5-9—91
11:7—64
11:31—94
12:1-3—94
12:1–25:10—94
12:3—12
12:10-20—94

13—94
14—94
15:1-6—94
15:5—94
15:6—94, 177
15:7-21—94
15:13—95
16—95
17:1—57
17:1-22—94
17:5—94
17:9-14—94
17:15—94
17:20—95
18—46
18:1-15—94
18:16-33—94
18:18—144
19:1—84, 280
19:26—181
20—94
22:2—95
22:11-18—35
22:13,14—95
24—95
24:7—282
25:5,6—264
25:23—95
29:16-30—95
29:21-30—266
30:23—265
31:19—94
32:28—95
36:15,16—258
37:28—95
45:26—95
50:20—51

## Exodus

1—96
2—96
3–14—96
3:2-6—35, 284
3:8—114
3:14—44
7:19–12:32—51
12:14—96

12:15—259
13:12—100
14:21-28—51
15:22–17:7—96
16—97
17:1-6—97
17:8-16—107
19:16-20:17—97
20—99
20:1-17—198
20:2-5—29
20:2-17—98
20:3—45
20:4-6—283
20:5,6—53
20:11—60, 61, 68
20:18,19—97
21:7-11—265
22:16—266
23:17—120
23:19—100
24:3—97, 103
24:10,11—46
25:9—102
28:1—13
28:30—259
29:9—101
30:30—101
32—103
32:9—13, 101
33:3—101
33:5—178
33:19—90, 189
33:20—45
34:6,7—55
34:9—101
35–40—97
35:4–38:31—102

## Leviticus

1–9—151
4:3—100
10:1,2—179, 180
12:7,8—100
16:2-34—102
16:11-14—210
18:6-17—266

18:18—266
18:21—112
19:9,10—147
19:29—264
20:10—266
20:13—266
20:26—100
21–25—151
24:5,6—102
24:16—255
25:23—100, 175, 253
27:30—100

## Numbers

1:16—258
1:50—101
4:1-3—121
6:24-26—58
14:1-10—103
14:30—178
17:10—102
19:11,12—100
20:10-12—103
21:21–24:25—103
23:19—48, 161
26:65—103
27:6-11—265
27:21—259
31:1-18—103
32:1-27—103
36:12—265

## Deuteronomy

4:2—98
4:24—53
5:32—217
6:1,2—29
6:1-12—12
6:4—58, 59
6:4,5—45
6:4-9—8, 31, 268
6:6-10—234
7:9—53
8:17—101
11:26-32—144
14:28,29—273
17:14,15—106

18:10-12—287
18:12—104
18:15,16—133, 134
21:22,23—137
22:22-24—264
22:23,24—119
22:25-27—264
22:28,29—264
24:1—266
24:19-22—273
25:5,6—265
25:13,14—200
25:13-16—4
26:8—46
28:1-13—78
28:15-68—12, 163
28:22—50
28:38-40—50
30:19,20—83
32:3,4—52, 59, 195
32:39—58, 104, 189

## Joshua

3—51
3–6—103
3:15—50
5:13-15—46
6:21—104
10:12-14—70
10:12-15—51
23:10—35
24:2—94
24:15—26-29, 236, 268
24:17—61
24:31—104

## Judges

2:1-4—35
2:16—259
6—46
6:11-27—208
6:36-40—255
13:2-25—208

## Ruth

112—273
114—265

## 1 Samuel

2:25—52
8:6,7—106
8:21—46
9:1,2—107
9:15,16—259
11:1-11—107
14:47—107
15:1-23—202
15:2—57
15:10,11—107
16:1—120
16:1-13—107
16:7—48, 200, 278
16:14—107
117—107
118–31—108
24:10—176
28:6—252

## 2 Samuel

2:4—108
2:8—108
3–5—108
7—12
7:11-17—144
7:16—15
12:13—247
15:25—46
23:1—108
23:1,2—13

## 1 Kings

1:13—108
4:32—13
12—109
12–22—109
16:31—109
17:1—112
18:21—191
19:18—178

## 2 Kings

1–25—109
6:5-7—51
6:18—51

10:31—61
11:1-3—111
15:34,35—111
19:35—51, 281

## 1 Chronicles

16:23—238
28,29—108
28:9,10—217
29:11—171

## 2 Chronicles

1–4—108
6:41—277
10–36—109
36:11-21—14
36:14-16—117
36:16—53

## Ezra

2:63—275
2:64,65—178
6:10—57
10—178

## Job

1:6-12—59
1:9-11—285
1:12—286
9:3—35
19:25-27—167
38–41—48, 88
38:8-11—77
38:32—69
41:11—222
42:12—271

## Psalms

1:1,2—29-31, 196, 223, 234
1:5,6—187
2:4—25, 46, 207
2:7—58, 61
8:4—55
16:3—277
18:30—52
19:12—248

19:12,13—201
22:1—138
22:16—137
22:18—137
24:1—174
31:19—55
33:7—196
34:20—137
40:8—187
44:20,21—200
50:10—35
50:12—212
50:15—252, 284
50:16,17—217
51:3—201
51:5—187, 240, 247
51:9,10—178
51:11—62
51:13—224
68:10—55
69:5—200
83:18—58
84:4—162
90:2—185
90:4—35
91:9,10—173
91:11—283
91:11,12—84, 226, 282
102:25-27—47
103:20—282, 283
104.24—54
104:27—77
104:27-29—50, 196
104:29—77
110:1—61
115:3—49
115:4-8—198
118:8,9—117
118:9—112
119:105—202
127:1—46, 77
127:1,2—49
130:1-4—252
132:11,12—108
135:5,6—49
139—48
139:7-10—46

145:9—54
145:15,16—251, 270
145:17—83
145:18—46

## Proverbs

3:5—224
14:34—199
15:3—46
16:33—174, 212, 261
22:6—235, 264
22:7—272
23:31,32—36
30:8,9—271
31:10—270

## Ecclesiastes

7:20—159
12:7—70, 157, 284

## Isaiah

1:11-17—14, 113
1:18—113, 203, 221
1:23—273
4:1—265
5:20—198
6:2—281
6:3—281
6:10—207
7:14—119, 120
8:19—252
9:6—208
10:22—113, 153
12:6—57
13:9—197
14:27—50
29:13—111, 133, 134, 259
29:16—222
32:6—53
37:7—51
37:36—85
40:8—215
40:13-15—171
42:1—58
42:6,7—125
42:8—44, 53, 279

43:10—58
43:10-13—44
43:13—49, 173
44:6-8—59
44:6-9—64
45:9—169
45:9-12—190
45:21—45
46:9,10—53
48:16—58
49:15,16—187
52:13–53:11—138
52:13–53:12—113
53:9—137
53:10—52
53:12—139
55:1—215
55:8,9—49, 54
55:9—22
55:11—235
58:11—78
64:6—202, 209, 217, 223
66:24—161, 210

## Jeremiah

1:4,5—173
6:14—113
9:10,11—114
17:9—25, 82
17:23—233
22:8,9—259
23:5,6—58
23:23,24—46
23:24—207
29:7—230, 257
33:2,3—195
33:20,25—50
36:2—113
43:1-7—147
44:15-19—111

## Ezekiel

1:23—280
2:5—113
3:16-21—180
13:6—246
16—21

20:13—206
33:11—190, 191
33:12-20—53

## Daniel

3—260
7:10—84
12:2—157

## Amos

9:1-6—46

## Micah

5:2—113, 119
6:7—222

## Nahum

1:6—49

## Zephaniah

1:18—210

## Zechariah

8:16,17—200
9:9—137
12:10—137

## Malachi

2:10—61
2:13-16—266
3:6—47, 209
4:5,6—118

## Matthew

1:20-23—119
1:21—120, 208
1:22—118
1:22,23—16
2:1—115
2:1-12—121
2:13-15—121
2:13-18—208
2:16-18—121
3:1-12—121

3:13-17—121
3:16,17—60
4:1—285
4:1-11—121
4:10—279, 283
4:17—247
5–7—221
5:16—271
5:20—123, 214
5:28—267
5:44,45—260
5:45—49, 77, 89, 174
5:48—52, 195
6:6—251
6:10—52
6:16—216
6:19-21—176
6:24—183
6:28,29—77
6:31-33—251, 254, 271
7:6—23
7:12—274
7:13—213
7:13,14—125, 182
7:18,19—84, 85
7:21-23—181
8:12—160
8:16—285
8:20—32
8:23-27—51
9:1-7—124
9:9-13—278
9:10—125
9:11,12—126
10:29—77
10:29,30—48, 186
10:34-39—134
11:4,5—125
11:20-24—123
11:28-30—221
12:24—285
12:32—62
12:34,35—220
13:13—129
13:15—126
13:18-23—219
13:19—235, 285, 286

13:24-30—182
13:35—128
13:41,42—210, 262
13:41-43—158
13:42—160
13:46—160
13:58—274
14:19-21—51
14:25-32—51
15:1,2—133
15:19—197
15:19,20—88, 217, 267
15:24—145
15:35-38—51
16:3—157
16:16—152
16:18—152
16:19—152
16:21—139
16:23—152
16:24—202, 219, 226
16:24-26—124
16:26—218, 247, 271
17:5—59
18:3—241
18:10—282
18:15-18—248
18:18—152
18:20—268
19:3-9—266
19:6—269
19:18-20—216
19:23—272
19:26—158
21:12,13—133, 134
21:23-27—135
22:14—123, 153, 177
22:15-22—135
22:21—260
22:23-33—135
22:30—85, 262, 280
22:35-38—45
22:37—98
22:37-40—198
22:39—98
22:41,42—120
22:44—61

23—134
23:4—133
23:8,9—152
23:13-36—200
23:37—123
23:37,38—78, 212
24—36
24:3—155
24:4-12—156
24:6—204
24:6,7—197
24:6-12—261
24:23-27—166
24:24—5
24:27—158
24:29-31—141
24:30—158
24:31—158
24:36—165, 281
24:36-39—77
24:36-44—157
24:38-41—165
25:1-13—157, 182, 223
25:14-30—182
25:21—209
25:31—156
25:31-45—184
25:31-46—156
25:32—159
25:34-40—159
25:41—59, 84, 86, 160, 190, 286
25:41-46—198
25:46—159, 163
26:3-5—135
26:14-16—136
26:26—242
26:27,28—144, 242
26:38—208
26:46—136
26:53—281
26:57-68—136
27:1,2—136
27:3-5—136
27:5—256
27:24—137, 212
27:42—138
27:46—210

27:51—138
27:51-54—138
28:13—139
28:18-20—61
28:19—59, 232, 240
28:19,20—6, 188, 220, 226, 231
28:20—141, 209

## Mark

1:22—16
1:27—285
2:27—133, 275
4:3-9—129
5:9—285
5:35-43—51
6:21-29—119
7:3,4—232
7:4—242
7:6-8—178
7:8-13—134
7:21-23—24
8:33—152
8:36,37—212, 215
8:38—282
9:47,48—160
10:2-9—263
11:21—122
13:32—155
14:7—273
14:22-25—242
14:49—212
14:50—211
16:16—201

## Luke

1:3,4—16
1:5-25—119
1:13—282
1:15—36
1:19—281, 284
1:26-38—51, 119
1:34,35—263
1:35—207
1:39-45—119
1:54—54
2:1,2—122
2:1-5—120

2:7—120, 208
2:8-20—120
2:21—120
2:22-38—121
2:41-51—121
3:1-20—119
4:1-13—286
4:16-22—231
4:16-30—216
5:32—122
7:11-15—51
7:11-17—126
7:47—202, 220, 233
8:43-48—126
10:21—214
10:25-37—23, 129
11:37-52—180
12:16-21—77
12:18-21—271
12:47,48—159
12:48—253
15:7—78
15:8-10—129
15:10—281
16:19-31—157
16:26—160, 161
16:31—13
17:20,21—172
18:9-14—123, 199, 222, 278
18:11—216
18:11,12—252
18:31-33—136
19:10—122
20:36—280
21:11—50
22:19—243
22:29,30—163
22:39-46—136
23:1-25—136
23:30—158
23:34—212
23:43—157
24:39—208, 280
24:44-48—5
24:45—143
24:46,47—145, 235

**John**

1:1—61, 134
1:3—60, 62
1:18—59
1:32-34—134
1:41—120
2:1-11—36
2:18-22—244
2:24,25—48
3:1,2—51
3:3—239
3:5—192
3:16—54, 187
3:17—156
3:17,18—33
3:35—59
3:36—33, 124, 159
4:1-42—135
4:22—145
4:24—45, 196
4:48—125
5:14—247
5:28,29—157, 284
5:39—31, 135
5:39,40—143
6:15—36
6:29—221
6:44–61
6:58—126
6:60—123
7:5—147
7:14-52—16
8:39,40—135
8:41—61
8:41,42—60
8:44—86, 287
8:58,59—135
9:4—188
9:14—133
9:16—134
9:39—126
10:22-39—64
10:27,28—224
10:27-29—189
10:28—188, 286
10:29,30—62
10:30—135

10:30,33—122
10:37,38—134
11:1-44—51
11:47,48—51
11:48—133, 211
11:50—51
12:6—211
13—32
13:2—286
14:6—135
14:16,17—6, 225
14:26—6, 143, 225
15:1-8—32
15:5—31-34
15:5,6—221
15:16—252
15:22—129
15:26—59, 60, 62, 64
16:12-15—6
17—225
17:1—60, 61, 64
18:36—36, 164
20:12—280
20:23—152, 246
20:25—139
21:15-19—139

## Acts

1:1-3—16
1:6—140, 164
1:7—38, 88
1:8—141
1:9-11—141
1:26—151
2:1-12—145
2:10—153
2:14-41—146
2:19,20—156
2:23—186, 211
2:34—61
2:37—199
2:42—229
2:42-47—146
2:47—146
4:13—140, 145
4:32-37—273
5:1-11—248

5:3,4—59, 64
5:17-41—146
5:29—176
6:1-6—150
6:1-7—146
6:4—244
6:5—151
6:8-7:60—146
6:15—282
7:5—94
7:22—12
7:51—191, 219
8:2—146
8:4—146
8:5-25—146
8:32—210
9:1-25—148
11:2,3—150
11:20—148, 244
11:22—148
11:25,26—148
12:23—282
13:4,5—148
13:22—108
14:8-18—149, 236
14:22—181
15—6
15:1—147
15:1-21—150
15:13—147
15:39-41—149
16:22—149
16:25-34—218
16:30,31—212
17:5-9—149
17:11—223
17:22-34—236
17:26—69
17:32—149
19:23-41—149
20:31—149
22:25—149

## Romans

1:1—151, 244
1:4—60
2:14,15—88, 98

2:15—283
3:3,4—53
3:20—199, 221
3:21,22—223
3:21-25—278
3:22-24—160
3:23,24—55, 233
3:24—189
4:25—139
5:8—54
5:18,19—191, 208, 232
6:11—219
7:4—33
7:18,19—225
7:22,23—201
8:5—241
8:20,21—70, 86
8:26—226
8:28—78, 181, 272
8:29,30—189, 192
8:31-39—227
8:33,34—167
9:11—189
10:3—213
10:9—240
10:10—241
10:17—180, 240
11:2—188
11:6—211
11:13—245
11:13-24—33
11:26—78
11:34,35—189
12:2—52
12:5—229
12:6-8—227, 244, 254
12:18—261
13—261
13:1,2—175
13:1-7—260
13:3,4—175, 260
13:5-7—230
15:4—68, 82
15:6—61
15:25—277
16:17—250
16:20—59

## 1 Corinthians

1:21—261
1:25—170
2:7—188
2:9—8
2:14—82, 210, 215, 218, 236, 241
2:16—185
3:2—201, 234
3:9—180
4:3,4—245
4:7—273
5:6—246
5:9,10—260
6:9,10—266
6:9-11—203, 227
6:13—183
6:15-7:6—264
7:8,9—268
7:22,23—226
7:29—155
7:32-34—267
7:34—269
8:4—58
9:20-22—236
10:12—223
10:13—226
10:16—243
10:17—243
10:31—255, 274
11:25—155
11:27—243
12:1-11—62
12:3—144, 188, 192, 218, 219, 241
12:4-6—254
12:14-26—231
13:1-3—199
14:19—183
14:40—238
15:5-8—139
15:9,10—16
15:22—263
15:52—158
15:55-57—139

## 2 Corinthians

3:6—144
3:14—129, 143

4:2—37
5:6,7—170
5:15—138, 139
5:17—225
5:18,19—124
5:19—211
5:20—144, 227
5:21—213
8,9—273
8:3-5—254
9:15—241
11:13—237
12:2,3—162
13:14—60

## Galatians

1,2—150
1:1—60
1:6—179
1:8—6, 179, 232
1:8,9—144
1:19—147
2:10—273
3:11-13—275
3:21,22—202
3:24—274
3:25,26—274
3:25-28—31
4:4—122
4:4,5—48, 56, 115, 118, 188, 207, 209
4:6—60, 62, 64, 65
5:16,17—226
5:18-21—225
5:22,23—226
6:7,8—114
6:10—252

## Ephesians

1:1—225, 278
1:9,10—205
2:1—70, 192
2:4,5—54
2:4-6—221
2:4-7—158
2:8,9—55, 124, 212, 223
2:11-22—178
2:20—150

4:4-6—245
4:30—64
5:15-17—52
5:22-29—269
5:22-33—264
5:28—268
5:28,29—263
6:1-3—258
6:4—264
6:10-18—227
6:10-20—229
6:11,12—286
6:12—227

## Philippians

1:10,11—205
1:23—157
2:5-7—209, 276
2:9-11—211
3:12-14—163
3:20—224, 261

## Colossians

1:1—278
2:13,14—218
2:16—255, 276
2:18—283
2:20-23—36, 255
3:1—244
3:16—235
3:23—272

## 1 Thessalonians

4:14—60
4:16—158, 280
4:17—159
5:16-18—251

## 2 Thessalonians

1:7,8—284
1:9—70, 187
3:10—183, 270

## 1 Timothy

2:1,2—253
2:1-4—261

2:2-4—187
2:5,6—251
3:1-13—245
5:1—258
5:8—265, 271
5:19—246
5:21—196, 282
6:6-8—226
6:7—100, 252
6:8—251
6:9—225
6:10—267, 286
6:15,16—172

## 2 Timothy

2:12—163
2:13—48, 52
3:16,17—7, 23, 64, 234
4:2—144, 237
4:2-4—181
4:3,4—236

## Titus

1:5,6—150
2:13,14—61
3:4-6—60
3:5—240
3:7—211, 219

## Hebrews

1:3,4—281
1:13—61
1:14—84, 280
2:16—285
2:17—209
2:17,18—272
3:3—133
4:13—48
4:15—207
6:17—257
7:12—257
7:27—243
9:15—145
9:22—101, 103
9:26—210
10:30,31—162

11:6—33, 159
13:2—280
13:4—267
13:17—246

## James

1:13,14—191, 267
1:23,24—217
1:26—217
1:27—272
2:1-13—200
2:10—202, 247
4:2,3—251
4:6,7—252
4:13,14—77

## 1 Peter

1:2—186
1:3—59
1:12—61, 281
1:20,21—186
1:24—207
2:9—251
2:10—229
2:16—275
2:17—276
3:15—185
3:20—178
3:21—240, 241
4:7—157
5:8—36, 157, 224, 285
5:13—147, 153

## 2 Peter

1:20,21—60, 62, 64
1:21—7, 150
2:1—199
2:4—160, 196, 281, 285
2:9,10—217
2:22—219
3:3-7—165
3:8—47
3:9—48, 55
3:10—182
3:11-13—182
3:15,16—37
3:16—179

## 1 John

1:7—103, 138, 247
1:8—233
1:9—233, 247
1:10—212, 247
2:2—144, 205
3:8—285
4:1—230
4:8—43, 54

## Jude

6—84
9—35, 284

## Revelation

2:10—225
3:15,16—203

5:11—35
7:14—126, 159, 184, 233
9:16—35
12:7-9—285
12:12—286
15:2,3—162, 163
15:3—53
19:4—281
19:6-9—163
19:16—57, 171
20—164
20:1-3—34-36
20:2—285
20:4—157
20:10—161, 285
20:12—159
21,22—162
21:4—163
22:20—157

# Subject Index

## A

Aaron, 13, 96, 101-103, 144
Aaronic blessing, 58
Abraham (Abram), 9, 12-13, 94-95, 127,
      134-135, 280
    promise to, 11-12, 26, 95-96, 144
absolution, 246-249
active obedience, 209-210, 213, 224, 278
Adam and Eve, 11, 69-70, 85-88, 93, 113,
      118, 121, 139, 144, 174, 177,
      187-188, 197, 206, 207, 253, 258,
      262-263, 270, 285-286
adiaphora (adiaphoron), 28, 255-256
adultery, 264, 266-267
Ahab, 109, 111
allegory, 38
altar-and-pulpit fellowship, 250
analogy, 131-132
    of faith, 37-38
    of Scripture, 28
Angel of the Lord, 34-35, 96, 284
angels, 34-35, 83-87, 119-120, 160, 177, 187,
      191, 195-196, 225, 252, 279-284
    guardian, 283
antinomianism, 201
Antioch, 17, 38, 148-150
Apocrypha
    Jewish, 15
    Pseudepigrapha (New Testament), 17-
      18, 121
approaching judgment, 156-158
argument from silence, 28
ark of the covenant, 102
atonement
    cover (mercy seat), 102
    day of, 102
    limited, 191
    universal, 11, 191

attrition (shallow repentance), 222
Augsburg Confession, viii-ix

## B

Babel, 91, 93
Babylon, 16, 114-115, 147, 153, 163
Babylonian captivity, 9, 13-15, 147, 178, 259
baptism, 239-242
    of Jesus, 121
Barnabas, 148-149
Becker, Siegbert, 47
Beelzebul, 285
Bethlehem, 119-120
Bible, 1-38
    approach to understanding the, 21-38
    false approach to the, 23-25
    inerrancy of the, 7-8, 23-25, 38, 64, 67, 72
    introduction to the, 1
    Jewish Apocrypha, 15
    New Testament, 6, 11, 16-19
    Old Testament, 6, 11, 12-15, 19
    Pseudepigrapha (New Testament Apocry-
      pha), 17-18, 121
    role of the, 5-10, 25, 67-68, 72, 176,
      198-199
    structure of the, 11-12, 19
    study of the, 234-235
    verbal inspiration of the, 23-25, 67, 72
binding key, 246
biogenesis, 80
*Book of Concord, The,* viii, ix
*Book of Mormon, The,* 8-9

## C

Caesar Augustus, 117
Cain, 88-89
call (within the ministry), 244-246

Calvin, John/Calvinism, 37, 191, 224, 244
catechisms
    Luther's Large, ix, x
    Luther's Small, ix, x
    Roman Catholic, 23
celibacy, 267-268
charismatics, 8
chiasmus, 22
Christian freedom, 255-256, 271, 274-276
church
discipline, 246-249
fellowship, 249-250, 260
first-century, 143-154
    to the Gentiles, 147-150
    invisible, 177-182, 229, 251
to the Jews, 145-147
    militant, 225
mission of the, 143-145, 231-256
    persecution of the, 146-148
preservation of the, 150-154
and state, 258-261
triumphant, 225
visible, 153-154, 172, 179-182, 229-256
citizenship, 260-261
civic righteousness, 34, 176, 199, 204, 278
civil disobedience, 176-177, 261
civil estates, 257-276
civil rights, 176
colloquy, 249-250
commandment, external, 86, 196-198
companionship in marriage, 262-264
concubine, 264-265
confession, 246-249
congregational life, 231-256
congregational organization, 256
conscience, 283
Constantine, 65, 260
contrition, 222
conversion, 148, 192, 216-224, 240-241
covenant, 11, 78, 91, 117, 127, 242
    Mosaic (old, two-sided), 12-15, 97-115,
        117, 127, 133, 134, 143-145, 150,
        151, 163, 178-179, 253, 265
    one-sided (new), 12, 91, 143-145, 155,
        254
    testament (another name for), 11, 12-
        15, 16-19
creation, 67-71, 83

creation science, 75-76, 79-80
cultural barriers, 22-23, 235-237
Cyrus (king), 114

## D

dated arguments, 80
David, 12-15, 30, 107-108, 111, 120, 145,
    164
death
    eternal, 70, 86-87, 198
    feelings about, 166-167
    Jesus', 137-140, 144, 188, 210
spiritual, 70, 86-87, 192, 223
    temporal (physical), 70, 86-87, 157-158,
        166-167, 197-198, 284
decision for Christ, 192
Declaration of Independence, 275
degrees of glory, 159
degrees of punishment, 159
democracy, 175, 261
demons, 83-87, 125, 161, 177, 179, 181, 183,
    223, 225-227, 246, 285-287
devil. *See* Satan
divine right of kings, 261
divorce, 263, 265-266, 269
double predestination, 190

## E

Easter, 139
Egypt, slavery in and rescue from, 13, 26-29,
    51, 95-97, 103-104, 137
election of believers, 177, 181, 188-192, 195,
    219, 224, 286
    errors regarding, 190-192
Elijah, 109, 112, 118-119, 125, 178
Elisha, 125
Elizabeth, 119
employment, 270-272
end times, 155-167
    false teachings about, 163-166
feelings about, 166-167
Enoch, 90
eternal punishment, 59, 84-86, 123, 160-162,
    177, 187-188, 198, 281, 285
Eucharist. *See* Holy Communion
Evangelical churches, 220
evangelism, 235-237

evolution, 73-76, 79-80
exaltation, Jesus' state of, 211
excommunication, 248
exegetical examples
    John 15:5, 31-34
    Joshua 24:15b, 26-29
    Psalm 1:1,2, 29-31
    Revelation 20:1-3, 34-36
external commandment, 86, 196-198

**F**

faith, 223-224
fall into sin, 70, 81, 93, 98, 101, 165, 263, 264, 270
Father, God the, 60, 61, 63-66
figurative language, 244
flood, great, 70, 77, 90-91, 93, 178, 258, 270
foreign righteousness, 124, 213
foreknowledge, 185-186, 192, 195, 205
Formula of Concord, viii-ix
fornication, 264, 266-267
*Freedom of a Christian, The*, 276
freedom of choice (free will), 83-85, 93, 177, 186-187, 196-197, 199, 206, 281

**G**

Galilee, 133, 135, 136
gender, 262
Gentiles, mission to, 147-150
Gnostics, 18
God, 39-80
    as Creator, 67-71
    essence of. *See* Trinity
    goodness of, 55
    holiness attributes of, 45, 51-54
    jealousy of, 53
    as King, 171-173
    loving attributes of, 45, 54-56
    names of, 44-45, 57, 69
    as Preserver, 77-78
    size and power attributes of, 45-51
    and the universe, 55-65
    will of, 52, 195-196
    wisdom of, 54
Golden Rule, 274
Golgotha, 137-139
good Samaritan (parable), 23, 129-130

good works, vii, 159, 166, 180, 199, 202-203, 212-213, 217, 219, 221-223, 271, 278
gospel, 5-7, 16-17, 35, 122-125, 129, 134, 143-144, 149, 177-182, 183, 188, 205-214, 215-223. *See also* plan of salvation
    Christ's obedience, 209-212
    fulfillment of the, 207-209
    God's commitment (promise), 206
    by grace, through faith, 212-213
    kingdom of grace, 177-182
    preaching of the, 201-204, 231-233, 235-237
gospel-first evangelism, 220
governing authorities, 175-176, 203-204, 217, 258-261
grace, 22, 54-55, 212-213
Great Commandment, 7-8, 30-31, 44-45, 98
Great Commission, 181, 188, 226-227, 231-233, 235-237, 240, 246, 261
great exchange, 213-214
guardian angel, 283

**H**

heaven (as a place), 157, 161-163, 182-184, 219, 278, 286
hell, 70, 84-87, 123, 138, 141, 157, 159, 160-162, 183, 184, 187-188, 190, 272, 281, 285-287
heresies, 179-182, 190-192, 198-199, 220-224, 246
hermeneutics, 21-38
    Bible not clear and inerrant, 23-25
    false approaches, 36-38
    Lutheran (historical-grammatical) approach, 25-36, 38, 223, 242-244
    rules for, 27-28
Herod
    of Galilee, 135-136
    the Great, 115, 121, 208
hidden God, 38, 172, 224
historical-grammatical approach to Scripture, 25-36, 38
Holy Communion, 223, 242-244
Holy Spirit, work of God the, 60-66, 143-144, 145, 150-151, 153, 215-227, 236-237, 239-242

homosexuality, 265-267, 269
humiliation, Jesus' state of, 209, 211

**I**

idolatry, 198-199, 278-279, 283, 286
image of God, 85, 88, 98, 187, 196, 206,
       208-209
Immanuel, 120
impenitence, 7, 246-249
incarnation, 207
indulgences, vii, 222
*intuitu fidei*, 192
irresistible grace, 191
Isaac, 95
Isaiah, 120, 125, 133, 137-138

**J**

Jacob (Israel), 12-13, 51, 95-96, 258
James ( Jesus' brother), 147
Jeroboam, 109, 112
Jerusalem, 6, 114, 120-121, 123, 133, 136-
       137, 145-154, 259, 273
Jesus
ascension of, 141, 211
baptism of, 121
birth of, 118-120
and the church, 150-154
death of, 137-140, 144, 188, 210
deity claim of, 132-135
earthly ministry of, 117-141, 231
       exaltation state of, 211
humiliation state of, 209, 211
       message of, 122-125
       miracles of, 125-128
       misunderstandings about, 122
name of, 120, 207-208
natures of ( human and divine), 208-209,
       211, 244
parables of, 128-132
       passion of, 135-139
       pre-ministry period of, 121
resurrection of, 139-141, 211
       return of, 158-160
Jews, mission to, 145-147
John, 147
John the Baptizer, 6, 16-17, 119, 121, 122,
       134

Joseph (husband of Mary), 119-121
Joseph ( Jacob's son), 95
Joshua, 26-29, 103-104
Judaism, 143, 148
Judaizers, 150
Judas Iscariot, 136, 211, 256
judges (period of), 104-106, 259
judgment, approaching, 156-158
judgment day, 36, 154, 155-156, 158-160,
       165-167, 182, 184, 211, 217, 253,
       282, 284

**K**

kingdom of God, 171-184
       earthly, 164
       eternity, 47, 154, 156, 162, 172-173,
       195, 205-206, 257, 282, 284
       of glory, 172-173, 182-184, 225, 257
       of grace, 172-173, 177-182, 184, 224-
       225, 231-256, 257
       of power, 172-177, 184, 257-276
kings (period of), 107-112, 258, 259

**L**

Lamech, 89
language barrier, 22-23, 232
law, 97-101, 195-204, 215-223
       ceremonial, 97, 99-101, 129-130, 133
       civil, 97-98, 217, 258-259
as curb, 198-199, 201, 216-217, 221, 233
       as guide, 196-197, 201-202, 221-222,
       233
       as mirror, 196, 199-201, 202-203, 217-
       218, 220, 233
       moral, 97-98, 196-198, 203-204, 216,
       230, 248, 266, 267, 272, 274-276,
       286
       Mosaic, 13, 97-115, 122, 126, 130, 147,
       255, 259, 264, 266, 272-275
       preaching of the, 202-203, 231-233, 236
law-law approach to salvation, 221
Lazarus and the rich man, 157
lectionary, 239
legalism, 275
Levites, 13-14, 15, 101-106, 109, 129-130,
       144
lifespan, 88-89

limited atonement, 191
liturgies, 237-239
loosing key, 246
Lord's Supper. *See* Holy Communion
lost coin (parable), 129
love of God, 54-56
Lucifer. *See* Satan
Luke, 6, 16, 146, 149
Luther, Martin, vii-x, 10, 15, 25-26, 38, 124,
    181, 213, 238, 276
Lutheran (historical-grammatical) approach
    to Scripture, 25-36, 38, 223,
    242-244

# M

magi, 121
marriage, 262-270
martyr, 278-279
Mark, 16
Mary (Jesus' mother), 119-121, 149, 152,
    207-208, 263, 284
mathematics, 26, 71-72, 78-80
Matthew, 16, 278
means of grace, 172, 183, 191, 223, 239-244,
    248, 253
mega churches, 221
Melanchthon, Phillip, viii-ix, 192
mercy, 54, 187-188
millennium, 35-36, 164-165, 172, 203
ministry of the Word, 244-246
miracles, 51, 70-71, 73, 103, 119, 125-128,
    134, 137, 150, 153, 173, 208, 273
Mishnah, 179
Mosaic covenant, 13, 97-115
Moses, 12-13, 96-97, 101-103, 125, 134,
    152, 198
Mount Sinai, 13-14, 44, 45, 97, 103
Muhammad, 9

# N

national law code, 203-204
natural disasters, 174
natural laws, 50-51, 70-71, 173
natural religion, 9, 39-41
natures of Jesus, 208-209
Nazareth, 119-121
New Testament Era, 155, 164

Newton, Isaac, 73
Nicene Creed, 65-66
Nicodemus, 134
Noah, 12, 90-91

# O

obedience (of Christ)
    active, 209-210, 213, 224, 278
    passive, 210-212, 213, 224
objective justification, 211, 215
office of the keys, 246-247
old Adam, 225
omnipotence, 43, 49-51, 52, 67-71, 79
omnipresence, 46-48, 209
omniscience, 48-49, 54, 55, 81, 84
omri, 109, 111
one flesh, 263, 264
ordination, 245

# P

parables, 128-132, 157
passive obedience, 210-212, 213, 224
Passover, 96, 135-137, 242
Pasteur, Louis, 80
patience of God, 55-56
patriarchs, 94-96, 177-178
patriarchy, 258, 265
Paul (Saul), 5-6, 16-17, 33, 147, 148-151,
    152, 218, 231-232, 236, 268, 273,
    275
Pentecost, 145, 164
Pentecostal churches, 220
pericope, 239
Peter, 145-147, 151-153
Pharaoh, 96
Pharisee and the tax collector (parable), 123-
    124, 148, 199, 222
Pharisees, 122-124, 133-135, 180, 278
Pietism, 220
plan of salvation, 13, 38, 54-56, 67-68, 70, 78,
    86-87, 90-91, 93, 100-101, 144-
    145, 155, 163, 165-166, 187-189,
    192-193, 205-214, 215-216, 233
    historical view, 81-167
    theological view, 169-227
poetry, 29-30
Pontius Pilate, 136-137, 211-212

poor, help for the, 273-274
pope, vii, 23-24, 152
prayer, 251-253, 283-284
preaching, 231-233
predestination, 185-193, 224. *See also*
          election
Pre-Flood Age, 83-91
preservation of faith, 223-224
priesthood (levitical), 13-14, 101-106, 109,
          114-115, 129-130, 144, 243, 259
priesthood of believers, 251-253
probability, 79-80
procreation, 262, 265, 267-268, 280
prophecies, 135-139, 211-212
prophets (period of), 110-111, 112-114
public ministry, 244-246
purgatory, 161-162
pursuit of happiness, 275

**Q**

quid pro quo approach, 222
Qur'an, 9

**R**

rapture, 165
real presence, 243-244
rebellion
          of angels, 84-86, 281, 285
          of humanity, 86-88
Red Sea, 51, 96
Reformation (Lutheran), 260, 268-269
Rehoboam, 109
repentance, 78, 112-113, 119, 122-125, 156,
          216-219, 222, 226-227, 247-249
resurrection of the dead, 157-158
rich man and Lazarus, 157
righteousness (two forms), 122-124
righteousness of God, 160, 212-214, 223,
          278
rock, 152
roles of men and women, 263-264, 265
Roman Catholic Church, vii-viii, 10, 23-24,
          30, 152-153, 161-162, 222, 238,
          243, 269, 278-279
Roman Empire, 148-149, 151-152, 259-260,
          278-279

Rosetta Stone, 9
Ruth, 265, 273

**S**

sacrament, 239-244
Sacrament of the Altar. *See* Holy Commu-
          nion
Sadducees, 122, 135
saints, 225, 277-279
of Roman Catholicism, 278-279
Samson, 106
Samuel, 106, 107
sanctification, 30, 180-181, 224-227
          broad sense, 226
          narrow sense, 224
Satan, 34-35, 70, 83-88, 121, 152, 157, 160,
          164, 177-178, 213, 223, 226, 234,
          235, 285-287
Saul (king), 107-108
Saul (Paul), 5-6, 16-17, 33, 147, 148-151,
          152, 218, 231-232, 236, 268, 273,
          275
science, 71-77, 78-80
          assumptions of, 72-77
          laws of, 80
limitations of, 73-77, 207
          nature of, 71-72
scientists, 72-80
          Christians as, 79
scribes, 13, 15, 122, 133
seat of doctrine (sedes doctrinae), 28, 33,
          36, 38
Secular Humanism, 37, 74-75
Septuagint, 15, 147
sermon, 231-233, 234
Sermon on the Mount, 123, 221
sexual relations, 262-270
signs of end times, 156-157
silent period, 114-115
similies, 129, 131-132
Smith, Joseph, 9
social responsibility, 272-274
*Sola Scriptura,* 28
Solomon, 13-14, 108-109, 112, 164
Son of God, 34-36, 60, 61-62, 63-66, 124,
          134-135, 207-209, 284
Son of Man, 208-209

sower and the seed (parable), 129

standards of truth, vii-ix, 3-5, 24-25, 30, 71-72, 98, 104, 196-198, 203-204, 206, 249-250, 257, 259-261

    Bible as a standard of truth, 5-10, 25, 67-68, 72, 176, 198-199

    false standards of truth, 9-10, 24-25, 72-77, 91, 176-177, 179-181, 198-199, 278-279

    need for conformity of, 3-5

    structure of, 4-5

state (national government), 175-176, 203-204, 230, 256, 258-261, 268-270, 273

state of exaltation, 211

state of humiliation, 209, 211

Stephen, 146, 147

stewardship, 253-255, 273-274

subjective justification, 219, 277

supernatural, 286-287

synergism, 162, 166, 203, 222-223

**T**

tabernacle (tent of meeting), 97, 102

Talmud, 9, 179

tax collectors, 123-124, 135, 278

teaching the Bible, 234-235

Ten Commandments, 30, 44, 97-99, 163, 198, 203

ten virgins (parable), 157, 223

theocracy, 101, 104, 106, 258-259, 261

thermodynamics, 79

theses, ninety-five, viii

thousand years, 35-36, 164-165, 172, 203

Timothy, 149

Torah, 30-31

total depravity, 12-13, 22, 68, 82, 117-118, 197, 202

transubstantiation, 243

tree of life, 198

tree of the knowledge of good and evil, 86, 174, 197

Trinity, 57-66

    false teachings regarding the, 62-65

nature of the, 58-61

    persons of the, 59-62

    symbols of the, 62, 63

**U**

universal atonement, 11, 191

Urim and Thummim, 9, 259

**V**

veneration of saints, 278-279

**W**

work and employment, 270-272

worship services, 237-239

**Z**

Zechariah (husband of Elizabeth), 119